ROAD TO REVOLUTION

ROAD
TO REVOLUTION

A Century of Russian Radicalism

By

AVRAHM YARMOLINSKY

PRINCETON UNIVERSITY PRESS

Princeton, New Jersey

PUBLISHED BY PRINCETON UNIVERSITY PRESS,
41 WILLIAM STREET, PRINCETON, NEW JERSEY 08540
IN THE UNITED KINGDOM: PRINCETON UNIVERSITY PRESS,
GUILDFORD, SURREY
COPYRIGHT 1957 BY AVRAHM YARMOLINSKY

FIRST PRINCETON PAPERBACK PRINTING, 1986
LCC 86-9374
ISBN 0-691-05478-9
ISBN 0-691-00809-4 (pbk.)

REPRINTED BY ARRANGEMENT WITH
MACMILLAN PUBLISHING COMPANY
AND HAROLD MATSON LITERARY AGENCY

CLOTHBOUND EDITIONS OF PRINCETON UNIVERSITY PRESS BOOKS
ARE PRINTED ON ACID-FREE PAPER, AND BINDING MATERIALS
ARE CHOSEN FOR STRENGTH AND DURABILITY. PAPERBACKS,
WHILE SATISFACTORY FOR PERSONAL COLLECTIONS,
ARE NOT USUALLY SUITABLE FOR LIBRARY REBINDING.

PRINTED IN THE UNITED STATES OF AMERICA
BY PRINCETON UNIVERSITY PRESS, PRINCETON, NEW JERSEY

For
BABETTE

CONTENTS

LIST OF ILLUSTRATIONS

FOREWORD

THIS book, intended for the common reader as well as for the student, chronicles the Russian revolutionary tradition. The account covers a little more than a hundred years, from the first serious questionings of the established order to the emergence, toward the close of the past century, of two major rival parties committed to a violent break with the past. It was first in the eighteen-thirties that a few Russian heads were turned by socialist theory, and the present work naturally records its fortunes under three czars. The development of Populism, the native variety of Socialism, is a dominant theme. The mutinies and popular rebellions of earlier times, among them the jacqueries headed by the Cossack firebrands, Stepan Razin and Yemelyan Pugachev, in the reigns of Czar Alexis and Catherine the Great respectively, do not belong to the story.

Of necessity the socio-political setting, changing with the passage of time, has been sketched in. Only thus could the sequence of events, including those of the intellectual order, be intelligible. Cut off by the autocracy from political experience, with no opportunity to subject theory to the harsh test of practice, the radical movement was to a large extent a matter of doctrine and dogma, the product of minds given to pursuing ideas *à outrance*. Hence the close attention to ideological trends and to the men who were responsible for them or gave them currency. Throughout emphasis falls, however, on clandestine activities, whether executed or merely planned, whether they took the form of peaceful propaganda or political assassination.

The men and, from the sixties on, the women, behind these efforts and exploits include a variety of human types. They illustrate what Pascal called 'the glory and the baseness in man,' and, of course, a mixture of the two, as also of insight and dunder-headedness. Along with zealots and triflers, there are a few crackpots and many innocents. And there is the sinister premonitory shadow of a being less than human that lies across these pages. In the later chapters the centre of the stage is held by idealists, in some cases willing to use any means for the sake of the end, people who have learned to forego pity and are ready to immolate others as well as themselves in the service of what they believe to be just. The tale is a tragic one, though not without moments of comedy.

I would have liked to bring the story down to the epochal turning point of the year 1917. But this would have required another volume. Attention centres here upon early stirrings, initial attempts, and pioneer endeavours. The narrative follows the headwaters of the revolutionary current and comes to a stop just before the rivulets join to form a sizable, if divided, stream. Yet this survey of 'unhappy, far-off things, and battles long ago' is not without relevance to what happened when the old order was finally overthrown, and should help to bring into sharper focus the Soviet phenomenon, if only because of the way it contrasts with all that the nineteenth-century radicalism dreamed of, stood for. The revolution has followed a course unforeseen either by the populists or their Marxist adversaries. Nevertheless there originated within the period examined some of the ways of acting and thinking that persisted into the current century and have influenced Soviet ideology and practice. Such, for example, is the concept of what may be called the telescoped revolution, involving seizure of political power and its dictatorial use to the end of enforcing socialism. Several Soviet historians have emphasized the debt Bolshevism owes to the cohort of populist propagandists and terrorists which went by the name of The People's Will. Indeed, it is doubtful if the doctrine of Leninism can be fully understood without taking account of the indigenous social-revolutionary tradition as it developed in the second half of the nineteenth century.

Over the years, and especially since 1917, the literature on that subject has grown enormously. It is mostly in the nature of monographs and papers on particular episodes and personalities, also of documentary source material, such as police reports, prisoners' depositions, trial records, texts of underground publications issued by the various secret groups and societies. The present study seeks to be a work of synthesis based on much of that literature. Practically all the necessary research was carried out in the New York Public Library, which has an unusually ample Russian collection. Grateful acknowledgment is hereby made for the friendly services of my former associates in the Slavonic Division of that library. I also wish to thank Boris Ivanovich Nicolaevsky for allowing me to draw, now and then, on his intimate knowledge of the Russian revolutionary movement. The dedication is an inadequate token of my indebtedness to my wife, who gave me every kind of help in the writing of this book.

A word should be said about chronology. Unless marked N.S. (New Style), the dates are according to the calendar which was used in Russia before 1 February, 1918 (Old Style); being of the nineteenth century, they are twelve days earlier than they would be if reckoned by the calendar now in general use. N.S. is omitted where it is clear from the context that the date is reckoned by the latter calendar.

A. Y.

September, 1956

CHAPTER I

THE ANCESTOR: RADISHCHEV

IN May, 1790, when Catherine II had been on the throne twenty-eight years, copies of a new book, entitled *A Journey from Petersburg to Moscow*, found their way into one or two bookstores in the Russian capital. The few people who bought it must have gaped as they turned the pages of the bulky volume duly provided with the censor's imprimatur. Indebted to the technique of Sterne's *Sentimental Journey*, this medley of narrative, argument, invective, and homily, enlivened by thumbnail character sketches sharply drawn and an occasional digression into surprisingly frank autobiography, was least of all a rambling travelogue. It was a political tract of unprecedented boldness. Here spoke, in the rhetorical and tearful accents of the period, not only a sensitive heart that bled at the sight of suffering and swelled with indignation—an indignation not free from self-righteousness—at the spectacle of injustice, but also a mind committed to the ideas of a revolutionary age.

While informed with the spirit of Western Enlightenment, the book is deeply rooted in the native soil. Never before had the seamy side of Russian life been so boldly exposed, nor the vernacular used to voice sentiments so unbecoming a subject of the Empress and a member of the Orthodox Church. One chapter intimates that the gaudy façade of Catherine's rule conceals a corrupt and cruelly oppressive régime. By innuendo her favourites, notably Potemkin, are told off as a pack of greedy, incompetent sycophants, mercilessly plundering the people. Nor does the author mince words in denouncing the criminal negligence and venality of lesser officialdom. He is no gentler with those who wear a crown. Of Emperor Joseph II he writes: 'He was a king. Tell me, then, in whose head can there be more absurdities than in a king's?' His political ideal, government by law, is compatible with monarchy. But there is not a little in the book to suggest that the nation would be best off if the throne were to be swept away.

1

His animus against autocracy is most apparent in the ode entitled 'Liberty', excerpts from which are inserted in the text. This clumsy and prolix piece—in its entirety it runs to fifty-four ten-line stanzas—celebrates freedom as the highest good, godlike in its creative possibilities. Apparently composed between 1781 and 1783, it was to some extent inspired by the American Revolution. The poet apostrophizes Washington as an unconquerable warrior guided by liberty. In lines omitted from the book he thus addresses the American States rejoicing at their newly acquired freedom: 'You jubilate while we suffer here, and all thirst for the same, the same.' If he could at least be buried in America! But no, let him be interred in his native land, so that youths, seeing his grave, may say: 'This man, who was born under the yoke of authority, and bore gilded fetters, was the first to prophesy freedom to us.'

The poet envisions a popular rising against a tyrannical king, his trial by the successful rebels and his death verdict. In this connexion the regicide Cromwell is praised for having taught the peoples to revenge themselves on rulers who violate the rights of man. An accusing finger is also pointed at the Church: in partnership with the State 'faith' oppresses society, the one seeking to enslave the mind, the other to obliterate the will.

The last stanzas are heavy with confused, dark augury, that brightens at the close. They have recently been read, not without some exercise of the imagination, as a foreshadowing of the Russian revolution. The Empire, the poet vaticinates, will go on expanding and, as a result, the bond uniting the several parts will weaken; then the country will pass through a great upheaval; fire and famine and civil strife will lay it waste and shatter it into fragments; they will reunite on a new basis, presumably as a federation, and under the ægis of freedom; this will be crushed by authority; in the fulness of time, however, the shackled people will rise, and on a day that will be 'the most elect among all days' liberty will shine forth.

In prose, and more soberly, the author calls for religious tolerance and the abolition of censorship, citing in this connexion the constitutions of four American states. He seems to be aware that equality before the law is not enough. 'Right, without power,' he remarks, 'has always been esteemed an empty word.' Indeed, on one occasion he mentions 'equality of possessions' as a desideratum. Both as a devotee of liberty and as an egalitarian he attacks the status and privileges of the nobility, particularly its right to own bondsmen. In fact, the main force of his protest is directed against 'the hundred-headed monster' of serfdom.

Solitary voices had called attention to the evils of this institution in the past, and the public prints that blossomed out briefly in the 1770's had helped to make it odious. The Freemasons, whose numbers had grown considerably since the lodges first appeared in the mid-century, had sought to humanize the treatment of the serfs. *A Journey* goes much further. Later abolitionists were to add nothing to the case against serfdom that is made out in the book. Episode upon episode builds up an accusing story of misery and oppression. 'Greedy beasts, insatiable leeches,' cries the author, 'what do we leave to the peasant? That which we cannot take away: air.' He offers no palliatives. He demands complete, if gradual, emancipation. The serfs must become fully-fledged citizens, owning the land they till.

How is liberation to be brought about? The author has an imaginary sovereign appeal to the owners to take the initiative in freeing the serfs. Morality, religion, the public good, the economic interest of the masters themselves are invoked in turn. There is yet another argument, which a czar will use in a later generation: if freedom does not come from above, it must come from below, the result of 'the very weight of enslavement'. Serfdom is bound to lead to a bloody uprising. The danger is imminent. 'Already Time has lifted his scythe awaiting an opportune moment. . . .' The author, far from being appalled by it, welcomes the prospect of a popular explosion, in which, he knows, the members of his own class stand to lose everything, including their lives. 'Oh, would that the slaves, burdened with heavy shackles, rose in their despair,' he exclaims, 'and with the irons that deprive them of freedom crushed our heads, the heads of their inhuman masters, and reddened the fields with our blood!' There are, in *A Journey*, other less bombastic passages which call to mind the motto coined by another rebel under different circumstances: 'War to the castles, peace to the huts!'

II

Either the censor approved the manuscript of *A Journey from Petersburg to Moscow* without looking into it, or he failed to grasp the meaning of what he read. In any event, he had permitted the release of a literary bomb.

It burst in a charged atmosphere, throbbing with the remote thunders of the French Revolution. We have it on the authority of the French Minister to Russia that the news of the fall of the Bastille made a great stir in Petersburg (now Leningrad), as it did in so many European centres. While it caused consternation at the court and in the mansions, it aroused enthusiasm among middle-class people and some scions of the gentry. Strangers embraced in the streets and congratulated each other. The event seems to have been the object of some sympathetic comment even in high places. One evening in the autumn of 1789 a secretary to the Empress arriving home—his apartment was in the Winter Palace—found the passage leading to his drawing-room flooded with the light of many candles. His daughter, a precocious child of seven, explained that she had arranged the illumination, a feature of all the parties at the Palace, to celebrate the capture of the Bastille and 'the freeing of those poor French prisoners'.

Citizen Edmond Genet, the new French chargé d'affaires, reported to his government that the Russian soil held 'the seeds of true democracy'. He was amazed at the signs of friendliness that he met in many quarters. When it became known that he had been forbidden the Court, many Guard officers called on him to pay their respects. Early in 1790 a Moscow review carried the observation that the preceding year had inaugurated 'a new epoch for mankind'. Even in the provinces news from France was eagerly followed. An alarmed ecclesiastic remarked that due to the emotions 'inflamed by the example of France . . . free talk against the autocratic power' was 'well-nigh universal'. This was in 1790. Two years later a Russian statesman, writing to another Russian aristocrat, deplored the effect of the French revolution, adding: 'Not that it hasn't many partisans among us, as elsewhere.' There was no doubt exaggeration in these statements. Yet it is probable that the French upheaval did stimulate whatever political discontent existed in Russia at this time. At any rate, the more enlightened segment of the literate public, a very limited group indeed, briefly displayed a considerable concern with politics.

Small wonder, then, that *A Journey from Petersburg to Moscow* attracted attention. It aroused particular interest among what a contemporary called 'the riff-raff'. Before many weeks had elapsed the book was brought to the notice of the Empress. She read it. She was mortified, she was enraged. She covered the margins with angry comment, in ungrammatical Russian. The wretch takes a black view of everything, has an ungrateful heart, is trying to teach his grandmother to suck eggs. He would rouse the people against their superiors. He calls war murder! He exudes French poison. The idea of bewailing the condition of the peasantry! Why, in Russia the lot of a serf owned by a good master is the best in the whole world. This pen-pusher has no regard for the laws, either human or divine, he threatens the foundations of the family, he is against the commandments. Nothing escapes his censure. If he contracted the pox in his youth, it was the Government's fault (the author blames the authorities for his disease because they sanction prostitution instead of trying to eradicate it). He extolls Cromwell and Mirabeau, 'who deserves not one, but several gibbets'. His dislike of monarchs stares you in the eye, he threatens them with the block. And he pins his hopes to the mutiny of the churls. Seditious, criminal pages!

A Journey had been completed, as the Empress was soon to learn, nearly a year before the fall of the Bastille. Also the single passage on revolutionary France in the text conveys a rather dim view of developments there. Noting that despite all the talk of liberty, the National Assembly has not abolished censorship, the author concludes that 'the French should weep, and mankind with them'. Nevertheless Catherine decided—and not without reason—that the book exhibited the temper that was turning France upside down. It was an incendiary work, besides being an affront to her person. The police were ordered to destroy all copies they could lay hands on. As a result, of the six hundred and fifty copies printed, only seventeen are extant. Nor could the author go unpunished. His name did not appear in the volume, but it was easy to identify him.

5

He proved to be an official in charge of the Petersburg custom-house, a widower, just over forty, by the name of Alexander Radishchev. As a boy he had attended the exclusive Corps of Pages, which partook of the nature of an educational establishment. The pupils served as pages at the imperial court and were instructed in sixteen subjects, all of them taught by a single pedagogue, a Frenchman. In his middle teens he had been sent abroad by the Empress to study law and related subjects. He spent five intellectually profitable years at the University of Leipzig, reading the works of the French *philosophes* more assiduously than his German textbooks. Back home, he entered government service, but continued to keep abreast of events in the West and of European thought, particularly in the field of economics and politics. He did not shed his radicalism with his youth. He also found time for writing, and among other things gradually composed the chapters that made up *A Journey from Petersburg to Moscow*. It was run off on his own printing-press by his own serfs, private printing establishments having been permitted in 1783.

Radishchev was arrested and handed over to a prosecutor infamous for his manhandling of prisoners. The outcome of the trial was a foregone conclusion: he was condemned to be beheaded. But he promptly and abjectly apologized, disclaimed any intention other than to acquire literary fame, and pleaded for mercy, protesting his loyalty to the Empress and enjoining his sons in his last will 'to love and respect her sacred person above all'. In view of his recantation, and because peace had just been concluded with Sweden, Catherine commuted the death sentence to a ten-year term of exile to Siberia. At the end of that time he re-entered the service, but soon committed suicide (in 1802, at the age of 53). In *A Journey* and elsewhere Radishchev had expressed his conviction that a man has the moral right to take his own life if he cannot live it with dignity.

III

After the Empress had finished reading *A Journey*, she concluded that, since the author's purpose was no less than to snatch the sceptre from the hands of the monarch, and since he could not carry out this design alone, he must have had partners in crime. Questioned on that point while under arrest, Radishchev's truthful reply was in the negative. He was rather unsociable, he added, and spent his leisure at home composing his 'vile book'.

If he had no accomplices, from the first his book was not without a sympathetic audience. As has been suggested, in the latter years of Catherine's reign her thirty-six million subjects included people infected with democratic ideas. Like so much else in Russian culture they were an importation from the West. French political literature, which played its part in throwing up barricades in Paris, was read and taken to heart in Russia. It helped to form the intellectual climate hostile to the established order. The Empress herself was instrumental in spreading European Enlightenment in her adopted country, particularly during those early years when it pleased her to play the part of a crowned philosopher. She opened schools, encouraged book publishing, sponsored a periodical press, though only as long as the satire in which it indulged remained innocuous. A peasant uprising at home and the turn events were taking in France helped to put an end to her flirtation with liberalism. The régime which had started out as an enlightened despotism ended as despotism *tout court*. But she could not wholly undo what was, in part, the work of her own hands.

The constituted authorities had nothing to fear from the men who were hospitable to Radishchev's idea and sympathized with the French Revolution. Intellectuals and semi-intellectuals born into the lesser nobility and the third estate, they were a tiny minority, impotent, nearly mute, alienated from their surroundings by education. Cruelly ill at ease, they could only dream of a distant future when, as they might have phrased it, man's natural right to liberty and happiness would be secured by laws grounded on reason and justice.

Some of the Russians staying in France temporarily succumbed to the revolutionary virus. The Russian ambassador in Paris complained that the priest attached to the embassy had got out of hand, the Rights of Man having gone to his head. Among those infected were several scions of the topmost aristocracy who were being educated abroad. Prince Dmitry Golitzyn, aged eighteen, is said to have taken part in the assault on the Bastille. Another raw youth, Count Paul Strogonov, heir to an immense

7

fortune, who was in Paris with his French tutor early in the Revolution, joined the Club des Jacobins—his membership certificate is dated 7 August, 1790. The idea of returning home, where he would have to breathe the air of despotism, horrified him. But, like Golitzyn, return he did, and eventually both made brilliant careers, one becoming a senator, the other—Governor-General of Moscow.

One of the women who ruled Russia in the eighteenth century had had to cope with an opposition that stemmed from the top of the social hierarchy. In 1730 a group of great lords, men of ancient lineage who owned vast estates and thousands of 'souls', attempted to force a charter on Empress Anna, limiting the sovereign's authority, guaranteeing certain basic rights to the population and giving the upper nobility a voice in the affairs of state. Had such a constitution been granted, it would in all likelihood gradually have developed along democratic lines, and the history of Russia and the world would have had a different complexion. But the aristocratic *frondeurs* failed, and by the time Catherine took power they had ceased to count. By and large, the upper classes, particularly the country squires, were as innocent of political ambitions as the infant third estate and the lower orders. They were solidly behind the autocratic régime, since it guaranteed their economic and social prerogatives, especially the exclusive right to live off the labour of the serfs. Catherine was at pains to formalize the corporate organization of the nobility as a privileged caste. In her reign the nobles had more reason than ever to feel that they were the backbone of the empire, the mainstay of the throne and, indeed, the salt of the earth.

As for the rural masses, they clung to the belief that the occupant of the throne, an anointed ruler, was their protector against the greed and inhumanity of the masters. By giving himself out to be Czar Peter III, a Cossack by the name of Pugachev succeeded in rousing a large segment of the peasantry against the landed gentry, and for two or three years (1773–75) a bloody *jacquerie* raged throughout the eastern section of European Russia. The rising was crushed, and the lot of the villagers only worsened. While professing liberal sentiments, the 'crowned Tartuffe in petticoats', as Pushkin called Catherine, actually extended the status of bondsmen to hundreds of thousands of State peasants by making generous gifts of lands that they inhabited to her favourites, as did also her successor. By 1782 the nobility owned fifty-three per cent. of the peasant population. Completely at the mercy of their masters, and more thoroughly exploited than ever before, the serfs were in an ugly mood, but their resentment found vent only in an occasional outbreak of insubordination or the lynching of an exceptionally harsh landowner. Cowed and brutalized, the peasantry was wholly absorbed in the task of keeping above the starvation line.

In short, while abroad revolution was smashing the edifice of absolute rule and feudal privilege, in Russia the finishing touches had been put to it, and it stood there, complete and seemingly impregnable.

Radishchev was, no doubt, aware of this situation. He knew that he had been born too soon, that he would not live to see 'the elect among all days'. He was a near-republican in a semi-Oriental autocracy, a democrat in a squirearchy, an egalitarian in a caste society, an abolitionist in an age that witnessed the expansion of quasi-slavery, a nobleman with a bad conscience in a period when the nobility accepted its privileges as its rightful due. A humanitarian, he denounced the evils of industrialism, describing mines as 'graves in which thousands of men are buried alive'. What sustained him was a sense of the historic significance of his work, the stubborn belief that subsequent generations were certain to heed his message. Like one of the imaginary characters that he used as mouthpieces in his book, he thought of himself as 'a citizen of the time to come'. He concludes his project for the emancipation of the serfs with these words: 'This is not a reverie: the gaze penetrates the thick curtain of time concealing the future from our eyes; I look across a century.' He could have said with Saint-Just: 'I cast my anchor into the future and press posterity to my heart.'

The excesses of the French Revolution quickly alienated the sympathies of not a few who had begun by applauding it. For some of these enthusiasts devotion to liberty, equality, and fraternity was a passing indiscretion, for others—a matter of fashion, like Jacobin hats and cravats. Besides, it was becoming distinctly unsafe for Catherine's subjects to show the slightest sign of anything but abhorrence for what she called the French *grabuge*.

The Empress watched the drastic course of the Revolution with growing dismay. Her reaction to the news of the execution of the King, as set down by her secretary, was that 'it was absolutely necessary to exterminate everything French, down to the name'. This sentiment, expressed in French, dominated the reporting of French affairs in the Russian press. Not even moderately objective comment on them was tolerated. Although in official utterances Catherine insisted that her empire was immune to the French infection, her fury was not unmixed with fear. She saw conspirators everywhere and imagined that her life was in danger.

The sense of insecurity was not confined to her. On 13 November (N.S.), 1792, Count Vorontzov, Russian Ambassador to Great Britain, wrote to his brother that the world was witnessing a struggle to the death between the 'haves' and the 'have-nots', in which the latter were sure to win, and that Russia too was in the end bound to become a victim of this universal epidemic, perhaps within his son's lifetime. 'I have decided,' he concluded, 'to teach him a trade, that of a locksmith or a cabinetmaker. When his vassals tell him that they no longer need him and wish to divide his lands among them, let him at least be able to earn his bread with his own labour.' A week later the Count returned to the subject of the irresistible onward march of the 'democrats', winding up dejectedly with the remark: 'Our turn, too, will come. . . .'

Several pamphlets by native authors, directed against the Revolution, made their appearance, and one versifier told the French that they could have enjoyed lasting peace if, like the Russians, they had known how to obey. But the Empress was inclined to rely on police measures rather than on ideological weapons to combat the menace of subversion.

She had always disliked the Freemasons. Now they fell under suspicion as harbouring political designs and she visited her wrath upon them. In vain did they go out of their way to deny any connexion with Radishchev—his book was dedicated to a prominent Mason—protesting that criticism of the constituted authorities was against their principles. Their lodges were outlawed and their leader, Nikolay Novikov, clapped into jail without a trial and publicly branded as a charlatan. The charitable and educational institutions established by the Masons were disbanded and many thousands of volumes published under their auspices went up in smoke. Among them were copies of a Russian version of Shakespeare's *Julius Caesar*. Book burning became a regular police occupation. The umbrageousness of the censors knew no limits. A new translation of Voltaire, the former protégé of the Empress, was confiscated by her order, and so was a tragedy by a native playwright celebrating the republicanism of medieval Novgorod. The French residents of the capital were forced to take an oath which amounted to disowning their country, and Russians staying in France were ordered to return home. Whenever possible, French instructors were replaced by Swiss. The royalist émigrés, received at Court with open arms, set the tone of polite society, in opinions as well as in sartorial matters. Rarely did a young gentleman display a Jacobin touch in his attire, just for the devil of it, and a lady was apt to wear her hair *à la reine* and a gown *à la contre-révolution* in black and yellow, the colours of the anti-French coalition.

Paul I, who succeeded his mother on the throne after her sudden death in November 1796, was at pains to undo her governmental system. But he continued to maintain the quarantine against the French contagion which she had instituted. His unbalanced mind was swayed chiefly by hatred of democratic principles. Russians were forbidden to go abroad, and the country was practically barred to all foreigners except aristocratic émigrés. An embargo was placed on foreign literature and music. Everything that smacked of Jacobinism in men's or women's apparel was expressly banned. A special decree proscribed the use in print of certain words, such as 'citizen', 'fatherland', 'society'. In the five black years of Paul's reign his subjects had an opportunity to learn more than ever about the abuse of autocratic power, though not as much as their descendants were to be taught in our time.

Official rigours were mitigated by inefficiency. There were chinks in the iron curtain between Russia and the West, rung down by Catherine and reinforced by her son. Intellectual contacts with the outside world did not cease even under Paul. All the French tutors could not be eliminated. Nor were the Swiss who had replaced some of them immune to liberal ideas. One, an instructor in a military college, taught the cadets the Marseillaise. The reactionary régime of the last years of the century silenced but could not, of course, entirely choke off the opposition.

In the summer of 1793 one Fyodor Krechetov, described officially as a dangerous political criminal, was confined until further notice to a solitary cell in the Fortress of Saints Peter and Paul, where Radishchev had spent some time before his deportation to Siberia. One charge against this retired lieutenant was that he had brought out a list of the works he had prepared for publication—the man was a graphomaniac—without submitting it to censorship. A more serious accusation was that he had been spreading subversive notions by word of mouth. It was alleged that he had made scurrilous remarks about the Empress and expressed the wish 'to overthrow the autocracy and make a republic or some such thing, so that all should be equal'. His head was full of plans for reforms, and on one occasion he had observed that if the authorities failed to put them into effect, 'a small band, uniting with the discontented, could do for the Government in the twinkling of an eye'. Krechetov and some of his acquaintances were readers of *A Journey from Petersburg to Moscow*.

Two manuscript copies of the book were in the possession of an army man arrested in 1794. Among his papers were found poems which, in a dithyrambic style resembling that of Radishchev's ode 'Liberty', urged the people 'to crush the walls of autocracy'. Another military man was overheard saying that all monarchs were 'tyrants and evildoers', and that all men were equal, which earned him exile to Siberia. This was in 1797. Two years later a small landowner of gentle birth was arrested in Kiev: he had been heard to say that people would be better off if they were 'free and equal', like the French. In 1798 the police discovered a group of army officers stationed in the province of Smolensk who were meeting secretly to read forbidden books, which, in the words of the official report, were certain 'to deprave weak minds and implant in them the spirit of liberty and sympathy with the French republic. . . .' The books in question apparently included *A Journey from Petersburg to Moscow*. Repeatedly Shakespeare's *Julius Caesar* was read aloud, and the scene of the murder of the Roman dictator elicited sanguinary remarks directed at the tyrant at home. In their letters the men liked to quote the phrase: 'Brutus, thou sleep'st,' adding: 'while the fatherland is in irons.' It is reported that a Major Potemkin volunteered to assassinate the Emperor.

A truly seminal work, Radishchev's book continued to be read, *sub rosa*, mostly in transcripts. More of these are extant than printed copies, and fabulous rentals are said to have been paid for them. The efforts of the authorities to consign Radishchev to oblivion were of no avail. Echoes of his ideas are discernible in the writings of several minor authors who were active at the turn of the century. Nor was his name unknown to the next two generations. But it was in mid-century, when the movement for political and social reform was taking shape, that the significance of his pioneering effort began to be widely appreciated. A reprint of his book appeared in London in 1858. Ten years later the ban on it was removed. Nevertheless, an expurgated edition of Radishchev's writings issued in Petersburg in 1872 was confiscated by administrative order. It was only early in the twentieth century that *A Journey* became freely accessible to the general public.

By that time his reputation as the first prophet and martyr of Russian freedom was firmly established. He was honoured as the Ancestor by both liberals and radicals. The former rightly read *A Journey* as the first programme of Russian political democracy. The latter hailed it as the fountainhead of Russian revolutionary tradition and Radishchev as the progenitor of radical thought and feeling. They stressed the fact that he sanctioned the use of force for political ends, that he was a militant by temperament as well as by conviction, that he sided with the downtrodden and had a deep faith in the masses as the prime mover of history, that he was indeed the first swallow of the populist spring that was to come generations after his death.

On 22 September, 1918, a statue of Radishchev was unveiled in the garden of the Winter Palace in Leningrad. It was the first of the monuments erected, at Lenin's suggestion, in the capital of the triumphant revolution. In recent years Soviet scholarship has heaped extravagant encomia on Radishchev. One author has blithely declared that he was the greatest political thinker of the eighteenth century. He was actually an apt disciple of Western Enlightenment in its later phase. Convinced that no ruler will give up an ounce of his authority voluntarily, he invoked the arbitrament of force without, however, losing faith in the power

13

of reason to deal with the sources of human suffering. He was clear-sighted enough to examine native realities in the light of his ideas and, his recantation notwithstanding, he was a pioneer in courageously speaking out against the twin evils of Russian life: autocracy and serfdom, although he knew that his was a voice crying in the wilderness.

CHAPTER II

THE DECEMBRISTS:
THE SECRET SOCIETIES

On the night of 23 March, 1801, Paul I was strangled in his bedroom by a group of titled conspirators. They acted on the pretext that the Czar's mental derangement was endangering the safety of both the dynasty and the State. It was the last of the palace revolutions to which the successors of Peter the Great owed the throne. Like those that went before, it left the régime intact.

At the outset, however, great changes seemed afoot. Grand Duke Alexander had been described by Citizen Genet as 'an ardent democrat'. When he became Czar he surrounded himself with a group of young reformers dubbed by the diehards 'the Jacobin gang'. Before long he had as his chief adviser Speransky, a Francophile statesman of liberal views, who wished to see the country industrialized, modernized, brought within the orbit of European civilization. The French influence strongly reasserted itself. 'You who abhor everything that upsets the social order,' wrote one dismayed Russian aristocrat to another the year after Alexander's accession, 'will be overwhelmed, on arriving in Petersburg, to see there hundreds of young men who deserve to be adopted sons of Robespierre and Danton.' An increasing number of people were exposed to Western ideas. The influence of English liberalism and, to a lesser extent, German romanticism, was beginning to make itself felt. At the same time a growing body of native literature was having a humanizing effect, which tended to render the iniquity of the sytem more distasteful to the literate public.

The Emperor revoked certain repressive measures, stayed the censor's hand, and encouraged popular education. He also planned to bestow civil rights on the citizenry by a special edict, which was to be Russia's Magna Carta, and in 1809 Speransky drafted something in the nature of a constitution. In the preamble to this document the serf-owners are described as 'a handful of parasites.' The adoption of some form of representative government would have gone far toward conciliating the progressive elements of the gentry and even the inchoate middle class, which was becoming aware of the political implications of its economic interests. Nothing came of these plans for reform, however. The instrument drafted by Speransky was laid on the shelf, as was also a charter, based in part on the constitution of the United States, which was prepared a decade later. As his people were not long in discovering, Alexander was not the man to lead them out of bondage. 'He would gladly have consented to set the whole world free,' an intimate said of him, 'on condition that the whole world gladly did his bidding.'

The Government's foreign policy served to alienate the affections of the agrarians, without winning over the industrialists. The alliance with France after Tilsit, and the adherence to the Continental System, ruined the country's export trade, which was confined to agricultural products, and brought the State to the verge of bankruptcy. Feeling ran so high among the nobility that it looked as though Alexander might end like his father. A memorial addressed to the Czar, which was circulated in manuscript, called attention to famine in the border provinces, high prices in the capitals, crushing taxes, onerous levies of recruits everywhere, universal indignation and despair.

At the outbreak of the so-called Patriotic War of 1812 the landed gentry was further disturbed by fears that the invaders were going to liberate the serfs, and rumours of such an eventuality seeped down to the peasantry. Here and there, in the occupied territory, serfs refused to obey their masters, saying that now they were under the French, they were free. But it soon became clear to all concerned that Bonaparte, like Hitler in the next century, had come not to liberate, but to conquer and pillage. As a matter of fact, in Poland and Lithuania the French crushed the peasant risings for which the war had been a signal. Speaking before the Senate on 20 December, 1812, about the Russian campaign, Napoleon said that he could have won over the majority of the people by proclaiming the liberty of 'the slaves' but, seeing the brutishness of that large class of the population, he had refrained from enacting a measure which 'would have doomed many families to death, devastation, and horrible tortures'. To his brother Jérôme he wrote that many villagers had petitioned him to issue an emancipation decree, promising to take up arms for him, but that in the absence of a middle class which could direct and moderate the popular movement that such a step would have started, he felt that to arm slaves would have meant 'to deliver over the country to frightful evils'.

One of the petitions mentioned by Napoleon has recently been brought to light. Dated Ruza (a town in central Russia), 30 September, 1812, and purporting to come from 'The Russian Provinces', it opens with the statement that it has been God's will to end serfdom among the Russian people with the aid of Napoleon's power, and concludes with assurances of allegiance to him. For the most part, however, the masses were hostile to the French and, as everyone knows, their passive resistance played a part in annihilating *la Grande Armée*.

The invasion laid waste the western and some of the central provinces and left in its wake much economic distress. The campaigns of 1813 and 1814, while adding to the lustre of Russia's arms, were a further drain on the country's resources and increased the heavy burden borne by the masses. There was a widespread feeling among the peasantry that their patriotic service to the country had earned them their freedom, and that they were going to receive it at the Czar's hands. He had another view of the matter. 'May our faithful peasants receive their reward from God', the Emperor said in his manifesto of 30 August, 1814, adding that, as regards privately owned serfs, 'we are certain that our care for their welfare will be forestalled by their masters' solicitude for them'. The institution of serfdom remained intact in spite of the fact that its drawbacks were beginning to show up with the development of a money economy.

Within a few years Alexander's early liberalism had virtually vanished and was replaced by the reactionary principles of the Holy Alliance. The ambassador to England, Count Semyon Vorontzov, writing to his son at the beginning of the reign, described the period as 'a suspension of tyranny', predicting that his compatriots, like the Roman slaves after the Saturnalia, would soon relapse into their normal condition of servitude. His words proved prophetic. The decade that followed the Napoleonic wars witnessed something like a reversion to the nightmare of Paul's reign. 'Emperor Alexander I', wrote Lafayette to Jefferson on 20 December, 1823, 'is now the head of the European counter-revolution.'

As a matter of fact, even while Alexander had been consorting with 'the Jacobin gang', he had also been depending upon his father's trusted servitor, Arakcheyev, who combined the brutality of a vicious martinet with the meanness of a small-minded bureaucrat. With this man as the all-powerful vizier, the country was again at the mercy of intolerant obscurantism. The press was terrorized, elementary schooling was curtailed, and on the pretext that education must be based on 'piety', the universities were emasculated. The few half-hearted administrative reforms, instead of leading to a parliamentary régime, only strengthened the hands of an incompetent and corrupt bureaucracy. The changes were 'a drama of feebleness and insincerity', to use the language of Jeremy Bentham when, in 1814, he turned down the invitation to assist the commission for the revision of the Empire's code of laws.

The Government did introduce one novelty: the so-called military settlements. These were initiated before the war, but it was only in the year marked by the formation of the Holy Alliance that they were started on their disastrous career in earnest. This was a pet scheme of the Czar's whereby, to the alarm of the other powers, he hoped to obtain an unlimited supply of cannon fodder, cheap. The maintenance of the armed forces swallowed up a large part of the State revenue—fifty-four and a half per cent of it in 1816—and the settlements are generally believed to have been an ill-conceived measure of economy. An attempt has recently been made by an American scholar to show that the Czar was inspired by high motives in launching this enterprise, that the colonies were to be 'spearheads of civilization', a boon to a backward people. Whatever the intentions behind the venture, its results proved a source of unmitigated misery to the population immediately concerned.

The plan called for the ultimate transformation of most of the Crown peasants into a military caste from which alone combat personnel was to be drawn, and which in time was to include a quarter to one-third of the country's male population. The members of this estate were to live in newly established settlements which were eventually to occupy a wide zone stretching across the Empire, from the Baltic to the Black Sea. Thither the bulk of the standing army was gradually to be transferred. Indeed, elements of several regular regiments were quartered in the

Alexander Radishchev, author of *A Journey from Petersburg to Moscow*. From an engraving by Francesco Vendramini

Colonel Pavel Pestel. From a portrait by his mother, 1813

Mikhail Petrashevsky

Nikolay Chernyshevsky at the pillory, 1864. The inscription
on the placard reads 'Political criminal'

settlements which actually materialized. In these communities all the males, from the age of seven up, wore uniform. The men were enrolled in battalions and received military training but, unlike ordinary soldiers, were expected to support themselves by agricultural work and handicrafts. The settlements formed a state within a state, with an autonomous administration and laws and courts of their own. They were a centrally planned, strictly regulated society, a nightmare Utopia of paternalism and regimentation. Life there was subject to a rigid army regimen, families living in barrack-like cottages, the men working in the fields in squads. Even the women's chores, such as heating the stove, were done at the signal of a drum. Marriages were arranged by official order, and expectant mothers had to report to head-quarters when they felt birth pangs.

From the first, the military settlements were abominated by the liberal-minded and eyed with apprehension even by con-servatives. 'In the nature of things,' wrote the Empress's secretary, 'sooner or later Russia will not avoid a revolution. . . . The conflagration will start with these notorious settlements.' The peasants involved resented them fiercely, and there were some outbreaks of violence. These were ruthlessly put down. Alexander is alleged to have said that the settlements would be maintained even at the cost of lining the road from Petersburg to Chudovo with corpses. It would have meant seventy-five miles of them. Although the enterprise proved a failure financially and other-wise, due in part to the corruption and incompetence of the administration, which was headed by Arakcheyev, the most hated man in Russia, the Emperor refused to abandon it. By the end of his reign, the settlements had a population of some three hundred thousand male souls.

II

Ground down as the masses were, they remained inert, their discontent finding expression in sporadic riots and killings of brutal serf owners, as also, obliquely, in religious dissent. The landed gentry clung to its privileged status and to the monarch as its guarantor. Of course, the squires grumbled, particularly those who exported much of their produce. For some time

Russia had been the bread-basket of Europe, and in the 'twenties the fall of world prices of grain, caused in part by the English Corn Laws, hit the agrarians hard. Because of disturbances in the Balkans, Turkey closed the straits to Russian shipping, thus further reducing the export of cereals. The government was blamed for failing to promote the nation's vital interests. The State, which was the chief buyer in the domestic market, fixed the prices it paid at so low a level as to make its purchases almost confiscatory. The industrialists, too, had their grievances. These were caused chiefly by a policy that see-sawed between protectionism and free trade. A manuscript pamphlet, purporting to come from the quill of a Moscow merchant, stated that business had no confidence in the government and complained that the merchants at home were treated worse than the Jews in Germany. Mme. de Staël had once told the Emperor that his character was his empire's constitution and his conscience the latter's guarantee. A few of his subjects, including some Petersburg shopkeepers, were now openly discussing the advantages of a more tangible kind of constitution, establishing representative government and civil liberties.

The opposition, such as it was, took shape, however, not in the nascent third estate, but in the Army and Navy command, particularly among the officers of the Guard regiments, the *élite* of the armed forces. Brought up by French tutors, many of these young aristocrats had been exposed to the humanitarian and liberal ideas of the age. The conflict with Napoleon gave their liberalism a nationalist tinge. During the War of 1812 the Army came to feel, as one general put it, that it served not the Emperor but the country. Actual warfare was a relief from the drudgery of drills which had been a fetish with Paul and was so with his son after him. Peace meant return to a discipline as meaningless as it was exacting. Moreover, higher appointments were being bestowed on drill masters and careerists, rather than on men with an honourable war record. Native Russians were passed over in favour of Germans from the Baltic provinces. Alexander probably preferred them for the reason given by his brother Nicholas: 'The Russian gentry serves the State, the Germans serve us.' Peace did not improve the lot of the common soldier. He was subject to corporal punishment, and he could reflect that while his term of service amounted to a quarter of a century (guardsmen served twenty-three years), a Pole served seven years and a Finn was free from military service.

The army men had cause to be disgruntled not only as professionals but also as citizens. The domestic scene was all the more shocking to them after they had something of a glimpse of life abroad during the foreign campaigns. They could not help noticing the difference between the standard of living of the French masses and that of the Russian peasantry. The officers, and to some slight extent even the privates, had breathed the freer air of Europe, had read books and newspapers, and had interested themselves in public affairs. Along with the souvenirs in their knapsacks, they carried back subversive ideas in their heads. The corps that remained in France until 1818 was considered so disaffected that upon its return it was disbanded. The Emperor had sanctioned the free institutions of Finland, recently annexed, and in 1815 granted a constitution of sorts to Poland. But the monarch who abroad wore the halo of a liberator of peoples, at home was a despotic ruler and the head of a system based on serfdom. Some of the officers took this discrepancy as an affront to national dignity, indeed, as treasonable to the country's interests, and in consequence their personal allegiance to their sovereign was sorely tried.

They also felt the impact of events in foreign parts. The uprisings in Spain and Portugal, the Carbonarist insurrections in Naples and Piedmont, the Greek rebellion, were so many object lessons to malcontents in Petersburg and Moscow. Several writers, notably a young scapegrace with a golden tongue in his head by the name of Pushkin, wrote saucy epigrams against those in power and lyrics celebrating liberty and tyrannicide.

In a communication to his Government dated April 1820, the French ambassador wrote that he could not think without horror of what would happen to Europe if forty million Russians, still half savage and brutalized by slavery, conceived a desire for freedom and proceeded to shake off their chains. True, the dangerous notion hadn't yet entered the heads of the lower orders, but it was already inflaming the well-born. 'The entire youth,' he went on, 'and particularly the Army officers, feed on and are imbued with liberal doctrines. The boldest theories are the ones that please the most. . . . Already they imagine, nay, approve, the excesses, the very crimes to which the love of freedom can lead.'

The ambassador had in mind the assassination of the Duc de Berry by the Parisian saddler, Louvel. 'Among these youths', he wrote, 'the infamous Louvel inspires less horror than in France, and his detestable crime has found apologists among the officers entrusted with guarding the Emperor!'

It was inevitable that young, impulsive, generous-minded patriots should attempt some kind of action. They began, meekly enough, by seeking political enlightenment in books, mostly foreign, and they read Radishchev's ode, 'Liberty', as well as his *Journey*, which had the attraction of forbidden fruit. They formed circles to discuss public affairs and wrote letters arguing the necessity of getting together to work for the good of the country. In those years Europe was honeycombed with clandestine groups plotting against the governments leagued in the Holy Alliance. Russia was not without its small quota of plotters.

III

The earliest Russian underground organization of a political character bore the high-sounding name of The Society of the True and Faithful Sons of the Fatherland. It was started in 1816 by a youthful Lieutenant-Colonel of the Guards. At no time during its brief existence did it count more than thirty members. Some of them were sons of the first families of the land, many were officers in the exclusive Guard regiments and veterans of the Napoleonic campaigns.

The Society was also known as The Union of Salvation. It was out to save the country by abolishing serfdom and introducing a constitutional régime. On that point there was complete unanimity. But there was no agreement on how to achieve these objectives. Should a petition be addressed to the Emperor? No, 'acting upon minds', influencing public opinion—that was the way to proceed. It may be that the end of the reign would provide an opportunity for action. Then the Union, grown strong and powerful, would emerge into the open, its members refusing to take the oath of allegiance to the Czar unless he repented the error of his ways and agreed to enact the programme sponsored by the Society.

But why not hasten the propitious moment? The association

was barely six months old when a member, who cherished a dagger he had meant for Napoleon, suggested that Alexander be assassinated by a band of masked men on one of his trips to Tsarskoe Selo. The proposal was turned down, but a year later there was again talk of regicide. A report had reached the Union that the Emperor intended to restore Poland within its pre-partition borders, which would have meant the loss to the Empire of the Ukrainian and White Russian provinces. According to other rumours, Alexander was planning to transfer the capital to Warsaw, and to free the serfs in a manner which was likely to provoke a disastrous *jacquerie*. In an excess of patriotic indignation a young Sub-Lieutenant, who was just then suffering from an unrequited passion, volunteered to shoot the Czar as he was leaving the Uspensky Cathedral in the Kremlin. The would-be assassin intended to use two pistols, killing the Emperor with one and himself with the other, so as to give the affair the semblance of a duel fatal to both noble combatants.

The group included other reckless spirits, but also some timid souls who were horrified by the thought of violence against the sacred person of the monarch. The regicidal plan was abandoned. Before long the Union of Salvation fell apart.

Early in 1818 another secret society, the Union of Welfare, came into being. To judge by its statutes, known as the Green Book, from the colour of its binding, the purpose of this association was to promote the public good by spreading enlightenment and 'true rules of morality'. The chief duty of the members was to conduct themselves virtuously and persuade others to do likewise. The closest that the statutes came to political matters was to suggest that official corruption be combatted by personal example and moral suasion. As for serfdom, the members were enjoined to incline serf owners to treat their peasants in a humane fashion, particularly not to break up families in selling them. Like its predecessor, the Union of Welfare affected oaths, rites, and a fairly elaborate hierarchy, which gave it a resemblance to a Masonic lodge. Freemasonry, though nominally prohibited, was tolerated and had a large following. But, unlike the lodges, the Union of Welfare nourished ambitions other than philanthropic.

The Green Book had a supplement which was shown only to a chosen few and which outlined a political programme of a fairly radical complexion. Here the objectives of the Society were declared to be: to infiltrate the armed forces and the civil administration and at an opportune moment force the Government to grant a constitution, free the serfs, shorten the period of military service, abolish the military settlements, remove 'foreigners', that is Balts, from important posts, and enact other liberal reforms.

The Union succeeded in enrolling up to two hundred members. Army men continued to be the dominant element. Headquarters were in the capital, and several cells sprang up in Moscow and in the south. It is doubtful if many of the members took their plotting very seriously or regarded it as a dangerous game. Some of them were not averse to collaborating with the Government. The belief lingered on that freedom in Russia would come from the Throne. Had not the Emperor declared in 1818 at the opening of the Warsaw Diet that 'he hoped to extend liberal institutions to all the lands under his sceptre'?

As time went on, it was becoming increasingly clear that the authorities were not likely to meet the would-be reformers half-way. The anti-Government trend within the Union grew more pronounced, and republicanism supplanted attachment to constitutional monarchy. The conviction was ripening that the whole system needed a thorough overhauling and that this could not be done peacefully. One of the most resolute advocates of a revolutionary programme and the tactics of force was Colonel Pavel Pestel, a veteran of Borodino and the European campaigns. The son of a thoroughly assimilated German who held the post of Governor-General of Siberia, this young man with a Napoleonic profile, of which he was rather proud, a Machiavellian bent, and the makings of a doctrinaire, stood out among the members of the Union. He headed a branch of it at Tulchin (in the Ukraine), which he had started when he was transferred to the Second Army, made up of line regiments and stationed in the south.

Pestel afterwards asserted that the society had from the first been a revolutionary organization. But, as a matter of fact, some of the members resisted the leftward swing. The men had been enrolled without much discretion, and there were among them too many faint hearts and lackadaisical spirits. What helped to intimidate them and to stimulate their exodus from the Society was the Semyonovsky affair, or rather its consequences.

In the autumn of the year 1820 the brutal behaviour of a newly appointed Colonel created a mild mutiny in the Czar's favourite Guard regiment, the Semyonovsky. In the barracks of another regiment copies of two leaflets were found. One was addressed to the Preobrazhensky guardsmen, the other to soldiers generally. The first described the Czar as 'a powerful brigand' and the gentry as another enemy of the people, and declared that the rule of these 'evildoers' must be replaced by *laws* 'deemed useful by the fatherland'. In the second, the men were urged to arrest their superiors and elect new officers from their own midst, and they were assured that failure to do so would lead to 'a terrible revolution'. The identity of the author or authors of these leaflets is a mystery to this day. It is certain that the Union of Welfare had nothing to do with them or with the mutiny. At most, the mutineers may have received moral support from members of the Society. Nevertheless, the Emperor believed that the disturbances had been fomented by officers—he had some inkling of the existence of the Union—and was greatly alarmed. The mutineers were severely punished and the regiment was disbanded, the men becoming a leaven of discontent in the units to which they were transferred. The entire Guard was subjected to the surveillance of a special secret police.

Membership in the Union now involved more danger than heretofore. The disintegration of the cells in the two capitals, which had been going on for some time, grew more rapid. Under these circumstances a dozen delegates from the several branches met early in 1821 and agreed to dissolve the Union.

This step was a ruse intended to rid the society of undesirables and to deceive the authorities. The handful of men who formed the core of the Union intended to carry on under cover of strict secrecy. They were known as the Northern Society. The branches located in the Ukraine, refusing to disband, assumed a quasi-independent status and the name of the Southern Society.

IV

For some time the Northern Society remained in a state of suspended animation. There were times when its active members could be counted on the fingers of one hand. By the summer of

1823 it began to show signs of life. It was headed by a three-man *Duma*. The triumvirs were all Guard officers: Prince Sergey Trubetzkoy, Prince Yevgeny Obolensky, and Nikita Muravyov, a senator's son and heir to vast estates and thousands of serfs. A reader of French political literature, notably the writings of Benjamin Constant, Muravyov was the most articulate member of the group. He composed 'a free man's catechism', in which the wickedness of autocracy and the advantages of representative government are demonstrated by passages from Scripture. He also drafted a constitutional charter, which he kept rewriting. Though he had at one time been a republican, this charter provides for an empire headed by a hereditary monarch with strictly limited authority. The country is organized, somewhat after the pattern of the United States, as a federation of thirteen regions (the number of the original American states). The bicameral National Assembly, as well as the regional legislatures are elective bodies, but the electorate is restricted by high property qualifications. The serfs are given their personal freedom, without being assured of land. Trial by jury is introduced, and civil liberties are guaranteed to the entire citizenry. To bring about this transformation, Muravyov advocated a long period of peaceful propaganda.

The rather infirm allegiance of the membership was divided between this moderate programme and a more radical one, which called for the establishment of a republican régime, possibly preceded by the extermination of the Imperial family. One retired Captain, a man of thrifty disposition, suggested, perhaps half jokingly, the construction of an 'economy gallows' tall enough to accommodate the Czar as well as the Grand Dukes, hanged one from the feet of the other.

The counsels of moderation were even less heeded in the Southern Society. It continued to be dominated by Pestel's vigorous personality. Content to leave the work of propaganda and organization to others, he was above all an *idéologue*, abreast of the currents of the time. 'Everywhere the spirit of change', he wrote, 'made the minds seethe.' Indeed, 'revolutionary thoughts' were the distinguishing mark of the age. Another feature of it was the struggle of the masses against the aristocracy of birth and the aristocracy of wealth. Both, particularly the latter, were inimical to the public good and could only be wiped out by a republican government. In contrasting the radical temper of the south with the timidity and inaction of the north, he was writing to Nikita Muravyov in 1823: 'Half measures are worth nothing; here we want to make a clean sweep.'

The one task to which he devoted himself wholeheartedly was the composition of a treatise entitled *Russkaya Pravda* (Russian Law, or Justice), which remained unfinished. This was meant to be a set of instructions for the guidance of the Provisional Government that the triumphant revolution would establish, in fact, a blueprint for the Russia of the future, conceived by a man who did not question his right to prescribe and command.

Pestel's thinking was a curious amalgam of liberalism and authoritarianism, with a preponderance of the latter. *Russkaya Pravda* advocates a republican representative régime based on universal suffrage. It is a centralized, monolithic, totalitarian state, exercising absolute control, in the name of public welfare, not only over the behaviour but also the minds of the citizens. To this end it relies on the clergy and a powerful police, including a secret service charged with spying on the population. Private associations, whether open or secret, are forbidden, and so are cards, drinking, all manner of dissipation. In industry free enterprise is the rule, and no provisions are made to safeguard against economic inequality. In fact, 'the rich will always be with us,' Pestel observes, adding, surprisingly enough: 'and this is good.' Private property is declared 'sacred and inviolable'. Yet no legal privileges attach to wealth: before the law all citizens are equal. Of course, this means the abolition of serfdom. The agrarian programme has socialist overtones: half of the land is owned privately, the other half is nationalized and periodically distributed on an equalitarian basis among the families engaged in agriculture. Indeed, every citizen has the right to the free use of acreage sufficient to give him a living. Apparently, Pestel thus hoped to prevent the formation of a landless proletariat, a prospect he abhorred. He was thus committed to a kind of 'mixed economy', with a private and a nationalized sector.

While Muravyov's constitution evinces respect for cultural pluralism and favours the federalist principle as reconciling 'the grandeur of nations with the liberty of citizens', *Russkaya Pravda* looks toward a Russia that would be one and indivisible, a country with a uniform culture, a single language, a common faith. The ethnic minorities must give up their separate identity, all except the Poles, who are to be granted independence conditionally. As for the Jewish citizenry, Pestel was not averse to seeing it leave Russia in a body. If the Jews fail to assimilate, he held, they ought to be helped to emigrate to Asia Minor and there set up a state of their own. Pestel may have borrowed the idea from a converted Jew who was a member of a clandestine group in touch with the Northern Society. This man, Grigory Peretz, used *Herut* (Hebrew for *freedom*) as a password in his cell and spoke of founding a society for the settling of the European Jews either in the Crimea or in the Orient 'as a separate nation'.

Russkaya Pravda, Muravyov's constitution, and similar attempts by other hands were the subject of much debate. Both the northerners and the southerners shared a weakness for planning what to do on the morrow of the successful overturn. Less thought was given to the ways and means of bringing it about. The one procedure that was ruled out was a popular rising. It was felt that the cause had as much to fear from a disorderly populace as from the forces of the existing order. In fact, at least some of the plotters held that it was incumbent on the society to act precisely in order to prevent the bloody popular revolution which the abuses of officialdom were bound to bring about. The sympathy of the masses was desired, but not their co-operation. Will not a popular revolution, it was asked, turn out to be a Frankenstein monster? 'Let us suppose', wrote one member of the Southern Society to another, 'that it is easy to bring the axe of revolution into play, but are you certain that you will be able to stop it afterwards?' Aristocratic army men could not help looking down upon 'the mob', but half acknowledged contempt was not unmixed with apprehension. Baron Steinheil, of the Northern Society, in questioning the desirability of a popular revolution, argued that 'in Moscow alone there were ninety thousand house serfs ready to seize knives, and the first victims will be their (the plotters') sisters, aunts, and grandmothers'.

According to one activist, the Society's intention was to set up a popular government even at the cost of 'a terrible torrent of blood'. Another was ready 'to exterminate twenty-five million to bring freedom to the other twenty-five million'. As a rule, however, the men were eager to avoid violence and believed in the feasibility of a bloodless overturn. Both societies pinned their hopes to a purely military action, a neat *coup* modelled on the Spanish insurrection of 1820, rather than on the French revolution. At the same time the possibility of coming to an understanding with those in power was not ruled out, the bayonets remaining in the background merely as a threat intended to exact concessions from the Government.

How were they to get hold of the bayonets? The plotters were vague on the subject. It was generally expected that the privates would do the bidding of their officers. One southerner, a Lieutenant-Colonel, said that if his company refused to join the insurgents he would drive the men to it with sticks. No systematic attempt was to be made to acquaint the soldiers with the aims of the movement or to win them over to the cause, but the officers were advised to secure the devotion of their men by all means. A leading southerner favoured appealing to their religious sentiment. A fellow member dissented, retorting that 'faith is contrary to freedom'. Many years were to pass before this became an article of the revolutionary creed.

Pestel, for one, was by no means optimistic about the ability of the societies to sway the soldiery. True, the ranks were bristling with discontent, but he knew that it was a far cry from grumbling to mutiny. Nor was he unaware of the immemorial habit of devotion to the Czar which dominated the simple folk. But, he told himself, if the people were faced with the fact of the end of the dynasty, the revolution might succeed. From the first, he had believed that the *coup* must be preceded by the assassination of the Emperor, indeed, of the entire imperial family. Accordingly, he conceived the idea of 'a lost cohort,' a small band of dedicated men, ready to act as regicides under orders from the Society. The plan found some adherents in the north as well. It was assumed that the regicides would be helped to escape abroad, but if caught they would be tried and mercilessly condemned even under the new régime, so as not to bring the Society into disrepute. For the sake of the cause, the terrorists must be ready to forfeit not only their lives, but their very honour. There is a curiously modern ring about this idea.

v

While the two societies had a separate existence, efforts were not lacking to bring them together. In May, 1823, an emissary from the South told the Northerners that the Southern Society was ready to act that very year and asked if it could count on their assistance. He received an evasive reply. The Northern group, still very feeble, was preoccupied with questions of ideology and internal organization.

In the spring of the following year Pestel himself appeared in the capital. His mission was to effect a merger between the two Societies. His republican platform appealed to some Northerners, but there was one plank in it to which all objected. What Pestel advocated was in effect the seizure of state power by the conspirators. The autocracy overthrown, the directorate of the Society should, he argued, become the Provisional Government, vested with authority to decree the new régime as outlined in *Russkaya Pravda*, and remaining in power a decade or longer. This dictatorial scheme, to which there was considerable opposition even in the South, was rejected in the North as a revolting usurpation of the people's sovereignty. Even the more radically-minded took it for granted that the Society would confine itself to destroying the old order and that the Provisional Government would last no longer than was necessary to arrange for the convocation of a National Assembly, which would adopt a constitution and guide the destinies of the country generally.

In spite of this disagreement with Pestel, a conference of the Northern militants resolved that the merger was 'both useful and necessary,' and directed the *Duma* to continue negotiating with him. But that ruling body was firmly opposed to amalgamation with the South and so did not carry out the mandate. Pestel seems to have attempted to split the Society, but did not succeed. He won the enmity of its leadership and the reputation of a potentially dangerous, self-seeking individual who would bear watching. All he achieved was an agreement that neither Society should start the insurrection without consulting the other, unless suddenly forced to act. The two organizations continued to function separately.

30

Pestel was greatly discouraged by his failure. He had no illusions about the strength of the organization over which he presided. Of its three subdivisions two had only a nominal existence. Alone the branch located in the town of Vasilkov, near Kiev, was fairly active. It was headed by Lieutenant-Colonel Sergey Muravyov-Apostol, formerly of the Semyonovsky Guard Regiment, and Lieutenant Bestuzhev-Ryumin. They shared Pestel's republicanism, but by no means subscribed to the rest of his programme.

In 1824 the Southern Society concluded a pact with a secret Polish organization. It was a half-hearted and wholly fruitless agreement between parties that distrusted each other's motives. In the summer of that year a member returning from a stay in 'warm Siberia', as the Caucasus was sometimes referred to, reported that the army corps stationed there harboured an independent clandestine league ready to support a revolution. Nothing further was heard of the matter.

An event of real significance was the absorption of the Society of United Slavs, an underground group with about fifty members that was active in the south-western provinces. It had been started as a 'Pythagorean Brotherhood', which affected the language and ritualism of Freemasonry. Eventually the fraternity, putting away childish things, set as its goal no less an objective than the establishment of a federation of Slav peoples liberated from 'tyranny'. This panslavist emphasis went hand in hand with a militantly democratic and libertarian disposition. 'Having passed through a thousand deaths', a member vowed in taking the oath, 'having overcome a thousand obstacles, I will dedicate my last breath to freedom and the brotherly union of the noble Slavs.' One of the rules of the Society was directed against serfdom. It read: 'Do not wish to have a slave if you do not want to be a slave yourself.' The United Slavs were mostly people in humble circumstances: army officers with nothing but their miserable pay to live on, government clerks, small landowners. One member is known to have been of peasant stock.

The two groups did not discover each other's existence until the summer of 1825. Without delay negotiations were begun to bring the United Slavs *en masse* into the fold of the Southern Society. The spokesman of the latter—it was Lieutenant Bestuzhev-Ryumin—painted a dazzling, if altogether false, picture of the power of the organization he represented, its immense backing at home, its high connections abroad. The entire army, he said, had been won over to the cause, Moscow and Petersburg were impatiently awaiting the revolt, and the constitution drafted by the Society practically guaranteed a speedy and bloodless victory. 'The fate of despotism would be sealed the following summer', he asserted, when the Emperor arrived in the South to review the Third Army Corps. 'At that time the hateful tyrant will succumb under our blows, we will raise the standard of freedom and march on Moscow, proclaiming the constitution.'

The United Slavs, though overawed, were not without misgivings. They had at heart a popular movement, believing that any change made without the participation of the masses was unsound. The Southern Society, as has been noted, advocated a purely military *coup*. Might not a revolution so initiated prove the grave rather than the cradle of liberty? And what measures were to be taken to prevent the projected Provisional Government with its dictatorial powers from resulting in a new tyranny? 'The Slavs' also disliked the highhanded way in which they were treated during the negotiations. In the end they gave in, apparently convinced that the Southern Society sought to establish a 'pure Democracy' in Russia.

During the meeting at which the fusion was effected Bestuzhev-Ryumin fired the audience with a speech. The present age, he declared, was one in which the peoples of the earth were endeavouring to liberate themselves from slavery. Would the Russians, who had freed Europe from Napoleon's yoke, fail to shake off their own? He bade his hearers look about them: the masses were oppressed, commerce had dwindled, industry had all but ceased, the army was restive. Was it surprising that almost all enlightened people had joined the Society or were in sympathy with its aims? It would soon act, and free Russia, perhaps all of Europe. 'The high deed will be accomplished,' he cried, 'and we shall be proclaimed the heroes of the age!' He took from his neck the small icon that, according to Orthodox custom, he wore next to his skin, and swore upon it to be faithful to the Society and to take up arms at the first call. The others did likewise and, amid embraces, there was a murmur of solemn vows, a burst of passionate outcries. 'Long live the constitution! Long live the republic! Long live the people! Perish the nobility and the rank of czar!'

The former 'Slavs' were guided by the maxim: 'Having bared your sword against your monarch, you must fling the scabbard as far away as possible.' Two days after the merger a dozen of them volunteered for 'the lost cohort', which was still only a project. The Society now had a considerable contingent of activists eager—perhaps too eager in the opinion of some Southerners—for drastic action. They were set the task of preparing the privates for the impending insurrection, without initiating them into the real aims of the movement.

Meanwhile there had been changes in the Northern Society, too. At the end of 1824 Prince Trubetzkoy was transferred to Kiev. He was replaced in the *Duma* by a retired Ensign, who had been enrolled the previous year. This man, one Kondraty Ryleyev, was an employee of the Russian-American Company, the trading corporation that was exploiting the Russian possessions in America. In his leisure hours he wrote civic verse, which enjoyed a measure of popularity. A thorough-going democrat, he abhorred Pestel's dictatorial plans, but shared his republicanism. He admired the United States as the only country, he once observed, that had a good Government. Yet he also dreamed of reviving the dubious glories of pre-Muscovite Russia.

His thinking shows traces of the emphasis on the exceptional and superior nature of Russia's manifest destiny, which was to mark Slavophilism and, to an extent, Populism and Bolshevism. On one occasion, in arguing against a fellow conspirator who maintained that the country was not ripe for a radical change and that a monarchy like the English suited Russia best, Ryleyev remarked that Great Britain, enslaved by an aristocracy as it was, could not be a guide on the road to liberty. In fact, he went on, that country would be the last to taste freedom. 'The European overturn must be started in Russia'; there the revolution could not be crushed by foreign intervention as it had been in Naples and Spain—witness the events of 1812. 'The world', he declared, 'must expect everything from Russia.' A friend of Ryleyev's chimed in: 'Russia will be transformed in a Russian way.'

An incandescent, if unstable, soul, capable of kindling people with his enthusiasm, Ryleyev soon came to occupy a dominant position in the Society, which was not remarkable for outstanding personalities. Nikita Muravyov was still a member of the *Duma*, but his influence was rapidly waning, and by the autumn of 1825 he had practically withdrawn from the organization.

The military continued to make up most of the membership. When Ryleyev suggested that merchants should be admitted, the retort was: 'Impossible! Merchants are ignoramuses!' The Society had members and sympathizers in several of the Guard regiments garrisoned in the capital. A foothold was also secured in the Guard *Equipage*, a special naval unit trained for amphibious combat. This was done with the aid of Midshipman Dmitry Zavalishin. At seventeen he had conceived the notion of founding an international knightly order to effect the spiritual regeneration of mankind and, incidentally, to annex California to the Russian Empire. At first he sought to place this society under the Czar's protection. But by 1825 he had reached the conclusion that nothing good could come from the Government. He became active in the Northern Society without giving up the pretence that the secret order which was the figment of his imagination was a force in world politics. By his own account, he became such a power in the Society that out of jealousy Ryleyev removed him from the capital by giving him an assignment to ascertain the state of public opinion in the provinces. Before departing from Petersburg—this was in November 1825—he wrote to the Emperor urging him to enact liberal reforms or face a revolution. At the same time he exhorted the *Duma* to disband the Society on the ground that too many members were motivated not by zeal for freedom but by thirst for power, and that consequently victory would merely substitute one despotism for another.

The conspirators wished to gain a toehold in the Navy so as to be able to deport the Grand Dukes and their families to a foreign country on board a man-o'-war. This alternative to a sterner method of disposing of the potential pretenders to the throne was under serious consideration. As for the Czar, it was generally held that his life could not be spared. When, in the summer of 1825, Captain Yakubovich arrived in the capital intent on killing the Emperor simply to avenge his transfer to the Caucasus after a duel, Ryleyev persuaded him to postpone action until the Society was ready. He had at his disposal yet another would-be regicide, a penniless and somewhat

Alexander Herzen

Pyotr Tkachev.   From a
photograph, 1868

Pyotr Lavrov

unbalanced former Lieutenant by the name of Kakhovsky. The man had come to Petersburg on his way to join the Greek insurgents, and the prospect of becoming a Russian Brutus caught his imagination.

Early in November, 1825, Prince Trubetzkoy was back in the capital. During his stay in Kiev he had kept in touch with the Vasilkov Branch of the Southern Society, which had assumed a dominant position. Before leaving for the North, he concluded something in the nature of an informal agreement with the Southerners. According to its terms, the insurrection was scheduled for May 1826 when the Czar was expected to review the troops stationed in the South. As the initial act, he was to be assassinated. Thereupon the Northerners were to arrest the Grand Dukes and ship them abroad. Then Pestel was to occupy Kiev, Bestuzhev-Ryumin was to march on Moscow, and Sergey Muravyov-Apostol take over the command of the Guards in the capital. The Northern Society was assigned the tasks of determining the composition of the Provisional Government and of drafting a new constitutional charter.

Events played havoc with these none too carefully laid plans.

CHAPTER III

THE DECEMBRISTS: INSURRECTION

ON 19 November, 1825, Emperor Alexander died at Taganrog, a town in Southern Russia. The news only reached the capital on 27 November, and as the Czar had been childless, the troops and the highest dignitaries of the Church and State immediately swore allegiance to Constantine, the eldest of his three brothers.

As a matter of fact, Constantine, who at the time was living in Warsaw, had previously renounced his claim to the throne in favour of the Grand Duke Nicholas, but the rescript which legalized this deviation from the order of succession had remained secret. Nicholas, though not unaware of the arrangement, acknowledged his brother as Emperor and took the oath of allegiance to him. On his part, Constantine failed to act promptly and unequivocally. He refused to make a formal announcement of his abdication or to come to the capital. This, coupled with delay due to slow communications, resulted in uncertainty and confusion. For over three weeks the country was 'in the strange predicament,' as the London *Times* put it, 'of having two self-denying Emperors, and no active ruler.' Not until 12 December was the situation clarified, and Nicholas felt free to signify his acceptance of the throne.

It will be recalled that from the first the plotters had looked forward to the Czar's death as the signal for revolt. Those at the helm of the Northern Society did not learn of Alexander's illness until the day before his demise became known in the capital, so that the news of his passing took them completely by surprise. At all events, Constantine's accession went off without any untoward incident. The Society was ready to suspend its activities. But when its leaders, who had informants in high places, became aware that the wrong Grand Duke had been proclaimed Emperor, and that the dynastic imbroglio had brought about a virtual interregnum, they could not help perceiving that here was an opportunity 'to obtain the rights enjoyed by other nations,' as one put it, that was not likely to recur for many long years. The moment had arrived for the two Societies to come out into the open. The Northerners found this all the more imperative since they believed that an explosion was certain to occur in the South. The hour for action had struck.

There was no unanimity as to the course to be followed. After much debating a plan was half-heartedly agreed upon. It hinged on the refusal of the troops garrisoned in the capital to take the oath of allegiance to Nicholas. A mutiny was to be engineered ostensibly in favour of Constantine as the legitimate Emperor. The plan was to be abandoned if Constantine arrived in the capital and made an unambiguous public announcement of his abdication. The conspirators took advantage of the fact that, of the two brothers, the elder was the one less disliked, perhaps because of his absence from the scene. The privates were to be urged not to swear allegiance to Nicholas on the ground that he was a usurper and that the real Czar was kept in chains, or that he was marching on the capital at the head of his loyal troops and would punish the traitors. Of course, the plotters knew all this to be untrue. Fraud cast its shadow across the cradle of the Russian revolution. The conspirators could have shaken all hearts with the slogan of liberty. They could have made capital out of the very real grievances of the rank and file in the Guards. Instead, they chose to play on the soldiers' legitimist sentiment. By pretending to defend the very essence of the old order, Zavalishin was to observe in retrospect, they had robbed the undertaking of meaning.

The square in front of the Senate building was selected as the rendezvous for the mutinous troops. Once the rising was under way and the insurgents had a sizable number of bayonets to back them, the Senate was to be forced to issue a manifesto announcing the end of the existing régime, proclaiming democratic reforms, and naming a provisional government. This was promptly to convoke a Constituent Assembly empowered to adopt a constitution for the Empire and decide the fate of the imperial family, which in the meantime would be kept under arrest. The plan of assassinating the Czar and his kin was given up. The majority envisaged the revolution as an armed demonstration intended to force the Government to come to terms with the

Society. It was to be an orderly, decorous affair, keeping as far as possible within legal bounds and avoiding bloodshed. Pestel's idea of the seizure of state power had no adherents in the North.

In case of failure the insurgents were to retreat to the military settlements in the hope of finding support there, and, if need be, retire farther into the interior. But this was a mere suggestion. There was something sketchy about all the particulars of the plan. Thus, the matter of arming and provisioning the troops was hardly given any thought. The conspirators apparently went on the assumption that the Government would yield before it came to a show of force. The person elected—not without misgivings—to head the insurrection was Prince Sergey Trubetzkoy. He was styled 'Dictator', a title that ill-suited this mild-tempered, rather irresolute man of notably moderate views and a stickler for legality.

During these decisive December days the Northern Society developed a feverish activity. Its directors, together with other militants, a dozen men in all, were virtually in continuous session. Ryleyev was 'the mainspring of the enterprise', as a fellow conspirator put it. One or two activists arrived from Moscow and some new members were recruited, but they scarcely made up for the defections from the ranks. On close inspection, these proved very thin indeed. The active membership did not exceed sixty, and the foothold the Society had secured in the army and navy was exceedingly precarious. Few units could be counted upon with any degree of assurance. Hardly anything had been done by way of propaganda among the soldiery, except to spread the rumour that in his last will the deceased Czar had freed the serfs and reduced the term of military service to ten years, and that Constantine, unlike Nicholas, intended to carry out the terms of his brother's testament.

The enterprise seemed doomed to failure. Many of the men were not unaware of this, and the 'Dictator', for one, was ready to give up or postpone the undertaking. But it was too late to withdraw. Those at the centre strongly suspected that the Society had been denounced to Nicholas. Since they could not escape the consequences, they felt that they must go through with their plan. Some of them seem to have been motivated by a zeal for self-immolation. At one meeting young Prince

38

Odoyevsky, who like Ryleyev, wrote verse, exclaimed: 'We shall die! How gloriously we shall die!' There were moments when waves of delirious enthusiasm swept over the conspirators. The important thing, they told themselves, was to take the first step; success was with the daring.

As a rule, the oath of allegiance was administered to the troops soon after the new reign was proclaimed by manifesto. The insurrection had to be timed for the interval between the promulgation of the manifesto and the administration of the oath. The conspirators believed that the soldiers could not be roused against Nicholas, once they had kissed the cross in swearing allegiance to him. Consequently, the date for the *coup* could be set only after it became known when Nicholas would be proclaimed Emperor. On the morning of 13 December he signed the manifesto, directing that it be made public on the morrow. The date was a strictly guarded secret. By noon the plotters were in possession of it. So Monday, 14 December, was to be the day!

The time was short. Impossible to make any but the scantiest preparations. Impossible to get in touch with the Southerners to obtain help or arrange for concerted action. And the manifesto which was to be forced on the Senate had yet to be put in shape. Some last-minute changes were made in the distribution of the parts to be played by the individual conspirators. Yakubovich was instructed to occupy the Winter Palace with the aid of a detachment of sailors. At the same time, as if in anticipation of his failure, it was arranged that the first contingent of troops to reach the Senate Square was to attack the Palace. Colonel Bulatov, the Dictator's deputy, was assigned to seize the Fortress of Peter and Paul—its guns covered the Palace and the centre of the city.

As the afternoon advanced Ryleyev was assailed by a dreadful thought: was it wise to have decided to spare the lives of the imperial family? Was it not a tragic mistake, likely to precipitate the horrors of civil war and jeopardize the cause? Acting on his own, and in violation of the adopted plan, he exacted a half promise from Kakhovsky to make his way into the Winter Palace early the next morning and assassinate Nicholas.

II

The fateful day dawned upon men armed with wavering courage and uncertain hopes. The first hitch in the plan occurred in the small hours. Yakubovich declined the assignment he had accepted the previous day to seize the Palace and put all the potential pretenders to the throne under arrest. A little earlier Kakhovsky had gone back on his pledge to stage a private overture to the revolution by killing Nicholas. Long before sunrise another blow fell: the senators held a brief session, heard the manifesto announcing Nicholas' ascension to the throne, promptly swore allegiance to him, and dispersed to attend a reception at the palace. It was then barely seven-thirty a.m. The conspirators had not counted on anything happening at such an ungodly hour. There was no sign of mutiny. The timetable had gone completely wrong.

Not until nearly eleven o'clock did the first unit of insurgents, some seven hundred bayonets strong, enter the Senate Square. At the head of the column Yakubovich marched gallantly, his plumed hat on the tip of his bare sabre. Nothing had been done about placing the imperial family under arrest, and so the mutineers should have attempted to seize the Winter Palace—a few blocks away. Instead, they drew up in battle formation, near the monument of Peter the Great, presumably waiting for reinforcements. Since the senators were not sitting, there was no reason why the Senate Square should remain the rebels' rendezvous. The situation called for a change of plan. But there was no one with authority to issue the necessary orders. Both Prince Trubetzkoy, the 'Dictator', and Colonel Bulatov, his alternate, had failed to show up.

The Czar, for his part, was on the alert. The conspirators' suspicion that he knew of their plans was well founded. An hour or so before he decided to accept the throne, the existence of the two secret societies had been disclosed to him in a report from Field Marshal Diebitsch. It was based on data supplied by informers. One of them was a non-commissioned officer by the name of Ivan (John) Sherwood, a native of Kent and the son of an English weaver established in Russia. The same day another informer acquainted Nicholas with the particulars of the conspiracy. 'In the early hours of the day after tomorrow,' he wrote to Diebitsch on 12 December, 'I shall either be the sovereign or a corpse.'

There were many anxious moments for the Czar that day, but he did not lose his head. He acted with intelligence and dispatch. Hours before dawn he received many generals and high officials and assured himself of their allegiance. He reinforced the guards at the palace, and when the mutineers appeared on the Senate Square he concentrated a large number of troops, including cavalry, in the vicinity. In directing operations against the insurgents he repeatedly exposed himself to the danger of assassination, and afterwards he marvelled at his luck in not having been shot at. Accompanied by a small retinue, he passed among the crowd that packed the area and read his manifesto aloud to one group after another. The reading was punctuated by shouts of 'Hurrah for Constantine!' from the insurgents.

They did nothing further until the Governor of the capital, a veteran of the Napoleonic wars, rode up to their ranks and railed at them: they were not worthy of the name of Russian soldiers, they should throw themselves at the Czar's feet. At that several shots rang out—one of them Kakhovsky's—and the General slid off his horse, fatally wounded. Another General who attempted to harangue the men was badly mauled by civilian sympathizers of the rebels.

The loyal cavalry then took the offensive. This attack was repelled with slight losses to both sides.

Force having failed, persuasion was again resorted to. Followed by deacons, two metropolitans in ceremonial vestments with uplifted crosses addressed the men, assuring them that Nicholas was the legitimate Czar. Their efforts were of no avail. The Emperor's younger brother, Michael, also tried to remonstrate with the men. A pistol was aimed at him, but it misfired, and the Grand Duke retired to safety.

About this time the ranks of the insurgents were swelled by a column of grenadiers and a large detachment of sailors. There were cheers, and the officers embraced. Ryleyev was the first to greet the commander of the naval unit with 'the kiss of freedom'. These ominous developments induced Nicholas to order carriages for his wife and mother, so that they could flee, if necessary, to Tzarskoe Selo (now Pushkin).

It was now about two p.m. A little later several more companies of grenadiers arrived. Contrary to the conspirators' expectation, these men had mutinied, even though they had already taken the oath of allegiance to the new Czar. A Colonel who had followed them to the Square in an effort to keep them from joining the insurrection was fatally wounded by Kakhovsky. On his part, the Emperor encouraged no effort to keep the units which turned against him from joining their comrades. He preferred to have all the bad eggs in one basket.

The second contingent of grenadiers was the last reinforcement received by the rebels. The students of one naval and one military college sent a delegation to the insurgents asking permission to join them. In reply the youths were thanked for their 'noble intention' and advised 'to spare themselves for future exploits'.

There was still no trace of the 'Dictator'. Ryleyev went to look for him and did not return. Without saying a word to his comrades, Trubetzkoy had left his quarters in the morning and spent the rest of the day wandering about the city 'in great fear and dejection', as he put it later. His deputy, too, was nowhere to be seen. Nor did a leader spring from the ranks.

The rebels managed to thrust back another cavalry attack, a half-hearted affair, in which both sides clearly spared each other. For the rest, they stood about idly as though on parade. Their shouts of 'Hurrah for Constantine!' mingled with 'Hurrah for *Konstitutzya* (constitution)!' That they believed this to be the name of Constantine's spouse is a widespread report which was probably originated by a loyalist wag. The privates and, for that matter, the populace that milled around them were perhaps not entirely in the dark regarding the real objectives of the uprising.

The conspirators had hoped against hope to be able to rouse six Guards regiments. Actually they succeeded in mustering only some three thousand privates and thirty officers. Furthermore, the sailors had failed to provide themselves with sufficient ammunition and had left their cannon behind. More troops had arrived on the Square, but had drifted away, discouraged by the confusion in the ranks.

Could bold action still have saved the day for the revolution? Possibly. There was doubtless some vacillation among the loyal troops. Eight hundred members of the Finnish Guard Regiment, who had taken up a position in the vicinity of the Square, were temporizing and waiting on events. Messages came from various military units asking the mutineers to hold out until after dark and promising to join them then. Also the vast throng of civilians, mostly of the lower classes, that filled the area was unmistakably hostile toward the Government forces. They hurled stones and chunks of wood at the Czar's retinue and the loyal cavalry and occasionally manhandled a police officer. 'Give us arms', voices were heard in the crowd, 'and in half an hour we'll turn the city upside down.' But mob participation was just what the conspirators were firm in rejecting.

Inaction, and confusion due to absence of central command, continued. The situation did not improve when Prince Obolensky, an inexperienced staff officer with a weak voice and a lisp, was chosen to fill Trubetzkoy's empty place. The day, mild at the start, had turned quite raw, and the men shivered in the icy wind. They were tired, both their patience and their ammunition were running low. And they were now completely ringed by imperial troops outnumbering them four to one, a force of ten thousand men being held in reserve by the Czar.

About mid-December in Petersburg the sun sets near three p.m. As twilight descended on the city, the Emperor decided that it was dangerous to leave the issue unsettled, for under cover of darkness some loyal units might go over to the rebels and the insurrection spread to the populace. Still reluctant to use drastic measures on the opening day of his reign, he gave the mutineers a chance to capitulate. They refused.

It was then that several field-pieces were trained on the Square and its environs. Half a dozen volleys were sufficient to clear the area. On the snow lay the dead and the wounded. Both insurgents and innocent bystanders were mowed down by grapeshot or drowned in the Neva, cannon balls having broken the ice to which some of the men had fled. Curiously enough, not a single conspirator was among the casualties. The police estimated the number of those killed at seventy to eighty, but there were probably more.

The first cannon shot thundered out about four p.m. A futile attempt was made to rally a group of men in the gathering dusk, with a view to leading them to an assault on the Fortress of Peter and Paul across the river. By five p.m. the uprising was over. It had lasted about six hours. All that remained for the authorities was to round up the fleeing mutineers and arrest the members of the Society.

Ten days later a battalion of infantry garrisoned in the town of Bryansk, central Russia, refused to swear allegiance to Nicholas, shouting 'Hurrah for Emperor Constantine!' The next day, however, the men were persuaded to take the oath. They had been instigated by several officers who belonged to a secret group, probably affiliated with the Northern Society.

III

On the eve of the uprising the Northern *Duma* had sent a communication to Colonel Sergey Muravyov-Apostol, informing him of the impending action. On the same day an emissary arrived from the South with the message that down there a hundred thousand men were 'ready'. Nothing could have been further from the truth. Preparations in the South were just as sketchy as in Petersburg, if not more so. Soldiers as they were, revolutionaries as they wished to be, some of those men had a curiously feeble sense of reality: they deceived themselves as easily as they did their comrades.

One of the reasons why the Northerners had felt compelled to act was the belief that the Southern Society was certain to come out into the open. Actually it remained quiescent. When, in September, Alexander had arrived in Taganrog, the idea was conceived of dispatching several men there on a mission of murder. Later on there was talk of assassinating Grand Duke Constantine on his way to Taganrog, where the Emperor lay ill. Nothing came of these terrorist fantasies. Nor did the Czar's death arouse the Society to action. The troops in the South took the oath of allegiance to Constantine without demur.

For some time the existence of the Society had been known to the authorities. On the very day that witnessed the rising in Petersburg they struck at the heart of the organization by placing Pestel under arrest. One of his comrades raised the question of freeing him by force. They contented themselves with destroying some of his incriminating papers and burying a copy of *Russkaya*

Pravda in the ground, so as to preserve it for future generations. Alone the former members of 'the United Slavs' intensified their propaganda among the privates. They stressed the hard lot of the soldiery and went so far as to point out the advantages that the common people would derive from a republican form of government. They even worked out a plan involving immediate, bold military action. It was turned down by the directorate of the Society. All that the activists were told was that the insurrection would occur sooner than had been planned, namely, that 'the voice of the fatherland' would summon its sons 'to the standards of liberty' by February or March of the following year. Actually, events took another course.

News travelled slowly across Russia's great distances. Not until 24 December did the Southerners hear of Nicholas's accession and the abortive insurrection in the capital. There could be no doubt that their organization was now an open secret to the authorities. And indeed, two days later the Muravyov-Apostol brothers, Sergey and Matvey, learned that an order for their arrest had been received by the commanding officer of the Chernigov Infantry Regiment in which they served. Bestuzhev-Ryumin, who, with Sergey, headed the Vasilkov Branch, was also to be arrested. The three men got the news on their way home after a visit to a neighbouring town. What was to be done? Fleeing or hiding was futile. Matvey suggested suicide. The others demurred. It was decided to continue on their way back to Vasilkov.

They had gone only as far as the village of Trilesy, some distance from Vasilkov, when, on 29 December, in the small hours, the brothers were placed under arrest. Bestuzhev-Ryumin was not with them at the time. They soon broke away from their captors, however, with the aid of several officers of their regiment who happened to be on the spot. It was largely under pressure from these men, all active members of the Society, that the military insurrection, so much debated and so little prepared for, was launched then and there. Like the Petersburg *Putsch*, it was a leap in the dark, a hastily improvised enterprise, stumbled into, rather than deliberately planned.

Sergey Muravyov-Apostol was trusted, indeed, all but idolized by the men under him, and so the two companies of the Chernigov Regiment stationed at Trilesy and in a nearby village readily obeyed his order to take the field. The soldiers were told that they would be fighting to free the people and to improve their own lot, and that the rest of the army was with them. Headed by Muravyov-Apostol, the insurgents reached Vasilkov the following day, having marched part of the time through a snowstorm, and occupied the town without firing a shot. There they were joined by four more companies. The men, over nine hundred strong, celebrated the occasion by consuming great quantities of vodka—according to the tavern-keepers, 186 buckets. There was also some pillaging, mostly of Jewish property.

The officers spent the night making plans, while the commander was chiefly occupied putting finishing touches to a composition entitled *The Orthodox Catechism*. At more than one point it vaguely echoes the American Declaration of Independence. The czars are accursed of God, the Catechism declares, for they have robbed the people of freedom, and without liberty there can be no happiness. The republican form of government is the only one in agreement with divine law. Jesus Christ must be the only king on earth as He is in Heaven. It is the duty of the Army and the people 'to take up arms against tyranny and restore faith and freedom in Russia.' An appeal to the people at large, expressing similar sentiments in similar language, was also drafted. Here all the misfortunes of the nation are attributed to autocratic government. The Czar's death is a sign that God wills the Russians to shake off the bonds of slavery. 'Henceforth Russia is free.' The Army will establish 'a popular government' in an orderly fashion and without internecine strife.

The next day, 31 December, the new régime was formally inaugurated with a short Mass in the market-place. It was served by the regimental chaplain. Then in a trembling voice the young priest read aloud the newly composed catechism to the assembled troops. Couched in somewhat archaic, ecclesiastical language, it was probably unintelligible to the men. But when the author addressed them briefly urging them to serve the cause of freedom loyally, their hurrahs were lusty, and that not only because some of them were drunk. They had complete confidence in their leader, even if they were not clear about what he wanted them to fight for. The story goes that one private said that he was all for a republic, but, he asked, 'Who is going to be our czar?' The anecdote, like the one about *Konstitutzia*, must have been a loyalist *trouvaille*, but it was not inapposite.

The officers could not help noticing, however, that the arguments against autocracy taken from Scripture made little impression on the soldiers, and later on they reluctantly fell back upon the lie regarding the usurpation of the throne by Nicholas (the men had taken the oath of allegiance to him on Christmas Day).

With Sergey Muravyov-Apostol were his brothers Ippolit and Matvey, who were deeply attached to him. One was an impulsive youth of nineteen, the other a timid, overscrupulous man who had no faith in the venture and was a liability to the command. This included Lieutenant Bestuzhev-Ryumin as well as the four officers who had freed the brothers from arrest, all former 'Slavs' and men of energy and courage. Between the commander and his aides there was little harmony. He was a high-minded idealist, though not free from the aristocrat's arrogance, a Christian without the fanatic's inhumanity. His religion sanctioned taking up arms against tyranny, but he detested the use of force. At heart he hoped that the rest of the army would come over to his side, and that there would be no need to give battle. He wished to conduct the insurrection on a high moral plane, in keeping with the sacredness of the cause. He made it clear to the men that they were at liberty to stay or go. This the 'Slavs' found quixotic. They held that those not with them were against them. They favoured swift action, hard blows, surprise movements; he hesitated, procrastinated, fumbled.

The religious service over, the little army of the revolution, looking far from trim, left Vasilkov. The 'Slavs' favoured marching on nearby Kiev. Instead, the commander decided to proceed westward to a town where he expected his forces to be augmented by several regiments which had been infiltrated by the Society. At dusk the insurgents halted in a village. They spent the night there, as well as New Year's Day, to the disgust of some of the men who felt that such dilatoriness was the height of folly. Discipline being lax, there was more drinking and some marauding by the men. The local peasantry, all privately owned serfs, were rather friendly, but no attempt was made to enlist their active support.

During the day a part of another company of the Chernigov Regiment—army units were scattered through the countryside—joined the rebel ranks. No other troops rallied to the cause.

Leaving the village, the men now marched South, suspecting danger in the West and still hoping for reinforcements. These did not materialize. The couriers that were sent out found no response. Some of the members of the Society had been arrested, while others went back on their pledged word to spring into action at the first call. The rebels seemed to be labouring under an evil spell. Their leader acted as though he were in a trance. Plans were formulated and no sooner tried than abandoned. Nothing succeeded. The march of the revolutionary cohort resembled a funeral procession, as Bestuzhev-Ryumin was to put it. Naturally, the faint-hearted began to drop away.

In the evening the column again halted in a village. That night the commander's two brothers had a long talk about man's fate. The rest of the officers took counsel about more immediate matters, and decided to change the route once more, heading for a town where some troops commanded by 'Slavs' were garrisoned.

The following day—it was 3 January—the insurgents again found themselves tramping from hamlet to hamlet, meeting no resistance but getting no help and cut off from the outside world. One of the reasons why the military authorities were slow in taking measures against them was that they were not sure of the loyalty of the troops stationed near the scene of the uprising.

Finally, in the afternoon, as the insurgents were trudging along a road across the snowy steppe, they caught sight of a detachment of cavalry in the distance. As the horsemen drew nearer, some of them were recognized as members of a company commanded by Colonel Pykhachev. A few months previously at a meeting of the Society this officer had proudly claimed for his men the honour of being the first to fire a shot for freedom. Obviously, these were friends hastening to rally to the banner of liberty. Word was passed to the soldiers, and there was general rejoicing. Without warning the 'friends' trained a cannon on the mutineers and opened fire. Colonel Pykhachev had been put under arrest the previous day, and his company took the field not with the mutineers but against them.

The cannon volley mowed down half a dozen privates and one officer. Another committed suicide. Sergey Muravyov-

Apostol himself was wounded. Ippolit was either killed or, believing his beloved brother dead in a lost cause, took his own life. The insurgents laid down their arms without firing a single shot, allegedly under orders from the commander, unwilling to precipitate a fratricidal conflict. Believing themselves betrayed, the enraged men seized their officers and handed them over to the attacking troops.

Thus ended the second, and last, abortive attempt at insurrection made by the gentlemen who were to go down in history as the Decembrists.

IV

Of the privates who took part in the uprising of 14 December, six or seven hundred were rounded up on the Senate Square and in the adjacent streets. The rest of the survivors returned to the barracks of their own free will. The official theory was that the men had acted out of an excess of loyalty to the throne. The only punishment meted out to most of them was transfer to active service in the Caucasus, where desultory warfare against rebellious natives was in progress. The soldiers who took part in the Southern mutiny did not come off so lightly. One hundred and twenty of them were court-martialled, and many were put to the rods. The flogging was, however, rather perfunctory, except in the case of two men. They were former officers who, having been demoted and deprived of their rank in the gentry, had become subject to corporal punishment. The common soldiers, who, as usual, executed the sentence, took a sadistic pleasure in beating them to within an inch of their lives.

Arrests of the ringleaders began while the blood on the snow and the cobbles was still fresh. Denounced by an officer seized on the Senate Square, Ryleyev was taken the very evening of the 14th. On being questioned, he named Trubetzkoy as the chief instigator of the mutiny. This led to the arrest of the Prince late that night. Ryleyev also revealed the existence of the Southern Society and identified Pestel as its head. He wanted to prevent the Southerners from making an attempt like that of which he had been the moving spirit. It appears that no sooner had the uprising collapsed than he lost the faith that had inspired it. Later on the honest penitent implored the Czar to execute him alone and pardon the rest. To the last he would pray to God, he wrote, that 'his recantation and the punishment meted out to him should forever deter his fellow citizens from criminal enterprises against the authorities'.

Some conspirators gave themselves up voluntarily. Thus Colonel Bulatov came to the palace and handed over his sword to the Emperor, telling him, it is reported, that he had intended to assassinate him and that several times during the fateful Monday he had approached him, armed with pistols and a dagger, but that he had not been able to bring himself to execute his design. He was incarcerated in the Fortress of Peter and Paul, which, it will be recalled, he had been assigned to occupy. Shortly thereafter he smashed his head against the wall of his cell and died. One officer vainly sought safety in hiding. No one tried to escape abroad. Before many days had passed two or three hundred men were behind bars in the capital. They included members of the Southern Society who had been shipped there in irons.

Nicholas appointed a special commission to investigate the conspiracy, but he personally interrogated some of the prisoners and gave minute instructions as to how they should be treated. There was nothing clumsy about his technique as a detective. He reproached, ridiculed, threatened, cajoled, bullied, and stormed. Some he broke down with harshness, he overwhelmed others with magnanimity. There were those whom he convinced that the whole wretched affair was a misunderstanding, that he practically shared the plotters' views. 'What do you want a revolution for?' he said to Zavalishin. 'I am your revolution.' He would astonish Europe, he insinuated indirectly, by pardoning all the culprits.

With Kakhovsky the Czar had a long heart-to-heart talk. He encouraged the prisoner to speak with complete frankness. Kakhovsky pictured feelingly the lamentable condition of the country and suggested that in his place the Emperor himself would have embraced the revolution. With tears in his eyes Nicholas promised to work for the public good, to be a Father to the fatherland. The following day Kakhovsky wrote to him from prison: 'Since yesterday I have loved you as a human being, and with all my heart I want to love you as my sovereign.' Apparently, in time he did, without ceasing to believe in government by constitutional law and in the blessings of freedom. One of his communications to the Emperor contains a pæan to liberty.

Having discovered in the Czar a kindred soul, the would-be regicide had turned into an ardent loyalist. Kakhovsky was by no means the only one to experience such a change of heart. Some prisoners, immediately upon their arrest, honestly repented what they had done or had intended to do, others cried *peccavi* after they had been broken by weeks of solitary confinement. The emotion that had inflamed the men during the days just preceding the *coup* burned out like fire in straw. A profound disillusionment possessed them. To many the enterprise now seemed utterly mad, or, worse still, ludicrous.

Undoubtedly not a few prisoners offered abject recantations in the hope of saving their necks. Men who as soldiers and nobles should have exhibited a keen sense of personal honour cringed and grovelled before their captors. Prince Trubetzkoy went down on his knees to the Czar, pleading for his life. Prince Odoyevsky, who, shortly before the uprising, had exulted in the prospect of a glorious death, was no sooner in prison than his exaltation gave way to hysterical terror. Half out of his mind, he frantically protested his devotion to the throne and offered to lead the authorities to 'the root' of the conspiracy.

The conduct of the Southern leaders was not very different. Sergey Muravyov-Apostol repented and recanted, but without self-abasement. This cannot be said of Pestel. He flattered himself, he wrote to a member of the Investigating Commission after seven weeks in prison, that the Emperor was pleased with him because of his complete frankness. He had hidden nothing, nothing at all. Yet he could not vindicate himself before the monarch, he could only beg for mercy. The thought that he had belonged to the secret society was for him a source of burning grief and crushing pain, though he drew some solace from the fact that he had not engaged in overt action. But he would atone for his crime: 'Every moment of my life will be filled with gratitude and boundless attachment to the sacred person of the Czar and to his most august family.'

It is reported that later he regained self-control and became rather defiant in dealing with his questioners. But he did not cease to regret his past. He had once been a deist troubled by doubts as to the existence of a benevolent Providence. Some of his fellow conspirators were free-thinkers. Like Ryleyev, and like the repentant revolutionaries of a later generation, he now turned to religion. 'Faith in our Saviour is at present my happiness and solace', he wrote to his parents.

Whether they were sincere penitents or simply terror-stricken men, the prisoners for the most part turned the chamber in which they were interrogated into a confessional. Not only did they reveal their own criminal activities and thoughts, but they informed against their fellow members at great length, naming names, reporting conversations, plans, and even rumours and suspicions, engaging in mutual recrimination. They went so far as to betray the simple-minded privates whom they had led astray. The foremost militants were no better than the rank and file. And none was a victim of third-degree methods, let alone the more drastic methods of persuasion perfected in our generation.

The fewest stuck to their convictions or took care not to incriminate fellow conspirators. One prisoner, a man of moderate views, who at first recanted, later wrote in a deposition: 'Shamefully I repudiated what has been the finest thing in my life. Our secret society consisted of men of whom Russia will always be proud. The smaller the handful, the more glory to them, for, due to the disproportion of forces, the voice of liberty sounded several hours only, but it is pleasant that it did sound.'

After labouring for six months the Commission of Inquiry turned over its findings to a special tribunal. Of the nearly six hundred persons investigated, only a hundred and twenty men, about equally divided between the two Societies, were brought to trial. Most of them were deported to Siberia, a number to serve terms of hard labour. Ryleyev, Kakhovsky, Pestel, Sergey Muravyov-Apostol, and Bestuzhev-Ryumin were singled out as the worst offenders. They were sentenced to be quartered, at the suggestion of Count Speransky, who, as a member of both the Commission and the Court, dominated the proceedings. This was the man whom the Decembrists had planned to include in the Provisional Government they were to set up. The three ecclesiastical members of the Court declared that while they recognized the justice of the death sentence, it did not behove them as churchmen to sign it. Thus they abandoned the condemned to the secular arm. The Czar neither confirmed nor cancelled the verdict. Following the precedent set by a certain Roman procurator, he washed his hands of the matter, leaving it to the tribunal. He merely ordered that the execution should not involve the shedding of blood. Accordingly, the quartering was commuted to hanging.

The sentence was carried out on 13 July, 1826, in the small hours of a Northern white night. A detachment from each of the regiments in which the condemned had served was dispatched to the Fortress of Peter and Paul to witness the grim ceremony. The executioners were so inexperienced—there had been no hanging for many decades—that either the ropes snapped under the weight of three of the bodies burdened with fetters, or else the nooses slipped. Ryleyev, Muravyov-Apostol, and Kakhovsky fell into the pit dug under the gallows and after a delay of half an hour were hanged again. Of the several sayings that legend attributes to these men as they waited, the words, ascribed to Ryleyev, may be recorded: 'I am happy that I shall die twice for my country.' The Czar wrote to his mother that a prayer for him was on Kakhovsky's lips just before he was hanged.

It is a matter for speculation how many men would have suffered torture and death for a similar attempt under the tyranny which in our own day has succeeded that of the czars.

V

No more than a handful of men were active in the secret societies and in the plot that led to the two risings. That in itself scarcely accounts for the failure of the Decembrists. A close-knit group of dedicated souls who know what they want and fight for it without sparing themselves or others can be effective out of all proportion to their numbers. But the Decembrists were never at one with regard to their principles or their tactics. Aside from a crackpot or two, there were among them naïve dreamers, and sober reformers, Jacobins like Pestel and *laissez-faire* liberals like Trubetzkoy, fanatics and opportunists, revolutionaries who would overthrow the Government and gradualists who would bring it to terms. They began by plotting 'between Lafitte and Veuve Cliquot', as Pushkin put it. Later on, a more serious mood prevailed. But hardly one of them was of the stuff of which conspirators are made; too few realized that there can be no conspiring by half. There was no lack of inflammable youths protesting their readiness to lay down their lives on the altar of freedom, but there was a dearth of men of steady convictions capable of sustained effort. Not a few, in spite of their military training and experience, were intellectuals touched with the Hamletic blight.

In the eighteenth century the Guard officers had played the part of the Praetorian cohorts who made and unmade Roman emperors. The Decembrists tried to effect a political revolution with the means that had been successful in producing palace revolutions. Their tactics were those of men born too late, their aims those of men born too early.

The Decembrist programme, vague as it was on some points, always spoke for the emancipation of the serfs. It reflected the attitude of those agrarians who were beginning to realize the economic advantages of free over servile labour. But abolitionist sentiment was by no means strong, and its growth was checked in the 'twenties by the depression, which removed the incentive to intensified agriculture. The country squires were firmly opposed to emancipation. They distrusted all change and were content as long as the state protected their God-given right to the fruits of serf labour.

Matters affecting the country's economy, particularly its rural sector, were not overlooked by the Decembrists. But they were above all political liberals. Their imagination was fired by the ideals of freedom, popular sovereignty, government by law. Hence their advocacy of a republican régime or, as the next best thing, a constitutional monarchy. But political democracy found scant support among the nobility and the nascent third estate. At the top of the social pyramid there were men who were inclined to favour a constitutional régime, but one that would serve the interests of the aristocracy. The peasants, with their long memory of feudal oppression, still regarded the czar's unlimited authority as their sole protection from the rapacity of the gentry. It has been seen that the lower orders did not figure in the strategic calculations of the Decembrists. Except for the 'Slavs', they viewed the masses as the passive object of political action.

Under these circumstances it is not surprising that the more clear-eyed among the members of the Societies were haunted by a sense of fighting for a hopeless cause. They suspected that, in words attributed to Pestel, they were trying to reap before they had sown. Nikolay Turgenev, at one time director of the Northern Society, made this entry in his diary: 'All feel, but do not yet understand their needs. Such an epoch foretokens a revolution, but is not one in which a revolution can succeed.' Nevertheless, the Decembrists appreciated that their effort was not to be wholly in vain. On the eve of the ill-starred rising Ryleyev is reported to have said: 'I am certain that we shall perish, but the example will remain.' This was also the opinion of such a disinterested contemporary observer as the Resident Minister in charge of the British mission in Petersburg. Shortly after the executions he was writing to Canning: 'The late conspiracy failed for want of management, and want of head to direct it, and was too premature to answer any good purpose, but I think the seeds are sown which one day will produce important consequences.'

The Englishman, like the Russian, read the future correctly. If the uprising failed to 'awaken Russia,' as Ryleyev had hoped, the memory of what he and his comrades had attempted proved a potent thing. Eventually their ideals became a dominant element of Russian political thought. And they bequeathed to posterity a heroic legend, as the defeated not seldom do. The Government itself helped to build it by forbidding all references in the press to the events of 14 December—the rising in the South remained in the background.

Radishchev was canonized as the first martyr of the revolutionary faith. The Decembrists came to be revered as the first to take up arms against the autocracy. They were seen as knights without fear and without reproach who challenged the monster to battle, though certain that they themselves must perish. The tragedy of their fate was enhanced by the devotion of the wives who followed them into Siberia. Some thirty-five years later Alexander Herzen, who believed himself to be their spiritual descendant, called them 'a phalanx of heroes . . . giants forged of pure steel from head to foot. . . .' In view of the evidence, some of which has only recently come to light, it is clear that they were of different stuff and stature. They were, by and large, perceptive, patriotic, public-spirited young men, but impulsive and unstable, with an enthusiasm for freedom and justice, half genuine feeling, half rhetoric. Pushed by the hand of chance, they fought, however ineptly and ineffectually, the opening skirmish in Russia's battle for democracy—the end of which seems further off than ever. It fell to their lot to be the founders of Russia's feeble tradition of political liberalism. The revolutionaries, too, including Lenin, have traced their lineage to these amateurish pioneers.

CHAPTER IV

THE COASTS OF UTOPIA

THE easy triumph over the rebels failed to give the victors a sense of security. On the day Nicholas ascended the throne he is said to have addressed these words to his younger brother: 'The revolution is at Russia's gate, but I swear that it will not enter as long as there is breath in me. . . .' If necessary, he was ready to lock up half the population to save the other half from revolutionary infection. There was in him no trace of the duality that marked his predecessor's character. The history of his reign is one of coercion and reaction. Across it lay the shadow of the gallows.

The military settlements were abolished. For the rest, the system remained intact. The Czar was not unaware of the drawbacks of serfdom. On one official occasion he observed that it was 'an evil perceptible and obvious to all.' The police reported to him that it was a 'powder magazine under the State,' that the idea of freedom was spreading among the serfs, and that cases of violence against the masters were on the increase. Some measures were enacted to improve the lot of the peasants, but they were half-hearted and largely ineffectual. The Emperor lacked the courage to take a step that seemed to threaten a social revolution, since emancipation would not only do away with the gentry's rights to the 'souls' they owned but would also encroach upon their claim to their lands. He heeded those of his counsellors who held the institution to be the keystone of the arch, the deep-rooted tree that afforded shade to Church and Throne alike, as one of the ministers put it in arguing against laying the axe to serfdom. Nicholas thus threw away the opportunity for reform offered him by the long period of peace following the suppression of the Decembrist movement.

An innovation was a special department of political police, known as the Third Division of His Majesty's Chancery. Its avowed purpose was 'to guard the foundations of the Russian State'. Placed outside and above the network of administrative offices, it had a wide jurisdiction and was responsible solely to the Czar. It had at its disposal the Corps of Gendarmes and a force of undercover men. The Third Division was the predecessor of the incomparably more infamous and efficient security agency, which, under various names—the earliest was the *Cheka*—has been the watchdog of the Soviet Government.

The schools were subjected to rigid supervision, and an effort was made to confine education, particularly higher education, to the privileged classes. The underlying sentiment, expressed by the Chief of the Third Division, was that in Russia learning should be dispensed, like a poisonous drug, by government prescription only. The head of the educational system wished the schools to be 'intellectual dams,' barring the influx of new ideas. He considered it his duty to retard the nation's mental development, so as to prolong its youth. Control over the Church was tightened and the persecution of religious dissenters intensified. A network of committees kept watch over native publications as well as over imported printed matter.

Occasionally a censor would assume the role of critic and even seek to lead an author in the way he should go. In 1836 a writer was pronounced insane by the authorities for having published an essay which clashed with the official view, as set forth by the Minister of Education, to the effect that 'Russia's past is admirable, its present more than magnificent; as for its future, it is beyond anything that the boldest imagination can picture.' There is a familiar ring about this formula. It fairly epitomizes the Communist party line on Russian history. Yet Nicholas's rule, while paternalistic and dictatorial, fell short of totalitarianism, certainly in the area of culture. The State made no systematic attempt to mobilize the artists in the service of its policies. They were allowed as a natural and unquestioned right the modicum of freedom without which the creative spirit cannot live.

The severity of the régime was, as usual, tempered by its inefficiency. Despite the stifling atmosphere, the intellectual life of the country made headway. Close contacts with the West were unavoidable. Russian students in the universities abroad were becoming less rare. Somehow or other, forbidden French and German books managed to get into the hands of eager readers in the capitals and even in the provinces. A remarkable body of native letters was growing apace, and a periodical press taking its rise. Literature offered one intellectual interest that could be cultivated in relative freedom by a leisured class cut off from all participation in public life. There was plenty of time for reading and philosophizing, for keeping diaries and writing letters.

Driven back upon themselves, unable to act, men thought and felt. It was an age of tender consciences and tenderer minds. The speculations of the German romantic philosophers, at second hand, enjoyed a great vogue, reaching even the half-educated. Circles were formed for the reading and discussion of Schelling, Fichte, Hegel. In the Moscow salons the talk often touched on abstruse points in metaphysics. Idealistic philosophy, exalting the inner life and the world of the spirit, was the fashion. Spurning ends of a material and transitory nature, such as social betterment, one aspired to what is eternally true and beautiful. One rapturously accepted the world as the incarnation of the Absolute. This 'metaphysical complacency,' as a contemporary called it, was a defence mechanism which enabled men to ignore evils against which they were powerless. A small group of intellectuals, alienated from the people, were chiefly busy searching their souls and comforting themselves the while with Utopian reveries.

II

Few mutterings and stirrings disturbed the torpor that paralysed the political life of the country in the first two decades of Nicholas's reign. The Marquis de Custine, who visited the country in the late 'thirties, remarked: 'Russia is a cauldron of boiling water, tightly closed and placed on a fire which is becoming hotter and hotter; I fear an explosion.' The cauldron was certainly covered, with officialdom sitting on the lid, but the water was hardly beginning to bubble. In the army the spirit of opposition was dead. It was in the schools that a ferment was beginning to work. A ferment of ideas.

The aristocracy still shunned the universities, and the student body, which was very small, came from groups on the middle rungs of the social ladder. In the 'thirties the University of Moscow, the oldest in the land, was attended by a handful of youths destined to leave their mark on Russian, and not only Russian, political thought. The majority, which included

Vissarion Belinsky and Michael Bakunin, were wrapped up in German metaphysics. But there was also a more realistic set. These boys considered themselves heirs of the Decembrists, recited the forbidden verse of Ryleyev, and scarved their throats in the *tricolore*. They were supported by serf labour, but hated serfdom as they did autocracy.

The outstanding figure among these 'politicals' was Alexander Herzen. Born of an irregular union between a wealthy Russian aristocrat and a German woman of humble birth, his childhood experiences predisposed him to rebellion. He early absorbed the radical ideas to which a precocious Russian boy, instructed by foreign tutors, one of them a former Jacobin, was exposed. He was thirteen when the Decembrist rising took place, and he was present at the thanksgiving service in the Kremlin after the hangings. The scene made a lasting impression on him. In time the Decembrists became for him the object of a cult.

Already in his early teens he felt himself dedicated to a high and hallowed cause. His enthusiasm was shared by his friend Nick, who was to be his lifelong comrade-in-arms. This Nikolay Ogarev, too, was the son of a wealthy landowner. One afternoon the boys—they were in their middle teens—found themselves on the Sparrow (now Lenin) Hills, the panorama of Moscow stretched out gloriously before them in the setting sun. In the exaltation of the moment, they embraced, swearing to devote their lives to the fight for freedom. They kept this vow.

Herzen entered the University in 1829 and applied himself to the study of the natural sciences. He readily became the leader of the small group of like-minded spirits that he found there. The news of fighting on the barricades in Paris in July 1830 and of the November uprising in Warsaw profoundly stirred them, and Herzen added the portrait of Kosciuszko to his 'icon-case' containing pictures of the heroes of the French Revolution.

Along toward the end of his university years he and his friends discovered the writings of Saint-Simon and Fourier, or rather of their disciples. Socialist teachings were just beginning to gain currency in Russia. In a dramatic dialogue couched in execrable verse, Ogarev recalled how he and Herzen and a third comrade had gathered in a narrow room and sworn on the Bible to dedicate their lives to the people and the cause of liberty 'upon the basis of socialism', and to that end form a secret society.

Thereupon they had fallen on each others' necks and 'wept in young ecstasy'.

What impressed these youths most was Saint-Simon's vision of mankind totally regenerated by a new Christianity, a faith that exalted both the individual and the community. Nor could they fail to be fascinated by doctrines that boldly denounced the failings of the existing order and promised to abolish the exploitation of man by man. They were somewhat repelled by the emphasis Saint-Simonism placed on the rôle of the State and were inclined to favour Fourier's plan for phalansteries which relied on private initiative and the free co-operation of workers. The failure of the French revolution and of the Polish insurrection had made them question the efficacy of purely political overturns, and now the teachings of the socialists further strengthened their feeling that the time was ripe for more thoroughgoing changes.

Herzen completed his studies in 1833, but the circle over which he presided broke up only the following year, when both he and Ogarev were arrested. The charge against them was that they belonged to a group of young men who gathered to sing songs containing 'vile and ill-intentioned expressions directed against the oath of allegiance to the monarch'. Herzen was discovered by the official investigators to be 'a bold free-thinker, very dangerous to society'. He and Ogarev were under suspicion of having founded a secret organization aiming to overthrow the existing order through the propagation of 'revolutionary opinions permeated with Saint-Simon's pernicious doctrine'. Not that the prosecutor was clear as to whether this Saint-Simon was the socialist or the courtier of Louis XIV and author of the well-known memoirs.

The two friends were deported to the provinces. In the isolation of exile Herzen had moods of despair and of religious exaltation. Yet neither mysticism nor despondency over his own lot could take his mind off the oppression he saw around him, and he continued to be a Christian socialist. A play in verse which he wrote in 1839 exalts Quakerism as a kind of Gospel communism. It ends with a scene in which George Fox gives his blessing to William Penn who is setting out to America to found 'an evangelical commune'.

Toward the end of his enforced stay in the provinces Herzen came upon the works of Hegel, which he had previously known only at second hand. In Petersburg and particularly in Moscow, where he was permitted to spend much time during 1839–41 and where he settled in 1842 after finally regaining his freedom, he found the German thinker all the rage. It is on record that one night in February 1840 a group of young Moscow philosophers, after attending a charity ball, gathered around a supper table to toast all the categories of Hegelian logic, from Pure Being, through Essence, to Idea. Spurred on by the general interest in Hegel, Herzen delved deeper into his writings. The quietist interpretation of the master's teachings was the prevalent one. His maxim: 'All that is rational is real, and all that is real is rational' seemed to justify the acceptance of things as they were. Conservatism thus had the highest philosophical sanction. Both Bakunin and Belinsky unflinchingly adhered to this interpretation. 'To revolt against reality is to kill in oneself the living source of life', the former wrote, blithely mixing his metaphors. And Belinsky, already an influential critic, did not hesitate to glorify the autocracy in print.

Herzen protested hotly against such a way of understanding Hegel's philosophy. To him the core of it was a sense of existence as an adventure opening up ever-widening horizons, a conception of the cosmos as an endless unfolding of the spirit, proceeding in stages of conflict and conciliation, and reaching in man the summit of self-knowledge and freedom. His instinctive aversion to quietism, his scientific training, his contacts with the seamy side of Russian life, all inclined him to a view of Hegel approximating that of his Leftist disciples in the West. While deploring the master's accent on contemplation and his neglect of action and 'creative reason', i.e. the will, he perceived in the dialectical conception of history a sanction for political and social change. If everything real is rational, he argued, then rebellion against an order of things grown oppressive is also justified by reason. Herzen reached the conclusion that he later formulated thus: 'The philosophy of Hegel is the algebra of revolution. . . .'

Bakunin, who had been in Germany since the summer of 1840, had arrived independently at the same conclusion. In October, 1842, he published in the pages of a Left Hegelian German review an impassioned essay proclaiming Hegelianism a revolutionary tool and winding up with the dictum which was to become the motto of international anarchism: 'The passion for destruction is also a creative passion.' Belinsky too had undergone a change of heart partly under Herzen's influence. He revolted against an idealism that in concentrating on lofty abstractions ignored the concrete individual, the suffering man and woman, and he turned a jaundiced eye on the phenomenal world about him.

III

What added zest to the intellectual life in Moscow at this time was the war of words between Westernists and Slavophils. The latter were romantic doctrinaires who found in German philosophy sanction for their distrust of the intellect, their religiosity, their traditionalism. They believed that Russia possessed a culture distinct from and superior to that of the West. It rested on the adamant foundations of the Orthodox faith and on the love which bound the people to the czar. Hence it was destined to supersede European civilization, built as this was on the legalistic principle of the social contract and infected with materialism and unbelief. Hence, too, it behoved Russia to look to herself alone, refusing to borrow from other nations. Only by cultivating her own patrimony would she achieve her salvation and that of the world.

Slavophilism was the backward-looking philosophy of an upper class that had seen its day. Yet the Slavophils were not wholly reactionary. They detested the bureaucracy, and in fact the authorities regarded them with suspicion. Their adherence to the monarchy was tinged with a kind of anarchism. The Russian people, they held, had an inborn distaste for statehood, with its servitude and coercion. Indeed, in their eyes the autocracy was only justified because it allowed the people to shift the burden of political power from their shoulders to those of one in-dividual and so, free of the guilt it entailed, devote themselves to the things of the spirit. The Slavophils abominated the prospect of the government invading the inner life of men. Nothing would have been more abhorrent to them than the modern totalitarian state.

All the early representatives of the school advocated civil liberties, particularly freedom of conscience. And they wished to see the serfs freed. Their thinking showed a strongly democratic, or rather populist, bias. They idealized the Russian folk at the expense of the privileged classes. While these had gone a-whoring after strange gods, the argument ran, the unspoiled peasantry alone had preserved intact the true Orthodox faith, with its living sense of equality and brotherhood. As a result, the daily life of the common people was permeated with a genuine and spontaneous collectivism, which was poles apart from the individualism of the West. The Slavophils made much of the fact—or rather what they believed to be a fact—that throughout the Great Russian area the land worked by the peasants had for centuries been held in common and periodically redistributed by the assembly of householders (*mir*) in each village according to the number of workers or family units (*tyagla*) in the household. They did not exactly discover the *obshchina*, as the rural commune was known, with its joint responsibility for the collection of the poll-tax and the fulfilment of the serf's obligations to his master. As far back as 1788 a book, printed in Petersburg, had described the institution. But the Slavophils were the first to focus attention on it. Indeed, they exalted it as the very foundation of that authentically Russian way of life on which Peter the Great had laid violent hands and which they were anxious to restore. They saw in it the people's school of ethics, a safeguard against the pauperization of the masses which was going on in the West, a bulwark against the class struggle that was tearing Europe apart. The *obshchina*, with the native *artel*—the guild of workmen sharing equally in the product of their labour—was the clearest indication that the destiny and mission of Russia, of the Slavic world generally, differed radically from those of the West.

The Slavophil doctrine of the decisive importance of the collectivist elements in peasant life seems to have originated in the late 'thirties. Elaborated in the years that followed, it achieved an extraordinary career.

As for the Westernists—the name, though thrust upon them by their opponents, was a fitting one—they were committed to the proposition that Russia moved within the European orbit and that its progress was bound to follow the general lines of European development. Their minds ran in positivist rather than pietistic channels, and they were free from the messianic streak that marked Slavophil thinking. They pinned their faith to institutional reform, where their adversaries were inclined to expect social betterment from a change of heart wrought by divine grace. Both factions, it must be kept in mind, were schools of opinion, representing rival historico-philosophical trends. Neither had formulated a programme of action. Two groups of advanced thinkers, they existed in a political vacuum.

The Westernist school had a mighty champion in the person of Vissarion Belinsky. He was the first prominent man-of-letters in modern Russia who was not a gentleman with a manorial background. The son of a naval doctor, he had to struggle against poverty all his life. With literary criticism as his sole medium of expression, the man, born to 'howl like a jackal', as he put it, could only coo about such seemingly innocuous subjects as Pushkin's verse or Gogol's prose. Nevertheless it was to his articles in *Otechestvennye zapiski* (Fatherland Notes) and, after 1846, in *Sovremennik* (The Contemporary) that, on the twenty-fifth of each month, young people turned first. After he had repudiated conservative Hegelianism, he managed to insinuate into his prolix essays and reviews a libertarian, democratic outlook, an anguished concern for man's well-being here and now.

This concern was at the heart of what he called his socialism. The doctrine, he wrote to a friend in September, 1841, had become for him 'the idea of ideas . . . the alpha and omega of faith and knowledge'. Collective ownership of the means of production was apparently not an essential part of his new credo. Least of all did socialism mean to him the supremacy of the community over the individual. Society was for him a means of securing and enlarging the life of its members. Towards the end of his short life he came to the conclusion that Russia's hope lay in the development of an industrial middle class, and even at the height of his infatuation with 'sociality' he described the Government of the United States as 'ideal'. He was a political radical, not without a nationalistic bias, who held respect for the dignity of every human being to be the cornerstone of morality and who dreamed of a golden age to come in which men would live in perfect freedom and equality under the rule of reason. There were moments when 'fierce Vissarion' was prepared to bring the millennium about by fire and sword. And—which was rather uncommon at this period among those who longed for a new social order—he was possessed of a strong animus against religion.

Naturally such thoughts could only be expressed in talk and private correspondence. One letter of his, a lengthy communication written ten months before his untimely death in May, 1848, and addressed to Gogol, gained wide circulation in manuscript copies. It was an outburst against a book in which the novelist revealed his pietistic and obscurantist outlook.

Belinsky's letter was at once his testament and the manifesto of liberal Westernism. He described Russia as a country which had for a government 'huge corporations of official thieves and robbers', and completely lacked guarantees protecting the person, the honour, the property of the citizenry. The Orthodox Church he denounced as 'a prop of the knout and a toady to despotism, an institution foreign to Christ, who was the first to teach mankind the principles of liberty, equality, and fraternity'. The Russians, Belinsky insisted, might be ridden by superstitions, but fundamentally they were a level-headed and deeply atheistic people. The country saw its salvation not in mysticism, asceticism, or quietism, but in the advance of civilization, enlightenment, humaneness; it required laws which would be in agreement not with the teachings of the Church, but with common sense and justice; its most pressing needs were emancipation of the serfs, abolition of corporal punishment, strict enforcement of the laws already in existence.

Another protagonist of Westernism was Herzen. As Moscow was the Slavophil stronghold, he took part in the endless disputations that raged in the literary salons there. Night after night he broke lances with Khomyakov, the formidable dialectician, with Konstantin Aksakov, the fighting fanatic, with the Kireyevsky brothers, twin pillars of Orthodoxy and nationalism. He found their theories absurd, chimerical, extremely dangerous, seeing in them, as he put it later, 'fresh oil for anointing the Czar, new chains laid upon thought'. And yet he was simultaneously repelled and attracted by 'the vile coterie'.

As time went on, the relations between the two groups worsened, and early in 1845 there was a complete break. Nevertheless, Herzen retained a certain affection for some of his adversaries, and that not only because their personal characteristics appealed to him. The fact is that at some points his own thinking came close to theirs. Years afterwards he wrote: 'Like Janus, or the two-headed eagle, we looked in opposite directions, but one heart beats in our breasts.' He shared the partiality of his Moscow opponents for everything Russian and their faith in the common people; he was stirred by their intimations of Slavdom's world mission; he was more deeply impressed than he knew by the Slavophil emphasis on the collectivist spirit of the Russian folk, as it was embodied in the *obshchina*.

His devotion to socialism remained steadfast. It involved an animus against 'capitalism'. An entry in his diary, dated 17 June, 1844, commends the Fourierists for condemning mercantilism and modern industrialism as 'a syphilitic sore infecting the blood and bone of society'. On the positive side, it was a commitment to a humane ideal, now free from supernaturalism. The goal was a secular, rationally organized society. Not that he was clear what form the organization ought to take. Certainly the available blueprints were far from satisfactory. In the writings of Saint-Simon and Fourier there were prophetic hints, he thought, but also *des niaiseries*. Proudhon's denunciation of private property appealed to him, but he was unable to rid himself of the feeling that private property was essential to a complete personality. As for communism, he could discover in it nothing but 'negation'. Before long he would describe it as 'Russian autocracy upside down'. In any event, socialism was not a subject one could deal with in print. As a writer, he inveighed against quietism in philosophy and indirectly advocated greater freedom in private life.

Some of the Westernists, like the Decembrists before them, assumed that if everyone were assured human rights and the opportunity to pursue his economic advantage, all would be well. Others found this view no longer acceptable. From the West came sinister rumours of the disastrous effects of the *laissez-faire* policy on the masses. These reports were echoed in the native literature. In a book of philosophic dialogues, published in Petersburg in 1844, one year before the appearance of Engels' *The Condition of the Working Class in England*, it was argued that unrestricted economic competition wreaks havoc on the health, the happiness, the morals of generations. In 1847 an instructor in the University of Petersburg published a study in which he commended 'the social school of economists' who would restrict freedom of competition, replace anarchy with order, and impose a just and rational organization on industry.

Socialism seemed to offer an escape from the prospect of falling from the frying-pan of quasi-feudalism into the fire of capitalism. It teased the imagination with the dream-like vision of a society where body and spirit were at ease. A contemporary notes that by 1843 the works of Proudhon, Cabet, Fourier, and Leroux were in the hands of everyone in Petersburg, forming 'the object of study, ardent discussion, questions, and all manner of hopes'. In Moscow Saint-Simon was popular. Herzen has it that there socialism went hand in hand with Hegelianism. Nor was the vogue restricted to the capitals. A young engineer, writing from a small town in the province of Yaroslavl, requested his brother to get him *La Phalange* or the works of Considérant, saying he would rather go without boots than without the books of one of Fourier's apostles. The importation of such literature was of course forbidden, but dealers were careful to stock up on the titles they found on the Index, and pedlars called at the homes of trusted customers, prepared either to lend or sell bootlegged books. Though Slavophilism had adumbrated a connexion between the European Utopias and such native realities as the *obshchina* and the *artel*, socialism was plainly an imported article.

As the 'forties wore on, signs of a change in the intellectual climate multiplied. The rise of Slavophilism and Westernism indicated that the contemplation and cultivation of the inner self were giving place to a sense of civic responsibility. Interest in metaphysics was beginning to be supplanted by a concern with the material conditions of life. Here and there young men were turning against the Church and transferring their affections from philosophy to economic theory and the natural sciences. The early stories of Dostoevsky and Turgenev, which belong to this period, carry an undertone of social protest, and occasionally one comes across a piece of fiction in which this note, in spite of the rigours of censorship, sounds clear. *Dead Souls*, as well as other writings of Gogol, who was a pietist and a religious humanist, were interpreted as satires directed against the system. Literary criticism, under the influence of Belinsky, was becoming a critique of life, hailing the realistic approach and emphasizing the author's duties as a citizen. The civic motif now appears for the first time in the visual arts, notably in the canvases of a group of genre painters. A leading Petersburg journal, in characterizing the spirit of the times, speaks of materialism and 'sociality'. The word was soon to be supplanted by its synonym, 'socialism'.[1]

IV

Although men did no more than read and talk, their interest in social theories and civic affairs drew them together. In Kiev a number of intellectuals marked the twentieth anniversary of the Decembrist uprising by forming a secret brotherhood, which in some respects resembled the Society of the United Slavs. It was inspired by a devotion to evangelical Christianity and a belief in the innate democratic virtues of the Slavic race. The programme called for the emancipation of the serfs and for other radical reforms. A distant objective was the overthrow of the autocracy and the establishment of a federation of Slav republics patterned on the United States of America. The Society, which chose Cyril and Methodius, the apostles to the Slavs, as patron saints, produced some propaganda pieces, which failed, however, to circulate, and after a year's existence it was wiped out by arrests.

A more noteworthy circle existed in Petersburg. Here, from 1845 on, a group of young men gathered once a week to spend a long evening together in the shabby drawing-room of a certain Mikhail Butashevich-Petrashevsky, hereafter referred to as Petrashevsky, a clerk in the Ministry of Foreign Affairs.

He was a man of unconventional and strongly-held convictions, not without a touch of the crank about him. 'Finding no one worthy of my attachment,' he wrote, 'I have devoted myself to the service of mankind . . . striving for the common good has supplanted in me egoism and the instinct of self-preservation,

---

[1] The term was apparently first used in a French Saint-Simonist review in 1832. Its earliest occurrence in English is dated 1835 in *The Encyclopædia Britannica*, 9th edition, and 1839 in the *Shorter Oxford Dictionary*. According to the *Oxford English Dictionary*, 'socialist' first occurred in 1833, but E. H. Carr (*Studies in Revolution*, p. 10) traces the word back to 1827, when it appeared in an Owenite publication.

and respect for truth has freed me from every trace of self-regard.' From the first he had a sense of election, a feeling that he was destined, like Atlas, as he put it, to carry the world on his shoulders. With boundless faith in man's progress under the tutelage of reason, he looked forward to the day when words like 'poverty, suffering, bitterness, coercion, punishment, injustice, vice, and crime' would be mere reminders of past ages like skeletons of antediluvian animals.

In 1841, at the age of twenty, he planned to publish a political review, but went no further than to jot down notes for articles. Several years later he attempted to spread his ideas through the unlikely medium of a dictionary of borrowed words, which he helped to compile. Here he found a way to expound briefly the doctrines of Robert Owen, Saint-Simon, Fourier, and even of the obscure seventeenth-century Utopian, James Harrington. The word 'opposition' gave him a chance to defend civil liberties and the jury system; 'nepotism' allowed him to set forth the advantages of elective government; under 'odalisque' he championed women's rights, under 'Negrophil' he attacked serfdom. The copies of the book, which had somehow slipped by the censors, were of course seized by the police. Petrashevsky now concentrated on the weekly gatherings he had started in his rooms. In connexion with these meetings he ran a co-operative lending library consisting chiefly of forbidden French and German books. He did not, however, confine his efforts to the educated. A born proselytizer, he is said to have joined an artisans' dancing class in order to make converts there. He estimated his acquaintances at eight hundred.

In good time his Fridays became something of an institution, a social and debating club, rather than a secret society. The gatherings were attended by at least a score of men: small officials, army officers, school teachers, several students, writers, including the young Dostoevsky. The company included no women, though they would have been welcome, for 'through women ideas spread faster', as one visitor put it. It was a group of a lower social status than that of the Decembrists. The talk was not exactly of the kind that befitted sons of the Orthodox Church and loyal subjects of the Czar. Political and literary news was retailed, the moves of the Government were discussed, high officials freely gossiped about, the latest abuses hotly denounced, the necessity for reforms urged. Republican, pacifist, abolitionist, internationalist sentiments were freely voiced; religion, and even the family, were questioned. Here were the first manifestations of the spirit of nihilism, which was to assert itself in the next generation.

The revolution of 1848 made a great stir in the circle. A more formal and serious note crept into the gatherings. It was decided to devote each evening to the study of a definite social problem. Sometimes a speech would be made or a manuscript read. There might be a chairman provided with a bell in the form of a hemisphere surmounted by the figure of Liberty. One evening Petrashevsky spoke on how men of letters could spread their ideas. Again, he argued the need for freedom of the press and discoursed on the difference between social and political liberty, insisting on the necessity for economic change. On one occasion there was a lecture on political economy. On another an instructor in a military college quoted Feuerbach on the harmfulness of religion. A man must know, not believe, and all things are subject to the test of reason—such was the tenor of a talk which led one visitor, a fervent Christian, to lose his faith. Petrashevsky himself was a freethinker. He once characterized Christ as 'a well-known demagogue who ended his career somewhat unsuccessfully'. But his guests included men who combined radicalism with deep religious feeling.

Often the conversation at the Friday meetings turned to socialism. While to some it was an object of intellectual curiosity, others embraced it as a faith. The core of it, Petrashevsky held, was organization, 'the reaction of the human spirit against the influence of liberalism, an influence which is anarchic and destructive of social life'. By liberalism he meant, of course, *laissez-faire* policy. He bracketed liberals and bankers as the masters of Western Europe. On another occasion, however, this unbeliever described socialism as 'the dogma of Christian love seeking realization in practical life'.

The particular variety of socialism that commanded the allegiance of many was Fourierism. Just at the time when the Fourierist colonies set up in the United States were falling apart, the French Utopian's doctrines were gaining enthusiastic adherents in Russia. While the Americans had a chance to test out his theories, the Russians had to content themselves with talk, and as a result there was no limit to the extravagance of their daydreams. One Friday Konstantin Timkovsky, a government official, proposed that some country, perhaps the world, be divided into halves, one to be turned over to the Fourierists, the other to the communists, for social experiments. 'Let them live in friendly neighbourliness,' he is reported to have said, 'and borrow from one another the good things each has.'

The host took offence at this concession to communism, a doctrine that neither he nor most of his guests favoured. In their minds it was associated with violence. The fewest shared the attitude of the visitor who looked forward to the time when people would own everything in common, 'just as reason which unites them is common to all men'. Petrashevsky wrote to Timkovsky that the communists had nothing but atheism to offer the Fourierists. The latter, he pointed out, sought to achieve 'gradually and naturally' the aims which the communists would accomplish by force. A square mile of land, he argued, and two thousand men and women were sufficient 'to turn the most fantastic dream of paradisal bliss into reality'. His enthusiasm for the master's teachings was unlimited. When he had first discovered them, he felt as though he had been 'born anew'. It is reported that he had attempted to set up a phalanstery on his own estate, but gave up the idea after his forty serfs had set fire to their paradise. He did not, however, give up the hope of living in a phalanstery himself.

Petrashevsky was resolutely opposed to violence and undemocratic methods. When one of his visitors argued that the transition to the new order might require a temporary dictatorship, he exclaimed that he would kill the dictator with his own hands. His conviction that socialism offered a painless way of solving the social problem and one that was possible under the existing régime was shared by many of his guests. As one habitué had it, Fourierism repudiated 'liberalism, demagogy, mutiny, and rebellion'. Among the frequenters of the Friday meetings there were, however, a few who were less unrealistic and, moreover, temperamentally impatient with Fabian policies. The hard facts of Russian life intruded upon Utopian fantasies. The French reformers' condemnation of capitalist society could not but sharpen the opposition of their Russian followers to the semi-feudal order under which they lived. Certainly not all of them shared Fourier's political indifferentism. As a matter of fact, Petrashevsky himself favoured the gradual transformation of the Russian Empire into a federated republic like the United States of America. There were intimations of using force against the Czar's Government, and he himself came in for a good deal of obloquy at the gatherings. An army officer was the author of an essay in which he described Nicholas as the anti-Christ spoken of in the Apocalypse and suggested that the Emperor be put for a few days on the diet of the Vitebsk peasants—their bread looked like dried horse-dung mixed with straw.

Of course, abolition of serfdom was a general desideratum. And there were those who believed that only a peasant uprising would bring it about. Unlike the Decembrists, some of Petrashevsky's visitors came close to seeing the masses as an active political force. He himself attributed peasant poverty to collective land tenure, but at least one of his guests held that the *obshchina* was potentially an important national asset.

It has been indicated that the Petrashevsky coterie was in no sense a formal association. Late in 1848 an army officer and another frequenter of the Fridays proposed to set up such an organized body. They spoke of it as 'a brotherhood of mutual aid', but were vague about its real purpose. Several men met privately to discuss the idea. One of them was Nikolay Speshnev, a substantial young landowner who had travelled abroad and there fallen under the influence of socialist theories. He advocated nationalization of land and government control of the country's entire economy. During the talks about 'the brotherhood' he expressed the desire to see it organized as a 'purely political society' planning for propaganda and 'insurrection'. Afterwards he explained that he had spoken so boldly in order to bring the discussion to an end by frightening the participants. If that was his purpose, he achieved it, for the matter was dropped.

It is doubtful, however, if he gave up the idea of a secret society. Unlike Petrashevsky, he seems to have believed that a revolution would occur in the near future. The police found among his papers a statement to the effect that 'the undersigned' had joined 'the Russian Society', and had obligated himself 'to participate openly and fully in the uprising and fight, when the Committee has decided that the time for the insurrection has arrived', also to enrol other members and have each sign a similar pledge.

Speshnev was not the only one to entertain the thought of an armed uprising. Early in 1849 he had a talk with one, Chernosvitov, who had attended a few Fridays. Imagining that the man—a former police official who had turned to gold mining in Siberia—belonged to a secret society, Speshnev, to draw him out, passed himself off as a member of an imaginary underground organization. Thereupon Chernosvitov developed a plan for engineering the revolution: it was to start in Siberia, spread to the Urals, where four hundred thousand men with easy access to arms were waiting for the first sign of revolt, finally reaching the capitals. One of Petrashevsky's numerous acquaintances kept a tobacco shop, which was frequented by young men with whom the proprietor discussed liberty and equality and the chances of a republican régime in Russia. One of these youths, a student by the name of Tolstov, spoke of surveying the capital with a view to finding sites for barricades. Another, when in his cups, volunteered to kill the Czar.

During the winter of 1848-49 some of the men who had attended the gatherings at Petrashevsky's also formed a more intimate 'salon', so as to be safe from the secret service agents who, they suspected, not without reason, were mingling with the guests at the Fridays. At a meeting of this group, which included young Dostoevsky in addition to several other men of letters, Speshnev offered to have the writings of the authors present printed abroad and smuggled into the country. At another gathering Filippov, a student, proposed that the members write essays on various aspects of Russian life and reproduce them secretly by lithography. Speshnev's offer was not taken up, nor did the essays or the lithographing materialize. But it appears that a clandestine printing-press was actually set up, though not used. The enterprise, which was a capital offence, was concealed from Petrashevsky. It was carried out by Speshnev and Filippov, aided by half a dozen others, including Dostoevsky.

If the press remained idle, it was not for lack of appropriate copy. Several of the manuscripts which were read aloud at the gatherings were apparently intended for circulation. Such was a story from the pen of a Lieutenant of the Guards, in which a veteran of the Napoleonic wars advised the soldiery to follow the example of the French who had recently got rid of their king. Filippov himself was the author of a propagandist piece in the form of a commentary on the Ten Commandments. It applauded violence against brutal masters on the part of serfs, and described a czar who did not side with the people as 'a ruler whose authority was not from the Lord but from Satan'. Another manuscript that fairly begged to be printed was Belinsky's letter to Gogol, which was mentioned previously. Dostoevsky received a copy of it from Moscow and read it at Petrashevsky's and elsewhere, arousing 'universal rapture'.

v

On 7 April, 1849,[1] Fourier's birthday was celebrated with a dinner. Eleven men met in a room decorated with a portrait of the master imported from Paris for the occasion. The first speaker pointed out that the event they were commemorating was destined to bring about the transformation of the planet and of the human beings inhabiting it. He held forth in exalted language on some of the more extreme and abstruse aspects of Fourier's teachings, but did not omit to refer to matters nearer home. 'My fatherland', he exclaimed, 'is in chains, my fatherland is enslaved; religion, ignorance—the companion of despotism— have obscured, have stifled its natural inclinations. There is no room, however, for despair. Transfiguration is at hand!' the speaker cried; and it would be brought about by 'pure science'. All applauded; two enthusiasts embraced him.

Then Petrashevsky rose. He referred to himself as one of the oldest 'propagators of socialism'. This doctrine, he explained, sought to harmonize the organization of society with the needs of man's nature. He urged his hearers not to try to invent a new social system, but merely to apply the principle of Fourierism. The difficulties that confronted its Russian adherents should, however, not be minimized, for an unhappy accident had made them representatives of socialism on 'the savage soil' of an ignorant country, and faced them with conditions that neither Fourier himself nor his Western disciples could have foreseen.

[1] In ignoring the fact that Fourier was born on 7 April according to the Western calendar, the Russians were twelve days late marking the occasion.

The next speaker, after a grandiloquent opening, painted a black picture of the life around him: 'We live in a vast, hideous capital, amidst a monstrous conglomeration of human beings languishing in the grip of monotonous drudgery, soiled by dirty toil, smitten by disease and depravity, a conglomeration broken up into families which injure each other, waste time and energy, and join together to perform useless labours. And yonder the provincial cities strive to imitate the capital, their only aim and highest ambition being to become populous, depraved, monstrous like the capital! Still lower, tens of millions of labourers toil all day long, in sunshine and rain, tilling the soil which is not theirs that it may give them of its scanty fruit. Not for this has man laboured so long, and this is not the crown of his labours; it awaits him, he deserves it, and he will soon take it and cover his tormented head with it, and arise, king of the earth.'

From this point on, the note of exultation dominated his speech. 'We are celebrating the coming redemption of mankind', he went on. 'To turn this life of torture, disaster, poverty, shame and disgrace into a life harmonious and abundant with joy, wealth, and happiness, and to cover all this poverty-ridden earth with palaces and flowers—this is our great task, than which there is no greater on earth. . . . We here in our land,' he concluded, with messianic pride, 'will begin the transformation, and the whole earth will accomplish it.'

The practical outcome of the dinner, the first political banquet in Russia, was a decision to undertake a translation of the master's *Théorie de l'unité universelle*. The plan was not carried out. Some two weeks later the banqueters found themselves behind bars.

The existence of the circle had long been an open secret. In March 1848, Petrashevsky was placed under surveillance. Early in the next year a secret service agent managed to gain his confidence and in March began to frequent the Friday meetings. The result was that on the night of 23 April, 1849, Petrashevsky and some thirty of his visitors were rounded up and imprisoned in the Fortress of Peter and Paul. Other arrests followed shortly. Altogether over a hundred men were examined. (When the conversation at the gatherings had touched on the question of the total number of 'socialists' in Russia, the estimates—probably over-generous—would range from four to eight hundred.)

Many of the prisoners behaved in much the same way as had the Decembrists under arrest. They recanted and pleaded for mercy. Tolstov declared in a written deposition: 'I am guilty not only of the crimes with which I am charged, but of much greater ones. . . . And I would be a scoundrel if I dared to beg the Czar to spare me. All the mercy I crave is that he should forgive me in his heart, or else life will be poison for me. I can only say, like the prodigal son: "Father, I have sinned against Heaven and in thy sight." '

Petrashevsky was among the few who bore themselves with dignity. He was deeply concerned over the fate of his comrades. He pleaded that if punishment was to be meted out, he alone should receive it: if he could not serve mankind as he had hoped, he wished to serve his country by such an act of self-sacrifice. He did not feel that he or his fellow prisoners had done anything unlawful. They were, he told his judges, not fanatics and monsters, but thinkers, cherishing the truth above all. Let them be shown that they erred and they would give up their convictions. He lectured and upbraided the court. In his memoranda he offered, among other things, to advise the Government on matters of public policy. One of his suggestions was that the Czar finance a phalanstery near Paris. He would thereby end the dangerous hostility between rich and poor in Western Europe, thus earning for himself a fame far above 'Napoleon's ruinous glory'. Believing that he was at the point of death, he bequeathed a third of his possessions to Considérant for the establishment of a phalanstery, and his body to an anatomical theatre.

For a long time Petrashevsky consistently denied any subversive designs. By the seventh month of his incarceration he was reduced to such a state that he declared himself willing to sign any confession presented to him. Solitary confinement, which all the prisoners had to endure, eventually affected his mind.

The Investigating Commission established the fact that a handful of young men met at Petrashevsky's and elsewhere to discuss socialist theories, air pernicious opinions of a liberal nature, and read revolting manuscripts. Nothing was discovered to indicate that they had formed anything like a secret organization with a programme of revolutionary action. At most, theirs was 'a conspiracy of ideas'. Credence was given to Speshnev's statement that 'the Russian Society' mentioned in the pledge found among his papers did not exist and that the pledge itself had neither been seen nor signed by anyone. No trace was found of the press which he and Filippov had confessed to having attempted to set up: it must have been removed from Speshnev's quarters after his arrest. Nevertheless twenty-three men were court-martialled and fifteen of them condemned to death by shooting. The verdict was reviewed by the Auditoriat General, the highest judicial body in the land. It handed down the decision that fully twenty-one of the defendants were liable to capital punishment, but recommended clemency. Accordingly, the Emperor commuted the death sentence to terms of hard labour of varying lengths. The men, including Dostoevsky, were taken to a public square, and there, in the presence of massed troops and a gaping crowd, they heard their death sentences and went through all the preparations for execution. At the last moment they were informed that the Czar in his mercy had made them a gift of their lives.

Petrashevsky and some of his fellow convicts died in Siberian exile. Others returned to European Russia after having served their terms.

VI

The severity of the punishment meted out to the group which was to become known as the Petrashevists was due to the fact that the upheaval of 1848, like the events of 30 July in Paris and the revolution of 1789, had caused a spasm of reaction in the empire. Russia, a contemporary observed, was Europe's whipping boy. The news of the establishment of the second French republic produced a panic at court. The Czar's first thought was to march his troops to the Rhine. A month later he issued a hysterical manifesto bristling with threats against the revolutionaries and concluding with the words: 'Heed ye, nations, and submit, for God is with us!' He contented himself with assisting the anti-democratic forces in Prussia and putting down the Hungarian insurrection. In conservative circles the growth of the Russian working-class had long been regarded with apprehension. The February revolution enhanced the fear that such a development might lead to a repetition of what was happening in the West. The Governor-General of Moscow ordered that no more factories be built in that city, and it took a good deal of special pleading to overrule him. A high official, writing about those days in his memoirs, noted the appearance of 'a party of Reds who dreamed of a republic even for Russia'. The party was a figment of the dignitary's imagination. The spectre of communism that, according to Marx and Engels, was haunting Europe was seen in the palaces of Russia as well.

While intervening abroad, the Government tightened the bonds at home. The chief of the gendarmerie suggested a war to embitter the people against the French and their teachings. The authorities contented themselves with a campaign against the press. It was forbidden to publish anything 'about working people in France and in other states where political disturbances occurred or could occur'. Never before had censorship been so strict. It was during these years that several authors, including Turgenev, made their acquaintance with jail. Death alone had saved Belinsky from arrest.

The schools too were subjected to new stringencies. The universities were ordered to base their teachings not on rational but on religious truths, and the rectors and deans were enjoined to see to it that nothing in the instruction favoured socialism or communism. The chair of philosophy was abolished on the ground that the subject, while not demonstrably useless, was possibly harmful. All thought of reform, particularly the freeing of the serfs, was abandoned. The country breathed an intolerably oppressive air.

Herzen was spared the experience of living through that period of white terror. He had gone abroad with his family in 1847, to escape the fruitless discussions, the choking atmosphere of despotism. His first contacts with life in Western Europe were disheartening. He discovered that France was dominated by the section of the population that had appropriated all the gains of the Revolution: *meshchanstvo* (bourgeoisie). Basically this was to him not so much a social class, but an ethical and aesthetic phenomenon: a spirit hopelessly crass, shallow, ignoble, the tyranny of the mindless mob, the twilight of the soul, the death of culture. The bourgeois, he wrote, had all the vices of the nobleman and the plebeian, and none of their virtues. Herzen was given to changes of heart, but he hardly ever wavered in his dislike of the European middle-class. As he did not put his light under a bushel, he contributed no little to the discrediting of the bourgeoisie in the eyes of his compatriots.

The February revolution found him in Rome and his friend Bakunin in Brussels. Bakunin immediately rushed to Paris and attached himself to the Republican Guard. 'The revolutionary movement,' he wrote, 'will only cease when all of Europe, including Russia, is transformed into a federated democratic republic.' And he went off to rouse the Germans and the Poles, only to be arrested in Berlin. By April, when Herzen arrived in the French capital, the political skies were already overcast. With deep interest and growing apprehension, he watched the course of events. During the June massacres he and his wife sat with their Russian friends in a candle-lit room, since the light of a lamp would have seemed too garish, talking in whispers like mourners. He wished he had died on a barricade so that he could have taken some beliefs with him to the grave. Ogarev was then in Russia, but kept abreast of developments abroad. His advice, given in verse, was that those who had not committed suicide flee to America. As, indeed, many Europeans did.

The thought of emigrating to America occurred to Herzen too, but he rejected it. Weren't the United States but an extension of Europe, a revised edition of a familiar text? Furthermore, although the French Republic was becoming a police state, not unlike Nicholas's empire, it still had freedom of the press. He stayed on, spending part of the time in France, part in Italy, his mind furiously at work trying to make out the meaning of the cruel events, to learn the lessons of 1848, 'a pedagogical year'. Chief among them was the failure of political democracy. Universal suffrage, he wrote to friends at home, had given a controlling voice to orang-utans. The omnipotent middle-class was interested not in liberty, but in protecting its property. Except for 'a holy minority', the masses were incapable of sustained protest. The liberals did not understand them and could offer them no guidance. Paris had become an extinct volcano, its crater filled with mud. Europe had reached an impasse. 'Repent, gentlemen, repent,' Herzen cried, 'the judgment day of your world is here!'

Well, perhaps the doomsday of the old order was not at hand. But the revolution would rise from its ashes, and its objective would be not a 'political revolution'—the masses would have learned to expect nothing from that—but socialism. This was what Europe would bequeath to the future as 'the fruit of its efforts, the summit of its development'. Herzen envisaged a vast and violent upheaval, which was bound to wipe out Western civilization. He mourned its end, but hailed 'the chaos and destruction' that would sweep into discard the exploitative society and the centralized state, sacrificing freedom to order, the individual to the collective. Exalting reason as 'the guillotine within man', he momentarily favoured Blanqui's programme of dictatorship and, with characteristic inconsistency, Proudhon's anarchism. Indeed, he wrote for the latter's short-lived organ, *La Voix du Peuple*, and backed it financially.

The *coup d'état* of 2 December, 1851, and the subsequent establishment of the Second Empire distressed but did not surprise Herzen. Events bore out his blackest anticipations. In his headlong fashion he decided that darkness had descended on Europe. Indeed, he concluded that the old world lay dying. Would the end come through 'the barbarism of the sceptre', or 'the barbarism of communism', that 'socialism of vengeance'? In any event, the conflict was inevitable. It might break out anywhere, in Paris or New York, and it would spread far and wide. Reaction having done its worst and wars having changed the face of Europe, the 'have-nots' would rise against the 'haves', and communism, tempestuous, iniquitous, bloody, would sweep across the earth. Then, he prophesied, amid the ruins of palaces, factories and government offices, there would appear the new tables of the law: a *socialist* decalogue.

Herzen did not rule out the possibility of Socialism being defeated. He also conceded that the masses, having achieved victory, might become infected with the middle-class spirit. On an earlier occasion he had prophesied that in the fulness of time a new revolution would destroy Socialism. Meanwhile he remained committed to it. Not that the concept lost its vagueness for him. He described or was to describe it variously as embodied Christianity, a stomach problem, man's coming of age, the application of reason to public economy, as imminent, as far-off. He was satisfied that it had the highest moral sanction. Yet he felt the need of finding some guarantee that the socialist ideal was not an insubstantial dream. He believed that he had found such a guarantee at home.

As his disillusionment with the West deepened, his own country appeared to him in a different light. 'Faith in Russia saved me,' he wrote, 'when I was on the brink of moral death.' The Slavophils were right: Russia was different. Unlike effete Europe, it was full of vigour, self-confidence, audacity. In later years he was to speak of the Russians' lack of pieties, their readiness to utter 'with a kind of joy those ultimate, extreme words' which their Western teachers 'barely whisper, blanching and glancing about'. The dead hand of the past did not weigh on this virgin land. Like most Slavs, Russians 'belonged to geography, rather than to history'. Peter had forced Western civilization on his subjects with the help of the knout, so there was little in it that they cherished, surely not the principles of property and authority. Above all, Russia possessed the *obshchina*.

This institution had its drawbacks: it did not make for the most productive agricultural economy and, which was more deplorable, it submerged the individual. Yet potentially it was of immense value. It was 'the life-giving principle of the Russian people'. With its immemorial tradition of equality, collective ownership of land, and communal self-government, Herzen argued, the *obshchina* was in effect the seed of a socialist society. Under its ægis the simple villagers practised in their daily living what the noblest minds of Europe only dreamed of. The *muzhik* was the man of destiny. Herzen had been haunted by the thought that just as Christianity had undone the Roman Empire, so socialism was destined to overwhelm and renew modern civilization. He now decided that since the *muzhik*'s whole being was keyed to a collective mode of existence, not the West but Russia, or rather Slavdom, was in a position to assure the triumph of the new faith. Certainly a purely political change could not tempt the Russians. Taking advantage of her backwardness and of Europe's experience, she might indeed bypass the morass of capitalism and middle-class culture on her way to Socialism. There was no historic necessity for her to follow in the footsteps of other countries.

During the early years of his stay abroad Herzen poured out these ideas in a succession of brilliant, if brittle and somewhat hysterical essays, published in German and French and before long brought out in Russian. Later on he kept returning to these speculations. They had the greatest resonance in intellectual circles at home.

Herzen's thesis regarding the socialist potentialities of the *obshchina* was corroborated by Baron August von Haxthausen, a Prussian sociologist of archconservative views, who spent most of the year 1843 in Russia investigating conditions there under semi-official auspices. He presented his findings in an imposing two-volume opus published simultaneously in German and French in 1847. In his foreword to this work the author mentions the *obshchina* and goes on to say: 'In all other countries muffled rumblings announce the approach of a social revolution directed against property. . . . In Russia such an overturn is impossible. There the Utopia of European revolutionaries is already realized.' In his third volume, brought out in 1853, the Baron treated the subject of the peasant commune at some length. Like others before him, he saw its main advantage in that it assured the Empire against the two evils that threatened the other nations with ruin: the proletariat and pauperism. His views on the subject were to play an important part in the controversy centring around the institution of the *obshchina*. A generation later Anatole Leroy-Beaulieu, another foreign student of Russia, was to write: 'A kind of virtual and latent Socialism, a vague and naïve Communism is current among the Russian people. . . . Russia is the only country in the civilized world where one can attempt to abolish private property by decree.'

As an ideologue Herzen had come home, but only in spirit. When the French police informed their Petersburg *confrères* that he had taken part in an anti-Government street demonstration, he was ordered to return to Russia. But he refused, thus burning his bridges. In 1851 he naturalized himself in Switzerland. But this citizen of the canton of Uri felt himself more profoundly a Russian than ever, with his life work cut out for him. On the one hand, he would acquaint foreigners with his country, which they feared but did not know. On the other, he would make himself the voice of those at home who were tongueless. Although at this time he put his faith in revolution, he knew that his weapon was not the pistol or the bomb, but the printed word.

He had arrived in London, the city of refuge for radicals from the Continent, in 1852, a bereaved and heart-broken man. One of his small sons and his mother had been drowned, and his wife had died in childbirth shortly afterwards. He urgently needed work into which he could throw himself body and soul. Having inherited a considerable fortune, he had an annual income of fifty to sixty thousand francs. He used some of his money to set up, in 1853, the Free Russian Press.

The first sheets to come off it were an appeal to the gentry to take the initiative in liberating the serfs. Otherwise, Herzen asserted, they would be emancipated by the Czar, which would strengthen his despotism, or else abolition would come as the result of a popular rising. The latter alternative meant a blood bath, but this was not too high a price to pay for freedom. Rather tactlessly he went on to tell the landlords that the country was on the eve of an overturn, which would be close to the heart of people living out their lives within the *obshchina* and that kind of mobile *obshchina*, the *artel*. 'Russia will have its rendezvous with revolution,' he concluded, 'in Socialism.' Before long Herzen returned to the subject of emancipation in a pamphlet entitled *Baptized Property*.

Shortly after the birth of the Second Republic, Fyodor Tyutchev, a diplomat who was also a poet, wrote to the Czar that only two opposing forces remained in Europe: Russia and Revolution, the Christian and the anti-Christian principle. And he pictured the sacred Ark of Empire riding the revolutionary flood which was to overwhelm the Western world. Far from collapsing, the West, coming to the aid of Turkey, dealt Russia a humiliating blow in the Crimean campaign.

The régime was unable to stand the test of war. The shell was splendid, the core rotten, as a contemporary observed. Since no initiative on the part of the public had been tolerated, the administration had to bear the blame for the débâcle alone. Its corruption was exposed to plain view and its general incompetence demonstrated with finality. There were patriots who welcomed the fall of Sebastopol, in the hope that national defeat would mean the doom of the régime.

To a degree Herzen shared this defeatism. In a leaflet addressed to the troops stationed in Poland he told them that this was an unjust war, brought on by the Czar's stubbornness and pride, and he urged them not to lift a hand against the Poles, should they start an insurrection. Several incendiary appeals to the peasantry, composed by another expatriate, were run off the

Free Press. In addressing his foreign audience, Herzen emphasized the fact that the Russian people were the victims, not the accomplices of their government, and he took every occasion to affirm his faith in Russia as the land peculiarly fitted to assure the victory of Socialism. At least in the beginning he felt that this war was not an ordinary military contest, but a 'fateful' clash destined to usher the Slavic world into the arena of universal history and to sound the knell of the old order.

On New Year's Eve, at a party welcoming 1855, he presented his son, then fifteen years old, with a flamboyant dedication of the Russian edition of his book, *From the Other Shore*. Herein he told the boy that the only religion he was bequeathing to him was that of revolution, enjoined him to go and preach it in good time to their people at home, and added his blessing, in the name of human reason, personal liberty, and brotherly love.

The boy did not become a revolutionary. The peasants did not rise. The soldiers did not mutiny. The Poles did not rebel—not yet. But at the close of the winter something occurred to spur Herzen's hopes. On the morning of 4 March (N.S.) he dashed into the children's room waving a copy of *The Times*. It carried a headline announcing the death of Nicholas I. Later in the morning he celebrated the event in champagne with other émigrés, Russian and Polish. The autocrat was dead, perhaps the system would not long outlive him. This end might mean a new beginning.

CHAPTER V

FREEDOM?

THE news of Nicholas's death brought a general sense of relief. All thinking people felt that the event marked the end of an era, and that there were bound to be decisive changes. The long winter had come to an end and the tumult of spring was sweeping through the political air. Tongues were loosened, minds were aroused. 'Whoever was not alive in Russia in 1856,' wrote Tolstoy, 'does not know what life is.'

At first the new Czar, busy bringing the war to an end, could not give thought to the great reforms awaited by the country. He did, however, show a concessive spirit in various small ways. Restrictions on the number of university students were lifted and difficulties in the way of foreign travel removed. Some Decembrists and Petrashevists were amnestied. One or two notorious obscurantists were dismissed from high posts. Each liberal or humane measure, however trivial, was greeted with enthusiasm and served to sustain the great expectations that buoyed up all hearts. Hints at coming reforms were read into official pronouncements. The time for patchwork measures seemed at an end.

The slogan of progress was on every tongue. It was the refrain of the books and periodicals that were appearing in greater numbers. The press was given licence to touch on questions of foreign and domestic policy, although certain topics, notably the abolition of serfdom—the pivotal issue of the day—could not be mentioned. Forbidden subjects were aired in manuscript pamphlets by both Slavophils and Westernists. In their eagerness to work for a regenerated Russia the two camps were ready to bury the hatchet. Not that the Westernists were all of one mind. They had a left wing with its own organ, the Petersburg monthly *Sovremennik* (The Contemporary). The magazine was controlled by Nikolay Nekrasov, a civic poet of great popularity, who was also a shrewd editor. He leaned heavily on a young man by the name of Nikolay Chernyshevsky.

The radicals had a somewhat uncertain ally in the handful of expatriates captained by Herzen. A few days after the beginning of the new reign he addressed an open letter to the Czar. Acknowledging himself 'an incorrigible socialist' and his addressee 'an autocratic Emperor', he declared that nevertheless the two had in common a love for the Russian people. In the name of this love he urged Alexander II to free the press from censorship, abolish corporal punishment and wipe out the blot of serfdom. He promised 'to wait, obliterate himself, speak of something else', as long as he could hope that the government would accomplish these great things. He did not know how to obliterate himself and he could not speak of other things, but he did observe a kind of private truce with the Czar during the years that preceded emancipation.

The open letter was printed in the first number of a review which Herzen issued from his Free Press in July, 1855, on the anniversary of the execution of the Decembrists. He called it *The Polar Star,* after the miscellany that Ryleyev had once edited, and he provided it with a frontispiece showing the profiles of the five who were hanged. His previous pamphlets lay on the shelves of a shop in Paternoster Row gathering dust. *The Polar Star,* however, found its way into Russia and was eagerly read. It was a year old when Herzen started another publication: *Voices from Russia,* in which he printed some of the political literature that circulated in manuscript.

He soon perceived that there was need of yet another organ which could more readily keep up with the rapid pace of events at home, and which, being less bulky, could be more easily smuggled across the border. Accordingly, on 1 July, 1857, he launched *Kolokol (The Bell),* first a monthly, then a bi-weekly. He now had the help of Ogarev, who had joined him in London the previous year. *The Bell* summoned the living—*Vivos Voco* was its motto—to bury the dead past and work for the glorious future. It undertook to be everywhere and always on the side of freedom and against oppression, for reason and against prejudice, for science and against fanaticism, for progressive peoples and against backward governments. Specifically, *The Bell* was devoted to 'the liberation of Russia'.

In addition to being an ideologue and a memoirist of high distinction, Herzen was a crusading journalist possessed of a powerful pen. And he had the inestimable privilege of freedom

from censorship. The office of *The Bell* was flooded with communications from home, and there was a constant stream of
Russian visitors of both sexes and all sorts and conditions to the
house in Putney where Herzen lived and worked. With their
help and that of scores of correspondents scattered through the
country, *Kolokol* conducted a most successful muck-raking
campaign. It cited particulars and named names. Minutes of the
secret sessions of the highest bodies appeared in its columns.
Fear of exposure there became a deterrent to administrative
abuse. There was talk in high places of buying Herzen off,
perhaps with an important post. The journal was read by all
literate Russia, from the Emperor down to high school boys.
The smuggled sheets were sold almost openly and were tran-
scribed or mimeographed to meet the demand. The handful of
London expatriates were a power.

When *The Bell* first began pealing from the shores of the
Thames, Russia had known peace for more than a year. As
soon as the war was over, the Czar had turned his attention to
domestic matters. He was not a reformer either by temperament
or conviction, but he was statesman enough to perceive that the
Empire could not muddle along in the old way. Naturally, the
peasant question was the first to engage him. It was increasingly
obvious that the system of serf labour was choking the life of the
country, economically and otherwise. Furthermore, the discontent of the masses was mounting. At the height of the war
there were peasant riots in several provinces. They were caused
by a rumour that the emancipation *ukase* had already been
signed but was kept from the people by the officials. According
to another rumour, the treaty that terminated the hostilities
contained a secret clause which obligated the Czar to free the
serfs.

The peace of Paris was signed on 30 March, 1856 (N.S.).
Less than a fortnight later the Czar startled a gathering of nobles
in Moscow by observing pointedly that while he did not intend
to abolish serfdom with a stroke of the pen, the existing order
could not be left unchanged, and that in any event it was 'better
that bondage should be abolished from above than from below'.
Nearly seventy years earlier Radishchev had had an imaginary
czar advance this very argument. The serf owners, however,
failed to take the hint. A secret commission was set up to study

88

the problem, but made no headway. Finally, on 20 November, 1857, the Emperor took a long step toward emancipation by authorizing the gentry of three north-western provinces to form committees to discuss the terms of the measure.

This first public move in the direction of the epoch-making reform was greeted with enthusiasm by all the progressive elements. It rejoiced the hearts of Westernists and Slavophils, liberals and radicals. Herzen delivered himself of a pæan to the Czar, saying that he was 'as much an heir of 14 December as of Nicholas'. He declared: 'We go with him who liberates,' adding cautiously: 'and as long as he liberates.' *The Contemporary*, too, called down blessings on the Emperor's head. Momentarily even the most radically-minded entertained the belief that the system could be overhauled under the existing régime painlessly and gradually, yet thoroughly.

II

The state of harmony between the Government and the public was short-lived. The Czar had wanted the initiative in the matter of abolition to come from the serf-owners, and he was willing to have committees of them debate the details of the measure. But he relied on the administration to formulate and carry out the reform and he made it plain that he would brook no nonsense from the gentry. In the autumn of 1859 delegates from a number of provincial committees were summoned to the capital to confer with the officials. They criticized the plans of the administration as both unjust and illegal. One of them wrote to the Emperor urging him to let the nobility have a hand in working out the measure instead of merely offering suggestions. The delegates were rudely reprimanded, and two or three of the bolder spirits, including a former Petrashevist, were deported.

Like the aristocratic *frondeurs* of the previous century, the malcontents among the gentry sought political power as a compensation for the threatened loss of economic privilege. To the Slavophils, wedded as they were to the principle of autocracy, constitutional guarantees limiting the sovereign's authority were anathema. But they allowed themselves to speak out for freedom of conscience and to harp on the necessity of an 'understanding' between the people and the state. As a result, some of their organs were hounded out of existence.

The deliberations dragged on. Were the freedmen going to be provided with land? How large would the allotments be? Would these be redeemed by the peasants or the Treasury? How onerous would the terms of redemption be? Would the *obshchina* be perpetuated? Would there be a transitional period, and of what duration? Would the landlords retain any of their authority over their former serfs? These momentous questions hung in the balance. They were guardedly debated in the press and were the chief subject of discussion in the publications issued by the London expatriates.

When Herzen had first considered the terms of emancipation, before any steps had been taken toward it, he had argued that in fifty years liberation 'without land' would turn Russia into another, and more wretched, Ireland. And, of course, he pleaded for the preservation of the peasant commune. This was Cinderella's dowry, the only precious possession of a backward, poverty-stricken nation. The salvation of Russia, perhaps of the world, lay in the *obshchina*. For did it not hold the germ of the collectivist society, toward which all mankind was striving? These views determined the position of *The Bell* on the peasant reform. Since what Herzen was to call the *muzhik*'s 'religion of land' had as its cardinal dogma a man's right to the land he tilled, it followed that, if the expectations of the freedmen were to be met, they must be allotted gratis at least the acres they had worked under serfdom for themselves. Naturally the land would be held collectively and redistributed periodically on an equalitarian basis.

Although Herzen lost no opportunity to repeat that he would welcome liberation, whether it came from above or from below, in reality he heavily discounted the latter alternative. At first he expected that the progressive elements of the gentry would exert a decisive influence in shaping the reform. He also conceived the curious notion that the Czar could be persuaded to establish a species of agrarian socialism with a stroke of his pen. Only reluctantly did he accept the principle of redemption, preferring a money settlement to the bloody insurrection that the landowners' resistance to even partial confiscation would provoke.

Whenever the Government seemed to yield to reactionaries

intent on sabotaging the emancipation, he would savagely turn
on the Czar. 'We have nothing to expect from the Government,'
he declared, when a notorious anti-abolitionist was appointed to
head the commission that drafted the emancipation statutes. And
he urged boycotting the reform. Nevertheless his confidence in
the Emperor's noble intentions persisted. He continued to imagine
that 'the imperial dictatorship' could embrace the cause of the
masses and overcome the resistance of the propertied classes
without danger to itself or a breach of the public peace, and a
Romanov become the crowned head of a Socialist state.[1]
Lassalle's notion of an alliance between the King of Prussia and
the working class comes to mind. For all his dislike of centralized
political authority, Herzen's thinking reflected the strong
tendency of native scholars to cast the monarchy in the rôle of
the protagonist in the drama of Russian history.

Herzen's stand earned him criticism both from the moderates
and the extremists. One liberal told him that no educated Russian
had any use for his chimerical theories, least of all for 'social
democracy'. What the country needed was freedom of the press
and a way to liberate the serfs without shattering the whole body
politic. And he pleaded with Herzen to stop telling the West
that the *muzhik* was destined to bring socialism into the world.
The plea went unheeded. In the columns of *The Bell* and elsewhere Herzen continued to harp—in general terms, as usual—
upon the promise of 'Communism in bast shoes'. Nor was
he any more willing to heed another liberal who reproached
him for philippics that only irritated the authorities who were
engaged in the delicate task of untying age-old knots. And he
continued to reflect on the sad state of the West, what with
political rights vanishing in Europe and slavery flourishing in
America.

On the other hand, the small contingent of radically-minded
intellectuals that sprung up during the first years of the new reign
was far from pleased by the course the London émigrés were
pursuing. The issue of *The Bell*, dated 1 March, 1860, contained a
letter to the editor signed 'A Russian'. It painted a black picture

[1] In 1890 Konstantin Leontyev, a reactionary thinker of some originality,
threw out the suggestion that some day a czar might put himself at the head
of the socialist movement and organize it, the way Constantine the Great had
organized Christianity.

of the way in which the peasant reform was being mishandled. The serfs were exploited more ruthlessly than ever by the masters, who knew that their days of power were numbered. The peasants were desperate and ready to rise. Meanwhile the liberals were babbling of peaceful progress. The writer reproached Herzen for echoing them. 'Our situation is terrible, intolerable', he concluded, 'only the axe can save us, and nothing but the axe! . . . You have done all you could to promote a peaceful solution of the problem. Now change your tune and let your *Bell* not call to prayers, but ring the alarm! Summon Russia to seize the axe! Farewell, and remember that trust in the Czar's good intentions has, for hundreds of years, been ruining Russia. It is not for you to support that faith.'

Herzen's retort, printed with the letter, was that the country really needed not an axe but a broom. In Russia the old order was without any genuine strength, and a painless transition to a better society was quite within the range of possibility. In any event, force was to be appealed to as the last argument. He confessed that since the butchery he had witnessed in Paris in 1848 he had conceived a horror of blood. (Had he forgotten his hosannah to 'chaos and destruction'?) True, the Government was cowardly and the serf owners were holding on to their 'baptized property' with the tenacity of a steppe wolf clutching a bone. Nevertheless, some progress had been made. Besides, there was no unanimity in the ranks of the opposition, and where were the troops of the revolution? It was possible that the people would swing axes without prompting. That would be a great misfortune, he wrote; 'let us do everything in our power to prevent it'. At any rate, he could not issue a call to arms from his safe retreat in London. 'And who, except the Emperor,' he asked, 'had in recent years done anything sensible for the country? Let us render unto Caesar,' he concluded, 'the things that are Caesar's.'

The identity of 'A Russian' has remained undisclosed. It was probably either Nikolay Chernyshevsky, the right hand of the editor of *Sovremennik*, or some member of the group that revolved about that publication, possibly Dobrolubov, one of its contributors. At the beginning of the new reign he had not reached his twentieth birthday, while Chernyshevsky was only half a dozen years older. Both came from ecclesiastical families and had attended divinity school. In fact, the elder of the two was expected to become a luminary of the Church. Like so many of their contemporaries, they lost their faith, not without help from Feuerbach and with no little travail of spirit. Chernyshevsky entered the University of Petersburg, Dobrolubov a normal school. But if they repudiated the beliefs and traditions in which they had been reared, they retained certain traits associated with the religious habit of mind: the dogmatism, the moral fervour, the missionary zeal, the sense of dedication.

A voracious reader, Chernyshevsky early became acquainted, for the most part at second hand, with the ideas of such writers as Louis Blanc, Proudhon, and Blanqui, and his contacts with Petrashevists further stimulated his interest in Socialism. As a student, he was nicknamed Saint-Just. Barely twenty when the revolution of 1848 broke out, he followed its course closely. Its failure did not lead him to turn his back on the West as was the case with Herzen, but the march of events in Europe confirmed him in his impatience with political liberalism. He disliked those gentlemen, he wrote in his diary, who paid lip service to liberty and equality, but would not lift a finger to destroy a social order under which nine-tenths of the people were 'slaves and proletarians'. The important thing, he reflected, was not king or no king, constitution or no constitution, but an economic system which would prevent one class from 'sucking the blood of another'. He fancied himself 'a partisan of socialists, communists, and extreme republicans, decidedly a Montagnard'. His distaste for palliatives and half-measures was to survive his youth.

The self-styled Montagnard confided to his diary the thought that for a caste society the best government was dictatorship or absolute monarchy, provided it championed the cause of the toilers and abdicated the moment it brought about real equality: 'paradise on earth'. Before long, however, he repudiated this fantasy, which was to have such a hold on Herzen. Monarchy, he decided, was the natural ally of the aristocracy, not of the masses. The people would only get their rights by fighting for them. The monarchy must perish, and the sooner the better. The monarch's authority gone, he argued, the plundering of the poor by the rich would become more shameless, and this would hasten the hour of reckoning.

He did not doubt that a revolution was imminent in Russia,

though he was not certain of its success. 'There is not a single forward step in history without convulsions,' he noted in his diary. Moreover, he felt that, in spite of the physical cowardice with which he was cursed, he was capable of 'the boldest, maddest, most desperate acts'. He would lay down his life for 'the triumph of liberty, equality, fraternity', and, he added, 'the abolition of poverty and vice'. He told his fiancée: 'We shall soon have an uprising, and if we do I am sure to be in it. Neither filth nor drunken peasants with cudgels, not even slaughter, will frighten me.' He was then teaching in a school in his native Saratov, but he said things in class that 'smelled of penal servitude'. He was also preparing for a university career. Having failed of his professorial ambitions, in 1856 he joined the staff of *Sovremennik*, to which he had for some time been a contributor.

Chernyshevsky was a man of wide interests and varied, if somewhat shaky, learning, incurably didactic and given to ex-cathedra utterances. Modesty was not his *forte*. In his youth he felt that he was destined to change the course of history, that he was 'one of God's greatest instruments for doing good to man-kind'. Not until he was twenty-five did he give up the idea of building a perpetual motion machine which was to abolish poverty and make him the greatest benefactor of man, in the material sense, as he put it in his diary. Later he dreamed of vast systematic treatises, the crown of which was to be an *Encyclopedia of Knowledge and Life*, and a popular, semi-fictional abridgment of it designed for those who read only novels; all these books were to be written in French, 'the common language of the civilized world'. His ambition was to be 'a good teacher of men during centuries', a second Aristotle. His fate was to be the most casual of authors. His writings are a huge miscellany of occasional pieces, loosely reasoned, clumsily thrown together and swollen with acrimonious polemics. Moreover, like all radical writers, he had to play hide-and-seek with the censor, as one historian phrases it. Consequently he was forced to resort to the 'Æsopian' language of indirection, allusion, camouflage. But then the public had to perfection the art of reading between the lines. It was possible to smuggle in a surprising number of ideas dangerous to the established order. In the matter of thought control, as in other respects, the successor of the imperial government has proved vastly more efficient.

Chernyshevsky had first won the public ear with a Master's dissertation on aesthetics. Submitted at the University of Petersburg the very year Alexander II ascended the throne, it was the earliest manifesto of the new era. His thesis, which delighted the iconoclastic young, was that the arts generally, and literature particularly, could justify their existence only by accurately depicting, explaining, evaluating the actual in terms accessible to all, by being 'a textbook of life'. It was an attempt to bring the Muses down to earth and put them to socially useful work, a protest against the prevalent conception of art as an autonomous transcendent realm. Unable to assault the established order on the political or economic level, the young man attacked the enemy's æsthetics. In the decades that followed, this utilitarian view exerted a strong influence. It assumed a quasi-official status under the Soviet régime, serving to sanction the regimentation of the arts by the State.

Chernyshevsky's venture into aesthetic theory was followed by a series of literary studies, in which he worked the vein of civic criticism opened up by Belinsky. His interest in *belles-lettres* fed on the conviction that in Russia they were the chief vehicle of intellectual energies. Before long, however, as virtual editor of *Sovremennik,* he handed over the department of literary criticism to Dobrolubov, himself concentrating on surveys of the domestic and foreign scene and on essays in philosophy, politics, economics.

His ethics, too, were utilitarian. He told his readers that at the root of human behaviour is self-interest. This doctrine eliminated hypocrisy and had the virtue of being 'scientific'—he fervently believed in the infallibility of what he mistook for science. But to pursue one's self-interest one must be free to do so and one must know wherein it lies. Chernyshevsky attributed the greatest importance to knowledge as a power for good. People were wicked, he believed, because they did not know that it was to their advantage to eschew evil. His shibboleth was *enlightened* egoism. This, he held, precluded narrowly selfish, anti-social acts. It led the individual, naturally and effortlessly, to identify his own happiness with the happiness of all, his private advantage with the public weal. Furthermore, he argued that since man belongs in the order of nature, he is a creature of circumstance, shaped as an ethical being by society. Consequently, in the last account, moral responsibility lies there.

He loathed the principle of *laissez-faire*. This is the clue to his, as to Lassalle's, anti-liberal animus. Unrestricted competition sacrificed the weak to the strong, labour to capital, he insisted. He laid at the door of free enterprise not only unfair distribution of goods, but failure to stimulate production. Both the theory and practice of what he called capitalism had in him an implacable if muddle-headed, enemy. Marx observed that Chernyshevsky 'had no conception of the capitalist mode of production', but he commended the Russian's critique of 'bourgeois' economics in no uncertain terms. Indeed, one of the reasons why he learned Russian was to read Chernyshevsky.

Having arrived independently at the conclusion that economic doctrine mirrored class interests, Chernyshevsky sketched out 'the toilers' theory', as opposed to the economics favouring the rich. By 'toiler' he meant both the industrial worker and the peasant. For him, as for Herzen, the *muzhik* was the man of destiny as far as Russia was concerned, and the welfare of the individual the supreme good. 'The toilers' theory' rested on the proposition that labour alone was entitled to the goods produced and called for economic equality and elimination of socially wasteful enterprises. Chernyshevsky was vague as to the nature of the controls that would achieve these ends. At any rate, he did not advocate a centrally planned, nationalized economy. If to a lesser degree than Herzen's, his thinking was tinged with wariness of Leviathan. What he wanted was a loose aggregate of communities resembling phalansteries: voluntary associations (*tovarishchestva*), each engaging in both industry and agriculture on a co-operative basis, and large enough to use machinery. They were to be autonomous units, democratically administered and free from dictation by a central authority. The state was to have a hand in financing the associations, but would wither away once they had brought about abundance, as they were bound to do.

This was Chernyshevsky's conception of Socialism. It plainly stemmed from Fourier and Louis Blanc. He set it forth, taking care not to call it by its right name, as the system that had the backing of reason and justice alike, and was favoured by objective conditions as well. Unlike Herzen, he did not reject Communism. In fact, he intimated that it embodied a higher ideal than a co-operative society.

He realized that capitalism, i.e., industrialization, was making headway in Russia. But he believed that the process would be less cruel than in the West, and that indeed it might be arrested, the country entering the socialist phase at a leap. What would enable Russia to do this? The *obshchina*, of course. Chernyshevsky believed with Herzen that this institution made a short-cut to the new order a distinct possibility. In the West, Socialism involved the extirpation of inveterate habits of thought and action (Herzen likened the old order there to an elephant's tusk, blackened, diseased, yet deeply rooted in the jaw). Not so in a country where collective land tenure was an immemorial custom. Unlike the expatriate, Chernyshevsky saw in the village commune nothing peculiarly Russian or Slavic. In his judgment it was a relic of mankind's common past, preserved because the Empire had failed to participate in the onward march of the European nations. Yet Russia's backwardness was an opportunity: the country might avoid the mistakes made by the older peoples. History, he wrote, like a grandmother, loves her youngest grandchildren best; she gives them the marrow instead of the bones, in the breaking of which their elders have badly bruised their fingers. Further, Chernyshevsky did not share Herzen's distrust of the revolutionary potential of the European working-classes or his messianic dream of Russia bringing the new order into the world single-handed. In fact, he had it that the transition from the *obshchina* to Socialism was contingent on the triumph of the social revolution in the West. The idea of Socialism-in-one-land was alien to him. He went beyond Herzen in suggesting that, by abandoning the repartition of its acreage and by mechanizing production, the *obshchina* could easily take the tremendous step from communal land tenure to communal cultivation. Chernyshevsky seems to have been the first Russian to recognize the nexus between Socialism and the machine.

In any event, Socialism was a distant goal and Communism belonged to an even more remote future. The issue of the hour was liberation of the serfs. He had hailed the initial step toward the reform with no less enthusiasm than had Herzen, trusting

97

with the latter to the Emperor's good intentions. Within the limits set by censorship, he fought with his pen for terms which he believed at once favourable to the interests of the peasantry and beneficial to the economy of the country as a whole. Realizing that the total expropriation of the landowners was out of the question, he pleaded for providing the freedmen with sufficient allotments on condition that the burden of the redemption payments should be borne by the entire population. That the peasants alone should pay for the land they had worked for themselves under serfdom he recognized as a crying injustice. Needless to say, he spoke for the preservation of the *obshchina*. After some two years, while the reform was still being shaped, he decided that the battle for true emancipation was lost, and he ceased to discuss the subject, except incidentally.

He continued to expound his ideas covertly in the pages of *Sovremennik*, often using an episode in recent European history as his text. He was at pains to drive home to his growing audience certain political lessons. The chief of these was that in the last account the masses had only themselves to rely upon. Their interests could only be secured through an independent organization formed by the people themselves and eschewing entangling alliances. The frank supporters of the existing order were, of course, the enemy, but so were also the counsellors of moderation and gradualism. In fact, one gets the impression that the liberal, rather than the conservative, was the villain of the historical drama, as seen by Chernyshevsky. He pictured liberals as born compromisers, ready to sell out at the first opportunity. At best, they were gullible triflers content with patchwork; at worst, adventurers seeking to fill their pockets while babbling of the rights of man. At heart they feared the masses and could only lead them astray. Confused souls, they failed to grasp that what the vast majority wanted was bread, not suffrage, that 'a poor man's freedom was a form of slavery'. Chernyshevsky was largely responsible for the fact that 'liberal' became a term of opprobrium in advanced circles. In a glossary of foreign words compiled by a budding agitator about 1861 a 'liberal' is defined as a liberty-loving individual, usually a landowner, who loves the liberty of idling and going to balls and theatres.

The masses from whom Chernyshevsky hoped so much remained inert and inaccessible. There were times when he must have felt as did the hero of an autobiographical novel of his who, looking about him, exclaimed: 'A nation of slaves, slaves from top to bottom'. The review that he directed had a relatively large following, but this was a political factor only potentially. The radical camp was still practically non-existent, and he had broken with the liberals, Slavophils as well as Westernists, and all but parted company with the London expatriates. Intellectually he owed a heavy debt to Herzen, but his admiration of this thinker was never entirely uncritical. And now he found much to his distaste in the policy of *The Bell*. Aside from the note of confidence in the Czar, he deplored the failure of the publication to espouse a definite programme of political action. As for the journal's denunciation of administrative abuses, he wondered if this did not help the régime, since the attack was directed against minor defects of the system, not against the very principle of autocracy, which was in substance a dictatorship of the upper classes. In the summer of 1859 Chernyshevsky visited Herzen in London, and it is reported that he left his host under the impression of having dealt with a craven liberal.

What Herzen thought of his visitor can only be guessed at. He had been annoyed by a tendency of some *Sovremennik* authors to dismiss the intellectuals of the previous generation— that to which he himself belonged—as blue-blooded drones and dreamers. Also he was angered by the fact that the review lampooned the mild muck-raking in which the press indulged. This campaign of ridicule, he wrote, played into the hand of reactionaries. He even insinuated that the jesters were officially inspired and were to have their reward. Herzen was moved to print a retraction, but as the months went by his irritation with the *Sovremennik* crew did not abate. There was something about these radicals of plebeian extraction that rubbed him the wrong way. They were morbid men, with mangled souls and 'curdled *amour-propre*'. Many things about them distressed him: they were ruthless, they took malicious pleasure in negation, they had no traditions, nothing of their own, 'not even habits'—this from one who rejoiced volubly that the dead hand of the past did not weigh on his compatriots—they viewed the present with such 'studied despair'. Perhaps he was inclined to misjudge the temper of these youths, whom he knew only by the few who visited him. If the immediate prospect filled them with despondency, they were buoyed up by the belief that the future would yet be theirs. Chernyshevsky, for one, was confident that many battles would be lost, but in the end the war would be won.

IV

The Emancipation Manifesto was signed on 19 February, 1861. Some twenty-three million serfs, owned by roughly a hundred thousand *pomeshchiks* (landowning nobles), were granted their personal liberty. For the loss of his 'baptized property' the master received no compensation, but he retained possession of the acreage of which his bondsmen had had the use. He was, however, required to provide them with allotments, including house-and-garden plot, ploughland, pasturage, and wood-lot. On their part, the freedmen were obligated to accept the allotments and keep them for at least nine years, recompensing the owner with services or money payments. Within two years of the date of the emancipation the size of the allotments and the rental were to be fixed by mutual agreement between master and men, or, failing that, by rather loose official regulations. This relationship, which rendered the freedmen 'temporarily obligated' might last indefinitely. Under certain conditions they might end it by purchasing their allotments, and the Government undertook to finance the transaction by remunerating the landlord and raising annual redemption payments from the peasants.

All agreements were made not with individual peasants but with village communities, which were often the old *obshchinas* under a different name. The householders who made them up were jointly responsible for their obligations to their former owners and the state. Thus where collective land tenure with periodic repartition had been in existence it was preserved and indeed strengthened by investing traditional practices with the force of law. What the radicals imagined to be the seed of Socialism the Emperor's advisers regarded as a pillar of the existing order: a guarantee against the rise of a proletariat and a means of assuring the Treasury (and later the *zemstvos*) of revenue and the landowner of his rent. The peasant class was accorded a form of self-government, but its institutions were under the thumb of the landed gentry and officialdom. Several *ukases* issued between 1859 and 1866 extended the emancipation to the millions of peasants settled on state and crown lands. (In 1857 they numbered close to eight million, and eight hundred and fifty thousand males respectively.)

This was scarcely 'the freedom' for which the peasants had waited. In their minds personal liberty was inseparable from owning either collectively or individually, the land that they and their forebears had worked for themselves and for their masters. And now they were required to pay for their plots, in fact more than what these were worth, since alike the statutory rent rates for 'the temporarily obligated' and the redemption payments were excessive. Moreover, the manor lords were permitted to reduce the acreage that the former bondsmen had previously worked for themselves, and in many other ways the law favoured the interests of the masters. Indeed, the status of the 'temporarily obligated' bore a striking resemblance to serfdom. Surely this was a false 'freedom'. The true one, written in 'a golden charter' signed by the Czar, had been concealed by the officials and priests whom the landlords had bribed. To the peasant a person clothed with authority, be it of Church or State, was an alien and hostile force, to be endured like heat or cold, but the half-mythical Czar was still the image of justice and mercy.

As a result, in many localities the peasants opposed the reform. Their resistance was largely passive. The freedmen refused to continue rendering services or paying money-dues to their former masters. Nor would they sign agreements with the landlords, as required by the new law. The notion had arisen that the true 'freedom' would be proclaimed at the end of the transitional two-year period, and that its benefits would be lost to the households that had acquiesced in the false one. Often the resisters believed that they were doing the Czar's will. According to one of the rumours that circulated in the countryside, he had been wounded by the hirelings of the gentry and had fled abroad, commanding the people to oppose their masters. In some instances violence flared up, but unlawful seizure of land and attacks on landowners and officials were not frequent.

The Government having made no effort to explain the intricacies of the new law in simple language, disorders were sometimes due to a fantastic interpretation of the statutes. The villagers, faced with a stout book couched in complicated legal phraseology, would hire some half-literate reader who would leave confusion worse confounded or discover in the text what his hearers wanted to find there. In some regions where Russian was understood imperfectly or not at all, no translation into the local vernacular was made available.

There was much nervousness in high places immediately after the publication of the historic *ukase*. The authorities anticipated trouble and took measures to cope with it. Special emissaries were sent to the provinces, instructed to deal firmly with peasant insubordination. The frequent use of troops made for some bloodshed; there was much flogging, and there were also arrests and deportations to Siberia. In the provinces of Penza and Tambov the disturbances assumed the proportions of an insurrection, involving hundreds of hamlets. The peasants had come to believe that the Czar had given them with their liberty all the land and the other possessions of the gentry. They occupied a manor house, seized a *pomeshchik*'s livestock, helped themselves to timber from another landowner's forest. There was talk of slaughtering the masters and setting their houses on fire. Leaders, including a veteran of the Napoleonic wars and a religious sectarian, sprang from the ranks and gave the movement the semblance of an organized attempt. Agitators visited neighbouring villages, carrying a red flag mounted on a wheel as a symbol of the true 'freedom'. A police officer who tried to make arrests was put in irons, and the peasants routed a small company of soldiers sent to subdue them. It took a large detachment of troops to restore law and order.

The most sanguinary incident occurred in the village of Bezdna, province of Kazan. Here the ringleader was a schismatic and visionary by the name of Anton Petrov. Having persuaded himself by reading the statutes that this was a false 'freedom', he enjoined his fellow villagers to stop working for the landowner or paying him quitrent and to disobey the officials. Crowds of peasants from all over the district flocked to him. He declared them free, told them that all the land belonged to them, and urged them to elect new *starostas* (village elders) and send the rural constables packing, which they did. When troops arrived on the spot to arrest Petrov, the peasants refused to surrender him, and as the crowd assumed a menacing attitude the soldiers fired. After the fourth volley Petrov voluntarily gave himself up. The police reported that the shooting had resulted in sixty-one killed and 112 wounded. The unofficial estimate of the casualties was much higher.

According to police records, in the course of the year some one thousand two hundred estates were the scene of disorders, and in putting them down, the troops killed 140 and wounded 170 peasants. 'During these three miserable months [after the emancipation],' wrote a radically-minded contemporary, 'the people endured so much sorrow, so many tears were shed, and so much blood flowed, that the joy of liberation was extinguished.'

The spring and summer witnessed a wave of disturbances in the villages. Autumn brought serious disorders in the universities. At the beginning of the reign the restriction on the number of students in the schools of higher learning was removed and their doors thrown open to all comers, irrespective of social status. Thereupon, crowds of young men had flocked to the universities, some of them deserting military colleges and divinity schools to do so. The capitals were veritable magnets. In the University of Moscow the number of students doubled; in that of Petersburg it grew fourfold. During the 'sixties two new universities were added to those already in existence. An increasing number of youths came from plebeian families that were unable to support them at school. They had left home, some of them travelling long distances on foot, in the hope of making their way by tutoring and odd jobs. But there were not enough of these or of government scholarships either. In 1859 only 360 out of the 1,019 students of the University of Petersburg paid the modest tuition fee; in 1863 half of the students of the University of Moscow needed financial aid. Some of the young people lived on the edge of starvation. Typhus and tuberculosis decimated the student body. All this exacerbated the unrest natural to youth.

The students gradually acquired various liberties and developed a strong *esprit de corps*. They got into the habit of publicly voicing their approval and disapproval of lecturers, held meetings on the campus, ran co-operative libraries and eating houses, had publications and even courts of their own.

Clashes with the authorities over the behaviour of some particularly unpopular professor or over a fresh effort to enforce a distasteful disciplinary measure had occurred in previous years, but they were minor affairs compared to the events of the autumn of 1861. During the spring semester the students had been in such a turbulent state that the Emperor had planned to close some of the universities. Instead, in May, he sanctioned a new university statute, which called for a drastic cut in the number of Government scholarships and the abolition of the students' right to hold meetings. In July the newly appointed Minister of Education adopted even more stringent regulations. As soon as the University of Petersburg opened after the vacation, the fat was in the fire. An incendiary leaflet, calling on the students to take 'energetic measures', appeared on the campus. Then a crowd broke into the locked auditorium and held a stormy protest meeting against the new rules. The next day the students, in a body, marched across the city to the home of the rector, who had refused to receive a delegation at the University. When the procession reached Nevsky Prospect, the French coiffeurs ran out of their shops and, excitedly rubbing their hands, shouted: '*Révolution! Révolution!*'

The authorities would not yield ground, and the students boycotted classes. In the end several hundred young men, some of whom had been roughly handled by policemen and soldiers, found themselves behind bars. The tedium of captivity was relieved by the singing of forbidden songs, political discussions, concerts, and private theatricals. One prisoner remembered those days as among the happiest of his life. A shadow was cast over the companionable hours by the news of the death of Dobrolubov. After being detained two months the youths were released. Some of them were deported to the provinces, and the University was closed. It did not reopen until the autumn of 1863. A group of liberal professors started a 'free university', but this was short-lived.

From the northern capital the disturbances spread to other cities. In Moscow a student demonstration in front of the Governor's residence resulted in arrest for many participants and for others in bodily injuries inflicted by gendarmes, plain-clothesmen, and a ruffianly crowd. The mob seems to have been aroused by a rumour that the students were either rebel Poles or young masters protesting against the abolition of serfdom.

The student movement did not achieve its objectives. The

new university statutes introduced in 1863 granted the faculty a large measure of autonomy, but banned all student corporate organizations.

It was suspected in high places that the disorders in the universities were part of a revolutionary conspiracy. As a matter of fact, they were literally an academic affair, with only faint political overtones, and quite spontaneous. It is true, however, that the students were more hospitable to radical ideas than any other group. As far back as 1860 they had made the first attempt to produce underground literature, chiefly reprints of Herzen's writings. They looked for guidance to the London expatriates, to Chernyshevsky, Dobrolubov and writers of that ilk. One campus sheet was entitled *Messenger of Free Opinions*, another was called *The Bell*. The students were already beginning to enjoy the extraordinary prestige that was to be theirs for generations. In 1861 a group of Moscow professors drew up a memorandum in which they noted disapprovingly that the public regarded these youths not as learners but as teachers, and looked upon them with pride and respect. For at least three decades the revolutionary movement was to be a youth movement, manned chiefly by undergraduates. If under Alexander I the army had been a hotbed of active insurgence, under his namesake that rôle was played, with a difference, by the institutions of higher learning. It should be added that the student body was very small. While figures on the total number of students are unavailable, it is known that as late as 1880 there were no more than 8,193 in all the universities of the Empire.

V

The Bell met the Act of 19 February enthusiastically. It hailed the Czar as 'the Emancipator'. Within three months it ran 'An Analysis of the New Serfdom' in several issues. Each instalment ended with the words that were to become the burden of every radical comment on the reform: 'The people have been deceived by the Czar.' The author, Ogarev, urged all 'honest men' to break with the Government. News of peasant resistance to the reform elicited from Herzen an article entitled 'The Giant is Awakening'. The massacre at Bezdna moved him to an angry outburst: 'You hate the landlord,' he wrote, addressing himself to the peasants, 'you hate the official, you fear them and you are right. But you still trust the Czar and the priest. Don't trust them! The Czar is with them and they are with him.'

Herzen's own distrust of the Emperor was not complete. The previous year, as he had watched the swing toward reaction, he had allowed that a constitution might restrain a despotism running wild, as a strait-jacket restrains a maniac. He agreed with Ogarev that before anything more drastic was tried in Russia, the various elements of the opposition should unite to induce the Czar to convoke a General Assembly—the term used was *Zemsky Sobor*, the quasi-parliamentary institution that had functioned in old Muscovy. A representative régime, he argued, might prevent a popular revolution and prove a stepping stone toward greater goals.

Such a united front was advocated by a short-lived group of self-styled 'Russian Constitutionalists', which appeared on the scene soon after the emancipation. In the summer and autumn they put forth three issues of 'a gazette' entitled *The Great Russian*, one of the earliest examples of underground literature produced at home. As a matter of fact, it was run off on the press of the General Staff in the capital. Speaking in the name of a 'Committee' not otherwise designated—its membership has remained a secret to this day—and addressing itself to *obshchestvo* (the educated public), it advocated the end of absolutist rule. Can a Romanov function as a constitutional monarch? The Committee had its doubts, but was willing to give the Czar a chance. Convinced that all would soon share this view, it counselled patience and moderation, and suggested a mammoth petition to the Emperor as the first step, adding airily that the undertaking involved no risk.

A draft of the petition was appended to the final issue of *The Great Russian*. It urged that the peasants' expectation of receiving gratis the land they had worked under serfdom should be met, the former owners to be compensated by the Treasury. 'Deign, Sire,' the petition concluded, 'to convoke representatives of the Russian nation in Moscow or Petersburg, so that they may draw up a constitution for Russia.'

The petition was still-born. Not that the constitutional movement completely lacked support. While the peasant reform was

106

still in the planning stage some liberal members of the gentry had come to believe that a democratic régime under a constitutional monarch was its logical consequence. Now that the serfs were freed and the bungling administration was sowing dragon's teeth, the sentiment in favour of representative government had grown. The nobles were able to address remonstrances to the throne through their corporate organizations. Here and there they were touched by something like the generous spirit that had animated the spokesmen of the French noblesse on the historical night of 4 August, 1789. Early in 1862 Ivan Aksakov, a leading Slavophil and the scion of a venerable house of gentlefolk, suggested in print that the nobility be permitted 'solemnly, in the face of the whole of Russia to effect the great act of abolishing itself as a separate estate'. The gentry of Smolensk passed a resolution to the same effect on the initiative of a prince. The nobles of Tver took a similar step. In their address to the Emperor they urged him to shift the burden of the redemption payments to the shoulders of the entire population and to initiate other reforms, concluding that these could only be successfully carried out by an assembly of representatives freely elected by the whole nation. Moreover, a group of Tver country squires who acted as arbiters between the masters and their former serfs, finding the emancipation statutes unsatisfactory, practically declared that they would not be guided by them. They were forthwith arrested and given prison sentences, which were, however, annulled.

The incident aroused much indignation. One member of the gentry, V. V. Bervi, of whom more later, expressed his disapproval in a communication to the Emperor and the marshal of the nobility of the Tver province. He also apprized the British Ambassador of his protest, requesting that he make it known to the people of the United Kingdom. 'For I do not wish,' he wrote, 'that so honourable a nation should believe that the despotic and oppressive actions of the Russian Government go unprotested by its victims.' The man was committed to an insane asylum for observation and eventually deported to Siberia.

The Slavophils held to the quaint proposition that civil liberties would be safer under a Czar than under a constitutional monarch. A parliamentary régime was opposed by some liberal Westernists on the ground that the people were not ready for it. A correspondent of *The Bell*, writing in the issue of 15 September,

1861, spoke for the leftist fringe when he said that the people were to be appealed to and counted on, not 'the educated classes'. The interests of these were identical with those of the Government. There were among them, however, individuals ready to go over to the masses. United in secret societies—the only weapon of men under the yoke of despotism—they would be a formidable force capable of leading the masses to victory. A limited monarchy guaranteeing civil liberties was preferable to autocracy, but it was not enough. 'We' should neither help nor hinder the Constitutionalists.

In his rejoinder Ogarev granted the need for secret societies, but pleaded for co-operating with all the elements of the opposition to the end of limiting the Czar's authority, for even a constitution favouring the upper classes, he argued, was bound to assume a democratic character. As a matter of fact, with Herzen's approval he drafted a petition to the Emperor, similar to that of *The Great Russian*. Turgenev found the piece somewhat Machiavellian in that it seemed to appeal alike to liberals and disgruntled anti-abolitionists, and refused to sign it. Printed abroad, the petition was circulated in Russia, along with other documents of the same sort, and with no more effect.

It should be noted that 'the Russian Constitutionalists' did not intend to limit themselves to peaceful methods. The last issue of *The Great Russian* contained a broad hint that 'the Committee' might resort to revolutionary tactics: 'Should we see that the liberals fail to act, we shall have no choice but to speak another language and talk of other things.' Before the summer of 1861 was over, an attempt to speak 'another language' was made by a group that gravitated toward Chernyshevsky and the periodical he directed.

Sovremennik had met the Act of 19 February with eloquent silence. Since criticism of the statutes was forbidden, this was the only course open to the review. The issue for March, 1861, commented indirectly on the great event by carrying a translation of Longfellow's *Poems on Slavery* and an article on the Negroes in the United States, asking what would happen 'if the enslaved Samson should rise'. How Chernyshevsky felt about the reform may be inferred from an autobiographic novel that he wrote after emancipation had been in force for half a dozen years and which was not intended for publication at

home. Taking the extremist's the-worse-the-better attitude—
years later Lenin will display it—the hero, who is the author's
alter ego, regrets that the terms of the loathsome measure were
not even more onerous, since that would have hastened the
hour of a popular explosion. 'The landowners haven't the right
to a groat of redemption,' he says; 'whether or not they are
entitled to an inch of Russian land must be decided by the will
of the people.'

At the time when Chernyshevsky wrote these lines he was
very sceptical about the prospects of a popular rising in Russia.
But early in 1861 he was in a different frame of mind. It was a
tense moment, electric with excitement. Together with several
other men, he appears to have become convinced that the
liberation of the serfs had precipitated a situation alive with
revolutionary possibilities. Accordingly they conceived the plan
of circulating inflammatory appeals, each addressed to a sector
of the population that could be relied upon to support revolt.
They were not backed by anything remotely resembling a
conspiratorial organization, and altogether the enterprise was an
example of premature action, against which Chernyshevsky
had been repeatedly warning his readers.

Only one leaflet, entitled *To the Younger Generation*, was
printed. It starts off by excoriating the peasant reform. What is
this freedom, it asks, but a bone you throw to an angry dog to
save your calves? The emancipation is the last act of 'a dying
despotism'. The Romanovs have disappointed the people and
must go. The liberals want a *laissez-faire* economy and a constitutional monarchy. This means a society burdened with a
proletariat, an aristocracy, an oppressive state power. That is
the way of the West. 'Why shouldn't Russia establish a new
order unknown even in America?' All that is necessary is to
develop the principles inherent in the life of the Russian folk,
above all that of collective land tenure. Sale and private ownership of land must cease. A peaceful change, while preferred, is
not the only one envisaged. 'If, in order to achieve our objectives,
to distribute the land among the people, it would be necessary
to slaughter a hundred thousand landowners, that would not
frighten us.' Supporters of the Government and champions of
privilege should no more be spared than you spare weeds when
you clear the ground for a kitchen garden. The hope of Russia

is 'the popular party', that is, the oppressed masses and the educated youth.

The pamphlet concludes: 'Speak oftener to the people and the soldiers, explain to them what we want and how easy it is to get it. . . . Form circles of like-minded persons. . . . Look for leaders capable of and ready for anything. Let the shades of the martyrs of 14 December lead you into battle and, if necessary, to a glorious death for the salvation of your fatherland.'

To the Younger Generation was a product of the joint efforts of two contributors to *Sovremennik*, Shelgunov and Mikhailov. It was run off at the Free Press in London and smuggled into Russia in the early autumn. Shelgunov also composed a leaflet addressed to the soldiers, but it remained in manuscript. So did an appeal to the peasants believed to have been written by Chernyshevsky himself. In simple language he told them that the so-called freedom the Czar had given them would turn them into paupers, that indeed under autocracy there could be no freedom, and that to get it they must gradually and secretly prepare for an armed uprising, making common cause with the soldiery. At the proper moment, he promised, the revolutionaries would come out of hiding and declare themselves to the people.

Betrayed by a comrade turned informer, Mikhailov was arrested in September, took upon himself the blame for the composition of both leaflets, and suffered an early death in penal servitude. The appeal to the peasants was soon to play a fateful part in Chernyshevsky's life.

A revolutionary situation failed to develop in 1861. By the fall of the year the disorders in the villages had subsided, while the disturbances in the Universities had resulted merely in the deportation of scores of youths to the provinces. In Government circles reaction was on the rise. The appearance of incendiary underground sheets naturally enhanced this trend, which, indeed, had set in as soon as the emancipation manifesto was published. It was as though the administration were recoiling before its own audacity in freeing the serfs.

CHAPTER VI

'GET YOUR AXES!'

THE belief in the imminence of a mass revolt persisted, though Chernyshevsky himself was greatly discouraged. The Government's arbitrary actions, it was argued, were driving the country to revolution. The point was made in a leaflet, copies of which were scattered in the chapel of the Winter Palace during the services on Easter Monday, 1862. It addressed itself to the army officers, urging them to side with 'the poor oppressed people' in the coming upheaval.

Then one morning in May people in Moscow and in the capital discovered on their doorsteps or in their mail a piece of underground literature entitled *Young Russia* that made their hair stand on end. 'Russia,' it ran, 'is entering the revolutionary period of its existence.' The interests of the masses are irreconcilable with those of 'the Imperial party': the landowners, the officials, the Czar. Their plundering of the people can only be stopped by 'a bloody, implacable revolution'. 'We are not afraid of it, although we know that a river of blood will flow and that innocent victims will perish; we greet its coming, we are prepared to lay down our lives for the sake of it, the long desired!' If necessary, the Russians would shed three times as much blood as the Jacobins. The Romanovs have failed to understand 'modern needs'. Some of these are: a federal republic; expropriation of the manor lords and assignment of the land to peasant communes; socialized factories run by elected managers; a national guard to replace the standing army; emancipation of women and public education of children; abolition of inheritance and, indeed, of marriage and the family; the closing of monasteries and nunneries, 'the chief sink of corruption'. To achieve these objectives, 'the revolutionary party' must seize power, set up a dictatorship and 'stop at nothing'. Elections to the National Assembly must take place 'under the influence of the Government, which shall see to it that no partisans of the present order, if any of them remain alive, become members of the Assembly'. Though the masses are relied upon, initiative is to be taken by the army and 'our youth'. The latter is urged to head the revolutionary movement.

The manifesto ends on a note of vehement rhetoric: 'Soon, soon the day will come when we will unfurl the great flag of the future, the red flag, and . . . move upon the Winter Palace to exterminate its inhabitants. It may be that the affair will end with the destruction of the Czar and his kin only, but it may also happen that the whole Imperial party will come to his aid. In that case, with full faith in ourselves, in the people's sympathy, in the glorious future of Russia, to whose lot it has fallen to be the first to effect the triumph of Socialism, we will shout with one voice: "Get your axes!", and then we will attack the Imperial party with no more mercy than they show us; we will kill them in the squares . . . kill them in the houses, kill them in the narrow alleys of towns, in the broad avenues of capitals, kill them in the villages and hamlets. . . . Who is not with us is against us, and who is against us is an enemy, and enemies one must destroy by all possible means. . . . And if our cause fails, if we have to pay with our lives for the daring attempt to give man human rights, then we shall go to the scaffold, and putting our heads on the block, or in the noose, repeat the great cry: "Long live the Russian social and democratic republic!" '

There were those who took this bloodthirsty pronouncement to be the work of an *agent provocateur* intended to discredit the revolutionaries. As a matter of fact, *Young Russia* emanated from a circle of Moscow students. They reprinted and distributed forbidden books—so sketchy was control of printing establishments that they could do this with impunity for some time—they set up 'Sunday schools', in which adults were taught their letters, and after the liberation of the serfs some of the youths attempted to carry the message of revolt to the peasants. The group was captained by Pyotr Zaichnevsky, son of a retired colonel in moderate circumstances, and Pericles Argiropulo, scion of an aristocratic Graeco-Russian family. In March, 1861, Zaichnevsky made a speech on the church steps after a Mass for the Polish demonstrators shot by Russian troops in Warsaw. He called on the Poles and Russians present to unite against the common enemy, the Russian government, under 'the red banner of Socialism or the black banner of the proletariat'. During his summer vacation he contributed to the political enlightenment of several town misses and tried to arouse some villagers by telling them that all the land was theirs but that they needed arms to get it. As the letters to Argiropulo in which he detailed these activities were read by the police, in the autumn the friends found themselves in a Moscow detention house.

The discipline in this jail was so delightfully lax that their cell became a kind of political club. Incredible as this may sound, it was there that Zaichnevsky, aided by Pericles and other comrades, composed *Young Russia*. The leaflet was printed on a press which had been removed from the city to a safe place in the country before the start of the arrests that wiped out the circle. These facts remained unknown to the police, and the two youths, together with a score of others, were tried on a charge of having disseminated forbidden literature of a less inflamatory sort. One of the judges noted in his diary that Zaichnevsky gave him the impression of belonging to 'the confessors of *Socialism*, a word the meaning of which is very vague to them, but for which they are ready to be martyred'. Argiropulo soon died in jail, but Zaichnevsky reached advanced middle age, never out of prison for any length of time, a rebel to the end.

He was nineteen when he composed that prophetic proclamation, but it was by no means an example of the transient extremism of adolescence. All his life he clung to the programme of enforcing Socialism by means of the dictatorship of a revolutionary party—an idea which after the lapse of many years was to become powerfully operative. In 1924, a leading Soviet historian described the *Young Russia* leaflet as 'the first Bolshevik document in our history'. This view was proscribed in later years, when emphasis on non-Marxist roots of the official ideology had become taboo. But unquestionably a place must be assigned to Zaichnevsky's thought in the genealogy of Bolshevism. Indeed, it has recently been suggested that a woman follower of his helped to dispose young Lenin to accept the idea that the seizure of political power by a revolutionary party was both feasible and desirable.

A few days after the appearance of *Young Russia* a succession of fires broke out in the capital. They culminated in a huge conflagration which razed a section of the city. Similar conflagrations occurred in the provinces. The fires may or may not have been accidental. According to *The Bell*, the police possibly had a hand in the arson, to the end of 'frightening the Emperor above and weak souls below', a thesis which has recently been advanced again. But popular rumour saw the fires as the work of students and Poles, and the press seized on the theory of revolutionary incendiarism. A cartoon in a public print showed burnt-out buildings and distressed men and women surrounding a statue of Herzen holding an axe in one hand and a torch in the other. The caption read: 'To Iskander [Herzen's pseudonym], a ruined people, 28 May, 1862.' Herzen relates in his memoirs how a breathless young thing came to London all the way from Petersburg to ask him if it was true that he had had a hand in the burning of the capital. Dostoevsky called on Chernyshevsky to beg him to restrain the radicals from such excesses.

The fires were a godsend to the government. The head of the secret police reported to the Emperor that they had aroused universal indignation against students and Poles and 'rebellious heads generally'. It scarcely needs saying that this climate of opinion favoured the reactionary trend that had set in just after the liberation of the serfs. 'If in 1812 Moscow by its fires freed the country from a foreign yoke,' Herzen jested, 'half a century later Petersburg, in the same fashion, freed the country from the yoke of liberalism.'

The embers were hardly extinguished when a number of repressive measures were enacted in rapid succession. Because subversive propaganda had been discovered in one or two 'Sunday Schools', all the three hundred of them throughout the country were closed, and so were the reading rooms and Petersburg's recently opened Chess Club, while *Sovremennik* and another radical review were suspended. Aroused by the appearance of underground literature of domestic origin, the police had for some time been more vigilant. In July a number of arrests took place. Among those seized was Chernyshevsky.

II

Chernyshevsky may have helped to form the Central Revolutionary Committee, in the name of which *Young Russia* spoke and which was never mentioned again. He was not, however, directly involved either in the composition or the dissemination of the leaflet. Indeed, he repudiated it as inopportune. Moreover, he did not share the intransigeance, the revolutionary fervour that it expressed. In fact, early in 1862 he wrote a series of open letters to an unnamed person who was clearly none other than the Emperor. Breaking his silence on the subject of the emancipation, he made bold to point out that the reform had changed the appearance of the relations between master and man, but had left the reality nearly intact. In his carefully 'Æsopean' manner he managed to insinuate the thought that revolution was the only way out of the crisis brought about by the abolition of serfdom. But he also professed a desire to prevent violence. And the very fact that the letters were intended for the Czar's eyes argued that the author expected some good to come from the throne. The censor prevented his message from reaching its destination.

For some time he had been under police surveillance. His name headed the list of political suspects, which the Chief of the Gendarmerie drew up in April, 1862. The immediate pretext for his arrest was supplied, inadvertently, by Herzen. In a letter intercepted by the police the expatriate wrote that he was ready to help Chernyshevsky publish *Sovremennik* in London or Geneva. Chernyshevsky was confined to a cell in the Fortress of Peter and Paul and spent two years there awaiting trial. To beguile the empty hours he wrote, among other things, a tale called *What's to Be Done?* The investigating commission found nothing bearing on the case in the manuscript, and so registered no objection to it. The censor, assuming that it had been approved by an official body of high standing, passed it without further ado. Thus it came about that the work of a prisoner held in solitary confinement on a grave political charge appeared in 1863 in the pages of *Sovremennik*, which had been permitted to resume publication at the beginning of the year. Only then did the authorities outlaw the book. It remained under the ban until 1905.

What's to Be Done? is plainly a problem novel, the effort of a man intent on teaching his public what to think and how to live. The subtitle describes it as 'a tale of new men and women'. The heroine is the 'new woman', as her two successive husbands represent the 'new man'. The story, which attempts to introduce the elements of a thriller, revolves around the trio's triumphant effort to make of marriage a comradeship based on equality, freedom, and reason. The accent is not, however, on the private complexities of what Henry James called 'the great constringent relation between man and woman', but on the pursuit of the public good.

The two male protagonists are intellectuals of plebeian stock, democrats by conviction, scientifically trained, tough-minded, self-assertive individuals. Adhering to the outwardly cynical moral code preached by the author, they reject such concepts as conscience, honour, duty, self-sacrifice, believing that they merely seek their own pleasure, which is man's natural bent. Anything but starry-eyed idealists, they have persuaded themselves that they are moved exclusively by cold and calculating egoism, but, as a matter of fact, their ethical standards are of the highest, they have hearts of gold, and they are selflessly devoted to the cause of the masses.

The 'new men' succeed in winning the heroine over to their way of thinking. She runs a co-operative tailoring shop, presides over a study circle for seamstresses, and studies medicine. In a dream she is granted a glimpse of the future that she and her friends are working to bring about. It beggars description. The deserts having been turned into gardens with the aid of science, the earth blooms like a rose. People live happily in the enjoyment of security, abundance, freedom, and equality of the sexes. Labour is a blessing. The workers inhabit sumptuous palaces built of metal and glass and provided with aluminium furniture, indirect lighting, and steam tables that render waiters unnecessary. Without being told in so many words, the reader knows that it was Socialism that had transformed a wretched land into an Eden.

What is to be done to turn the dream into a reality? The answer could not be specific, and it is not unambiguous. Speaking through his characters as well as in his own person, the author calls on his readers to emerge from their narrow, self-centred existences. Then, he tells them, light and joy will fill their days. Life can be wonderful. But they must love the future, reach forward to it, work for it, carry some of its elements into the present. And this is not difficult, it demands no sacrifices. On the other hand—and this is more in keeping with the general tenor of his writings—Chernyshevsky intimates that the transition to the new order will require the utmost efforts of a band of dedicated souls.

Such a one is Rakhmetov, a minor character. Unlike the other 'new men', he is an aristocrat who has gone over to the people body and soul. He eats only such food as is the habitual fare of the peasantry, works with his hands, is proud of his phenomenal physical strength and completely disregards the proprieties. The money he has inherited he uses to help poor students. He travels abroad, not, Heaven forbid, for pleasure, but to inform himself about social conditions. He has no personal life, choosing celibacy, so as not to be deflected from his purpose. To test himself, presumably in anticipation of possible torture, he spends a night on a piece of felt studded with sharp nails, so that in the morning his back is a mass of bleeding wounds. Most of the time he leads the life of an athlete in training. In training for what? For Armageddon, of course; the battle on the great day of revolution. He is a man possessed, with something in-human and superhuman about him. 'A sombre monster', the heroine calls him, whereupon the author observes: 'A man with an ardent love of goodness cannot but be a sombre monster.' And he extols Rakhmetov as one of the chosen few, without whom life would lose its flavour. In creating this character the novelist drew, however awkwardly, a prophetic image. Here was the literary prototype of the professional revolutionary.

The influence exercised by *What's to Be Done?* was totally out of proportion to its literary merit, which is negligible. Writing years later, a competent observer asserted that since the start of printing in Russia no other book had achieved such an immense vogue. Much of this was due to the fact that it was a trumpet-call to action. Herzen noted that the young people who came from Russia in the 'sixties were all out of this novel with a dash of Bazarov in their make-up (Turgenev's *Fathers and Children* preceded Chernyshevsky's tale by a year). Denounced as lewd and immoral by the pillars of society, *What's to Be Done?* long remained the Bible of the radical youth. For all its glaring defects as a work of fiction it made effective propaganda for woman's emancipation, for Socialism, and, indirectly, for revolution. Be free in your personal relations and dedicate yourself in a disciplined realistic fashion to the cause of the people—this was Chernyshevsky's answer to the query in his title. At the age of eighteen Lenin pored over its pages for weeks and later kept returning to it. He compared its effect on his mind to that which a second ploughing has on a field, and called it one of those books the impact of which lasts a lifetime. To judge by the reminiscences of Georgy Dimitrov, the Bulgarian revolutionary who was the hero of the Reichstag fire trial, the influence of the novel was not confined to Russia.

To come back to the prisoner, on the basis of documents forged, with the knowledge of the investigating commission, by a young protégé of his who had turned informer, Chernyshevsky was convicted of composing the appeal to the peasants mentioned above and of an attempt to have it printed, as well as of 'an evil intent to overthrow the existing order'. The verdict also stated that he was 'a particularly dangerous agitator', since his writings, steeped in 'extreme materialistic and socialist ideas', had a great influence upon the young. He was condemned to fourteen years of hard labour and to Siberian exile for life, but the Emperor cut the term of penal servitude in half. There was widespread indignation at the sentence.

As a convict and as an exile staying in a small town lost in the Siberian wilderness, Chernyshevsky continued to write, but confined himself to fiction and allegorical skits, some of which have, fortunately, been lost. Absent, he was not forgotten. In revolutionary circles the question of freeing him was repeatedly mooted. One futile attempt was actually carried out, thereby worsening his position. When, in 1883, he was allowed to return to civilization, he was a broken man. Only half a dozen years were left him.

His martyrdom invested his name with a glory that time was slow in dimming. Early death had had the same effect on the reputation of his comrade, Dobrolubov. The Bolsheviks firmly clasped Chernyshevsky to their bosom. He had absolute revolutionary sense, Lenin declared privately, the way a singer has absolute pitch. He prized him particularly as an adversary of liberalism and as a thinker who demonstrated that every reasonable person must be a revolutionary. Lenin extolled him in print as 'a seer of genius', an author whose works 'breathe the spirit of the class struggle', as 'the great Hegelian and materialist' who prepared the best minds in Russia for the acceptance of Marxism. Lesser lights have been at pains to amplify and document these remarks. Chernyshevsky's leading Soviet biographer proclaimed him 'the founder of Russian Communism'. Some of his pages are required reading in the schools. In his native Saratov his statue has replaced the monument to the Czar who sent him to Siberia.

In order to establish him as an Ancestor, Soviet scholarship has had to distort the facts somewhat, a procedure in which it has had no little practice. True, he made his readers feel that they lived in an impermanent society which was in a state of deep crisis and which could and should be forcibly replaced by one resting on different foundations. Abominating the liberal temper, he came perilously close to extolling the revolutionary who is not squeamish about the means leading to his end, and is ready to soil his hands with mud or blood. But he was not free from the fear that revolution might be too costly a method of social change. Nor did he favour a centrally directed economy. He had a streak of the doctrinaire fanaticism that Herzen abhorred. Believing that material well-being is the sovereign good, he did not flinch from declaring that 'our Siberia' under the knout, where nevertheless people were well off, was 'much superior to England' with its Magna Carta, where 'the majority of people suffer need'. Yet he was certainly a determined enemy of the knout. As certainly he opposed compulsion where social and economic goals were concerned. 'Without a man's free consent,' he wrote, 'nothing truly useful can be done for him', and he has made a character in his novel say that 'there is no happiness without freedom.' It is impossible to imagine him at ease in the society that has emerged from the revolution for which he laboured.

III

The gap made by Dobrolubov's death and Chernyshevsky's removal from the scene was partly filled by the meteoric career of another publicist who was destined to leave his mark on the thinking of young Russia: Dmitry Pisarev. Possessed of the verve, the truculence, the merciless dogmatism of a perennial adolescent, he had leapt into the limelight with an essay in which, following in Herzen's footsteps, he attacked scholasticism. He was then twenty-one (he was born in 1840). Chernyshevsky invited the youth to join the staff of *Sovremennik*, but Pisarev preferred to stay with another Petersburg monthly, *Russkoe slovo* (The Russian Word), which soon became an influential organ of radical opinion.

The following year he was arrested. In a fit of indignation he had tossed off a vitriolic retort to a pamphlet against Herzen inspired by the police. 'The Romanov dynasty and the Petersburg bureaucracy,' he wrote, 'are ripe for the grave; all that is necessary is to give them the last push and cover their stinking corpses with mud.' Before the manuscript could be run off on an underground press it got into the hands of the authorities, and the author received a four-year prison term. It was from his cell in the Fortress of Peter and Paul that he contributed to *Russkoe Slovo* the brash, spirited commentaries and lay homilies that endeared him to a large segment of the intelligentzia.

He was only briefly and half-heartedly committed to revolution. The outburst that had landed him in prison was but a momentary frenzy, as he phrased it. He came to realize that it would be long before a frontal attack could be made on the existing order and that the task at hand was to act upon people's minds. To this task he devoted himself heart and soul.

'Here is the ultimatum of our camp: what can be smashed should be smashed; what will stand the blow is good; what will fly into smithereens is rubbish; at any rate, hit out right and left—there will and can be no harm from it.' Thus said Pisarev in the early essay mentioned above. Such advice couched in such forthright language thrilled the radical youth. He went on employing his pen to discredit authority, tradition, all the pieties and taboos that restrain the individual. This did not keep him from upholding an extreme determinism which robbed the same individual of his freedom. The stand was forced upon him by his adherence to a materialism cruder than Herzen's or Chernyshevsky's. It was Pisarev who greatly contributed to the vogue, in *avant-garde* circles, of Büchner's *Matter and Force* and of Buckle's *History of Civilization*, with its assumption that human affairs, no less than the processes of nature, are subjects to scientific laws.

Indeed, while himself incapable of scientific detachment, he ardently championed science as a cure-all, the power that could give the people both bread and freedom. Technological knowledge, he repeated, was Russia's greatest need. The country could not afford to divert its very limited intellectual cadres to any pursuits that did not increase the productivity of labour. As a result, this young man whose eyes would fill over a page of *Crime and Punishment* called for the abolition of arts and letters as a luxury that a poverty-stricken nation could not afford. Some civic-minded artists and poets—Pushkin was not among them—he did exempt from proscription. He conceded reluctantly that a novel could serve as a medium of instruction or indoctrination and thus make itself useful to the common man, but warned that literature 'begins to demoralize society the moment it ceases to move it forward'. His advice to the general run of *literati* was to popularize the findings of the scientists. At this task he tried his hand himself, producing an exposition of Comte's philosophy and Darwin's theory of evolution. He ardently embraced the doctrine of the survival of the fittest in its crudest interpretation and, incidentally, ranged himself on the side of spontaneous generation, against Pasteur.

While the other leaders of radical opinion stressed man's duties toward society, Pisarev, when he began writing, accentuated self-cultivation and self-fulfilment. He even appeared to speak for a socially aloof and hedonistic individualism. Without, however, surrendering his belief that selfishness was man's prime mover, he came to hold that the enlightened egoist just naturally had at heart the good of all. In fact, Pisarev decided that the 'problem of the hungry and the naked' was the central concern of the age, the one toward which everyone's thought and action should be directed.

How was this problem to be solved? Pisarev's answer differed substantially from that offered by other radical thinkers. Exposed to the ideas of Saint-Simon, Fourier, and Proudhon, as well as those of Herzen and Chernyshevsky, he had naturally not remained immune to Socialism. He could speak deprecatingly of competitive economy and remark that some day 'the tyrannical domination of capital would fall', as had theocracy and feudalism. On one occasion he observed that this consummation could only be effected by the workers themselves. Yet there is little in his writings to suggest that he wanted a popular revolution, either political or social. Nor did he have faith in the collectivist tradition or any other native virtue of the peasantry. Salvation, he was convinced, lay in going to school to the West, in assimilating the more tangible fruits of European civilization. Repeatedly he argued that the country's greatest need was a large contingent of private *entrepreneurs* equipped with technological and managerial skills, but also well-meaning, cultivated, enlightened people. An industrial economy run by these paragons under the ægis of science in the interests of labour—not that these clashed with the interests of capital—such was Pisarev's solution of the problem of the hungry and the naked. To the state he assigned purely police functions.

The plea for a quasi-technocracy scarcely impressed his readers. They were more receptive to his emphasis on the rôle of the intellectual *élite*. The majority, poor because it was ignorant or ignorant because it was poor, was helpless, he argued, without the leadership of the educated minority. This pet idea of Pisarev's found a climate in which it could slowly but surely thrive. Did a member of the *élite* owe his first duty to himself or to society? Pisarev was uncertain. It was one of those loose ends that give his doctrine an untidy look.

This rather ramshackle system of ideas Pisarev called realism, or critical realism. He was also content to let it go by the name of 'nihilism'. The term had occasionally been used before both in Russia and abroad, but it was popularized by *Fathers and Children*. In a lengthy review of Turgenev's novel he had hailed Bazarov, 'the nihilist', as a model of the man who was Russia's hope: the hard-working, tough-minded empiricist and pragmatist, to whom Nature was not a temple but a workshop. The designation 'nihilism' was obviously a misnomer. The views of Pisarev and his followers were anything but a philosophy of a moral wasteland. If the accent was on ruthless criticism, the negations were nearly balanced by affirmations, and both were professed with a passion verging on fanaticism.

Some word was needed to label a type of young person set apart by peculiar mannerisms and opinions, that had emerged in the late fifties, and Turgenev had supplied the need. To the conservatives frightened by the threatening effects of the new freedom, nihilism connoted atheism, free love, sedition, the outraging of every decency and accepted belief by men and, as often, by the unwomanly 'emancipated' woman. A report by the head of the Third Division for the year 1869 contains this thumbnail sketch of her: 'She has cropped hair, wears blue glasses, is slovenly in her dress, rejects the use of comb and soap, and lives in civil matrimony with an equally repellent individual of the male sex or with several such.' The official had nothing against women's striving for education and economic independence. It was not only for ideological reasons that they gave their fathers and husbands what James Barrie called 'the twelve-pound look'. As the decay of the gentry proceeded apace, the need for gainful employment was beginning to weaken the dogma that woman's place was in the home. But he lamented the fact that emancipation had taken on a character that made it a menace to 'everything that should be sacred to the sex: family, religion, womanliness'.

The stereotype bore some resemblance to the true picture. The nihilists did make a point of defying the conventions in appearance, manners, and address. Scorning decorum as hypocrisy, they affected forthrightness to the point of rudeness. An irreverent lot, impatient of all restraints, questioning all authority, they flattered themselves that they were hard-headed, cynical, materialistic, where their elders were sentimental, soulful, idealistic. They wanted to believe that they lived by the precepts of enlightened egoism, and they sneered at delicate feelings and fine words, looked down upon the arts, dismissed speculative thought as cobweb-spinning, and worshipped crude empiricism, under the name of science.

Nihilism was an aspect of the revolt of a generation with no deep roots in any cultural tradition against the values of a quasi-feudal past. It was a manifestation of what, in the words of Ecclesiastes, was a time to break down. Indirectly it reflected the naturalistic trend that asserted itself in mid-century Europe, as well as the change in the social structure of the intelligentzia. Ever since the beginning of the new reign the educated class had been rapidly expanding, due to the growth of the school system, the rise of the legal profession, the extension of the public health service. At the same time the group, while remaining alienated from the masses, was losing its upper-class character. Its ranks were being increasingly invaded by *raznochintzy*, i.e., newcomers from the middle and lower strata of society: scions of *déclassé* gentry, sons of professional men, of petty officials, manufacturers, tradespeople, and especially of the clergy, which had a low social status.

To a certain extent nihilism was a fad. This applies less to its plebeian than its genteel variety. The parlour nihilist flourished after the manner of the parlour pink. Many a nihilist, having sown his intellectual wild oats in his youth, settled down to a humdrum career or made the most of the new opportunities for getting rich that the growing industrialism offered. Enlightened egoism was likely to turn into egoism *tout court*, and the emphasis on individual freedom and on realistic thinking could be useful to those bent on elbowing their way to a place in the sun. On the other hand, nihilism was obviously a possible road to political insurgency. The attitude of criticism and revolt could shift from manners and morals to the socio-political level. Pisarev died in 1868, two years after he had regained freedom and before it became clear in which direction he would have moved. But several other contributors to *Russkoe Slovo*, who had shared his views, eventually found themselves in the revolutionary camp. The police report cited above stated: 'From the nasty prankishness of a few young people of both sexes who saw in the rejection of accepted conventions a means of proving their independence, nihilism has become a positive doctrine pursuing definite social and political aims. . . . It acts in the name of an idea, and that lends its followers the character of sectarians, i.e. eagerness to spread their teaching and readiness to suffer for it. . . .'

The ideological trend of which Pisarev had been the chief exponent did not long survive him. Nevertheless, the term lingered on, the conservative public finding it a convenient synonym for extreme and distasteful notions. Years after the word 'nihilist' had fallen into desuetude on its native heath, it continued to have currency in the West as a designation for the dangerous intellectual, the soberly dressed, serious-faced, long-haired man or short-haired woman, peering at a wicked world through dark spectacles, a book in one hand, a bomb in the other.

IV

Alone the half a dozen years that followed the suppression of the 'conspiracy of ideas' associated with Petrashevsky's name form a virtual blank in the history of Russian radicalism. The lull ended when Alexander II ascended the throne. As has been seen, the beginnings, however faint, of action 'in the name of an idea', mentioned by the head of the Third Division, go back to the early years of the new reign. It was chiefly a matter of disseminating underground literature, at first produced abroad, later run off on clandestine presses at home. These activities were carried on by a few small groups, ephemeral, loose, having no connexion with each other. Not seldom they were offshoots of the ubiquitous 'circles for self-education', the members of which—mostly high-school and university students—sought to improve their minds with respect to matters that the schools deliberately ignored. The situation finds its parallel in the French 'societies of thought' turning from discussions of the works of the *philosophes* to political propaganda.

The idea of gathering the scattered forces into a secret society on a national scale was not slow to sprout. It seems to have been considered by the London expatriates as early as 1857. An attempt to realize the idea was launched shortly after the liberation of the serfs. It was not a very serious or sustained effort, and Land and Liberty, as the organization that resulted from it was called, had only a shadowy existence. In theory it was a network of cells, each numbering five members and controlled from regional centres. In practice it was a congeries of several autonomous groups of young intellectuals located in the two capitals and in some of the provincial cities.

In the autumn of 1862 the society established contact with a group that called itself the Committee of Russian Officers in Poland. A list of sixty-four names, including that of Lenin's father-in-law, apparently members of this organization, has recently come to light. The Committee's propaganda aimed at persuading the troops stationed in the North-Western provinces not to use their arms against the Poles and to prepare to fight shoulder to shoulder with them for the freedom of the Russian and the Polish people. The previous spring the authorities uncovered the subversive activities of a circle of Russian officers in Warsaw, and three of the men were shot.

Land and Liberty survived the severe blow dealt it by the arrest in July 1862 of its chief organizer and of Chernyshevsky, who seems to have lent a hand in directing its activities. That winter a central committee was functioning in the capital. It is alleged that the society used the Petersburg Chess Club as a rendezvous. Perhaps because the society was trying for a united front, it was chary of a programme couched in anything but general terms. Ideologically the leadership followed Chernyshevsky in repudiating reformism. The first of the two issues of a sheet called *Freedom*, which were brought out early in 1863, contains an appeal to the educated classes. But while the *Great Russian* group had urged them to become politically active as an independent and decisive force; Land and Liberty sought to persuade the intellectuals to go over to the side of the masses and assume the leadership of a popular movement aiming at the expropriation of the landowners and the overthrow of the autocracy.

From the beginning, the enterprise had had Ogarev's sponsorship. In fact, the organization took its name from an article of his which answered the query: 'What do the people need?' with the words: 'Land and liberty'. But Herzen held aloof. Extremists continued to look askance at him. In fact, *Young Russia* dismissed *The Bell* as a liberal organ and 'a puzzle to truly revolutionary people'. Yet his prestige was still great. A leaflet that was circulated in Odessa in August 1862 ended thus: 'Long live the Republic! Long live the great dictator of Russia, A. Iskander!' But A. Iskander (Herzen's pseudonym, the reader will remember) was not cut out for the part of a dictator or revolutionary leader. He was an ideologue, not a man of action, a publicist, not a conspirator. Secret societies were not after his heart. Furthermore, he had not given up the notion that Alexander II was capable of heading a peacable social revolution. In denouncing the *Young Russia* manifesto as a rhetorical mixture of Babeuf and Schiller, he wrote, addressing the Russian youth: 'Should the fateful day [of revolution] arrive, stand firm and lay down your lives, but do not hail it as a desired day. If the sun does not rise amid blood-stained clouds, so much the better, and whether it wears a crown or a liberty cap—it's all the same.' Another article of his, written about this time, concluded with the reflection that Russia's 'predestined saviour' might be 'an emperor who, renouncing the system inaugurated by Peter the Great, combined in his person a czar and a Stenka Razin (leader of the seventeenth-century *jacquerie*)'.

In addition to Ogarev, *Land and Liberty* had in London another and far more ardent promoter in the person of Bakunin. He had joined the two expatriates shortly before 1862 was ushered in, and from then on the outside world came to think of Herzen, Ogarev, and Bakunin as a triumvirate, with the first of them as the master mind. Bakunin had escaped from Siberia to Japan, and on his way to Europe had stopped off in the United States long enough to declare his intention of becoming an American citizen and to have dinner with Longfellow, who described the Russian in his diary as 'a giant of a man with a most ardent, seething temperament'. The previous twelve years he had spent in the prisons of two countries besides his own and in Siberian exile. He had plotted with the Poles, had had a hand, it will be recalled, in the Paris revolution of 1848, made an abortive attempt to organize a secret revolutionary International, campaigned for a Czech revolt, participated in the Dresden uprising of 1849, been twice sentenced to death, and in 1851 extradited to the Russian authorities.

It was now his intention, he declared, to devote all his energies to fighting for the freedom of Russians and all Slavs. He had not yet formulated his anarchist doctrine, and he found himself echoing some of Herzen's views. But temperamentally the two men were so incompatible that they could not be comrades-in-arms, though they remained friends. Bakunin's instincts were all against moderation, and conspiratorial intrigue was his element. Small wonder then that he wholeheartedly embraced the cause of Land and Liberty and plunged into plotting with immense zest. He had plans for agitating in the army, among the peasantry and among the religious dissenters, and he toyed with the idea of a vast revolutionary organization ringing Russia with a network of its agents placed at strategic points on the border. Siberia was to be served by a branch located on the West coast of the United States.

Bakunin had long been convinced that a revolution was imminent at home. He was given to mistaking the second month of pregnancy for the ninth, as Herzen put it. It was then a common enough error. European radical circles were not free from it, and Bakunin's belief that the end of the old world was at hand had adherents in Russia. The explosion was expected to occur on the second anniversary of the emancipation. The peasants, it was said, looked for a new and better 'freedom' at that time, and the disappointment that was sure to follow was as sure to provoke a rising.

Meanwhile all through the summer and autumn of 1862 preparations for an armed insurrection were going on in the Polish provinces. The separatist movement there had revived with Alexander's accession, and now the situation was rapidly approaching a crisis. With Russian radicals and liberals sympathy for Poland's independence was traditional. It went back as far as the Decembrists. The Polish conspirators were naturally at pains to secure alliances with friends in the enemy camp. *The Bell* for 1 October, 1862, carried a manifesto by the People's Central Committee of Warsaw stating that the objectives of the movement were democratic. The editors declared that the Polish cause had their enthusiastic support. Shortly afterwards the Warsaw Committee concluded a pact with Land and Liberty, whereby the latter obligated itself to assist the insurrection by propaganda and diversionary tactics. The Poles seem to have believed that they had acquired a powerful ally. Herzen did what he could to dispel that delusion. He urged the conspirators to postpone action, at least until the spring of 1863, when, as has been said, the Russian villages were expected to be in a. turmoil. With a sinking heart he watched the gathering of the storm, expecting nothing but calamity.

The course of events justified his worst fears. To force the issue, the Russian authorities suddenly declared conscription in the Polish cities, and on 22 January, 1863, the revolt broke out. *The Bell* had urged the Russian officers not to spill Polish blood, and its issue dated 22 October, 1862, contained an address from the previously mentioned Committee of Russian Officers to the Governor of Poland, warning him that in case of an insurrection the troops would go over to the Polish side and 'no power on earth could stop them'. Actually only one man, the Sub-Lieutenant who headed the Committee, took this step (and was killed in action against his own people). The troops both in and out of Poland remained loyal to the Czar, and the Poles were left alone to fight a losing battle.

In the midst of these events Herzen, finally yielding to the pressure of Ogarev and Bakunin, consented to give aid and comfort openly to Land and Liberty. In January, an emissary of the Society had arrived in London to secure the support of *The Bell*. According to Herzen's caustic account, the youthful envoy treated the expatriates—the entire triumvirate was present—'as the commissars of the Convention of 1793 treated generals of distant armies'. Land and Liberty, the emissary declared, counted hundreds of members in the capital and three thousand in the provinces. Even the gullible Bakunin doubted these figures. The whole affair was distasteful to Herzen. Yet *The Bell* for 1 March ran an editorial which solemnly announced the formation of *Land and Liberty* as a result of the fusion of circles in the capital and the provinces with committees of officers, and extended a fervent greeting to it. Herzen was named the Society's chief representative abroad, and *The Bell* became in effect its organ.

This did not improve its fortunes. Except for printing an appeal to the troops not to bear arms against the rebels, it proved incapable of action. The emissary who had come to London failed to return home, and another member of the Central Committee also escaped abroad. Herzen could do nothing save inveigh against the Petersburg Government, while Bakunin kept evolving fantastic schemes, among them one for a rebellion in Finland. He actually took part in the quixotic expedition of a foreign legion which set out from Paris to join the Polish insurgents but disbanded before reaching its destination.

Seeing that no help was forthcoming from Land and Liberty, the Warsaw Committee decided to start on its own an uprising in the Volga region by way of creating a diversion in the enemy's rear. Kazan having been chosen as headquarters, in March several Polish patriots who served in the army and were stationed in the city persuaded a local student group affiliated with Land and Liberty to launch the insurrection by seizing the city. The conspirators had at their disposal four hundred roubles, fourteen revolvers without cartridges, and a number of copies of a fake imperial manifesto, composed by a Moscow student and printed abroad, which granted the peasants real 'freedom'. As one of the students turned informer, the plot was nipped in the bud, five Poles losing their lives and the Russians receiving prison terms.

As the months wore on, the Polish insurrection turned into guerrilla warfare which rapidly lost ground. Spring came and went, and nothing happened in Russia. Instead of being ablaze with revolt, the country was swept by a tide of reaction. The diplomatic intervention of foreign powers on behalf of the Poles caused a burst of chauvinism, and those who had sponsored the Polish cause were thoroughly compromised. Herzen had warned the Polish spokesmen: 'Our sympathy will do you no good at all, but will ruin us.' This is exactly what happened. Overnight the London expatriates had lost most of their following. They were denounced as traitors to their country. Towards the end of 1863 the circulation of *The Bell* dropped from two thousand five hundred copies to five hundred. Land and Liberty had ceased to exist. Herzen estimated the situation correctly when he wrote that before the insurrection a revolutionary organization was in the making, but that the impact of the explosion had destroyed it.

CHAPTER VII

'MEN OF THE FUTURE'

SECURE from the revolutionary menace, the Government might now have let well enough alone. But Alexander went on enacting reforms. These included the abolition of corporal punishment that Herzen had urged, and a year later, in 1864, the introduction of self-government for rural districts in the form of so-called *zemstvo* boards. These measures were effected in an atmosphere of reaction which made it easy for the administration to emasculate them.

Early in 1865 the nobles of the Moscow province presented an address to the Czar in which they voiced their satisfaction with the newly created *zemstvos* and also urged him to convoke a National Assembly 'for the discussion of the needs of the entire state'. Alexander's reply was that the right to initiate reforms was part of his God-given autocratic power, and that no one was privileged to intercede before him for the whole nation. This was the last stirring of the constitutionalism of the 'sixties.

The revolutionary movement appeared to have been stillborn. Clandestine printing ceased. *Sovremennik* gave much space to labour and Socialism in Western Europe, but was timid in dealing with matters nearer home and spent much energy in polemics against *Russkoe Slovo*. It lacked the enthusiastic following it had had in Chernyshevsky's day.

After the failure of the Polish rebellion Bakunin settled in Italy and kept aloof from Russian affairs. As for Herzen, in the columns of *The Bell* he continued to berate the administration and to hold up to scorn the chauvinism, 'half rapacious, half rhetorical', that prevailed at home. 'The public is worse than the Government,' he wrote to his daughter, 'and the journalists are worse than the public.' And he urged the convocation of a *Zemsky Sobor*. In and out of his review he also continued to preach what he called 'Russian Socialism', stemming from the *muzhik*'s way of life and reaching out for that 'economic justice' which is a universal goal sanctioned by science. And he harped on the antithesis of Europe, nearing the end of its vital cycle, and Russia, a country bypassed by history and knowing no cherished traditions save that of collectivism, possessing no accumulated wealth, belonging wholly to the future, resembling a woman heavy with child, a child that might prove, he hinted, the saviour of mankind. These were variations on old themes, but Herzen also sounded new notes. Perhaps the *obshchina* was not really the germ of the new society, he intimated, but rather a factor making the Russian soil ready to receive the Socialist seed, an article imported from the West. Might not an alliance between the *muzhik* and the European proletarian be the hope of the future? Possibly Russia, too, would succumb to 'the bourgeois pox'. On the other hand, *meshchanstvo* was conceivably just a passing phase in the development of Western societies. Herzen could not bear the thought that all the rivers of history must lose themselves in the swamp of a vulgar, property-worshipping middle-class civilization.

But *The Bell* had now neither readers nor influence. The editor antagonized the many who had drifted to the right, as well as the few who had moved further to the left, and he was too skittish to satisfy those who stood still. He found himself in no-man's-land. In 1865 he transferred the offices of the journal and of the Free Press to Geneva, 'the crossroads of Europe'. He hoped to find there a more congenial atmosphere than London could offer and, above all, closer contacts with home.

This step failed to improve matters. The city of Calvin harboured a number of recent arrivals from Russia, mostly young people of plebeian background. They had crossed the border chiefly in 1862–64 to avoid the police net or to escape from it. For some time Herzen had looked with favour at these radicals. They were half-baked, but there was a certain toughness about them. He had perceived that the intellectuals of gentle birth to whom he had once pinned his hopes were a weak reed to lean upon: bold in the realm of thought, they wavered and compromised when it came to action. His personal contacts with the new émigrés were, however, galling. Twice had 'the Geneva puppies', as he called them, approached him with a plan to make *The Bell* the official organ of a general-staff-in-exile, which would direct the revolutionary movement at home. The negotiations had come to nothing. Herzen gained the impression that these young people were merely out to get their hands on the review and also on the Bakhmetev fund for revolutionary propaganda. This had been entrusted to him in 1858 by a wealthy Russian landowner before he went off to the Marquesas to found a Communist settlement in that island paradise. 'The puppies', for their part, looked down upon their celebrated fellow expatriate as a muddle-headed liberal and a man whose professed convictions were at variance with his lavish way of living.

One of them said, publicly, as much and more in a scurrilous pamphlet which came out in 1867. His ire had been roused by a remark made by the editor of *The Bell* to the effect that his message complemented Chernyshevsky's. No, the pamphleteer indignantly asserted, the two men had nothing in common: Chernyshevsky had formed 'a whole phalanx of socialists', his ideas had struck deep roots; as for Herzen, he was a poet, an artist, a raconteur, a novelist, anything you please, but not a political thinker, and the notion that he was a leader of the youth was ludicrous. He understood nothing of what was going on around him. And what had this millionaire done for the cause? When young militants, covered with 'holy wounds', had arrived in Switzerland fleeing from hard labour or the gallows, he had refused to work with them and had treated them with 'haughty contempt'. The younger generation had perceived that he was but a self-adoring phraseur and had turned away from him with disgust. 'You, Herzen,' the author of the pamphlet concluded graciously, 'are a dead man.'

The attack cut Herzen to the quick. These young people, he fumed, were shallow, arrogant, and ignorant; they were moved by low passions. In a letter to Bakunin of 30 May, 1867, he stigmatized his reviler and his kind as 'swindlers whose scoundrelism justified the Government's measures against them'. Bakunin took up the cudgels on behalf of these youths. Their defects, he argued with a perceptiveness of which he was rarely capable, were due to the fact that the old morality was gone, while the new had not taken shape. 'But this should not conceal from us the serious, nay, great qualities of our younger generation: it has a real passion for equality, work, justice, freedom, reason. Because of this passion, tens of them have already laid down their lives, while hundreds have gone to Siberia.' And he warned Herzen against senile hatred of youth.

By this time the two men had moved far apart in their thinking. Bakunin had now given up the idea that anything but oppression and enslavement could be expected from czarist autocracy, or indeed from any form of statehood. It was his conviction that the salvation of the Russian masses, as of the people everywhere, lay in an upheaval which would make a bonfire of both the political and the social order. To foment a total world revolution, which, he held, the combined efforts of the peasantry and the city workers were bound to bring about in the near future, he had for some time been busy organizing a secret International Brotherhood.

Herzen scarcely needed Bakunin's admonition against one of the infirmities of old age. Wholesale condemnation of the radical youth was far from his mind. Quite the contrary. When, at the end of 1868, *The Bell* was silenced for good, he wrote in an open letter to Ogarev, which was his parting word, that, in the main, their most precious convictions were secure. 'There are young people, so deeply, so irrevocably devoted to Socialism, so rich in logical audacity, so strong by virtue of their scientific realism and their rejection of all clerical and governmental fetishism that there is no more fear: the idea will not perish. The younger generation . . . is of age, and knows it.'

Here was an example of wishful thinking. One looks in vain for intimations of maturity in the ideas and behaviour of the radical fringe of the intelligentzia of the late 'sixties. There was something adolescent about its attempts at political action and at living the good life. Here and there co-operatives sprang up, often dress-making establishments, like the one run by the heroine of *What's to Be Done?* They did not last. The professional seamstresses, who worked while the others talked, were apt to take the initiative in breaking up the shop. Sometimes they would carry off the sewing machines for which the idealistic amateurs had paid. Had they not been taught, they argued, that the tools belonged to those who used them?

Occasionally young people attempted to set up communal households. Earnings were shared and even such personal belongings as boots and coats. This was by way of honouring Chernyshevsky's precept of importing the socialist future into the present. These 'communes' failed invariably and promptly, even though some of them were a useful form of mutual assistance. But they bequeathed to the revolutionary circles the habit of comradely sharing of possessions.

As the 'communes' included both men and women, rumour pictured them as dens of promiscuity. Such was not the case. True, among 'nihilists' there was a tendency to unions without the benefit of clergy. What particularly scandalized the public was the fact that to secure her independence from parental tutelage a girl would contract a fictitious marriage. One apologist for the practice pointed to the legal disabilities of the unmarried woman. On the other hand, the nominal unions involved no hazards since, as he put it, 'the relations of men and women in these circles are based on mutual confidence and respect, which exclude the very possibility that men will ever think of abusing their rights'.

II

A few clandestine 'circles' managed to carry on. An active one existed in Moscow and was in touch with a group in the northern capital. The members included several government clerks and school teachers, men of mature years, but for the most part they were university students. One member was a former house serf, another a scion of an impoverished princely family. A leading rôle was played by a merchant's son, Nikolay Ishutin, a hunchbacked youth, nicknamed 'the General'. For him, as for his comrades, Chernyshevsky was the object of a veneration that verged on a cult. Ishutin is reported to have named him, together with Jesus and St. Paul, as 'one of the world's three great men'. A wild scheme hatched by the circle was a plan to free him from captivity and smuggle him out of the country, so that he could edit a revolutionary review abroad. Herzen was looked down upon not only as a liberal but as one whose way of life belied his professed convictions, and Pisarev was dismissed as 'an empty phraseur'. These youths lacked the nihilists' respect for science, believing that a man's duty was total devotion to the people's cause. 'The masses are uneducated,' one of them observed, 'therefore we have no right to an education. You don't need much learning to explain to the people that they are being cheated and robbed.' With this anti-intellectualist bias went an ascetic streak.

At first the circle engaged in activities that kept more or less within the law. It ran a co-operative bindery and a dressmaking establishment. Further, it had plans for other producers' co-operatives, as well as a workmen's mutual loan association and— an Owenite colony on the Amur in Siberia. It also set up a school for boys in the slums of Moscow. Here a slanted variety of elementary instruction was offered. Thus, the teacher, after pointing out that the eagle was a bird of prey, would observe that a government flaunting the eagle on its coat of arms (Russia was, of course, such a one) only proved thereby that it was as rapacious and bloodthirsty as that bird. The arithmetic teacher, having led his pupils to admit that one was less than seventy-two million, indeed, an insignificant quantity in comparison, would say: 'Well, we have one czar, but there are seventy-two million of us.' Ishutin is said to have remarked: 'We will make revolutionaries out of these boys.'

The Petersburg group inclined toward a political orientation. Its head, a young scholar who had several works on Russian folkways to his credit, addressed a memorandum to the Emperor, urging him to grant the country civil liberties. Only a revolution from above, he argued, not unlike Herzen, could prevent a revolution from below. He was willing to accept the hazards of a democratic order, believing that it was a prerequisite for Socialism. In Moscow a different view prevailed. Ishutin, for one, held that a constitutional régime would only worsen the condition of the masses: while guaranteeing personal liberty, it would hasten pauperization and the growth of a proletariat. When, in 1865, two years after the young people had first come together, a smaller group, of a distinctly revolutionary character, crystallized within the Moscow circle, the objective of this so-called 'Organization' was a purely 'economic revolution'.

On the subject of tactics there was no unanimity in the Organization, and this resulted in sharp friction. Some favoured peaceful propaganda cautiously conducted, others were eager for drastic action. Ishutin pleaded for 'bang, bang', instead of talk. He was all for shocking the people out of their apathy by some violent deed, such as the blowing up of the Fortress of Peter and Paul. Perhaps a series of assassinations could frighten the Czar into decreeing a social revolution.

Half a dozen of the more audacious spirits discussed at length a plan for forming a terroristic band. They called it Hell. Each member of this secrecy-shrouded body was to be a dedicated and doomed man. He had to give up his friends, his family, his personal life, his very name. To disarm suspicion, the one chosen by lot to act was to abandon himself to dissipation, even play the informer. The deed done, the terrorist must destroy himself by squeezing a pellet of fulminate of mercury between his teeth, so as to make his features unrecognizable. In addition to political assassination, Hell's projected function was to liquidate traitors within the group. An all-powerful, all-controlling secret body, it was to be maintained even after the revolution had triumphed, so as to keep a watchful eye on the new government and, if necessary, use terror against it.

When the moderates got wind of this plan, they considered taking some rather stringent measures against the would-be terrorists, not excluding denunciation to the authorities. As for the extremists, when a refractory youth was reported to have spoken sharply against a certain proposal, it was suggested that he should be killed, since he knew too much and could be dangerous if he withdrew from the Organization. Apparently neither the moderates nor the extremists were inhibited by moral scruples or by a sense of comradeship. They believed that the end justified the means. Their amateur Machiavellianism did not stop at fraud, theft, murder—at least, on the planning level. To provide the Organization with funds one member was to hire himself out as a valet to a rich merchant and rob him; another was to loot the mails; a third was to poison his father for the sake of the inheritance. To carry out his intention, this last plotter actually obtained arsenic.

Ishutin was given to mystifying his comrades so as to add to his prestige and to bolster up their morale. He spread fantastic rumours, such as that Siberia was ready to secede from the Empire and that the United States had promised to assume a protectorate over it as soon as the garrisons in the Urals had been exterminated. Again, he told the members that their society was affiliated with a secret all-powerful European Revolutionary Committee organized for the purpose of assassinating the monarchs of Europe. This was an invention of his own, which some of his less gullible comrades disbelieved. It was possibly suggested by news of the establishment of the International (in

1864). Information about it may have been conveyed to the circle by the emissary who had been dispatched abroad to establish contact with the émigrés—a step that failed to bring results.

Certainly here was an explosive mixture of irresponsible talk and adolescent thrill-seeking.

III

The few who were initiated into the plans for Hell included Ishutin's cousin, Dmitry Karakozov, a morose, self-centred youth, deaf in one ear, whose grey eyes were set in a lean, sickly face. At the gatherings he listened carefully, but hardly ever opened his mouth. The talk of self-immolation, of daring action, fascinated him. He was a soul possessed. The cause of the common people was his ruling passion.

Born into an impoverished family of gentlefolk, the youth was hard put to it to keep body and soul together. He had been expelled from the University of Kazan in 1861 for participation in the disturbances there, and in the summer of 1865 he was dropped from the University of Moscow for failure to pay the modest tuition fee. He was not sorry. The diploma would give him a place among the privileged, where a revolutionist scarcely belonged.

In the winter of 1865–66 he was taken ill and spent two months in the university infirmary. He was suffering from an intestinal disease, but he came to believe that his ailment was mental. He imagined that his days were numbered. And to think that he would die without having done anything for the cause! One day in February he vanished, leaving behind a note which hinted at suicide. On returning to town he said that he had visited a neighbouring monastery. Then he stunned his comrades by declaring that he had decided to make an attempt on the Czar's life. Regicide had by no means been excluded from the terrorist's plans. In fact, it seems to have been the main objective of Hell. It is possible that Ishutin nurtured the idea in his cousin's sick mind, intending to use him as a tool for the execution of his design.

Some of Karakozov's fellow members tried to dissuade him:

talk of assassination was one thing, action was another. Yet the thought obsessed him. At the beginning of Lent he secretly went to Petersburg with a pistol in his pocket, apparently bent on carrying out his intention. Here he composed, or possibly had written for him by the head of the Petersburg group, a personal if unsigned statement addressed 'To Worker Friends', which was at once a defence of his intended act and his testament.

He had long been tormented, he began, by the question as to why Russians tolerated an order that kept the toilers poor and the idlers rich. By dint of much reading and reflection he had come to the conclusion that the czars were at the bottom of the trouble, that they were indeed the people's worst enemies. 'And so,' he went on, 'I have decided to destroy the wicked Czar and die for my beloved people.' If he failed, others, inspired by his example, would succeed. Once the chief enemy has been eliminated, the lesser ones will lose their power. Then real freedom will come: the people will govern themselves without the Czar, the land and all capital will belong to associations of workers. 'Everyone will have plenty, and there will be no one to envy, for all will be equal, and the Russian people will live happily and honestly. . . . This is my last word to worker friends. . . .'

Karakozov made several copies of this leaflet and with a fine disregard for caution scattered them near factory buildings. Roaming the streets, dressed as a man of the people, he also handed the sheet to students he encountered. One copy was turned over to the police, but they paid no attention to it.

On hearing of these goings-on, two members of the *Organization* came to Petersburg to persuade him to abandon his plan. He did go back to Moscow, but abruptly returned to the capital. In the afternoon of 4 April, as the Czar, having left the Summer Garden, a public park, was walking toward his carriage, Karakozov fired a shot at him. Either because the cheap pistol was defective or because his aim was poor, the shot went wild, and no one was hurt. A bystander by the name of Komissarov, a cap-maker of peasant stock, claimed credit for saving the Czar's life by striking the assassin's arm, and the authorities went out of their way to spread this rather questionable story. Surely it was providential that the Liberator should have been saved by a liberated serf. It happened that the cap-maker was a native of the province of Kostroma, birthplace of Ivan Susanin, the peasant who, according to a firmly established, yet somewhat dubious tradition, had sacrificed his life to save the first Romanov from murder by the Poles, and this was taken as added proof that the Emperor had escaped the assassin's bullet by a special act of Providence. The event produced a great outburst of expressions of loyalty to the Czar. The common people generally took the attempt on his sacred person to be an act of revenge on the part of the disgruntled serf-owners. This interpretation gained currency abroad as well. In the joint resolution passed by the United States Congress, congratulating the Emperor and the Russian nation upon his escape from danger, the would-be assassin is described as 'an enemy of emancipation'.

Papers incriminating his comrades were found on Karakozov, and one member of the circle turned informer. Arrests followed, and since the prisoners confessed abjectly and volubly, they implicated others. As a result, all the members of the organization were rounded up and some innocent bystanders besides. Practically all of the former recanted and begged for mercy. Ishutin burst into tears and kept repeating that he had nothing to do with the shooting. As for Karakozov, shortly after his arrest he wrote to the Czar that in acting as he did he had been moved by a desire to bring happiness to 'the great majority of people' whose lot is ceaseless toil, suffering and degradation. He predicted that the masses would soon rise in their wrath at the injustice of the system and, further, that from time to time men would lay down their lives in order to show the people that their cause was just. 'As for me, Sire,' he declared, 'I can only say that if I had not one but a hundred lives, and if the people demanded that I should sacrifice all the hundred lives to promote their welfare, I swear that I would not hesitate a minute to make the sacrifice.'

While in prison he showed signs of mental derangement, which the authorities chose to disregard. For hours he was on his knees in prayer. He declared that he had carried out the attempt in a state bordering on insanity and also that he had been influenced by what he had learned of 'the Constantine Party'. During his stay in the capital he must have heard about the existence of an aristocratic clique that, in the event of the Czar's death, intended to turn the throne over to Grand Duke

Constantine, reputedly a liberal, who was sure to grant the country a constitution.

After a lengthy preliminary investigation thirty-five people, some of them mere boys, were arraigned before a special tribunal. Ishutin and Karakozov were condemned to die, the rest receiving terms of penal servitude of varying length. On hearing the verdict, Karakozov addressed a petition to the Emperor. His offence was so monstrous, he wrote, that he dared not think of any alleviation of his lot, but he swore that he would not have committed the crime if it were not for his abnormal state of mind. He begged the monarch's forgiveness 'as Christian of Christian and man of man' and signed himself his well-wisher. The Czar's indirect response was that personally he had long since forgiven the man in his heart, but as a sovereign he did not believe he had the right to pardon such a criminal.

Princess Dagmar of Denmark, the fiancée of the Heir Apparent, was expected in the capital for the wedding, and it would have been awkward to carry out the hanging during the solemnities, which were scheduled to last for weeks. It was decided to speed up the execution. On 3 September, two days after the verdict had been pronounced, Karakozov was hanged by one of the peasants for whom he wished to lay down his life. At the last moment, when Ishutin was already in his shroud, he was told that the Czar had commuted his sentence to hard labour for life.

Karakozov's shot, while missing its target, was fatal to the circle. Just about the time when he was getting ready for the attempt in Petersburg, his comrades in Moscow had composed their differences and agreed on a programme of action. In the summer they were going to leave town and carry the revolutionary message to the peasantry, combining propaganda with a study of economic conditions. Arrests disposed of these plans and brought to an end all the activities of the circle, but did not entirely obliterate its influence. With its score or two of members, it was a tenuous link in the chain of which Land and Liberty was the beginning and which was to remain long unbroken. The thinking of these youths vaguely foreshadowed the revolutionary trends that asserted themselves in the next decade.

IV

The attempt on Alexander's life intensified the political reaction which had been gathering strength since the emancipation, and particularly since the Polish rebellion. For a while the two capitals were in the grip of what a contemporary pamphleteer described as 'white terror'. In vain did *The Bell* argue that the attack was not the result of a conspiracy, but the act of an unbalanced boy. In vain, and for the last time, did Herzen in a personal message appeal to the Emperor to reverse his illiberal policy. Men who favoured the strong arm were raised to power. A shining exception among the obscurantists and mediocrities who now surrounded the Czar was the Minister of War. Eventually he succeeded in humanizing the discipline, shortening the term of military service, and democratizing it by introducing universal conscription. This, and a limited form of municipal self-government, were the last of 'the great reforms' with which Alexander's name is associated.

Dejection and disillusionment overtook the liberals. The *zemstvo* and town elective boards, being at the mercy of the bureaucracy, were not an attractive field of activity. Those who belonged to the landed gentry applied themselves to planting their cabbages. Others settled down to careers in the civil service, or joined the scramble for the mad money which was being made in railway construction, banking, and the rapidly expanding industries. During the late 'sixties life in Petersburg suggested the atmosphere of Paris during the decline of the second Empire, even to the popularity of Offenbach's operettas. Here, too, though on a smaller scale, there was private extravagance; here, too, there was scandalous corruption in Government offices. Only the republican opposition was missing.

Shortly after Karakozov's attempt, an imperial *ukase* enjoined all agencies of the Government to help in combating the pernicious ideas directed against 'religious beliefs, the foundations of family life, the rights of property, obedience to law, and respect for the established authorities'. Even before this declaration of war against ideas, panic had seized the republic of letters. Every author, particularly every journalist whose published opinions were not quite orthodox, considered himself a marked man. And indeed many a writer saw the inside of a prison cell in those days. Nekrasov, whose character did not match his literary genius, lost his nerve and went so far as to read, at two successive dinners given by the aristocratic English Club, a patriotic poem in honour of the Czar's saviour, Komissarov, and a pæan to Count Muravyov, a former Decembrist, who had been nicknamed The Hangman for the way he had treated the Polish rebels. The editor made these genuflexions in order to save *Sovremennik* from the axe. They were futile. On 1 June the review was suppressed and with it *Russkoe Slovo*. The opposition lost its two most influential organs.

As the schools were considered to be another source of infection, they too were in the first line of attack. The liberal Golovnin, who had headed the Ministry of Education, was replaced by a former Procurator of the Holy Synod, and an arrant reactionary. Under his direction mechanical drill in Greek and Latin crowded out the natural sciences and social studies in the secondary schools. He also enacted a set of special regulations applying to the schools of higher learning. They were aimed at the corporate organizations which continued to exist in the universities in defiance of the law. The student body was subjected to strict police supervision.

The new regulations were applied in a high-handed and tactless manner which was bound to bring on trouble. With the opening of the academic year 1868–69, the capital was the scene of numerous gatherings at which the problems of student life were heatedly debated. There was general acceptance of the programme that had rallied the student body in 1861. While many of the youths were reluctant to resort to any but lawful means in obtaining these rights, others favoured drastic, defiant action. Indeed, there were those who wanted to direct the movement into a revolutionary channel, turning their comrade's discontent with certain conditions in the schools into discontent with the entire system.

The extremist faction included the several underground groups that managed to lead a precarious existence. One of them grew out of a 'commune' set up by a few former members of the defunct Ishutin *Organization*, after they had served short prison terms. It became known as The Smorgon Academy,

which was the popular name of a forest where Gypsies trained
bears for performances at fairs. Presumably there was something
bearlike in the appearance and manner of these youths. The
Academy attracted a few radical intellectuals and semi-intellectuals.
A novel feature at the gatherings was the presence of young
women, who until then had not ventured into associations for
political ends.

In a sense an offshoot of the *Organization*, the Academy
followed in its footsteps. It made preparations to free Chernyshevsky from captivity and helped to pay for reprinting his
works in Geneva. A plan for bankrupting the Government by
flooding the country with counterfeit money was under discussion, and so was regicide. By way of actual performance, the
group sent an emissary abroad to establish contact with the
European Revolutionary Committee which, it will be recalled,
had figured in Ishutin's talk. Of course, the man failed to discover
the mythical body, but after being mistaken for an *agent-
provocateur*, succeeded in gaining the confidence of some of his
compatriots in Switzerland, and in the autumn of 1868 he
returned, bringing with him copies of the first issue of a new
Geneva journal *Narodnoe Delo* (The People's Cause), edited and
largely written by Bakunin.

It called upon the student youth to rally to the banner of the
social revolution. The latter was the only way out of the *impasse*
created by the failure of the reforms to improve the lot of the
masses. Rejecting Herzen's emphasis on the antinomy of Russia
and the West, the veteran conspirator argued for a close link
between Russian and world revolution, since both had the same
objective: to free the people from 'the yoke of capital, hereditary
property, and the State'. Bakunin had lately formulated the
doctrine for which he is best known, and in the pages of the little
review he lost no occasion to expound his anarchist creed. 'The
business of every government,' he wrote, 'is to strangle the
people in order to preserve itself; by the same token, the business
of revolutionaries is to destroy the State in order to free the
people.'

A segment of the student body proved unusually receptive
to the bold message of *Narodnoe Delo*. The issue was copied and
recopied and read to pieces. One article, which dealt with the
rôle of enlightenment, received particular attention. Bakunin

admitted that knowledge could set the people free, but not under the existing system. Alone the destruction of Church and State would enable the masses to come by the enlightenment. From this thesis some of the youths apparently drew the conclusion that it was incumbent on them to give up their studies and, merging with the common people, work for the revolution. That winter the matter was the subject of much excited discussion at the student gatherings in Petersburg.

V

Count Shuvalov, head of the Third Division, in the report for 1869, which has already been quoted, commented on the disturbances in the universities. He was willing to concede that the corporate organizations demanded by the students were in themselves innocent and could indeed be useful to the less fortunately circumstanced youths. The economic status of the student body had not improved with the years. In the early 'seventies three-quarters of the students in the provincial universities needed subvention. The house searches conducted in 1869 revealed living conditions that were officially described as 'truly shocking'. Yet the authorities were forced to forbid the reading rooms, the co-operative eating places, etc., for the reason, the official explained, that they were apt to become centres of anti-government propaganda. What with the young men dropping out of the universities for lack of means or being expelled for insubordination, the country faced the prospect, he observed, of being burdened with half-baked intellectuals who entered life with a deep-seated grudge against the established order. He deplored the presence of former divinity students in the institutions of higher learning: they were particularly apt to become 'fanatics and propagandists', and being more mature than the graduates of secondary schools and more inured to privations by the harsh regimen of the seminaries, were an admired and influential group. However, much of the trouble in the universities, Count Shuvalov insisted, was due less to the students than to outside agitators whose only interest was to compromise as many innocents as possible, have them expelled and thus add to the ranks of potential revolutionaries.

One such outside agitator was a journalist whose student years were behind him. This Pyotr Tkachev was born into a moderately circumstanced family of gentlefolk. After a short stay behind bars, he was expelled from the University of Petersburg at the age of seventeen for his part in the disturbances of 1861. He continued to move on the periphery of radical groups, including the Smorgon Academy, and made a living by contributing reviews and miscellaneous articles to the periodicals.

From the first his thinking was tinged by a not too consistent adherence to economic determinism. He expounded this theory in a book review. It had been formulated, he wrote, by the well-known German exile, Karl Marx, and was now the common property of all decent thinking people. He was one of the earliest Russian radicals to be influenced by Marx's writings. Like Chernyshevsky, whom he acknowledged as his master, he used his censored pages as a vehicle for intellectual contraband. Like him, Tkachev harped on the failure of the programme of liberalism to meet the needs of the unpropertied masses. A revolutionary both by temperament and conviction, he missed no opportunity to point out the futility of moderation and gradualism in trying to alter social relations. Hatred of the existing order was his consuming passion. Alone, acts directed toward its destruction, he contended, might be called truly moral. Furthermore, he allowed that the revolutionaries—he called them, euphemistically, 'men of the future', as Chernyshevsky had dubbed them 'new men'—were not bound by conventional ethics in their fight for the happiness of all. The doctrine was popular in the Ishutin circle and was soon to be acted upon by another underground group.

Chernyshevsky lodged some of his more daring ideas in notes to his rendering of John Stuart Mill's *Political Economy*. On his part, Tkachev concealed ideological dynamite in the introduction and notes he appended to his translation, published in 1869, of an obscure German book on the labour problem. The author advocated the establishment of workers' co-operatives by the existing States. Engaging in polemics against him, the translator argued that the State would not act in the interest of labour until it became the workers' State, virtually a dictatorship of the proletariat. Only then could the communist dream become a reality: a society free from competition and strife, guaranteeing the worker the full product of his labour, assuring economic and every other kind of complete equality to all. And though he had to resort to Aesopian language, he managed to make it clear to his readers that the workers' State could come into existence solely as a result of a break in the historical process, 'a jump', as he put it, i.e. social revolution. 'The way of peaceful reform, peaceful progress,' he wrote, 'is one of the most unrealizable Utopias that mankind has devised to ease its conscience and lull its mind.' The book was, naturally, confiscated and eventually earned the translator a prison term.

It was in Tkachev's lodging that the hot-heads held their meetings. An informal committee seems to have been set up for the purpose of organizing, enlarging, and radicalizing the student movement. The group elaborated an ambitious 'Programme of Revolutionary Action'. Calling for a political upheaval as a preliminary to the social revolution, it envisaged a swift and vigorous propaganda campaign winning over the intellectual *élite,* the urban poor and the peasant masses—all within the space of a year. The climatic event was scheduled for the spring of 1870. Until 19 February of that year, that is, the ninth anniversary of the Emancipation, the ex-serfs were legally bound to hold the parcels allotted to them by agreement with the landlords. After that date they had the option of either continuing in the state of temporary obligation to their former masters, or terminating all connexion with them by restoring their allotments to the owners. Thus, in the spring of that year, millions of peasants would have to face the problems of their relations with the manor-lords, and it was thought that, what with the anticipated worsening of the peasants' lot, the result would be many local clashes which might lead to a general uprising.

When the institutions of higher learning reopened in January, 1869, after the Christmas vacation, the police broke up some of the student meetings and took down the names of the participants. Some arrests were made. The academic air became dangerously charged. A spark could set off an explosion. It occurred in March, when a student of the Military Medical Academy was expelled for a breach of discipline. In defiance of regulations, stormy meetings were held, at which his fellows demanded his reinstatement. It was refused. On the 14th of the month a number of students were arrested, and the Academy was closed until

further notice. Then the disturbances spread to the Technological Institute and the University. The students broke up
lectures and held meetings in the lecture-halls. On the 21st, five
students were expelled from the University. On that very day
there appeared a printed leaflet setting forth the students' demands
and urging the public to come to their support. 'Our protest,'
the appeal concluded, 'is firm and unanimous, and we are ready
to perish in exile and dungeon rather than suffocate and cripple
ourselves morally in our academies and universities.' While the
leaflet failed to elicit any response from the public, it did arouse
the police, for here, after a lapse of five or six years, underground
literature of domestic origin was making its reappearance.

The author of the sheet was Tkachev. It was run off secretly
on a press owned by the young woman with whom he was
living and who eventually became his wife. She was the
illegitimate daughter of an army captain, and had some modest
means. One of the first women to embrace the revolutionary
faith, she conceived the idea of opening a printing shop that
could turn out clandestine literature. As a minor, she could not
dispose of her capital unless she became a married woman.
Tkachev either could not or would not marry her at this time.
She decided to contract a fictitious union, and Tkachev took her
to Moscow to find her a nominal husband. An accommodating
party was discovered in the person of a radical-minded guard
in a detention house, but he was too young, and the priest refused
to perform the ceremony. The girl then abandoned her matri-
monial project and bought a small printing establishment with
borrowed money. Here was a case to illustrate Count Shuvalov's
contention that nihilists of the female sex were 'as harmful
politically as they were socially'.

The appearance of the leaflet led to Tkachev's incarceration.
After serving a prison term, he was deported to a provincial
town, from which he escaped abroad at the end of 1873. The
arrests of the early months of 1869 wiped out the group that
centred around Tkachev, as well as the Smorgon Academy. The
student movement spread to Moscow. More expulsions, arrests,
and deportations followed. Hundreds of young people, many of
them quite innocent, found themselves in the dragnet of the
police.

CHAPTER VIII

FORCE AND FRAUD

THE meetings in Tkachev's lodging had been attended by a friend of the host, Sergey Nechayev, a non-matriculated student. The youth kept in the background and spoke little, but always to the point. His tone was ironic and cutting. He advocated action: open protest, street demonstrations, resistance to force. And he had no patience with democratic procedure.

As has been seen, in January 1869 the police stepped into the picture. They obtained a relatively large number of names of the bolder youths. It happened in this wise. After the Christmas vacation an attempt had been made, at Nechayev's suggestion, to collect the signatures of students who were ready to back a written demand on the authorities, a daring step indeed. The enterprise came to nothing, but the paper with ninety-seven signatures, which had been in Nechayev's hands, found its way into the files of the secret service. It has been conjectured that it was Nechayev himself who turned the list over to the authorities in order to compromise the signers, thus swelling the ranks of potential soldiers of the revolution.

He seems to have been summoned by the police for questioning or even detained for a short while. Be that as it may, he decided to withdraw from the scene. He made his exit in a characteristic manner.

At the end of January he vanished from the capital. Shortly afterwards a girl of his acquaintance, Vera Zasulich, received a communication from a stranger to the effect that just after a police coach carrying a prisoner had passed him by, he had found on the pavement a note, which he enclosed. The note, in Nechayev's hand, informed his friends that he had been arrested and was being taken to prison. The inquiries made by his sister were futile: the police knew of no such person under arrest. Then the rumour spread that he had escaped from the Fortress of Peter and Paul—an unprecedented feat. During the weeks that followed it was whispered that he had been seen in Odessa,

Kiev, Moscow, that he had been arrested again and broken jail a second time.

These arrests and escapes he had fabricated out of whole cloth in a deliberate effort to build himself up as a hero and a martyr in the eyes of his comrades. He impressed them all the more easily because of his background. He belonged neither to the gentry nor the middle class, but wore the halo of a child of the people. A native of the town of Ivanovo, the Russian Manchester, he was the son of a seamstress and a sign painter. In his teens Sergey worked as an office boy and also helped with sign painting. At the same time he was acquiring an education by dint of dogged tenacity and determination. Before he was twenty he became a grade teacher in a Petersburg parish school, where he taught religion, among other subjects. In the autumn of 1868 at the age of twenty-one he entered the university, a young man with the look of a peasant lad somewhat polished by city life. A voracious reader, he pored over many volumes, including the writings of the native radicals and—'the works of the latest American historians'. He is said to have known, at second hand, Buonarotti's description of Babeuf's 'conspiracy for equality', the first attempt to set up a communist dictatorship. The book made a profound impression on the students who gathered in Nechayev's room.

Early in March Nechayev went abroad. This move, at least, was no invention. His destination, when he crossed the frontier, was Geneva. The most famous of the Russian expatriates, who had found a haven in that city, was no longer there. Herzen had left Switzerland soon after *The Bell* ceased publication. That fighting review did not long survive *Sovremennik* and *Russkoe slovo*. With the issue of 1 July, 1867, which marked the paper's tenth anniversary, it was suspended. It failed to reappear. An effort to continue it as a French language publication was also unsuccessful, and so was the attempt to revive, after a lapse of six years, *The Polar Star*.

But when Nechayev arrived in Geneva, another émigré who was beginning to enjoy great prestige at home was living there: Bakunin. Before long the two met. The veteran rebel was fascinated by this 'young savage', as he called Nechayev. Here was a man, he believed, through whom he could make his ideas felt at home. He saw in this 'tiger cub' a true representative of the new Russian youth, which he described about this time as the most revolutionary in the world, charming young fanatics, believers without a God and heroes without phrases, who knew neither doubts nor fears. Once more Bakunin found himself up to his neck in Russian events.

In a speech at the second congress of the League of Peace and Freedom, which had taken place the previous autumn at Berne and given him his first opportunity to proclaim his anarchist views in public, Bakunin declared that the people had lost their faith in the Czar, and that there was an army of forty or fifty thousand revolutionaries in Russia ready to turn against the State. He rather fancied the idea of assuming the generalship of this army. Shortly after this meeting with Nechayev he wrote: 'Two years will pass, one year, perhaps several months . . . and we shall have a revolution [in Russia] that will undoubtedly surpass all the revolutions seen hitherto.' It will be a social revolution 'such as the imagination of the West, which has been moderated by civilization, scarcely dares to picture.' Nechayev must have considerably strengthened Bakunin's belief in the imminence of this event. The young man spoke of himself as a representative of a powerful revolutionary body at home, with connexions in the army and ramifications everywhere, though he could produce nothing more tangible to support his claims than the Programme of Revolutionary Action mentioned above.

Bakunin repaid him in the same coin. He was at this time at the head of two organizations: the International Brotherhood, noted earlier, and the less exclusive but equally secret International Alliance, which had infiltrated the International Workingmen's Association for the purpose of combating 'the authoritarian communists' led by Marx. Yet he did not initiate his new friend into either of these bodies, which had a precarious yet real enough existence. Instead, he enrolled him in a society which was wholly the figment of his imagination. Under date of 12 May, 1869, he issued to Nechayev the following credentials: 'The bearer is one of the trusted representatives of the Russian Section of the World Revolutionary Alliance. No. 2771. (Signed) Michael Bakunin.' In the seal the parent organization is named, more modestly, *Alliance Révolutionnaire Européenne*.

Whether or not Nechayev believed in the reality of this organization, he used the document to further his own ends.

Bakunin took one more step to add to the young man's prestige. Ogarev had written a poem in memory of a dead friend of his childhood, in which that student is pictured as a fighter for the people, a martyr who perished in a 'snow-bound Siberian prison'. Bakunin persuaded the poet to dedicate the piece to 'his young friend Nechayev'. With this dedication the poem was printed and circulated in Russia (a stanza from it is reproduced in Dostoevsky's novel, *The Possessed*).

Each sought to use the other as his tool, and to achieve his ends neither scrupled to resort to fraud. A mere boy, a nobody, Nechayev nevertheless dominated his curious partnership with the celebrated firebrand. The slight young man exercised a strange ascendancy over the shaggy giant. There is a reliable story that Bakunin gave Nechayev a written pledge to the effect that he would obey him in all things as the representative of the Russian Revolutionary Committee (an alias of the Russian Section of the World Revolutionary Alliance), and that in token of his complete submission he signed himself: Matryona (a woman's name).

While Herzen would have nothing to do with the two plotters, they found an ally in Ogarev. No attempt was made, however, to recruit the other expatriates. Nechayev's eyes were on Russia, and his efforts were directed toward producing literature for home consumption. Even before he formed an alliance with Bakunin he had issued an appeal to Petersburg students. Signed 'Your Nechayev', it was in the nature of a personal message, opening with a reference to the author's lucky escape from 'the frozen walls' of the Fortress of Peter and Paul. He urged the comrades he had left behind to intensify their fight, to offer armed resistance, if need be, remembering that they had allies in the toilers and that there was no struggle without sacrifice. They must invite to their meetings representatives of all the discontented elements, except, of course, the liberals. They must think in terms not of the problem of youth but of the larger problem of Russia, for all questions come down to one: the necessity for renewing Russian life through a revolution.

About ten other leaflets were run off a Geneva press. One of them, which called for the annihilation of the entire social order, ended with a pæan to the highwayman, 'the sole real revolutionary in Russia'. An appeal to the peasants, in verse, invited them to get ready stout nooses for the thin necks of the gentry, and urged them to burn the cities and plough up their sites. 'We must devote ourselves wholly to destruction, constant, ceaseless, relentless, until there is nothing left of existing institutions.' Thus runs a passage in the pamphlet entitled *The Principles of Revolution*. This sanctions every weapon in the revolutionary struggle: 'poison, the knife, the noose, and the like.' The émigrés are bidden in accents of authority to return to Russia and join the ranks of the activists. An exception is made for those who had established themselves as workers for the European revolution. The reference is obviously to Bakunin.

Furthermore, a little review, *Narodnaya rasprava* (The People's Vengeance) was started in the name of the Russian Revolutionary Committee. The first issue anathematized science and civilization as instruments for exploiting the masses, and declared: 'We prize thought only in so far as it can serve the great cause of radical and ubiquitous destruction.' It listed the several groups of public enemies who never would be missed. Venal journalists should be silenced in one way or another, perhaps by cutting out their tongues. The Czar himself was to be spared 'for a painful and solemn execution before the eyes of the liberated masses'. Nevertheless, Karakozov's act was applauded as 'the beginning of our sacred cause', a prologue to the great drama.

II

Much of the propaganda literature produced in Geneva found its way into Russia through the mails. Between the end of March and the beginning of August, 1869, 560 packages of leaflets addressed to 387 persons were seized at the Petersburg post office alone. Nechayev's purpose seems to have been to compromise the addressees rather than to convert them. It is not clear how these activities were financed. Not before July did the promoters of the Russian Revolutionary Committee come in for a windfall in the form of four hundred pounds. This sum represented half of the Bakhmetev fund. Herzen had turned the money over to Bakunin and Ogarev, yielding to the latter's importunities.

He did this with great reluctance and against his better

judgment. Nechayev's personality was repugnant to him, and the leaflets brought out in the name of the Russian Revolutionary Committee horrified him. He could derive some comfort from the fact that not all the émigrés were haunted by adolescent dreams of conspiracies and bloody upheavals. A group of them had taken over *The People's Cause*, the journal launched under Bakunin's ægis, and used its pages to excoriate the Russian Revolutionary Committee and all its works. An implicit critique of the Committee's programme is to be found in a series of essays Herzen wrote during the year 1869 in the form of open letters addressed to 'An Old Comrade', that is, to Bakunin.

In these pages Herzen unequivocally repudiated the revolutionary way of achieving a socialist economy. He did not shrink from calling himself a gradualist, and indeed maintained that the old order held things that were fine and beautiful. Not only human beings should be pitied, he wrote, but also objects, products of men's toil, which were bound to perish in the cataclysm. What was this outcry against books and learning, this clamour for universal destruction, but demagogy of the most ferocious and dangerous kind? It could only unleash the low passions. The strength of fighters for freedom had always lain in their being pure of heart. As for the State, eventually it must pass away, but to abolish it before the people were ripe for a stateless existence was to invite disaster. Lassalle had been right in asking: why destroy a mill which could grind *our* flour? Not until the foundations of bourgeois society had been undermined from within, Herzen argued, would violence avail against it. Certainly, force could not break the nexus between private property and liberty which existed in the mind of the European. There must be no more civilizing by the knout and liberating by the guillotine. The workers' league, the future 'free parliament of the fourth estate'—an allusion to the International— this was the first step toward the coming economic order. The need of the age, he insisted, was not soldiers and sappers, but apostles. The eyes of the enemies must not be put out, but opened, so that they might see and be saved. While his addressee was rushing on, moved by the mistaken belief that the passion for destruction was a creative passion and deferring to the future alone, he, Herzen, was seeking to gauge the people's normal speed so as to keep in step with them.

These letters, which were not published during Herzen's lifetime, were in a sense his last will and testament. He must have known that his message of pity and patience, his appeal to reason and tolerance were likely to fall on deaf ears. The future belonged to the expedient of force. A man of a truly seminal mind, he combined an empirical habit of thought with a passionate, mercurial temperament, and consistency was not his hobgoblin. At heart he was a romantic, drawn to what is spontaneous, generous, grand. Ambivalence marked some of his attitudes and opinions. He did indulge in the rhetoric of revolutionary violence, but certainly in his later years his sympathies were not with Babeuf, the surgeon, but with Robert Owen, the accoucheur.

On one occasion he observed that Russia, unlike the West, would have Socialism before it had liberty. This must be accounted a temporary aberration. A libertarian by instinct, he appreciated that freedom is antecedent to and prerequisite for the blessings promised by the new order. 'A Socialism that would want to do without political liberty and equality before the law', he wrote toward the end of his life, 'would quickly degenerate into authoritarian Communism.' His Socialism was a strategy for assuring the welfare of the individual here and now, and his concern was perhaps more with man's moral than with his physical well-being. 'The subjection of the person to society, nation, mankind, idea,' he wrote, 'is a continuation of human sacrifice.' While he abominated a government over which the governed have no control, he also perceived the dangers of popular sovereignty. It was part of his credo that the Slavs had an instinctive aversion from the centralized State. He wanted to restrict its authority and he looked forward to its disappearance. Since he rejected State control of national economy as 'industrial despotism', the question of how to preserve personal freedom under collectivism did not present itself to him in all its acuteness. Yet on occasion he did speak of it as the excruciating problem of the age. Further, he had an inkling that the socialist order was not immune to the curse of the vulgarity that he so loathed in the bourgeois world, and to the danger of tyranny, including the doctrinaire variety, which he hated heart and soul. It was fitting that his concluding word should have been an affirmation of that humaneness which, he had said early in his career, was his banner.

The final 'Letter to an Old Comrade' was penned in the autumn of the year. That winter his eldest daughter, Natalie, the only one of his children with whom he felt a spiritual kinship, was struck down by a mental illness, which he mistakenly believed incurable. In January 1870 he died, a lonely and broken man. Ogarev, inactive and indeed extremely decrepit, survived him by seven years.

Soviet scholarship has been at pains to stress Herzen's aspersions of political democracy, his detestation of the bourgeosie, his adherence to philosophical materialism, yet on the whole its attitude toward him has been lukewarm. Lenin had it that there wasn't 'a grain of Socialism' in Herzen's 'Russian Socialism', but allowed that the man 'has played a great rôle in the preparation of the Russian revolution'. It was a very different revolution from the one captained by Lenin that Herzen had hoped he was helping to prepare.

III

To return to Nechayev, early in September, 1869, he was back in Russia. He was out to destroy the Empire and found a new social order on its ruins almost single-handed, with no ammunition save a few leaflets in his luggage. To those who had heard of him at all he had now become a semi-legendary figure. And he carried credentials from Bakunin himself. He also brought from Geneva a super-secret opuscule printed in cipher, apparently a product of Bakunin's pen. It was in the nature of a preamble to the statutes of a most exacting underground society. The document is called, inappropriately, since it is not in the form of questions and answers, *The Catechism of the Revolutionary*. Its twenty-six paragraphs, divided into four sections, echo some of the ideas that were current in the Ishutin group. The first paragraph opens thus: 'The revolutionary is a doomed man. He has no interests, no affairs, no feelings, no attachments of his own, no property, not even a name. Everything in him is wholly absorbed by one sole, exclusive interest, one thought, one passion: revolution. He must train himself to stand torture and to be ready to die every day. The laws, the conventions, the moral code of civilized society, have no meaning for him. He lives in it the sooner and the more surely to destroy this vile order. To him, whatever promotes the triumph of the revolution is moral, whatever hinders it is immoral, criminal.' The sentiments of gratitude, friendship, love, honour itself must be sacrificed to 'the cold passion for the revolutionary cause'. It is a passion that must go hand in hand with callous calculation. When the question arises as to whether the life of a comrade should be saved, considerations of economy alone must prevail.

The Catechism divides 'all this foul society', i.e. the upper and middle classes, into several categories. One, consisting of influential and intelligent notables, is sentenced to immediate systematic extermination. The lives of the members of another category are to be temporarily spared, so that their bestial conduct may drive the people to rebellion. A third—highly-stationed, wealthy, stupid creatures—are to be exploited by blackmail and other means. The ranks of the liberals are to be infiltrated with a view to compromising them and using them ruthlessly. Radical phraseurs should be constantly urged on and placed in situations which will ruin most of them and turn a few into revolutionaries. Women are singled out for special attention. Those who have wholeheartedly accepted 'our programme' are 'our most precious treasure'.

The organization, the Catechism declares, has no other objective than the liberation and happiness of the people, that is, the common labourers. And since this cannot be achieved save through a crushing popular revolt, it pledges itself to spread by every means the miseries and evils that are bound to put an end to the people's patience and bring about a general uprising. This upheaval, unlike the revolutions in the West, will completely wipe out the political and social order. What will take its place? The answer is left to the future. 'Our business is passionate, complete, uniquitous, ruthless destruction.' To this end an alliance with the highwaymen, the sole true revolutionaries in Russia, is essential. 'It is our task,' the Catechism concludes, 'to consolidate the brigands, who for centuries have been the only active opponents of the social order, into an invincible, all-destructive force.'

Nechayev was the first Russian professional revolutionary, a man who gave to the cause not a spare evening but the whole of his life. His task was cut out for him: to bring into being the

Russian Revolutionary Committee, which had two aliases but existed only on paper. It was to be a hierarchical network of cells, all doing the will of an omnipotent centre shrouded in the strictest secrecy. The individual member was not permitted to know more than was necessary for him or her to execute the particular task assigned. As in the Programme of Revolutionary Action mentioned in the preceding chapter, the uprising was scheduled for the ninth anniversary of the Emancipation. The seal of the society, with an axe as its symbol, read: 'The Committee of the People's Vengeance, 19 February, 1870.'

Identifying the cause with his own person—*la révolution c'est moi*—Nechayev used others as his working capital. He could twist everyone round his finger. His ascetic habits—he lived on bread and milk, and slept on bare boards, at least while staying at the homes of his followers—could not but make an impression. Those he did not fascinate he ruled by fear. His energy was unlimited, his vigilance unremitting, and he acted with lightning-like rapidity. Theorizing was not to his taste, and he was suspicious of it. He demanded complete and unquestioning obedience from his comrades. He arrogated to himself the right to destroy those who did not see eye to eye with him. He would not spare even those for whom he would lay down his life. 'To love the masses,' he told a comrade, 'is to expose them to grape-shot.'

Nechayev could make but little headway in Petersburg. In Moscow he was more successful. Here he chose the Agricultural Academy as his main field of activity. The discipline there was lax, and the students enjoyed extraordinary liberties. He persuaded the members of a clandestine study circle that existed in the college to join the revolutionary organization he said he represented. A founders' cell was set up, and the members, in their turn, formed subsidiary units. In all, perhaps as many as eighty men and women were enrolled.

A skilful and resourceful proselytizer, he appealed to the idealism of some and to the cowardice of others. He had an impressive way of telling prospective members that the time had come to stop idle talk and put their shoulders to a man-sized task. Everyone must begin in the ranks, he insisted, must learn to take orders. He set the members spying on each other, and before long they felt that they were under the eye of a severe, if invisible, authority. He would suddenly appear at meetings with sealed orders from the Central Committee. To no one would he reveal the composition of this committee, of which he was in fact the sole member. Indeed, he said very little about the objectives and the tactics of the society, and showed the Catechism to the fewest. He insinuated, however, that the converts were allying themselves with a powerful international organization.

Nechayev deceived his fellow conspirators at home and he intended to go on deceiving his partners abroad. He assumed various parts and had his fellow conspirators also change their rôles. He paraded one youth before the uninitiated now as a member of the mysterious Central Committee, now as a rank-and-file activist with a message from forty thousand Tula gunsmiths, whom no power on earth could keep from rising. He told the Muscovites that there was a strong organization in Petersburg, and to the few Petersburg members he spoke of the mighty Moscow body. At least one member of a cell adopted this method of deception on his own part and gained a considerable reputation with his comrades by submitting fraudulent reports of his activities. In order to fill the cash-box, money was collected ostensibly for the relief of expelled students. At the height of its career the society is said to have had no more than three hundred roubles on hand. In October a large cheque was obtained from a sympathizer by blackmail, but it was never cashed.

The General Rules of the Organization, a document which, unlike the Catechism, was passed around in manuscript rather freely, called for establishing relations with 'the so-called criminal section of the society'. One of the first converts was an un-employed middle-aged government clerk who drank heavily. This Pryzhov was also a gifted and passionate student of Russian history and folkways, with several studies, including a monograph on pot-houses, to his credit. He was assigned the task of propagandizing the porters, drivers, bakers, and letter-carriers. As he was a familiar figure in the slums and low haunts of Moscow and its suburbs, it was through him that Nechayev tried to get a foothold in the underworld. Pryzhov put a fellow conspirator in touch with some prostitutes and thugs, but the man hastily withdrew when he was warned by a woman to whom he had given a meal that his prospective proselytes were planning to rob him. Some preparations seem to have been made to carry propaganda into the provinces.

The members of the cell were known by number. No. 2 of the founders' cell was a certain Ivanov, a student in the Agricultural Academy. A strong-minded youth, who wielded a considerable influence in his circle, he allowed himself to contradict Nechayev, disobey his orders and question his authority. He had an infuriating way of teasing the man, and he went to the length of expressing doubts as to the existence of the august Central Committee. He seems to have guessed the truth about its composition. It appears that he even spoke of seceding from the organization and forming another based on more democratic principles.

Ivanov's revolt, Nechayev felt, was a grave threat to his own authority and so to the cause. Perhaps he believed that the youth was capable of betraying them all to the police. He was about to leave for Petersburg, but postponed his departure and set about persuading Ivanov's comrades that it was necessary to kill him. Possibly he wished to test them and to seal with blood the bond that united them.

His task not was a difficult one. He was dealing with people who, once they accepted a principle, adhered to its consequences no matter how painful these were, or how much at variance with their instincts. It had previously been decided that the organization had the moral right to take the life of any of its members. Moreover, these men were in an exalted state of mind, ready to immolate themselves and so, of course, their comrades. On 21 November, 1869, Nechayev, aided by three members of Ivanov's cell, brutally murdered the youth in a grotto situated in a park on the Academy's grounds and threw the body into a hole in the ice of a nearby pond.

For years the cry to kill the people's enemies had repeatedly been raised by the handful of would-be liberators. The only victim turned out to be one of their own small number who had aroused the leader's hostility.

Some hours after the assassination Nechayev was showing several people the revolver from which he had fired a bullet into Ivanov's brain when the body was already lifeless. It went off, almost killing Pryzhov, one of those who had had to be dragooned into participating in the murder. Nechayev blithely remarked that if Pryzhov had been killed, they could have pinned the murder on him. The incident is related in the man's reminiscences with the implication that the shot may not have been accidental. The suspicion was shared by another participant in the murder. Shortly thereafter Nechayev left for Petersburg, apparently to plan for the assassination of the Czar. He believed that forty or fifty resolute men could break into the Winter Palace and exterminate the Emperor and all his kin.

The discovery of Ivanov's body a few days after the murder, and a search accidentally made about the same time in the flat of one of the murderers, led to the arrest of hundreds of people. The organization was crushed. Needless to say, the spring of 1870 was uneventful. The precautionary measures taken by the authorities were unnecessary. There was not a sign of the heralded revolt.

IV

The chief culprit was not among the prisoners. As soon as the arrests started, Nechayev escaped abroad. Preceded by contradictory rumours, he turned up at Geneva in January, 1870. There had been no correspondence between him and Bakunin during his stay in Russia, but Ogarev wrote to him at least once. In this letter 'from grandfather to grandson' the expatriate asserted that the eastern section of the country was ripe for rebellion and that the best strategy would be to have two columns march on Moscow: one, from the Urals, containing a Bashkir contingent, the other, with Kirghiz insurgents, from the Don. Siberia and the Caucasus, he was certain, would always prove faithful allies. And he warned his 'grandson' to be sure to tear up rails in order to interfere with the movement of loyalist troops, and meanwhile to organize the rear, setting up communes and introducing exchange tokens so as to break up the power of money. The years had not subtracted from Ogarev's revolutionary zeal or added to his meagre stock of common sense.

When Bakunin heard of the young man's arrival, he jumped with joy so violently that, as he wrote to Ogarev, 'he nearly broke the ceiling with his aged head.' He was then living at Locarno, and Nechayev went to see him there. The visitor behaved with the self-assurance of the leader of a powerful organization and treated his old master rather cavalierly. Yet the relations between the two remained close. Bakunin did not leave a stone unturned to assure his friend's safety: the Russian authorities having demanded Nechayev's extradition, the Swiss police were after him. Now that Herzen was dead, Ogarev was the sole trustee for the Bakhmetev fund, and Bakunin had no difficulty in persuading him to hand over part, if not all, of the money to Nechayev, who received it in the name of the non-existent Central Committee. To a limited extent he was also helped by Natalie Herzen, who had recovered from her mental breakdown. Nechayev may have become interested in her because of the small fortune she had inherited. He contemplated augmenting his funds further by organizing a band of robbers to despoil tourists. It is said that he planned to enrol in this band the son of the English prostitute who was Ogarev's mistress.

In these early months of his second stay in Switzerland he was as active as ever. He issued appeals to burghers, merchants, women, the rural clergy, all in the name of the Committee and of another equally mythical body. In a proclamation addressed to 'Russian students' he told them that many of his comrades had fallen prey to 'bloody reaction', though fate had again spared him. 'Apparently I am destined to outlive this vile Government,' he wrote, and he summoned them to action. There had been talk in the Ishutin circle of getting out a provocative leaflet purporting to come from an aristocratic source and suggesting the restoration of serfdom. Nechayev now issued a manifesto addressed 'To the Highborn Russian Nobility,' which listed the grievances of the gentry and urged it to overthrow the degenerate imperial power in knightly combat.

Nechayev also put out the second, and last, number of *The People's Vengeance*, dating it: Winter, 1870. It announced that in October of the previous year Nechayev had been strangled without a trial at the personal order of Mezentzev, head of the Third Division. He had been caught, the statement added, as a result of information lodged with the authorities by a Petersburg liberal. It is difficult to see what purpose was to be achieved by this clumsy stratagem, which directly contradicted Nechayev's appeal to the students. Least of all could it deceive the police.

The opening article, which brought the news of Nechayev's death, contained a veiled reference to the murder of Ivanov and

Michael Bakunin

Alexander Mikhailov

Sergey Nechayev at the time of his trial, 1872

Vera Zasulich, acquitted of the attempted assassination of General Trepov, 1878

a vague attempt to justify it by observing: 'the austere logic of the true workers for the cause cannot stop at any measure that leads to success.' The second article began by asserting that it was no longer possible for people to travel along the middle of the road. Well-meaning liberals must choose between joining our ranks or becoming police spies. The glorious time of popular self-liberation was approaching, and all honest people should share the sweet labour of preparing for the Great Day. But the workers for the cause were subject to harsh discipline. Anyone violating the rules or in any way deviating from them due to doubt of their wisdom and justice was to be expelled, and 'expulsion means elimination from the list of the living'. The last sentence was plainly another apology for Ivanov's assassination.

In contravention of the principle enunciated in the Catechism, the third, and last, contribution to the journal describes 'the main foundations of the future social order'. Karl Marx called it 'an excellent example of barracks Communism.' All the means of subsistence are in the hands of 'our Committee', and under it are bureaus having charge of production, consumption, education. Physical labour is obligatory for all, including mothers, even if they choose to care for their children themselves, instead of entrusting them to communal nurseries. Everyone must join a workers' association, or lose the right of admission to a communal restaurant and communal dormitory. 'He, or she, has only one choice: work or die.' No contracts between persons or groups are recognized; the relations between the sexes are entirely free. Under these circumstances all ambition and pretence will vanish; everyone will seek to produce as much as possible for society and will himself consume as little as possible. For further details of a theoretical nature on the subject under discussion the reader is referred to the *Communist Manifesto*. The previous year the first Russian translation of it, made by Bakunin, was issued in Geneva from the printing establishment which had succeeded Herzen's Free Russian Press.

Nechayev's most ambitious literary enterprise, an attempt, with Ogarev's blessing, to revive the defunct *Bell*, is typical of his protean disguises. The six weekly issues which he succeeded in bringing out in April and May, 1870, preached a united front against the monarchy and affected a moderate tone completely at variance with the extremism of the other writings he had sponsored. He could even impersonate a liberal when he chose.

One looks in vain for Bakunin's influence in the revived *Bell*. Some of its pages breathe an authoritarian spirit which is incompatible with anarchism. His only contribution to the issues was a letter to the editor criticizing the policy of the paper. Obviously a rift had occurred between the two men. The disagreement was not entirely on ideological grounds. It appears that Nechayev either ignored or refused to meet the financial demands made on him by Bakunin. They were all the more legitimate since, in order to devote his time wholly to the cause, he had, at Nechayev's instance, given up his sole source of income, a translation of Marx's *Capital*, ordered by a Russian publisher. He had taken a sizable advance, but this little difficulty was disposed of by Nechayev, who wrote a threatening letter to the publisher demanding that he relinquish all claims on the translator. Bakunin may also have been influenced by an *exposé* of Nechayev as a charlatan made by a former associate who had escaped from Russia. Finally, he may have been exasperated by Nechayev's unscrupulousness.

The relations between the two came to a violent end in July, just before Nechayev left for London. If Bakunin's words are to be credited, it was indeed he who forced Nechayev to leave Switzerland. But the young man must have had reasons of his own for getting out of Geneva: what with the attention of the police and the arrival from Russia of people who knew too much about him, the place was becoming uncomfortable. Before bidding it farewell, he stole a number of compromising papers belonging to Bakunin, Ogarev, Natalie Herzen, and others. They would come in handy if he wished to blackmail these erstwhile comrades. Confronted by his victims, Nechayev declared imperturbably: 'Yes, that is our system. We regard as enemies and are obliged to deceive and compromise all those who are not wholly with us.' He did not restore the papers.

Bakunin now turned violently against Nechayev. He dispatched warning letters to friends and associates to whom he had highly recommended the tiger cub. He characterized him as a dangerous fanatic, guided by the precept: 'For the body only violence; for the mind, lies,' and apt to ruin all who came in touch with him. Except for a few men at the top, all comrades were to him meat for conspiracies, whom it was permissible, nay compulsory, to compromise, deceive, rob, even murder. 'If you introduce him to a friend,' Bakunin wrote, 'he will immediately proceed to sow dissension, scandal, and intrigue between you and your friend and make you quarrel. If your friend has a wife or a daughter, he will try to seduce her, and get her with child, in order to snatch her from the power of conventional morality and plunge her despite herself into revolutionary protest against society.' Eventually the disclosures at the trial of the Nechayev group so outraged Bakunin that he advised one of the man's former comrades to make known his identifying marks, including the scars on his fingers where they had been bitten by Ivanov during the struggle preceding the murder.

Arrived in London, Nechayev started another review, *Obshchina*. The first, and only, issue carried a letter from him to Bakunin and Ogarev demanding that they deliver to him the remainder of the Bakhmetev fund which had remained in Ogarev's hands. The journal preached popular revolution, and incidentally dismissed Herzen's radicalism as a frail hothouse plant.

Before long Nechayev recrossed the Channel. He was in Paris during the siege, but not during the Commune, having returned to Switzerland in March, 1871. He tried to join a group of Russian followers of Bakunin in Zürich. He proposed to start a journal with the interest on the Bakhmetev fund, which, he claimed, the Herzen family still owed him. Should the money not be forthcoming, he would bring into play the compromising papers he had in his possession. The Zürich group could not stomach such methods. Besides, Bakunin resolutely opposed any collaboration with the man. Nechayev then allied himself with a tiny circle of Russian 'Jacobins' there. He eked out an existence by working as a sign painter.

Most of the émigrés shunned him. At home his former comrades were bitter against him. One of them offered to act as a decoy to secure his arrest abroad; another undertook to assassinate him, promising to return to prison after the deed was accomplished. He was betrayed, however, by an outsider, a sign painter like himself, who was at once the secretary of a Polish revolutionary organization and an agent of the Russian police. Nechayev was arrested in August, 1872, and subsequently turned over to the Russian authorities.

He was tried as a common criminal. In protest he stubbornly refused to answer questions or testify. In certain radical circles it was rumoured that he was an *agent provocateur*. Indeed, a former comrade of his wrote a pamphlet to prove it. This remained unpublished, however, perhaps because the twenty years of hard labour to which Nechayev was sentenced invalidated the author's thesis.

When the trial was over, Nechayev sent a communication to the head of the secret service which, surprisingly enough, breathes a humane and liberal spirit. 'I am a child of the people,' he wrote. 'My first and foremost goal is the happiness, the welfare of the masses.' He did not hail the impending political overturn. 'Such cataclysms,' he observed, 'while they hit the upper classes, are a heavy burden on the common people.' Therefore he urged the authorities to put an end to administrative arbitrariness and brutality, for they sowed the seeds of future revolutionary terror and sharpened the blade that would descend on the government's neck. Alone the introduction of a representative régime could avert a catastrophe. 'I am going to Siberia,' he concluded, 'with the firm conviction that soon millions of voices will repeat the cry: "Long live the *Zemsky Sobor!*" '

Nechayev did not go to Siberia. According to regulations, he had to hear the verdict announced while he was tied to a pillory in a public square for ten minutes. On his way to the square he kept calling out: 'Down with the Czar! He drinks our blood!' When he stepped onto the scaffold, he cried out that on that very spot there would soon be erected the guillotine which would cut off the heads of those who had brought him there. Tied to the pillory, he shouted: 'Down with the Czar! Long live freedom! Long live the free Russian people!' As a result, the Emperor changed the court sentence to solitary incarceration for life in the Fortress of Peter and Paul.

V

Nechayev entered the fortress prison on 28 January, 1873. He was confined to the Alexis Ravelin, which had housed Decembrists and Petrashevists. At this time the entire population of the dreaded prison included one more inmate, who was

demented.[1] The two were guarded by some sixty officers and
men. So strict was the isolation in which Nechayev was kept
that his identity was unknown even to his jailers, and in official
correspondence he was referred to as 'a certain prisoner' or by
the number of his cell. Nevertheless, his fare was tolerable, and
he was supplied with Russian and French books of his choice,
some of them specially purchased for him, and he was allowed
to occupy himself with literary labours. He gave his keepers no
trouble, except on one occasion when General Potapov, head of
the Third Division, visited him and threatened to have him
flogged as a common criminal. He slapped the General's face,
apparently with impunity.[2] In 1875 the authorities requested
Nechayev to set forth his views, perhaps in the hope of discovering that he had undergone a change of heart. He composed
a statement in which he elaborated the thesis that absolutism had
seen its day and that only a liberal constitutional régime was
likely to mitigate the violence of the impending revolution. He
continued to believe in revolution as others believe in God.

On the third anniversary of his incarceration he petitioned
the Emperor to have his case reviewed, since he was, he insisted,
the victim of a miscarriage of justice. As a result, he lost the
privilege of having writing materials, and all his manuscripts
were taken away from him. He grew violent and was put in
chains, remaining handcuffed for two years. He was able to keep
his mental balance, perhaps because he continued to get the books
he wanted.

His writings were destroyed and all that is known about them
is what may be gathered from an official review of them. They
included prison impressions, political essays, and sketches for
two novels, one dealing with the Paris Commune, the other
with Russian student circles. According to the reviewer, the
fictional attempts revealed complete absence of moral sentiment

[1] This was Mikhail Beideman, who, on receiving his officer's commission,
deserted, and for a while worked at Herzen's press in London. Arrested on
his return to Russia in 1861, he told the police that his intention was to assassinate the Czar and arouse the peasants by means of a fake imperial manifesto.
He was kept in the Ravelin for twenty years without a trial and died in an
insane asylum.
[2] The General was known for his abhorrence of the printed word. The
story goes that whenever he travelled in Germany he made a point of stopping
in Mainz to stick out his tongue at the statue of Gutenberg.

and 'a kind of selfindulgence in the contemplation of the strength of the author's hatred of the wealthy'. Men belonging to the upper classes, even if they worked for the revolution, were depicted as villains, and upper class women as 'monsters of depravity'. The era of peaceful development would not begin, these writings suggested, until all those above the masses were destroyed.

Nechayev had been in prison half a dozen years when an important change occurred in his situation. Taking advantage of the incredibly lax discipline that prevailed in what passed for the Empire's most carefully guarded place of confinement, he succeeded in making friends with some of his keepers. He knew how to overawe these simple-minded peasants in uniform. He told them that he was suffering because he had stood up for the common people, he hinted that he was a very important personage and that the Heir was on his side. He harangued, cajoled, threatened, and managed to secure the men's sincere devotion. They called him admiringly their 'eagle' and, in defiance of strict regulations, engaged in talk with him. They kept him abreast of what was going on in the fortress, ran errands for him, and even supplied him with newspapers and writing materials. Astonishing as it is, underground literature circulated freely within the walls of the Ravelin. With the aid of the guards, this man, supposedly buried alive, was able to communicate with his fellow prisoners, of whom there were now two, and with the outside world.

One icy evening in January, 1881, a member of the People's Will, a revolutionary organization which for once was not an invention of Nechayev's, came to the secret quarters maintained by the society. Removing his snow-covered cap and coat, he dumbfounded the comrades present by placing on the table several slips of paper and saying: 'From Nechayev, out of the Ravelin.' In this coded letter the prisoner laid before the People's Will a scheme for setting him free and simultaneously seizing the fortress, as well as the Czar and all his kin. This was to be accomplished while they were attending services in the fortress cathedral. The organization was just then concentrating every ounce of its strength on a plan of its own for putting a violent end to the life of Alexander II, and refused to be diverted from it.

After the Emperor's death, some weeks later, Nechayev

continued to communicate with the People's Will. He urged it to print a fake imperial *ukase* decreeing the restoration of serfdom and the extension of the term of military service, also to disseminate a circular marked 'Secret' and purporting to come from the Holy Synod. This was to apprize the clergy that the new Czar had lost his mind and to enjoin it to offer prayers for his recovery. A bogus manifesto was to follow, proclaiming that since the old Czar had been killed and the new one was insane, the country was now ruled by the *Zemsky Sobor*, which forthwith ordered the peasantry to seize all the land, slaughter the landlords and make short shrift of the police.

The People's Will did not heed this advice. Nor was it strong enough to offer Nechayev help in his plans for escape. He continued, however, to make preparations for it. And then in the autumn of 1881 the collusion between him and the guards was discovered, almost certainly owing to the treachery of a fellow prisoner. Over sixty men were arrested and tried, while Nechayev himself was subjected to a murderous regimen, which before long broke him in body and spirit. He died of scurvy on 21 November, 1882, the thirteenth anniversary of the murder of Ivanov.

It is scarcely astonishing to find that with the advent of Soviet power an attempt was made to rehabilitate Nechayev. One author described him as the originator of a new morality, a grandiose figure who left his imprint on the revolutionary movement. A book by another Bolshevik writer offered an apologia for Nechayev and indeed exalted him as a genius who anticipated the objectives and the methods of militant Communism. There were those, however, who opposed such unqualified glorification of the man. While commending Nechayev's revolutionary ardour and devotion to the interests of the masses, they condemned his tactics. This has become the approved Soviet attitude toward him.

CHAPTER IX

POPULISM

IN a sense the dozen or so years after the Crimean War, that are somewhat improperly termed the "sixties", were the Russian equivalent of the Enlightenment, 'our brief eighteenth century', as Leon Trotsky labelled the period. It was the seedbed of radical ideas. In his report on the state of his see for 1859, Metropolitan Philaret deplored the prevalence of 'censorious and blasphemous literature', resembling the writings that had prepared the way for the French Revolution. Bakunin called Herzen 'our mighty Voltaire.' Indeed, Herzen, Chernyshevsky, Dobrolubov, Pisarev came close to being the counterpart of the Encyclopædists. Like the latter, they attacked feudal privilege, absolutist rule, and Church authority, they professed materialism and attributed to the intellect a leading part in the dynamics of social change. But while the *philosophes* stopped short of questioning the right of private property, by and large the Russian ideologues were democrats committed to Socialism.

That doctrine, it has been pointed out, had secured the allegiance of a segment of the Russian educated public as far back as the 'forties. In the virtual absence of *laissez-faire* liberalism, it filled an ideological void for a tiny intellectual *élite*, alienated alike from the masses and from the emergent middle-class, cut off from political experience by a jealous government, and so doomed to spin out theories in a vacuum. From the first, the effort was to adapt socialist principles to Russian conditions, real or imaginary. The resulting incompletely integrated complex of ideas had as its core an ethically and emotionally motivated agrarian Socialism. It dominated the radical scene from the 'sixties until nearly the end of the century, when it found a formidable rival in Marxism. The name by which it went was *narodnichestvo* (populism). The term, which gained currency in the 'seventies, suggests the important part played in this ideology by the concept of *narod* (people), in the sense of *demos,* the broad social base, the great body of manual workers, specifically the peasantry. With concern for the material welfare of the masses went a mystique which surrounded 'the people' with a halo. Some viewed them as potentially or actually an irresistible historical force; others as the repository of all the virtues, the sole source of spiritual energy and thus the hope of the world.

The tendency to idealize the lower orders may be traced back as far as Radishchev. It was central to Slavophil thinking and cropped up among the Westernists, too. Under serfdom it was a manifestation of abolitionist sentiment and a symptom of the guilt felt by the more sensitive souls among the serf owners. The feeling was particularly widespread after the emancipation. Indeed, it was first recognized and labelled during the 'seventies. Perhaps 'the penitent noble' was a sign of the advanced decay of the gentry as a socially useful group. In any event, during the last third of the century the thinking of the intelligentzia revolved around 'the people'. 'Ideas, ideals, movements, tendencies,' writes a historian of the period, 'were accepted if deemed beneficial to the people, and rejected if considered useless or harmful to the people. A stern judgment from which there was no appeal weighed down upon Russian thought, conscience, and creative effort.' The populist motif runs through the body of major Russian fiction. In Tolstoy it was linked with a Rousseau-esque impulse to slough off the trappings of civilization; for Dostoevsky 'the people' were a vessel of grace and a haven of salvation. It may be noted that while the populists who were moved by a feeling of guilt sincerely desired to humble themselves before the people, they were not free from the pride of humility: a sense of belonging to an *élite* destined to lead the oppressed out of bondage.

A vision of the poor rising against their oppressors to possess the earth, *narodnichestvo* involved the conviction that by virtue of their temperament, their history, their folkways, the Russians were peculiarly fitted to realize the socialist ideal. The proposition had been formulated by Herzen, the begetter of Populism, which he called 'Russian Socialism'. As has been stated, it was he who had announced to the world that the *muzhik*, in the *obshchina* and *artel*, practised, in rudimentary form, the Socialism which was only preached in the West. He had concluded—and Chernyshevsky agreed—that in Russia the new society could grow from native roots, while elsewhere it could only be brought into being by a series of catastrophes.

At several points the theory was at variance with actuality. The village commune was not a manifestation of the Slavic folk genius and the survival remaining from a hoary past that Herzen believed it to be. The great age of the *obshchina* was under suspicion in his own lifetime, and the opinion now prevails that the institution was created by the State for fiscal purposes no earlier than the age of Catherine II. Furthermore, he disregarded the fact that hereditary land tenure existed in a large section of the Empire. Nor did he take sufficient account of the evidence— it had been accumulating since the 1830's—to the effect that the commune was in a precarious condition. In sum, Herzen's fantasy-laden conception of the *obshchina* was a social myth. As such, it possessed the effectiveness that creations of the kind often have. It helped to sustain faith in Socialism. The *artel*, too, was scarcely the model for a workers' co-operative that Herzen pictured. 'If you haven't worked in an *artel*,' wrote Turgenev, quoting a remark he had heard from a member of such an association, 'you don't know what a noose is.' It may not be irrelevant to note that the chief exponent of the doctrine of peasant collectivism was an expatriate who had never been close to the actualities of Russian rural life.

That the village land commune could become the foundation of the socialist order was the cardinal dogma of the populist creed. Herzen realized, it will be recalled, that the institution was not faultless, and in defending it Chernyshevsky stipulated, as a condition for its development, a successful revolution in the West. But the reservations suggested by the twin pillars of Populism were lost on their followers. For them the *obshchina* was a battle cry, a sacrosanct principle, for which one should be ready to lay down one's life.

The populist version of Socialism did not call for the nationalization of the country's economic resources and State control of production and distribution. Partly due to Bakunin's influence, the *narodnik* was hostile to centralized political authority. He wanted sovereignty to rest with the small, self-governing economic unit. The body politic held together by force he would replace with free productive communes spontaneously banded together in a loose confederacy. This is what was meant by social revolution, as against a change-over resulting in a representative régime. Far from Herzen's ambiguous feeling toward a political revolution was the conviction that this was unnecessary and indeed harmful, both as a distraction from the main goal and in its results. The argument ran that once economic equality was assured, the superstructure of autocracy was bound to crumble; on the other hand, political democracy by itself would favour the development of a competitive economy resting on private ownership of the means of production, and so benefit solely the propertied classes.

Eventually the populists abandoned their anarchist bias and apolitical position. Capitalism remained for them a veritable 'bugaboo', a source of unmitigated evil. They feared that it would bring the horrors of pauperization and proletarianization, create a powerful bourgeoisie, undermine the collectivist tradition of the peasantry, and thus delay the advent of Socialism, if not make it impossible. A reassuring thought, fathered by the wish, was that Russian capitalism was an artificial growth without a future. Furthermore, there was nothing in the nature of things to prevent Russia from by-passing the capitalist phase. The country might develop in a way for which there was no precedent in the West, turning the curse of its backwardness into a blessing. This was a basic tenet of populism, vigorously upheld alike by Herzen and Chernyshevsky. To them, as to their followers, history was a matter of genuine choices, 'dishevelled improvization', not 'a providential charade', as Herzen put it. Socialism, like every human aim, was to be achieved by a victory over the force of circumstance in a combat of uncertain issue. Populism combined enthusiasm for the collectivist principle with exaltation of the individual who, however dependent on his physical surroundings, was yet capable of 'changing the pattern in the carpet', to use Herzen's phrase.

II

One of the ideologists of populism did not come into promin-ence until the very end of the 'sixties. At that time Pyotr Lavrov was on the shady side of forty. By birth and psychological make-up he belonged to 'the repentant gentry'. For years he taught mathematics in military colleges, and to eke out his rather meagre salary he did a good deal of writing for the reviews, displaying varied learning and mildly radical leanings. He was involved with the *Land and Liberty* Society and in 1861-63 edited an encyclopedia, which was discontinued by official order after a reviewer in an ecclesiastical journal had likened it to the eighteenth-century *Encyclopédie*.

During the reaction that followed Karakozov's shot he spent some months in prison and was subsequently deported to a remote province. It was there that the middle-aged ex-professor composed a series of politico-philosophical essays entitled *Historical Letters*, which were serialized in a review in 1868-69. They struck a responsive chord and, somewhat to the author's surprise, at once became, in the words of a contemporary, 'a revolutionary gospel'.

The book was written primarily to combat certain trends that prevailed among the provincial intellectuals of the author's acquaintance and that he attributed to Pisarev's influence: a puerile scientism, a narrow individualism shunning social responsibilities, a breakdown of morals (which was soon to bear such evil fruit in the Nechayev incident). It appealed not to people's enlightened egoism, but to their sense of moral duty. Its main thesis was that the masses had paid with much sweat and blood for the existence of an intellectual *élite*, and that the time had come for the latter to liquidate the historic debt by leading the fight for social justice. Lavrov's readers took this to be a clear call to devote their lives to the cause of the people, and they responded eagerly.

He certainly had at heart the material welfare of the masses. Yet he assigned the chief part in the drama of history not to them, as other populists were apt to do, but to the intellectual minority. This, he told his readers, embodied *thought*, the truly creative principle which gives meaning to action by rendering it conscious, and is indeed the prime mover of progress. His hero was 'the critically thinking person', a man or woman capable at once of perceiving where the true interests of the people lay and of formulating ideal goals. These persons must inevitably associate, act together, consider themselves parts of a larger whole. This whole was not the nation, not the State, but—and here Lavrov was announcing a theme familiar to the present generation—*the Party*.

His clamour for the repayment of the debt incurred by the

intelligentzia was seconded by another unsystematic, if more prolific and effective author, a younger man, who early chose journalism as a career and refrained from casting his lot with active revolutionaries: Nikolay Mikhailovsky. He, too, was a 'penitent noble'. In fact, it was he who gave the phrase currency. He was convinced that the amortization of the debt must take the form of economic, not political, democracy. Like other exponents of Populism, he failed to perceive that the first was impossible without the second. Though prizing the blessings of freedom, he was ready to repudiate civil rights and liberties at the thought that they might only increase the age-old debt to the people, as had happened in the West. Such at least was his stand in the 'seventies.

His extreme animus against capitalism fed on the belief that it separated the producer from the means of production and, worse still, that by division of labour it tended to reduce the worker to a fractional human being and limit his solidarity with his fellows. More than any other champion of Populism, Mikhailovsky stressed the importance of the individual. For him man's attainment of his full stature was indeed the be-all and end-all of progress, and he was convinced that a society made up of units like the *obshchina* offered the individual the best chances for self-fulfilment. Nor did he doubt that Russia was free to choose between Capitalism and Socialism, since he held with Herzen that history is the realm of the possible. No other populist thinker was so deeply preoccupied with the ethical principle. In dealing with human affairs, he insisted, the quest of truth was inseparable from the pursuit of justice. Like many of his contemporaries, he felt that Socialism was likely to succeed for the reason that it was morally right.

It is clear from the foregoing that the populist ideology was poles removed from Marxism. Soviet opinion has branded *narodnichestvo* as ﹨a petty-bourgeois idealistic pseudo-socialist doctrine. Herzen seems to have been unacquainted with the writings of Marx, and the two expatriates were separated by personal enmity, for which Marx's feud with Bakunin was only partly responsible. The works of Marx and Engels were apparently unknown to Chernyshevsky before his imprisonment. In 1872 a copy of *Das Kapital* reached him in his Siberian exile, and he is said to have found a word of praise only for the historical passages. Lavrov came under the influence of Marx and, in fact, acknowledge himself his disciple, but the Marxist conception of Socialism as, in the words of G. D. H. Cole, 'a summons to men to understand the irresistible historic tendencies and to work with them', remained alien to him no less than to other *narodniks*.

Populist sentiment fed on the verse of Nekrasov, which pictured the virtues and sorrows of the peasantry, as well as on the semi-fictional prose of a school of authors who depicted the life of the urban and rural masses. Some of these writers viewed the scene through rose-coloured spectacles, others were realistic in their approach. Gleb Uspensky, for one, told his readers many bitter truths about the brutality and servility of the peasant, his lack of group solidarity, his tendency ruthlessly to exploit his fellows. He made the discovery that the *obshchina* was disintegrating and throwing up a predatory bourgeoisie, the *kulaks*, not a foreign body, but flesh of the flesh of the people. His audience failed to grasp the devastating import of the testimony marshalled in his sketches. What was prized in his pages was his compassion for the underdog and the feeling that deep within the soul of the people their moral sense was alive.

Factual reports on the conditions under which the masses lived also found eager readers. The work of this kind that made the greatest impression in advanced circles was by V. V. Bervi, who had first attracted the attention of the authorities by his protest against the arrest of thirteen Tver arbitrators and who was now writing under the pen name of Flerovsky. His book, *The Condition of the Working-Class in Russia*, appeared simultaneously with *The Historical Letters*. It was a sprawling, loose account, personal, direct, full of concrete details, the work not of a professional economist but of a man with an immense and first-hand knowledge of folk life.

By the working-class the author meant not only the wage-earners, but, above all, the peasantry. His books disposed for good and all of the argument that the masses in Russia were more fortunately circumstanced that their fellows in the West. He showed that the Russian miners and factory hands were worse off than the English proletarians. He found large-scale industry particularly destructive of the well-being of the workers. He also drew an appalling picture of the pauperization of the villagers as a result of the Emancipation — a development anticipated by Chernyshevsky and others. To save the situation the author urged that the redemption payments be abolished and the *obshchina* freed from State tutelage and protected from *kulak* depredations.

Few books were as effective in arousing sympathy for the masses. Marx, after dipping into it—he had started to learn Russian primarily to read this work—gained the impression that 'a collapse of Russian might' was impending.

Flerovsky was the author of another book which enjoyed great popularity in radical circles: *The ABC of the Social Sciences* (1871). In its author's opinion a contribution to 'scientific' ethics, it is a survey of the history of civilization leading to the conclusion that solidarity, co-operation, and altruism are the sole factors of progress, and, incidentally, seeking to discredit the doctrine of natural selection as applied to man, which was also both Chernyshevsky's and Mikhailovsky's *bête noire*.

Although the two books were free from overt socialist and revolutionary tendencies, they attracted the attention of the police. In 1873 the author was arrested on suspicion of membership in a secret circle and deported to a distant northern town. Many years later he expatriated himself.

III

With the collapse of Nechayev's venture, the revolutionary cause suffered a setback. What momentarily helped to hearten the would-be insurgents was the Paris Commune. Lavrov attributed great importance to the impression it made. Acting on his own, a former member of the Smorgon Academy responded to the news by composing and printing secretly four numbers of a periodical leaflet entitled *Gallows* and signed 'Communist'. The first issue declared: 'The world revolution has begun! Rising over the ruins of Paris, it will make the round of the capitals of the world. The longed-for, the holy one will also visit our peasant hut. . . .' The last number, issued during the agony of Paris, wound up with a call to honest men everywhere to 'respond to perishing Paris, that it may know that its cause will be taken up again and advanced bravely and heroically. . . . To arms! To arms!'

The crushing of the Paris Commune was followed by a stirring event nearer home: the trial of the Nechayev group. After a delay of a year and a half it opened on 1 July, 1871, in the capital, and it lasted nearly three months. The defendants, who numbered eighty-seven, included Pyotr Tkachev. Nechayev's chief accomplices were given long terms of penal servitude. By a grim kind of poetic justice, one of them, after spending some ten years in a Siberian prison, was hanged by his fellow convicts on the mistaken suspicion that he had turned informer. Tkachev received a prison term of sixteen months.

The courtroom had been open to the public, and a full account of the proceedings, as well as the text of the *Catechism of the Revolutionary*, had been printed in the official gazette. The effect of all this publicity was not entirely what the authorities had expected it to be. The defendants spoke with 'the eloquence of fanatical conviction,' as a detective put it, 'that fascinated some of the students and young officers who found their way into the courtroom, in spite of the efforts of the police to fill it with respectable folk.' In the eyes of a few the Moscow Agricultural Academy, the chief theatre of Nechayev's activities, became almost holy ground.

The disclosures at the trial made a painful impression, however, on the majority of the radically-minded. To them Nechayev and his followers, far from being martyrs worthy of emulation, were a horrible example. The very idea of a centralized secret society was discredited. Alone, informal 'circles for self-education' and 'communes' persisted. Sometimes such a confraternity was a substitute for home and family, as the populist faith was a substitute for religion.

This did not satisfy the more earnest spirits. Since manual labour alone, preferably tilling the soil, was considered honest work and all exploitation was abhorrent, they concluded that the good life could be lived only in an agricultural settlement run on strictly communist principles. They knew, however, that such establishments would not be tolerated by the authorities. Thus it was that a number of young people began thinking of emigration, and to America. The remoteness and strangeness of the land made the enterprise more difficult, but also more attractive. Rumours of the astonishing liberty enjoyed in the United States and of the communist settlements existing there had

Ignaty Grinevitzky, who threw the bomb that fatally wounded Alexander II

Sofya Perovskaya

Andrey Zhelyabov. From a pencil sketch made by Konstantin Makovsky during his trial, 1881

The scene of the assassination of Alexander II, immediately after the explosion of the first bomb

reached the shores of the Neva. Like Russia half a century later, America was at this time regarded in advanced circles as a laboratory for social experiments.

By 1871 there was an American Circle in Kiev with a score of members and ambitious plans for establishing a network of communes in the United States. Some of the settlers were expected to return home armed with American passports and go on with the good work without fear of molestation by the authorities. The following year three young men sailed for the United States as scouts, but did not stay there for any length of time and failed to promote the plans of the Circle. Two other members started out for America, but got no farther than Switzerland. Returning home before long, they found that nothing remained of the group.

A much less ephemeral affair, and one that was an important link in the succession of revolutionary associations, was a group which originated in the late 'sixties as a 'commune': the Natanson Circle. It was so called after one of its founders, Mark Natanson, a Petersburg student like the rest of its members. From the first they had opposed Nechayev, and the trial only served to confirm them in their detestation of his programme and his tactics. The Circle established branches in Moscow and half a dozen other centres, and in the spring of 1871 the membership was swelled by a number of young women.

'The liberation of the people' was the ultimate objective. But conscious of their inability to reach the masses and believing that these were not ripe for revolutionary action, they were content, for the time being, to labour among people of their own kind, relying on the long-range method of indoctrination. They concentrated on supplying study groups with an appropriate selection of literature. The Circle purchased books in quantity from publishers at a discount and sold them at cost. Already in the summer of 1871 the works it disseminated could be found as far south as the Crimea and as far north as Vyatka (now Kirov). It also engaged in a little publishing on its own account, issuing a reprint of *The Historical Letters*, a revised edition of *The Condition of the Working-Class in Russia*, and a book on the Paris Commune. Being full-sized volumes accessible to the learned only, these publications were exempt from preliminary censorship, but the police confiscated all the copies they could lay their hands on.

Natanson was arrested in November, 1871, and deported to a distant province.

The group then became known as the Chaikovsky Circle, after a member who represented it in business dealings. Not that this young man, a senior at the University, had any special prerogatives. 'Generalship', hierarchy, blind obedience in the name of secrecy were anathema. There were no rules, no written statutes. Decisions were made by unanimous consent. From first to last the Circle was an informal association of men and women united by friendship, mutual confidence, the belief that their work must be done with clean hands. An atmosphere of ethical rigour and dedication to the populist idea dominated the group. The members were expected to maintain exacting standards in their personal conduct. Even moderate drinking was frowned upon. Chaikovsky later called the organization 'a knightly order'.

The flock was not, however, without a black sheep. The group owned a small printing press in Zürich. It was run by V. Alexandrov, a one-time medical student and a founder of the Circle, with money supplied by Pisarev's sister, a young woman who worked as a typesetter at the press. When the five thousand roubles, which was all she owned, gave out, Alexandrov suggested that she obtain more funds for the establishment by selling herself to an old man. This she did, and then committed suicide (in 1875).

Throughout the existence of the Chaikovsky Circle thirty men and women belonged to the Petersburg centre and forty or fifty to the branches. Not a few of the members were outstanding personalities. Among those whose names will be met with again were Sergey Kravchinsky and Leonid Shishko, both officers who had early retired from the army, Dmitri Klemenz, a science student, Prince Peter Kropotkin, scion of one of the first families of the land and graduate of the Corps of Pages, the most exclusive military school in the country, which had ties with the imperial household. At the age of thirty he had given up a brilliant scientific career as a geographer to devote himself to the revolutionary cause. The Moscow cell included Nikolay Morozov, son of a rich landowner, and Lev Tikhomirov, a law student, both still in their teens, as well as Mikhail Frolenko, a student of the Agricultural Academy. The most prominent of the women was Sofya Perovskaya. In 1870, at the age of seventeen, she had run away from an aristocratic home—General Perovsky was at one time Governor of the capital—to join a 'commune' of women, some of whom were nominally married, and all of whom attended the pedagogical courses recently thrown open to women.

This handful of intellectuals developed an activity which made it the centre of populist propaganda in the early 'seventies.

IV

The Chaikovsky Circle was not content to confine its activities to the student youth. The populist faith demanded an effort to reach the masses, that is, above all, the peasantry. But how was this to be done? As a clerk in a *zemstvo* board, a teacher, a rural nurse, one could get opportunities for propaganda among the village folk. Yet revolutionaries were temperamentally unfit for the patient, humdrum routine which this method demanded. Proselytizing among the men employed in the mills and factories of the capital was a more rewarding, if also a more hazardous, task. From the summer of 1872 onward, several members, Sofya Perovskaya among them, took time off from other duties to devote themselves to it. Meeting secretly with small groups of workmen, they taught them their letters and indoctrinated them with Socialism. The branches of the Circle, too, turned their attention to wage-earners.

In spite of the paucity of propagandists and the unsystematic character of their truly pioneering effort, it continued to bear ample fruit until the end of 1873, when both the proselytizers and many of their converts found themselves in prison. The embryo of a labour organization, which was beginning to form under the guidance of the Circle, was destroyed. This helped to centre attention on the village. The agitators could not but notice that they were most successful in dealing with unskilled workers, recent arrivals from the countryside, who had a peasant mentality and had not lost touch with their rural background, returning to their native hamlets for holidays or during the slack season. These raw semi-proletarians were indeed sought out, since it was hoped that they would act as intermediaries between the intellectuals and the peasants.

As a matter of fact, when the arrests began some of the proselytized workmen returned to their village homes, and at least one of them for months busied himself spreading the gospel of revolt among the peasants. Similar attempts were made by more than one member of the Circle. In the autumn of 1873, two woodcutters appeared in a Tver village. One of them was Kravchinsky, the other was Dmitri Rogachev, also a member of the Chaikovsky Circle. He had undergone a kind of religious conversion to the people's cause after hearing a workman in a tea-house tell the grim story of his life. The two men let no opportunity for propaganda slip. One day as they were walking down the road, they were overtaken by a peasant, driving. At once they started urging him to refuse to pay taxes and quoted Scripture to prove that it was right to rebel. The *muzhik* whipped up his horse, which broke into a trot. The propagandists trotted after. He set his horse to galloping, but the pair could gallop as fast as his bony nag. They did not stop haranguing until they were out of breath.

They were not long allowed to carry on in this uninhibited fashion. At the end of November they were arrested, but managed to escape the rural police. When, in the small hours, they reached a forest, they embraced, not to celebrate their temporary safety, but their permanent outlawry: henceforth, they said to each other, their lives belonged to the people.

For propaganda among peasants appropriate literature was required: pamphlets couched in simple language and sparing the religious sentiments of the folk. Half a dozen of them were run off on the Circle's Swiss press, mentioned earlier, and smuggled into the country. In addition, several leaflets were printed secretly in a village near Moscow on the initiative of another populist group.

The idea of carrying the revolutionary message to the masses was not a new one. The slogan 'To the people!' was launched by Herzen in *The Bell* back in 1861, when, with the closing of the University of Petersburg, many youths had been left without an occupation. It was echoed with a strong conviction by Bakunin and Nechayev. They had urged the students to leave their books and 'go to the people', live among them, merge with them and fight for their interests. Excursions into the countryside for propaganda purposes were either planned or attempted by individuals and groups throughout the 'sixties. It has been seen that in the winter of 1868–69 the issue was under discussion among the undergraduates in the capital. In the years immediately following, the debate grew in volume and liveliness. There was near unanimity on the necessity for the agitators to identify themselves with the people, but no agreement as to just what the immediate objective of the propaganda should be. Two trends asserted themselves, producing a factional schism, which first took shape among the Russians who had gone to Switzerland as political refugees or as students.

A large number of them were concentrated in Zürich. The University and the Polytechnic there attracted young men expelled from schools of higher learning at home and young women who were still disbarred from them. One hundred and forty Russian girls registered at the University for the year 1872–73. Not a few of those who arrived abroad without any radical convictions quickly acquired them there. A case in point is that of Vera Figner, a young married woman who was studying medicine in order to alleviate the sufferings of the poor. Before long she made her own 'the ideal of the prophets and martyrs of the socialist evangel', as she phrased it in her memoirs.

The revolution haunted the thoughts of many of these young Russians. Small wonder then that when Bakunin came to Zürich for a short stay in the summer of 1872 he made a great impression there. He was about to be expelled from the International because of his opposition to the policy of the General Council led by Marx. Two years previously that organization had included a tiny Russian section which supported Marx and was indeed represented by him in the General Council, so that he jestingly signed a letter to Engels, 'Secretary for Russia'. But by now the handful of Russian Marxists had faded away, while Bakunin's followers, enrolled in a secret Brotherhood, formed a small, but influential group in Zürich.

Not long after Bakunin had left the city Lavrov had arrived there. He had escaped abroad two years earlier, in order to join a woman whom he loved and to devote himself, without being molested by the police, to an ambitious History of Thought. In Paris he enrolled in the local section of the International, and he visited London in a vain effort to obtain help from that body for the Commune. On that occasion he made the acquaintance of Marx and Engels.

He seems to have intended to hold aloof from the struggle in Russia. Yet in March, 1872, at the request of the Chaikovsky Circle he undertook to edit a revolutionary organ for home consumption. It was to be called *Vperyod!* (Forward!) and printed in Zürich. As a radical leader Lavrov left much to be desired. Essentially a theorist and a pedant, he was at home in the study, not at a gathering of plotters. Furthermore, his faith in revolution was of recent date: in *The Historical Letters* he had assigned to 'critical thought' the task of preventing, not calling forth, a social upheaval.

Lavrov shared Bakunin's fear and hatred of Leviathan, but on one important point he failed to see eye to eye with the anarchist: he did not believe that Russia was ripe for an immediate over-turn and envisaged a lengthy period of peaceful propaganda. As a result, in Zürich he became the eponymous head of the anti-Bakuninist faction. In the superheated, unhealthy air breathed by the expatriates there the division between the Lavrovists and Bakuninists became a violent feud. For a time feeling ran so high that Bakunin's followers dared not venture into the street unarmed. Then a split occurred in the ranks of his own Brother-hood. In the summer of 1873, shortly before that group had fallen apart, it printed a collection of Bakunin's essays under the title, *Statehood and Anarchy*. The book was to become the chief vehicle of anarchist propaganda in Russia.

Almost simultaneously with this work the first issue of *Forward!* came off the press. Some zealous Bakuninists con-signed copies of it to the flames and even accused Lavrov of being in the pay of the Russian police. Only one other volume of the miscellany appeared in Zürich, in March 1874. The previous May the Petersburg Government gazette carried a notice to the effect that if women students continued to attend courses at the University of Zürich after the first of the following year, on returning home they would be debarred from all occupations the exercise of which required official sanction. The reason given was that these young women had fallen under the pernicious influence of revolutionary agitators, and, further, that they were scandalizing the local population by practising 'the communist theories of free love'. As a result, some women

students transferred to other foreign universities, some went home
to attend courses recently opened to the sex in Moscow. The
Russian contingent in Zürich rapidly dwindled, Lavrov removing
himself and his review to London in the spring of 1874.

Bakunin had stayed on in Switzerland. While he kept aloof
from Russian affairs, his ideas were achieving a considerable
vogue in the country of his birth. In September 1873 he announced publicly that he was withdrawing from the political
arena and would no longer disturb anyone's peace. This did not
prevent him from taking a hand a year later in a futile attempt
to start a social revolution in Italy. The short time that was left
him was a period of dejection and disillusionment. He lost his
faith in the revolutionary passion of the masses and in human
decency. 'If there were only three people in the world,' he is
reported to have observed, 'two of them would unite to oppress
the third.' And Nechayev's former ally wrote to a would-be
Russian activist that nothing solid can be built on fraud and
that without a high humane ideal no revolution can triumph.
Abandoned by most of his comrades-in-arms, the father of
international anarchism died at Berne in 1876.

In the early years of the Soviet era there was a tendency to
exalt Bakunin as a towering revolutionary figure. In a monu-
mental biography he was described as a forefather of the Russian
Communist Party, a man who had foreseen the course of the
October Revolution and had 'laid the foundation for the concept
of Soviet power', in fact, a forerunner of Lenin. But the part of
an ancestor of Bolshevism scarcely fitted the arch-foe of the
authoritarian State for whom freedom was the highest good.
Since the 'thirties he has been under official anathema as an
enemy of the working-class and a betrayer of the revolution.

v

Copies of *Forward!* and *Statehood and Anarchy* reached Petersburg in the autumn of 1873, and presently the feud between
Lavrovists and Bakuninists was being carried on at home. The
former were the smaller faction. There were probably no more
than thirty active Lavrovists in the capital and a few in Moscow.
They dressed better, their hair and speech alike were smoother

than their opponents'. Using less vehement language, they were apt to come off badly in debate. Altogether they were too tame for the times. Bakuninism had a much greater appeal. Indeed, it won the sympathy of the impetuous Kravchinsky and several other members of the Chaikovsky Circle, which had originally sponsored Lavrov and his review.

That group was drifting to the left. There was talk of replacing the loose coterie with a formal association. The task of formulating a plan for it fell to Kropotkin. The two documents he drafted postulated the complete and irrevocable identification of the activist with the people, and reflected a strong Bakuninist bias natural to a man who was convinced that to place the means of production in the hands of the State was suicide for society, since this was likely to result in 'economic despotism, far more dangerous than merely political despotism', as he put it in his memoirs. The reorganization failed to materialize because by March, 1874, arrests had deprived the Circle of its most active members, including Perovskaya and Kropotkin. He was seized the day after he had delivered a brilliant paper on the glacial period before a session of the Imperial Geographic Society, of which he was a member.

This did not act as a deterrent. Since the prison gates might close upon them at any moment, the activists felt that they must bestir themselves. This meant 'going to the people', or at least preparing for it. Enthusiasm for this course was infecting hundreds.

Student meetings, milling with noisy crowds, followed one another in the capital. Other centres, too, were agitated. Discussions were endless. The Lavrovists' stand was that the would-be propagandist must undergo a long, arduous intellectual training to fit himself for his task. Moreover, since the people did not understand their own interests nor know their friends from their enemies, a lengthy period of peaceful indoctrination was necessary.

The Bakuninists dismissed all that as an attempt, dictated by cowardice and sluggishness, to relegate the revolution to an indefinite future. The idea of placing so much emphasis on book learning! Did the prospective agitator have to master all the sciences listed in Comte's classification, from astronomy on down? Why, the 'three R's' were sufficient baggage for him. One man gave the opinion that the accumulation of knowledge was as immoral as the accumulation of material goods. And surely the peasants needed no enlightenment. They lived by a traditional philosophy grounded on belief in equality, and hostility toward private property and centralized political authority alike. Undoubtedly they would be the first to get rid of the State. Hadn't the master written: 'The Russian people are socialists by instinct and revolutionaries by nature'? All the agitator had to do was to organize their revolt.

Bunt (revolt, mutiny) was the Bakuninists' open sesame. Hence they liked to speak of themselves as *buntars*. They believed that even localized and abortive uprisings were desirable because of their educational influence and cumulative effect. But if they used the language of violence, it was without realizing what the words meant. 'Our "blood",' as a contemporary put it, 'was not accompanied by pain. Our "rebellion" was more of a moral rebirth than a bloody reshuffling.' By the same token, the militant slogans represented not so much a programme of action as a dream of freedom and equality on earth which was a substitute for a lost faith in Heaven.

The two factions were not without common ground. Both emphasized the economic aspect of the coming upheaval. To the first issue of *Forward!* Lavrov contributed an essay in which the American Revolution was contrasted with the Pugachov *jacquerie*—the two events occurred at about the same time—and dismissed as belonging to a dead past, since it had left the social and economic status of the colonies intact. Again, the Lavrovists and the *buntars* shared the conviction that to be at all effective the propagandist, if he belonged to the privileged classes, as was nearly always the case, must completely identify himself with the common people. He must give up his own way of life and adopt the occupation, dress, food, habits, even Kropotkin for one believed, to church-going and keeping the fasts.

Agreement on this point left not a few debatable details. Should an agitator settle in a given community or travel from place to place? Should women be encouraged 'to go to the people'? By and large, the consensus was that a manual skill would be useful to the intellectuals in their new life and might come in handy in exile, too. Besides, working with their hands would help them 'rub off civilization', as the phrase went. Late in the 'sixties a circle was planning to open a shop where its members could learn a trade. Now such establishments had become a reality. Headed by Shishko, a group of students allied with the Chaikovsky Circle set up a locksmiths' shop in the capital. Two separate carpentry shops and a cobblers' shop were functioning in Moscow. In the provinces, too, there were places where one could learn how to handle an axe, a saw, an awl. Sometimes a workshop would serve as a secret meeting-place. Attached to it there might be a 'commune', i.e. a dormitory, with Spartan beds and a few other pieces of furniture.

Even the matter of proper diet for the propagandist was a subject of argument. Should he indulge in meat, which seldom figured in the people's regimen? Many, no doubt, recalled that Rakhmetov, in *What's To Be Done?* by Chernyshevsky, ate oranges in town, but not in the country, since they were not part of the customary fare of the peasantry. And what of personal relations? At least one *narodnik*, of gentle birth, reached the conclusion that it was his duty to marry a peasant woman.

Preparing to 'go to the people', some youths left the university before they received their diplomas. Others tore them up. Kropotkin, in bidding farewell to his scientific career, explained that to have continued his geological studies would have been to take the bread out of the mouths of the people. Those who clung to their books or were sceptical about what a handful of transmogrified students could achieve in the villages were apt to be branded as reprobates. What may be called the populist fixation was at its height. Mikhailovsky cited the case of a revolutionary who reproached a comrade with having spent three years in prison, since he stayed there at the expense of the people. The same author imagined a *narodnik* asking himself, on the eve of being hanged, if he wasn't thereby robbing the people of the birchwood and the labour that had gone to make the gallows.

Narod, the people, their grandeur and their misery, were the object of adulation, the focus of attention. The major famine of 1873-74, which gripped the Volga region, could not but sharpen the sense of compassion and the urge to action. Oh, the joy of becoming one with the masses, of drowning in that great sea! The sentiment was mixed with the urge to set the sea on fire. History itself, as Chaikovsky had put it, had placed upon that generation the responsibility of announcing to the people the truth that would make them free.

CHAPTER X

THE CHILDREN'S CRUSADE

AND now at last people had had enough of doubting and questioning. The time had come to act.

It was the spring of 1874. The ice on the rivers was breaking up and wild geese were flying north. The season itself was a spur. For several weeks there was an exodus from the two capitals and other centres of young people wearing the coarse clothes of the peasantry. On being asked by friends where they were going, they answered simply: '*V narod*' ('To the people'). Here, for the first time in the history of Russian radicalism, was something that approached a mass movement. Hundreds of men and women, perhaps two or three thousand, which is Kropotkin's estimate, were on the march.

They travelled singly or in small groups, often on foot. Strong legs are mentioned as essential to an agitator's equipment. A man would have a few roubles in his pocket or between the double soles of his footgear and a false passport stuck in the cuff of his boot, together with a tobacco pouch. His bundle might hold a map, some pamphlets, a few tools, which he did not always know how to use. He would perhaps have the address of a place where he could spend the night, receive messages, collect mail. In many cases his adopted rôle was that of an itinerant craftsman, but occasionally he would attach himself to a work gang, say of carpenters or stevedores, establish himself as a village shop-keeper or hire himself out as a farmhand, often at the risk of betraying his incompetence. Some joined the migratory workers who streamed south at harvest time.

There were not a few women among the propagandists, and they were models of courage and endurance. Such a one was Catherine Breshkovsky, who had deserted husband and child to head a circle known as 'the Kiev commune' and who eventually became 'the little grandmother of the Russian revolution'. Men and women travelled together on a comradely footing, and sometimes a couple settled in a village as man and wife, though the relation might be nominal.

189

For some the occasion may have been in the nature of a lark. For many the propaganda expedition was also a pilgrimage to the living shrine of the People or a cross between a reconnaissance and a field trip: an attempt to learn at first hand what the masses were like and to get a taste of the life they lived. There were those who felt that they were missionaries of a new gospel and, in fact, not without satisfaction they anticipated martyrdom. One young woman had a fixed idea that a revolutionary was most effective when he *suffered* for the cause. A participant in the movement reports that he saw some propagandists pore over the pages of the New Testament. A wooden cross stood on a shelf in the headquarters of a tiny circle the members of which were the first to 'go to the people'. They dreamed of a new faith that would at once steel the intellectuals with fresh courage and enlist the religious sentiment of the masses on the side of revolution. Lavrov has it that the intention of the agitators was not to accomplish something of practical value, but to perform a *podvig*, a deed of self-abnegation and spiritual merit. At the time, he wrote, Populism resembled a religious sect rather than a political party.

If the 'going to the people' was something of a crusade, it was a children's crusade. Those who participated in it had no clearer idea of what they had to cope with than the followers of the shepherd boy Stephen had had. Their enthusiasm was only exceeded by their ignorance and *naïveté*. The movement was spontaneous and unorganized. In the capital an attempt was made to set up a central directing committee and a common treasury, but within a few weeks these dissolved into thin air. No leadership came from the Chaikovsky Circle. It had been seriously weakened by arrests, and at the outset of the crusade Chaikovsky himself abandoned the cause of revolution, joining a newly founded religious sect that preached non-resistance to evil.[1]

Each of the little local groups acted more or less on its own.

[1] Together with the founder of the sect and a number of his followers, Chaikovsky spent some time in a rural commune established in Kansas by a compatriot who had gone to America back in 1868. He found the experience deeply disappointing, and in 1879 settled in London. Having repatriated himself many years later, he headed the short-lived anti-Soviet Government of Northern Russia, and in 1919 left Archangel for Paris, dying in exile.

The means at their disposal were meagre, wealthy supporters being few and far between. A printing press in Moscow turned out pamphlets and blanks for bogus passports, and here and there quarters were provided which could be used by agitators as hideouts and supply bases. Of course, there were always sympathizers who could be counted on for assistance. On one occasion the niece of the Governor of Moscow enabled Nikolay Morozov to change into peasant clothes in the Governor's mansion.

In good time the authorities reported that they had found evidence of propagandist activity in thirty-seven (out of the forty-nine) provinces. The figure was an exaggerated one, but the agitators undoubtedly wandered over an extensive area. From the two capitals they travelled into the central provinces. The Volga and Don regions were their particular goals: the land of the Razin and Pugachov rebellions, it was held, was bound to be fertile ground for revolutionary propaganda. From Kiev and other southern cities the Ukrainian territory was invaded as far as the Crimea. Half a dozen students, having gained the impression from a book on the prison system that gangs of escaped convicts were roaming the Ural Mountains, went there to organize the fugitives into a revolutionary fighting force.

Several men made the sectarian villages their goal. The notion that the religious dissidents were apt to prove especially susceptible to propaganda against the existing order had originated in Herzen's entourage. In 1862–4 *The Bell* had carried a special supplement intended to win over Old Believers. As a result of his contacts with them, the man chiefly active in this field ended by losing his own faith in revolution.

Siberia and the sections of the country inhabited largely by non-Russians were not visited by the propagandists. What could be expected from people who lacked the collectivist tradition of the Great Russians?

Theoretically, the choice of locale was of no importance, at least to the *buntars*. So much dynamite had accumulated all over the country, they assumed, that an explosion was bound to occur no matter where the match was applied. They intended to foment local revolts. The Lavrovists, on the other hand, planned to prepare the peasants gradually for eventual action. The former wanted to work on people's emotions, the latter would appeal to their intelligence. All that the propagandists of either persuasion did was to hand out the same pamphlets and talk in the same general terms of the ultimate objectives: land to the peasants, mills and factories to the workers, freedom and equality for all.

II

They had started out in the full flush of enthusiasm. At first, in addition to the moral satisfaction of having broken with the ugly past, there was the pleasure of ready camaraderie, the delight of tramping the open road in the soft air of spring, of sleeping under the stars, and the thrill of being mistaken for a genuine man or woman of the people. But as the days wore on, roughing it proved too much for the less sturdy souls, and some turned back.

Those who were able to bear the privations discovered other difficulties. Often there was no work to be had. Babes in the wood found themselves in strange predicaments. Those who had rigged themselves out in the shabbiest clothes, hoping thus to gain the peasants' confidence, discovered that villagers were unwilling to give a night's lodging to such ragged strangers, suspecting them to be thieves. Morozov all but betrayed himself when he sat at table with his peasant hosts. They ate out of a common bowl, and he disgraced himself because he did not know that they took turns in dipping their spoons into the dish. Two 'peasants' travelling together were forced to flee the countryside because Easter had come, and one of them being a Protestant and the other a Moslem, they did not know how to behave.

The most disheartening difficulties presented themselves when the actual business of propaganda was attempted. The pamphlets available for distribution were unsatisfactory. Besides, few villagers were literate. A man might accept a booklet gratefully, but only because it made such fine cigarette papers. The peasants may have been born socialists, but did not behave like them. They definitely plumped for private ownership. Oddly enough, it was the ancients who proved the least unresponsive to socialist, anarchist, egalitarian ideas. The younger men were, as a rule, rugged individualists. One householder, having heard an agitator picture the coming repartition of land, exclaimed: 'Won't that be great when we divide up the land! I'll hire two farmhands and live like a lord!'

The peasants listened to the talk of the new order as to Church sermons or fairytales that did not touch reality. They had apparently given up the belief that the charter of 'the true freedom' was being concealed from them. Yet the hope that there was to be a general redistribution of the land had not died out. Universal military service had been introduced early in the year, and the peasants argued that if all were to serve, all were to have an equal share of the land. It was expected, however, that the initiative would come from the Czar. His prestige was still enormous.

The *artel*, allegedly a germ of Socialism, on closer acquaintance turned out to be little else than a crew of workmen hired by a contractor and exploited by him to the limit. At the end of a day's work the men were too tired to take any interest in the message of revolt. Equally futile were attempts to proselytize the schismatics. Smug and bigoted, they proved even less receptive than the Orthodox folk. The Volga country disappointed all expectations. The peasants there had profited by the emancipation and so were even less susceptible to subversive influences than the rest.

The propagandists who tried to rouse the people to immediate action fared no better than their more moderate comrades. The peasants who agreed that something must be done would say: 'Let someone else start, we shan't lag behind.' Here and there an agitator gifted with personal magnetism and natural tact succeeded in winning the devotion of a group of simple men, so that they were prepared to follow him through thick and thin. But such instances were rare. One man who was working in a smithy roused the workmen to such a pitch of indignation that they were ready to fight. But there were no arms forthcoming, and if there had been, plans for action were wanting. He could only bid them wait, and they had not waited long before their enthusiasm evaporated. The youths who had set out to recruit escaped convicts into a revolutionary army returned after a month's stay in the Urals without having seen a single convict.

The authorities gave currency to the report that the peasants themselves handed the troublemakers over to the police. This was not generally the case. The crusaders were undone by their own carelessness. They conducted copious correspondence in an easily decipherable code and took few precautions of any kind. Spring was hardly over when the police were on their trail. On the last day of May the gendarmes raided a cobblers' shop at Saratov. The place was a receiving station for boxes marked 'lemonade', which contained underground literature in sheets. They came from Moscow, where they were printed on a press owned by one, Ippolit Myshkin, who had put his legitimate establishment at the disposal of the local circle. He seems to have made his first acquaintance with revolutionary ideas while acting as a court stenographer in the Nechayev trial. The sheets were stitched together at the Saratov shop and thence shipped to various points for distribution. Among those arrested at the cobblers' shop was a fifteen-year-old boy, who blabbed. From Saratov the trail led naturally to Moscow and other centres. The police made the most of the clues. In July they were considerably helped by an informer. Before autumn was well under way most of the propagandists were in prison.

III

Looking back on what Kropotkin called 'the mad summer of 1874', one of the crusaders observed that if they had been let alone, with autumn they would have returned to the lecture halls and laboratories in a chastened mood. Another propagandist eventually came to the conclusion that if he and his comrades had been allowed to live among the people a year or two they would have lost their faith in the peasant revolution. But they were not let alone. Arrests spared them the bitterness of disillusionment and robbed them of the lessons of experience.

A few, notably Kravchinsky and Myshkin, escaped the net by crossing the border. Abroad, they prepared themselves for resumption of work among the people. Others managed to elude the police without expatriating themselves. Catherine Breshkovsky was arrested, but not her companion, Yakov Stefanovich, a former seminarist turned medical student. Rogachev was at liberty, towing barges on the Volga, roaming the countryside as a huckster, acting as a Bible reader in a sectarian village. But those who persevered wanted the old enthusiasm. It was, as one man phrased it, 'like building a battery under fire'.

New converts were not entirely lacking, but they came from the intelligentzia. The effect of the crusade had been less to rouse the peasantry than here and there to win over to the cause a member of the educated public. By the following spring a sadly depleted band had re-formed ranks and was prepared to make a second attempt, in the face of grave discouragement.

By then the Chaikovsky Circle was no more. It was replaced by a semblance of an organization known as the Moscow Circle. Its nucleus was a coterie of young women most of whom had studied medicine at the University of Zurich. They had been known as 'the Frietsch girls' because they all lodged with a certain Frau Frietsch. The sorority had included Vera Figner, Sofya Bardina, three Subbotina sisters. A curious figure at its meetings was grey-haired Mme Subbotina, 'mother of the Gracchæ', who shared the radical convictions of her daughters. After the official warning to women students the members of the group scattered, but continued to keep in touch. In the summer of 1874 some of them were staying in Geneva.

The event of the season was a conference of Caucasian separatists. A handful of students, mostly Georgians, opposed secession from Russia on the ground that a concerted effort of all the peoples of the Empire to overthrow the existing order would be of greater benefit to the suppressed national minorities They found kindred spirits in 'the Frietsch girls'. These were now interested in curing the ills of society rather than bodily ailments. Just then news of mass arrests were coming from Russia. The Caucasians discovered that their new friends, like themselves, were troubled by the thought that it was their duty to leave their books, return home and step into the breach. Before the year was out both the young men and the young women were entraining for Russia. Vera Figner alone remained behind to complete her studies.

The Moscow Circle came into being early in 1875 as a result of a merger between some of the former 'Frietsch girls' and the Caucasian students. Mme Subbotina was missing: she had been arrested for propaganda among the peasants and held up officially as a horrible example of the encouragement that the young received from their elders.

The group began as an informal band of like minded people. The fear of centralized control, left by Nechayev, was still potent. But these young people were so ambitious—they aimed at nothing less than a revolutionary society on a national scale—that they had to overcome their distaste for organizational bonds. In February 1875 a constitution was adopted, together with the high-sounding name of the All-Russian Social-Revolutionary Organization. At the time it comprised twenty-one persons. They enjoyed complete equality and were obliged to serve in rotation for one month on the executive committee. A member was required to divest himself of all possessions and personal ties and to become a worker or a peasant, if he was not one already. As the purpose of the Organization was to gather within its fold all existing revolutionary elements, it refrained from formulating a credo, steering a middle course between Bakuninism and Lavrovism. A new feature was a plan to form organized bands, intended, on the one hand, to rouse the people, and, on the other, to *terrorize* the Government and the privileged classes and arrange for the escape of imprisoned comrades. The Circle thus sanctioned the use of force against the old order, but it did so reluctantly. It favoured the employment of persuasion in dealing not only with potential friends, but even with actual enemies, and it insisted that, while the necessities of the struggle forced a revolutionist to cut himself off from the body politic, he remained subject to the dictates of morality. The ghost of Nechayev still had to be laid.

Although the group aimed at carrying propaganda to the peasantry, it began by approaching city workers. Several young women hired themselves out as factory hands. The first to do this was Betty Kaminskaya, daughter of a Jewish merchant, or Maria Krasnova, soldier's wife, according to her forged passport. She was seen off by three comrades in the small hours of an icy January morning. As the frail young thing, huddled in a peasant *sarafan*, disappeared behind the bleak walls of the old paper mill, her escorts felt as though they had accompanied her to her execution. Indeed, Betty, and those who followed her example, had to endure an ordeal. They lived in dismal barracks attached to factories, slept on vermin-infested mattresses, ate wretched food, and slaved for intolerably long hours. The work itself was extremely trying. The young women suffered their martyrdom cheerfully. It did not last long. As they talked to their fellow workers freely and distributed underground pamphlets, within a few weeks they drew suspicion on themselves and had to leave the factories.

The results of the first two months of activity were gratifying. Cells had been formed in a score of large mills and in some small plants. Preparations for the departure of members to various centres on propaganda assignments were under way when, early in April, a third of the membership were arrested at the headquarters of the circle, and this for lack of elementary precautions. Undismayed, the others set out for their respective destinations. They were now more circumspect, but the police had names and addresses, as well as the key to the code they used. By August the All-Russian Social-Revolutionary Organization was wiped out.

IV

The Moscow group, like the Chaikovsky Circle before it, had given attention to city workers chiefly because it hoped that these barely urbanized peasants would carry the socialist message back to the countryside. The first revolutionary organization made up of wage earners and seeking to represent them as a distinct class was formed in Odessa late in 1874. This South Russian Union of Workers owed its existence to the initiative of E. Zaslavsky, a university graduate and a follower of Lavrov, who after 'going to the people' had lost faith in the revolutionary potentialities of the peasantry. 'The liberation of the workers' was the objective and revolution the means of obtaining it. In addition to spreading socialist ideas among factory hands, the Union conducted several strikes. Arrests put an end to its activities a few months after the Moscow Circle had met a similar fate.

The Union, with its proletarian complexion, was an isolated phenomenon. The village continued to hold the centre of the stage. In the spring of 1875, as has been noted, 'going to the people' was resumed. The results were no less disappointing, and the thin ranks of the propagandists continued to be decimated by arrests. Profound disillusionment with peaceful propaganda and a mood of despondency set in. 'Already we are bankrupt,' wrote Kravchinsky to Lavrov in the autumn. 'Life is barely stirring. Soon it will cease altogether.' He attributed this state of affairs to the Fabian policy of his correspondent. 'If persisted in,' he declared, 'the forces of revolution would entirely be wasted, and the burning embers of the intelligentzia extinguished without having kindled the masses. One mutinous act, even if unsuccessful, would achieve more than a decade of indoctrination.' In a subsequent letter he told Lavrov that an overwhelming majority had realized this and had turned away from him.

Indeed, the moderate sector was shrinking. The extremists were strongest in the South. Romantic idealization of the tradition of Cossack insurgency had not died out there. Kiev and Odessa harboured small, close-knit groups of *buntars*. They had given up careers open to university graduates and, in fact, looked askance at intellectuals. Some of them were 'illegals': men and women who were wanted by the police and so had gone underground. They had forged identity papers or none, and lived the lives of the hunted. The status involved such prestige that occasionally an activist who had not been compromised would go illegal just for the glory of it. At this time the secret service was rather lax in the South, and the illegals felt fairly safe.

In the summer of 1875 an Odessa group launched a plan to incite the peasants of the village of Korsun, Kiev province, to expropriate the landlords and offer armed resistance to the authorities. The place was chosen because it had been the scene of a spontaneous rising during the Crimean War. The *obshchina* did not exist in the South and the agitators were not unaware that it was a far cry from dividing the land among individual households to Socialism. But they were willing to let the future take care of itself. Seizure of land, they said to themselves, was a revolutionary act, which might prove the spark to start a larger conflagration. Kiev *buntars* offered a helping hand, and by Lent, 1876, a foothold was secured at Korsun and several other villages, and underground literature was being peddled at country fairs. As only a few of the conspirators proved equal to the task of recruiting villagers for the impending clash with the troops, the others decided to busy themselves collecting funds for weapons, ammunition and horses. Moreover, a fake imperial manifesto urging the peasants to revolt was to be printed.

The hope was to arm ten thousand men. Before long the number was scaled down to one thousand. Actually, enough cash was obtained to buy thirty cheap revolvers. The manifesto did not materialize. The recruiting of prospective insurgents proceeded at a snail's pace. And then came the *coup de grâce*. A participant, on being arrested, turned informer and was released. Up to this time renegades had been left alone. But now the mood had changed. On the night of 11 June, 1876, three men assaulted the traitor in a street in Odessa and left him for dead. But the job was botched, and the man remained alive. He continued to betray his former comrades, and there was nothing left for them to do but to abandon all the settlements. They gathered in Kharkov and then scattered, a disheartened and demoralized lot. Soon thereafter many were arrested.

In one instance the *buntars* did come near starting a popular rising. For some years a number of villages in the Chigirin district, not far from Kiev, had been in a state of turmoil owing to a bitter feud between two groups of peasants. At the time of the emancipation some families managed to secure more land than they were entitled to, and with the years the inequality of holdings had increased. The more prosperous villagers wanted to legalize this state of affairs by signing deeds which would grant them ownership of their present holdings in perpetuity. The less favoured peasants, on the other hand, demanded an equable redistribution of the land according to the number of male souls (*dushi*) in each family, as had been the rule under collective tenure. They came to be known as *dusheviks*. Furthermore, influenced by rumours, some of them began to doubt the legality of the payments they were required to make for their allotments, and the old story about an imperial manifesto, granting the people the entire land, which the gentry and the officials had concealed, took on a new lease of life among them.

If only the Czar himself could be reached! He was sure to be on their side. Delegates went off to the capital with a petition, but they were stopped en route and sent back under guard. One of them escaped arrest and on returning home reported to his fellow villagers that the Czar had admitted inability to help them and enjoined them to seize the land by force and set up *obshchinas* to ensure equality. The peasants did not take this step, but, in the firm belief that they were acting in accordance with the Czar's will, they refused to put their mark on the official deeds and some would not make the customary payments. In May, 1875, troops were called in, and many of the recalcitrants were flogged. Yet nothing could break their spirit. Then about a hundred men were jailed, their allotments auctioned off and their families reduced to beggary.

Learning of the situation in the Chigirin district, the agitators in the Kiev province saw an opening. They recognized that if they claimed to act in the Czar's name, they were bound to be listened to. The use of fraud was distasteful to them, but they overcame their scruples. A group was formed for the purpose of turning the *dusheviks'* passive resistance into an insurrection.

The soul of the enterprise was Yakov Stefanovich, the youth who had accompanied Catherine Breshkovsky on her propaganda tour and who had also played a leading part in the Korsun affair. In the winter of 1875–76 he succeeded in gaining the confidence of some of the *dusheviks* imprisoned in Kiev. As they received no maintenance, they went out to work during the day, returning to jail to sleep. Striking up an acquaintance with these men, he represented himself as a delegate to the Czar from the *dusheviks* in a certain village (which he had visited at great risk), and he overwhelmed the simple souls by offering to intercede before the Czar for their village as well. He promised to be back from the capital in May. In June he sent word that his mission had been successful and that he was returning with important papers. Winter had already set in when Stefanovich faced the peasants. He brought with him two gilt-edged printed documents, the contents of which he communicated to them under a most solemn oath of secrecy.

One was an 'Imperial Manifesto'. Herein the Czar declared that by the *ukase* of 1861 he had given the peasants all the land gratis, but that the gentry had defrauded them of the better part of it. He had finally become convinced, the manifesto went on, that he was powerless to fight the landlords single-handed, since the Heir Apparent was on their side. He therefore ordered his faithful subjects to form secret *druzhinas* (bands) to prepare for an uprising. Once the people had won, land would become as free a possession as water or sunlight, and liberty and happiness would reign.

The other document was the *druzhina* Statutes. They required a member to take a solemn oath of allegiance to the *druzhina*, to arm himself with a pike, and to pay small monthly dues. Treason was punishable by death. A 'band' was to consist of twenty-five men, headed by a *starosta* (elder). These were to elect an *ataman*, who was responsible to a *soviet* (council) of commissars, appointed by the Czar. Stefanovich styled himself 'Commissar Dmytro Naido'. Both the Manifesto and the Statutes bore the Emperor's signature and were provided with a large gold seal, inscribed: 'Seal of the Soviet of Commissars' and showing a pike and an axe crossed. The two documents seem to have been printed in Geneva and reprinted at a secret press in Kiev.

The papers made an immense impression. Doubters were swept off their feet. *Druzhinas* sprang up like mushrooms. On a single night three hundred men, meeting secretly, took the oath. One of them was so overcome by what was happening that he went mad. By the middle of 1877 the membership had reached about one thousand. In spite of the number of people involved, there was not a single case of defection or betrayal, although the *ataman*'s enthusiasm for the cause did not prevent him from embezzling the funds entrusted to him. Finally, when the organization had been in existence nine months and at a time when preparations for the rising had not yet started, the police discovered the conspiracy owing to the indiscretion of a member while under the influence of *horilka* (brandy). Stefanovich and his comrades were apprehended in September, 1877. For months the ringleaders were being hunted down. The last arrest was made in May of the following year.

V

The Bakuninists, with their emphasis on direct action and their feeble interest in theory, wrote and printed little. In 1875 they launched a monthly entitled *Rabotnik* (*Worker*), printed in Geneva. It was the first revolutionary journal addressing itself to Russian proletarians and peasants. During the fifteen months of its existence the paper had an extremely limited circulation and scarcely reached its intended public, few members of which, indeed, were literate.

More people read the bi-weekly *Vperiod!*, which Lavrov launched in addition to the miscellany under the same title. The initial issue, like that of *Rabotnik*, was dated 1 January, 1875. The journal was, in a sense, a sequel to *The Bell*, but did not achieve either its popularity or prestige. The editor, some contributors, and the printers all shared a London flat, forming a kind of lay brotherhood. From the *Forward!* press, as from that of *The Worker*, came propaganda pamphlets both for intellectuals and the masses. The pieces for the latter were like those that the Chaikovsky Circle had produced. In one of them the devil, intent on plaguing mankind, invents the priest, the noble, and the merchant.

The bi-weekly recorded the revolutionary struggle at home and had much to say about the international socialist and labour movement, even reporting strikes in New York and Chicago. Occasionally it printed verse, such as 'The New Song', from the pen of Lavrov himself, which eventually became the Russian Marseillaise. It opens with a call to spurn the old world, and the refrain to its five octaves summons the worker to rise against his enemies. The last stanza predicts that after the struggle is over, the sun of justice and brotherhood will rise, blood will have bought the happiness of children, falsehood and evil will have been banished forever, and the nations will be as one 'in the free realm of holy labour'.

Considerable space was given to theoretical discussion. It was directed against Bakuninism with its assumption of Russia's readiness for revolution, its reliance on blind action, its appeal to elemental passions. In the West the future of Socialism was bound up with the evolution of capitalism and the political activity of the industrial proletariat, but in Russia, Lavrov held, Socialism was a movement of ideas deriving much of its authority from ethical imperatives. He did not blink the fact that the eventual overturn, of necessity a social cataclysm, meant war with all its horrors, but he insisted that the conflict must be carried on within the bounds of revolutionary morality, the heart of which was justice and love of humanity. His belief in the efficacy of peaceful indoctrination was unshaken. In the issue of the journal dated 1 June, 1876, this trained mathematician presented a piece of computation whereby he arrived at the conclusion that within six years one hundred propagandists could secure 35,950 converts. Even a third of this number, he argued, would constitute a formidable revolutionary army.

He wanted it to be an army of workers and peasants. The intellectuals must take the initiative, but Lavrov fervently hoped that when the hour of decision struck, leadership would be in the hands of the people. *Forward!* firmly opposed the idea of a small band of conspirators seizing political power and decreeing the new order into existence. With an insight of which he was rarely capable he pictured the result of the dictatorship of a revolutionary minority. The abolition of private property by such a régime, he wrote, would be only nominal. Actually the capital owned by the propertied classes would pass into the hands of 'a gang of ten thousand acting under the red flag of the social revolution'. On the morrow of the *coup* a struggle for power would begin, with disastrous effects. An overturn carried out by the masses before they had received a sufficient amount of socialist enlightenment, or by a dictatorial minority, would only lead, he concluded, to an exchange of one set of exploiters for another.

These shafts were aimed at the few Russian disciples of Auguste Blanqui who enlivened the radical scene. Back in 1873 Zürich held, in addition to Lavrovists and Bakuninists, a tiny group of Blanquists, also known as Jacobins, who were committed to a programme of dictatorship by a revolutionary minority. The cell, which Nechayev may have helped to form, found an articulate leader in the person of his former associate, Pyotr Tkachev. Having served his prison term and been deported to a provincial town, he had escaped abroad with the aid of members of the Chaikovsky Circle, who had hoped that he would contribute to *Forward!*. From the first, however, he and Lavrov found themselves at odds, and in the spring of 1874 he issued a pamphlet in which he savagely attacked the editor as, horrible to say, a preacher of peaceful progress, a man who unwittingly played into the hands of the police. Delaying the revolution might prove fatal, he argued. For while in the West the growth of capitalism brought the hour of the triumph of Socialism nearer, in Russia it had the opposite effect. Hence, it was now or never.

In his reply Lavrov denounced his critic as an irresponsible demagogue who did not realize how disastrous a revolution without the participation of the people would be. Friedrich Engels took up the cudgels for Lavrov and drew a vitriolic retort from Tkachev, to the effect that Russia was closer to the social revolution than the West: if she had no proletariat, neither did she have a bourgeoisie, and the people were communist by tradition and revolutionary by instinct. (He was echoing Bakunin.) Engels dismissed these remarks as puerile, but conceded that the Russian revolution was on the way and could only be retarded by a successful war or a premature uprising. There the debate rested.

By the end of 1875 Tkachev had acquired a medium for spreading his ideas: *Nabat* (Tocsin), a journal sponsored by a group of Russian and Polish Blanquists and printed in Geneva. In the leading article of the opening issue he again attacked Lavrovism, pointing out the dangers of procrastination and calling for immediate action. The revolutionary cohort, he insisted, must be ready to risk defeat, in the conviction that severe discipline, centralized command, swift action, utter intransigeance would assure it victory. 'The preparation of a revolution is not the work of revolutionaries', he wrote. 'That is the work of exploiters, capitalists, landowners, priests, police, officials, conservatives, liberals, progressives, and the like. Revolutionaries do not prepare, they *make* a revolution'. They were of necessity a minority, Tkachev went on. For only the few were morally and intellectually advanced enough to cherish the ideal which is the final goal of progress: absolute, 'organic', as he put it, equality, the foundation of the society of the future. This superiority entitled them to material power. The transformation of moral into material power was indeed 'the essence of every true revolution'. Since power is concentrated in the state, the *élite*, a close-knit fighting body, must take possession of it, not to destroy it, as Bakunin's followers demanded, but to use it in the interest of the cause.

Tkachev's conception of the revolution was not entirely dictatorial. The new government, he held, must *persuade* the people to accept its policies, propaganda following, not preceding the overturn. Furthermore, he had it that once the citizenry had been re-educated and the socialist order firmly established, the State would lose its *raison d'être* and wither away. He conceded that the conquest of power could not be achieved without popular support. But he saw the Russian masses as a purely destructive force, and the belief that, left to themselves, they could bring about their own liberation was to his thinking a dangerous delusion. History, he maintained, had placed the task of organizing the revolution, initiating it and directing its course upon the shoulders of the moral and intellectual *élite*.

Variations on this authoritarian, anti-democratic theme dominate the pages of *Tocsin*. The Lavrovists and Bakuninists alike abhorred Tkachev's doctrine as a scheme to impose the new order on the people by force, to drag them into the millennium by the scruff of their necks, as it were. What, they asked, would keep the socialist dictators from abusing their authority? The *Nabat* programme was, in Kravchinsky's words, nothing but vileness and *political* revolution. The fact that Tkachev remained abroad in safety, while urging others to risk their lives, did not go unnoticed. In any case, the circulation of his paper was extremely limited, and his followers both at home and abroad were a negligible splinter group. His seemed a lost cause. Before many years passed, however, his programme won adherents, and eventually it was to be carried out, with what results the world now witnesses. Writing in 1902, Lenin said that the attempt to seize power, *prepared by what Tkachev had preached* —he had in mind the effort of the People's Will—was 'majestic'.

VI

By the beginning of 1875, 770 propagandists (612 men and 158 women) had been ordered to be arrested, 717 had actually been seized and 267 of them remained in custody. The number of converts to revolution made at this cost was estimated at twenty to thirty. Between the middle of 1873 and the end of 1876, 1,611 political suspects eighty-five per cent of them men, were questioned; 557 of them were dismissed for lack of evidence, 450 were placed under police surveillance, 79 were deported to distant parts of the Empire and 525 were held for court trial. The majority of these, the more serious offenders, were under twenty-five years old and one out of four was a minor. More than half belonged to the privileged, though not necessarily well-to-do, classes and fully half were high school and university students. The official investigator reported that students of medicine and the natural sciences were the most hardened criminals, and the 46 women awaiting trial were more fanatical than the men.

The majority of the defendants were not allowed to face their judges until 1877. Two mass trials were staged in the capital before a special session of the Senate.

The first, known as the Trial of the Fifty, and involving former members of the Moscow Circle, was held in March and lasted three weeks. The public was admitted in limited numbers, and sympathizers eager to gain admission went so far as to print counterfeit tickets. The defendants were charged with having formed an illegal association aimed to overthrow the existing order and with dissemination of printed matter inciting to revolt. During the proceedings they behaved with a courage and dignity which won general admiration. The presence in the dock of attractive and obviously high-minded young women was particularly affecting. The prisoners boldly asserted their convictions. In fact, at the conclusion of the trial, when, in accordance with accepted procedure, they addressed the court, they turned the dock into a rostrum.

Sofya Bardina was the first to speak. In a low, soft voice she denied the intention of undermining the foundations of property, family, religion, and the State. She and her comrades, she said, merely defended the worker's right to the full product of his labour. As for religion, she personally 'had always been true to its spirit and essential principles in the pure form in which they were preached by the founder of Christianity'. And neither she nor her co-defendants wanted to destroy the State. They were peaceful propagandists working for universal happiness and equality.

The next defendant to speak was a tall, lean workman in a loose peasant blouse belted with a narrow strap. This was Pyotr Alexeyev, a weaver, who had been won over by Sofya Perovskaya and had joined the Moscow Circle. In vehement tones he pictured the intolerable lot of the wage-earner, concluding that the working people must depend on themselves and expect no help except from the student youth. 'They alone will be our inseparable comrades until the moment when millions of working people raise their muscular arms . . .' Here the presiding Senator made an attempt to stop the speaker, but he went on: 'and the yoke of despotism, protected by soldiers' bayonets, will be pounded to dust.' Both speeches, which had been carefully edited and rehearsed, were excised from the court records, but they were printed secretly and became revolutionary classics.

Prison terms, Siberian exile, hard labour were the lot of the condemned. The severity of the sentences intensified public sympathy for them. Money and other gifts poured in, and, as one of the Subbotina sisters put it, the women held 'a salon' in jail, receiving a number of titled ladies. Poems were written to the prisoners, and a dirge composed three years earlier by the now dying Nekrasov was circulated, with the report that he had composed it on his sick-bed as a lament for the condemned.

The cases were appealed, and the sentences rendered less onerous. Before the prisoners separated to go to their various places of confinement, each received a crucifix, the only personal possession a convict was allowed. It was inscribed on the reverse side with the initials of the Russian Social-Revolutionary Association. All that remained to many of them was an obscure martyrdom. Shortly after leaving prison, Alexeyev was murdered by Yakut robbers, whose crime might have gone undiscovered if they had not made a song about their exploit. Sofya Bardina, after some years in Siberia, escaped abroad, where, in 1883, at the age of thirty, she took her own life. It is said that one of the things that drove her to suicide was her inability to stomach the terrorist phase of the revolutionary movement.

A few weeks after the Trial of the Fifty, members of the South-Russian Workers' Union faced the court. Then came the Great Trial, which lasted from 18 October, 1877, to 23 January, 1878. The case of Revolutionary Propaganda in the Empire, as it was officially called, involved many of those who 'had gone to the people'. The preliminary inquiry had dragged on for some four years. It has been estimated that 3,800 persons, including witnesses, were drawn into this mass trial. Scores died of disease in prison, committed suicide or went mad there. After indictment, a few escaped. Only 198 were finally brought to the capital from the various parts of the country, to be tried by a special tribunal. In the course of the trial, death further reduced the number of defendants to 193. Some of them had but a remote connexion with the revolutionary movement, and indeed, there were those who were initiated into it by being dragged into the case. As one historian put it, the trial was a conference of activists arranged by and at the expense of the government. What was in fact the result of the unco-ordinated efforts of separate groups was presented by the prosecution as the concerted action of a single secret society, and this in spite of the fact that the authorities had a clear picture of the actual situation.

Nominally the proceedings were public, but the courtroom was only large enough to hold the judges, the prisoners, and their counsel. The defendants protested. Thereupon the prisoners were divided into groups, each of which was to be tried separately. Since they were being tried as a body, many objected to this arrangement and decided to sabotage the proceedings. They had to be dragged before the judges by main force and then they refused to answer questions. They delegated one of their number, however, to speak for them. This was Ippolit Myshkin, accused, with three others, of having organized the Society. In the courtroom, the four occupied a raised, railed-off platform which the defendants called Golgotha.

Against a barrage of interruptions from Senator Karl Peters, the presiding judge, Myshkin delivered a vigorous declaration of his and his comrades' convictions, which they had composed jointly. Acknowledging himself a member of the Social-Revolutionary Party, by which he merely meant a company of like-minded men and women, he said that their aim was to establish a free union of autonomous communes. It would come about through a popular rising against an intolerable system.

The climax of the speech came when Myshkin, prevented from relating the tortures to which he had been subjected in prison, cried out that this was no trial, but 'a farce, indeed something worse', and, in defiance of Senator Peters' orders to remove him, went on to declare that the Senators were prostituting themselves by selling 'everything dear to humanity for promotion and fat salaries'. The courtroom was in an uproar. Women became hysterical; some fainted. The judges, appalled, filed out, Senator Peters forgetting to declare the court adjourned.

Nearly half of the defendants, Sofya Perovskaya among them, were acquitted. The others received sentences varying from five days in prison to ten years of hard labour. Furthermore, the court petitioned the Emperor to free sixty-two of those found guilty, in consideration of the fact that they had served their term during preliminary detention, and to reduce the penalties of the others, except Myshkin. Contrary to custom, the court's petition was not granted, and it was said that the penalties were indeed increased in a dozen cases.

Two days after the verdict had been handed down in its final form, a group of the condemned signed a statement which was, in effect, a last testament. It was subsequently printed abroad and smuggled into Russia. The signatories reaffirmed their allegiance to the 'Popular-Revolutionary Party', and urged the comrades who remained behind to carry on the fight against a system which was the misfortune and shame of Russia.

The greater number of those acquitted were deported to distant parts of the empire by administrative order. Myshkin was executed in 1885 for attacking a prison warden.

The revolutionaries used the public trials as a forum from which they proclaimed the high motives that prompted their actions. In this way they added considerably to the moral capital accumulated by the cause and ultimately bequeathed to wastrel heirs. The government had hoped to arouse public opinion against the rebels. The opposite effect was produced. As a result, during the life of the old régime political cases received a minimum of official publicity.

CHAPTER XI

LAND AND LIBERTY

NEITHER the Lavrovists nor the *buntars* had anything to show for their pains. As the year 1876 wore on, the mood of disillusionment and discontent deepened. When autumn came, the activists still at liberty gathered in the capital and other centres as if by prearrangement. People who had been in various sections of the country had an opportunity to mingle and compare notes. It was plain that, as Kravchinsky put it, socialist propaganda was making no more impression on the masses than a beanshooter would on a stone wall. Why had they failed to win the ear of the peasant? Had their message been too remote for his needs? Was there something basically wrong with their whole outlook? Both factions, as well as Tkachev's followers, agreed that the lack of co-ordination and centralization was a source of great weakness. What could be achieved, it was asked, by scattered handfuls of people, without a general staff, without a plan of concerted action? Each group, indeed, each individual had carried on independently, but was so linked with others that the mistakes of one endangered many. The slogan of the moment became: 'Let us organize!'

Out of this searching of souls came a revision of the programme and tactics of the movement. Out of it came also an attempt to bring the dispersed forces together in a secret society conceived on a national scale. For some time Mark Natanson, founder of the Chaikovsky Circle, had been applying his uncommon organizing abilities to that end. Having served his term of forced residence in a provincial town, he came back to the capital late in 1875 and immediately set to work. To establish connexions and gain recruits he visited the radical centres at home and travelled abroad, conferring with Lavrov in London and persuading several expatriates to return to Russia. His efforts led to the formation, in 1876, of the first fairly substantial revolutionary organization on Russian soil: the Society of Land and Liberty. Sometimes this league and those that succeeded it were spoken of as the Social-Revolutionary Party. In careful usage, however, that high-sounding phrase designated merely those who sympathized with the radical ideology. The Party, in this sense of the word, formed the loose medium within which associations of fully committed militants functioned. The name, Land and Liberty, it will be recalled, has already figured in these pages as that of a secret society which had a shadowy existence in the early 'sixties.

In June, 1877, arrest put a period to Natanson's activities. His wife stepped into the breach, but she, too, soon found herself behind bars. This was not an irreparable loss, for the society included several other able and zealous organizers. One of them was a former engineering student, Alexander Mikhailov, of whom more later. Another was Aron Zundelevich, who accomplished miracles as a smuggler of men and literature, and so was known as the society's Foreign Office. The membership's ranks were swelled by the prisoners released after the Great Trial. For a while they had formed a separate circle, headed by Sofya Perovskaya. Before long, however, she herself and most of her following were within the fold of Land and Liberty. Certain individuals and groups, particularly in the South, retained their distaste for the discipline that goes with organizational ties and preferred to remain unaffiliated, but they were under the influence of the Society and occasionally worked with it. In fact, its statutes provided for 'separatist' members who joined the Society on a contractual basis for the execution of a definite task and were otherwise free from any obligation to the Party.

At the outset Land and Liberty formulated its platform. 'We narrow down our demands,' this began, 'to those that can be realized in the near future, that is, to the demands and desires of the people.' The first and foremost of these was that the entire land be turned over to the peasants and distributed equally among them. 'We are convinced,' a parenthesis followed, 'that two thirds of the land will be held communally.' Another plank in the platform had to do with centralized State authority. The statement, as revised in April, 1878, opened thus: 'Our ultimate political and economic ideal is anarchy and collectivism.' The membership, however, was far from unanimous in favouring the abolition of the State. There were those who were content to leave it to the people to determine the political structure of the future society. Some were even prepared to retain the monarchy, if the citizenry so desired. The people were trusted to do right, or rather, it was assumed that right resulted from the exercise of their will.

The Society's objective, it was stated, could only be secured by means of a violent overturn. Herzen's ambivalent attitude toward the use of force had been overcome. The revolution must be carried out by the masses. Nothing should be forced upon them, or done behind their backs. All the Party could do was to offer the initial impetus and some guidance. And speed was of the essence of the matter. The growth of capitalist economy, sedulously fostered by the Government, was undermining the *obshchina* and perverting the people's ideas about land ownership and the ordering of society.

Populism now lost much of its vagueness. The loose ideological complex had become the credo of an organized revolutionary body. In the process the centre of gravity shifted from Socialism to the demands and beliefs of the people. 'Realizing the impossibility, under present conditions, of inculcating in the masses other and, from an abstract viewpoint, perhaps nobler ideals, we have resolved to write on our banner the historic formula. "Land and Liberty!" ' Thus the revised platform of the Society. It was a deviation from what Herzen, Chernyshevsky, Bakunin, and Lavrov had taught, a deviation made at the end of a road strewn with disappointments. Those who were uneasy about the compromise had a ready poultice for their consciences. Since the Russians were inherent collectivists, they said to themselves, the satisfaction of the people's aspirations must inevitably lead to Socialism. Some felt that the Society's programme was simply the Russian variant of the foreign doctrine that Socialism was. Kravchinsky, who had joined Land and Liberty in the summer of 1878, wrote shortly afterwards: 'Five years ago we cast off German [i.e. European] clothes and put on homespun *kaftans* in the hope that the people would admit us into their midst. Now we see that it is not enough—the time has come to strip the German clothes off Socialism itself and dress it, too, in homespun.' Whether or not these populists felt that they were making a concession to the force of circumstance, they believed that they were being wonderfully practical, indeed, that they were playing the game of *Realpolitik*.

Their programme met with some criticism. In a journal issued at Geneva by a group of Bakuninists, a dissenter warned against throwing Socialism overboard and acting in the name of popular ideals. For one thing, the liberty the masses desired was vague enough to admit of worship of the Czar. As for communal land ownership, it could easily bolster a state more conservative than any in existence. Did not the reactionaries themselves prize the *obshchina* as an insurance against social upheaval? And even if it were possible to effect an agrarian revolution, what of the growing proletariat in the cities? The working men, who were without a collectivist tradition, might well wreck the whole enterprise.

Land and Liberty could get little aid or comfort from the Lavrovists. Numerically they had always been weak, and they were rapidly losing ground. In December, 1876, delegates from the several circles met in Paris. This was the first, and the last, Lavrovist conference. In the course of it Lavrov resigned his editorship of *Vperiod!* The relations between him and his flock had become strained for reasons not only ideological but personal as well. His predicament was not unlike what Herzen's had been a decade earlier. Furthermore, the financial support received by the review had become irregular, and its staff was reduced to semi-starvation.

Thus, by the end of 1876 the faction was without a leader and without an organ. The miscellany bearing the title *Forward!* managed to come out once more, in 1877, but the bi-weekly folded up. Lavrov withdrew temporarily into private life. A few of his former disciples continued to spread Socialism among factory hands and called themselves Marxists. Others argued that the work of organizing the proletariat could not begin until the liberals had obtained political freedom for the people. In the meantime they confined themselves to peaceful activities of a cultural nature. According to Lavrov himself, by 1878 the group lowered its flag and ceased to exist.

It was the Bakuninist faction that lived on in the Society of Land and Liberty. The revolutionary populists were *buntars* who had come to see things in a less unreal light and who, moreover, showed less resistance to organizational discipline.

II

According to the statutes of the Society, it consisted of regional and functional groups, with a Centre or Basic Circle, situated in the capital. This was in effect a close-knit body of professional revolutionists. Completely dedicated men and women, they could own no property and were subject to the control of the organization in personal matters, but they were not required to adopt the people's mode of living. They elected a small executive committee and were supposed to meet in plenary session from time to time. The Centre imposed a certain amount of discipline on the subsidiary groups, but left them a large measure of autonomy. Their activity was confined to a definite area or to a special type of work, and the demands made on the members were, apparently, not exacting. There was considerable opposition to tightening the organizational ties. One gets the impression that not a few of the provisions of the statutes remained on paper.

No more than a score of activists made up the Centre. The rest of the membership, including 'the separatists' mentioned above and fellow travellers, probably never exceeded two hundred. This handful comprised nearly all the most earnest and energetic spirits that the revolutionary cause could muster at the time.

Attached to the Centre was an establishment for the forging of identity papers, which was called, with an unwonted attempt at humour, the Heavenly Chancery. There was also a clandestine press. This was a precious possession, a symbol of power, at once a rallying ground and a sanctum. Kravchinsky recalled that he entered the dingy flat where it was installed 'with the sense of awe experienced by the faithful crossing the threshold of a temple'. The establishment was presided over by middle-aged, near-sighted Maria Krylova, nicknamed 'Mother of God'. She and her assistants led a life of voluntary imprisonment in the quarters which housed the shop. The fewest persons were permitted to enter the premises, in order to bring supplies and take away the printed matter. The press managed to carry on for four years under the very noses of the gendarmes. From it came an account of the Great Trial, some two score leaflets and pamphlets, as well as the Society's two organs. Some of the issues of the latter ran to three thousand copies. The Party no longer depended on the émigrés for underground literature.

The revolutionaries were acquiring mastery of some of the elements of conspiratorial technique. They had learned certain tricks to throw off undercover men. For meetings they maintained special quarters, which were also used as hide-outs and communication posts. Such a *kvartira* was usually a modest flat rented by an actually or nominally married couple who kept a 'maid'. Hers was the most difficult part, for she had to deal with the other servants in the house, the porter and the tradespeople. Every effort was made not to arouse the suspicion of the neighbours. Care was taken to choose a lodging with windows facing the street or courtyard. A signal in one of them was a warning.

Counter-espionage was carried on for the Society by a member who was a Government clerk. At Mikhailov's suggestion, this Nikolay Kletochnikov entered the service of the Third Division and, having access to the secret files, kept the organization informed of the activities of the police.

Contributions from sympathizers formed a considerable part of the Society's income. Another source was the sale of publications. Twelve hundred copies of the first issue of *Land and Liberty* were sold on the day of its appearance. Of course, the Party had at its disposal the property of the members of the Centre. Among them was 'the millionaire', also known as 'the saint of the revolution', Dmitry Lizogub,[1] who had inherited a fortune worth 150,000 to 180,000 roubles and who wished nothing better than to devote all he had to the cause. But before his possessions could be turned into ready cash he was arrested, and in the end the Society got only a sum estimated between a few hundred and a few thousand roubles. The recently published expense account of Land and Liberty shows that during the last ten months of its existence the total outlay amounted to 5,964 roubles and 95 kopecks.

The act by which Land and Liberty first drew public attention to itself was a meeting on 6 December, 1876, in front of the Kazan Cathedral in Petersburg. This was the first open revolutionary demonstration to take place in Russia. Three or four hundred participants, mainly students, gathered in the cathedral,

[1] Under a transparent pseudonym he figures in Tolstoy's story, 'Human and Divine,' as a revolutionary whose heart is open to the message of Christ.

where they ordered a prayer for the health of 'God's slave' Nikolay, meaning Chernyshevsky, and others, all martyrs to the people's cause. When the crowd emerged from the cathedral, an impromptu speech was made by a fiery young student, one Georgy Plekhanov, whose name was to become inextricably linked with the history of Russian Socialism. He excoriated the Government for rotting the country's best sons in prison. Thereupon a peasant lad, waving a red banner on which the words 'Land and Liberty' were embroidered in white silk, was hoisted on the shoulders of the crowd. A girl with flowing hair cried 'Forward!' and the demonstrators, swelled by the curious, moved down the Nevsky, shouting: 'Long live Land and Liberty! Long live the people! Death to the czars!' A few minutes later the procession was broken up by policemen, plain-clothes men and hoodlums. Some of the marchers were severely beaten. Over thirty men and women were seized, a few of them innocent bystanders and none of them members of the Society. They were given a speedy trial and received heavy penalties.

It appears that the demonstration had originally been planned by a group of workmen as a protest against the hardships of their lot, but that the students had taken it over, much to the disgust of the factory hands. The 'seventies were a period of rapid industrial expansion, and, what with the shameless exploitation that prevailed, there was considerable labour unrest. The decade was marked by sixty-six strikes in Petersburg alone. The Society did not fail to take advantage of the situation. It had a hand in several of the strikes that occurred in the capital. A leaflet that it printed was composed by the strikers themselves and entitled: *The Voice of the People Housed By and Working For the Rascal Maxel* (Maxwell, a manufacturer of British extraction). The populists no longer sought to convert factory workers in order to provide agitators for the villages. It was beginning to be realized that the wage-earners, though a product of the evil bourgeois order, had great revolutionary potentialities and could become a valuable ally of their rural fellow workers.

Already at this time there existed in the capital the nucleus of a revolutionary organization of a purely proletarian complexion: The Northern Union of Russian Workers. An offshoot of a workmen's circle, it came into being late in 1878 and was headed by two men of the people. The metal workers, who made up most of the membership—this amounted to some two hundred men—were a refractory lot. They were rather antagon-istic to their mentors, the students, resenting particularly the factional strife to which these intellectuals were addicted. The Union lasted only a year. Two secret service agents, a married couple, found their way into it, and as a result the police were able to crush it. A remnant of the organization managed to start the first Russian underground paper written for and by city workers. The proof sheets of the initial, and last, issue of *Rabochaya zarya* (Workers' Dawn) were seized, together with the Union's press, in March, 1880.

Work among various sections of the population was conducted by special groups. A futile attempt was made to win over religious sectarians. The notion that they were particularly accessible to revolutionary propaganda had a strong hold on the radicals. Apparently nothing was done to enlist highway robbers, described in the statutes as a promising social category. Much attention was given to the student body. This was in a constant state of unrest. The Society had a hand in the disturbances which occurred in the universities in 1878. A member composed the petition requesting the right to form corporate organizations, which the students of the Medico-Surgical Institute in the capital handed to the Heir Apparent. The disorders resulted only in arrests and deportations.

The peasants continued to be the main object of concern. As few propagandists were available, it was decided to confine activities to the section of the Volga region extending from Nizhny-Novgorod (now Gorky) to Astrakhan, as a land where the tradition of rebellion was believed to be still alive. Flying propaganda tours were now no longer in order. The agitators were to live among the peasants and become 'citizens' of the locality where they were settled. It was not essential that they should disguise themselves as men or women of the people. They might choose an occupation that befitted an educated person. Once they had gained the confidence of the people, they were to take advantage of their position to stimulate in the villagers a sense of dignity and solidarity, to bolster up the prestige of the *mir*, to teach them how to protect their interests in the day-to-day struggle against landowners and officials. This was called 'propaganda by facts'. The settlers were also to seek out malcontents and born leaders, and form fighting units in preparation for local risings which were to be a prelude to a general overturn. The idea of using fraudulently the people's faith in the Czar for purposes of agitation was broached but resolutely rejected. The Chigirin affair was generally frowned upon. It had been carried out by men outside the ranks of Land and Liberty.

Ambitious plans were made: the agitators in each province were to be directed by a 'centre' in the provincial capital, and all the threads were to converge in the Basic Circle. Actually no more than a score of men and women established themselves in several villages. They did not stay there very long. Some found their humdrum tasks uncongenial; others had to leave their posts because they were compromised by the arrest of a comrade or because the hostility of the local powers proved too much for them. Vera Figner's was a case in point. It will be recalled that she had remained in Switzerland, when the rest of 'the Frietsch girls' left, to complete her medical course. But in response to Natanson's call she had returned home a few months before graduation. Now a member of Land and Liberty, she settled as a nurse in a Samara (now Kuibyshev) village. Overwhelmed by the poverty and squalor in which the villagers lived, she was too busy with her hordes of patients to think of anything but the immediate task. 'As far as propaganda was concerned,' she wrote in her memoirs, 'I didn't even open my mouth.' In the midst of her absorbing work she had to disappear because a letter involving her was found on an arrested comrade.

By the end of 1879 there wasn't a single clandestine rural cell in existence. Populism had suffered another defeat.

III

Aside from propaganda, which fell under the head of 'organization', the Society's statutes called for disorganizing activities. These included the liberation of prisoners. On 11 August, 1876, even before Land and Liberty had come into being, several of Kropotkin's comrades contrived his escape from a prison hospital located on the outskirts of the capital. Smuggled out of Russia, he remained an émigré until in his old age the Revolution enabled him to repatriate himself. He died in 1921, a staunch opponent of the Soviet régime. After the conclusion of the Great Trial a futile attempt was made to free Myshkin. The escape of Stefanovich and two of his comrades from a Kiev jail was engineered, in May 1878, by Frolenko, who had hired himself out as a prison guard and came to be entrusted with the keys to the cells.

Doing away with informers was another 'disorganizing' practice. An unsuccessful attempt to kill one was made in June, 1876. The same year a spy was killed. The following year a renegade turned informer was dispatched. The youthful idealists were developing a cold cruelty. By its high-handed and often brutal treatment of propagandists, the Government was 'turning flies into hornets,' as one of them phrased it. They took to carrying concealed firearms, and sometimes these went off. In 1878 and 1879 there were several cases of armed resistance to arrest.

Under the heading of 'disorganization' the statutes prescribed 'systematic destruction of the most harmful or prominent members of the Government, and in general of people who are the mainstay of the political and social order we hate'. There was nothing systematic about this terrorism. It began as spontaneous acts of self-defence and revenge.

The first official thus attacked was General Trepov, Chief of Police in the capital. On 25 July, 1877, he visited the House of Preliminary Detention, where political prisoners were held pending trial or transfer to another jail. Annoyed by the behaviour of a certain Bogolubov, who had just been condemned to fifteen years of hard labour for demonstrating before the Kazan Cathedral, he ordered him flogged. Although Trepov's order was illegal, it was carried out with the approval of the Minister of Justice. Bogolubov's comrades in prison were roused to a frenzy of protest. When the news leaked out, indignation in radical circles knew no bounds. Several men came from the South, bent on vengeance. They were forestalled by Vera Zasulich, the young woman first mentioned in connexion with Nechayev's exploits.

Because of a letter received from him, she had been imprisoned for two years, then deported, and afterwards, while she was in Kharkov studying to be a midwife, kept under police surveillance.

Eventually she fell in with a group of *buntars*. Since the spring of 1877 she had been in the capital, working as a typesetter on the press of Land and Liberty. When she heard of the outrage committed against Bogolubov, who was a complete stranger to her, she inquired if the Society was planning any action against Trepov, and received an evasive answer. Time was passing, and nothing was being done. She decided to take matters into her own hands.

She was staying with another girl, and the two made up their minds that on the same day they would attempt to assassinate both Trepov and the prosecutor in the Great Trial, which was then drawing to a close. They postponed action until the verdict was handed down, so as not to influence it adversely. Vera Zasulich described her state as neither life nor death, but she was completely self-possessed. The trial came to an end on 23 January, 1878, and the following morning she called on the Chief of Police while he was receiving petitioners and fired a shot at him point-blank, inflicting a grave, though not fatal, wound. To avoid injuring anyone else, she promptly dropped the revolver and gave herself up. Her comrade failed to get her man: he happened not to receive visitors when she called at his office.

Curiously enough, the would-be assassin was held to be not a political, but a common criminal. And so the case was tried publicly by a jury. There was no doubt in anyone's mind as to the verdict. It happened that the counsel for the defence, unlike the prosecutor, was a brilliant lawyer and the presiding judge a man of liberal sympathies. During the proceedings there were moments when it seemed that Trepov, not the assailant, was on trial. Nevertheless, the verdict of not guilty brought in by the jury on 31 March came as a complete surprise to the prisoner, while delighting a large segment of the public, including some highly stationed functionaries.

Vera Zasulich became the heroine of the hour, admired even in the salons, though there was some disappointment at her being a dowdy girl with somewhat Mongoloid features, past her first youth, who had the unpleasant habit of shouting like one deaf when she forgot herself. 'Glory to the Russian nation that has produced a woman capable of such a deed!' wrote Plekhanov in a special leaflet issued by Land and Liberty. Another underground sheet declared her acquittal to be the beginning of a new era. According to the *Revue des Deux Mondes*, for forty-eight hours Europe forgot everything to talk only of the new Judith, the Muscovite Charlotte Corday. There were sanguine spirits who saw the jury's amazing verdict as the fall of the Russian Bastille.

The Bastille stood firm. An hour or two after the court was emptied, the Czar issued an order for the girl's rearrest. The word was late in reaching the prison, to which she had returned to fetch her belongings, and she emerged from the gates unmolested, to be greeted by an enthusiastic crowd and borne down the street. Police and gendarmes soon appeared on the scene. They placed her in a carriage and attempted to disperse the assemblage. A scuffle ensued, in the course of which several shots rang out, and when it was over, there remained on the spot the body of a nineteen-year-old boy. Land and Liberty blamed the gendarmes for his death. Vera Zasulich believed that he had committed suicide. If so, he acted either in a state of hysterical exaltation or in an effort to distract the attention of the police from their quarry. As a matter of fact, in the confusion the girl was whisked off, and a few days later escaped abroad, settling in Geneva, where Henri Rochefort, the Communard, found a room for her.

In one sense her shot did open a new era: it initiated a series of acts of violence on the part of the revolutionaries. In February a spy was killed and an attempt was made on the life of the assistant public prosecutor in Kiev. In May the Chief of the Gendarmerie in the same city was assassinated. The Government was not intimidated. Political prisoners continued to be mistreated, and on 2 August there was an execution in Odessa of a revolutionary who in resisting arrest wounded some of his captors. Two days later Kravchinsky, who had returned from abroad to edit the organ of Land and Liberty, stabbed to death General Mezentzev, the head of the Third Division, in broad daylight in the very heart of the capital. He had attacked his victim as he did on the chivalrous theory that only a hired murderer struck from behind, and he escaped in a carriage drawn by the very racehorse that had carried Kropotkin to liberty. The effect of this terrorist act was stunning. It was as if the city woke up that morning, the assassin wrote, to find 'that the ground under it was mined'. Years afterwards a comrade of Kravchinsky remarked that in view of the utter inefficiency of the police under Mezentzev, every effort should have been made to protect the man.

The Government's reply to this assassination was a *ukase* handing over all political offences involving the use of force to military courts. This proved no deterrent. In February, 1879, Prince Dmitry Kropotkin, cousin of the anarchist and himself Governor-General of Kharkov, who was held responsible for the brutal treatment of politicals in the Kharkov Central Prison, was fatally wounded, and in March there was an unsuccessful attempt on the life of Mezentzev's successor. This was General Drenteln, who had erected deportation to the dreaded Yakutsk tundras into a system.[1] Also two spies were done away with. Then, on the morning of 2 April, Alexander Solovyov, an 'illegal' who had returned to Petersburg from a village settlement, discharged a revolver at the Emperor as the latter, in taking his constitutional, was crossing the Palace Square, but did not injure him. The assailant was seized, court-martialled, and, on 28 May, hanged. 'He combined the courage of a hero,' Vera Figner wrote of him, 'with the self-abnegation of an ascetic and the kindness of a child.' Earlier in the month Valerian Osinsky, a fragile youth who was the leading Southern terrorist, was executed after watching the capital punishment of two comrades. Before the end of the year eleven men, including Lizogub, were put to death.

IV

At first the 'disorganizing' activities were warmly acclaimed by the membership of Land and Liberty. Soon, however, 'terror', as these acts came to be called, began to be frowned upon. Some held that it was using up too large a share of the Society's severely limited resources, both human and financial. Moreover, along with the emphasis on terror went an ideological shift that was heresy and, indeed, apostasy in the eyes of simon-pure populists. These believed that 'disorganizing' should play a

[1] The attack was carried out by Leon Mirski, a twenty-year-old student. He is said to have been motivated, in part, by the desire to impress his fiancée, who had been thrilled by Kravchinsky's exploit. Arrested several months later and incarcerated in the Fortress of Peter and Paul, it was he who is believed to have informed against his fellow prisoner, Nechayev.

subordinate part and be employed only as a weapon of self-defence. It was not the business of Land and Liberty, they argued, to kill high Government officials, but to arouse the masses to active protest in the name of their economic interests. The propertied classes—they were the enemy. 'Let the Government take a neutral stand in the duel between the revolutionists and the exploiters,' Kravchinsky, for one, was naïve enough to say, 'and it will not be molested.' In any event, political régimes were a matter of indifference to the people. When the forest was cleared away, the wolves perished of themselves: once the iniquitous social order was destroyed, the monarchy would collapse of its own weight.

This strict apolitical stand, an aberration characteristic of populism, was, however, beginning to be seriously challenged. The idea of an offensive against the monarchy in the name of political democracy was coming to the fore. The attempt to rouse the masses had obviously failed. And that in spite of the fact that the agitators were no longer callow youths and that they had adopted what they considered a practical programme. In an effort to find a way out of the impasse, the populists were beginning to question some of the dogmata of their faith. Might not a constitutional régime guaranteeing civil liberties prove a blessing, after all? The propertied classes could not be expected to battle for such a régime. The monarchy gave them all they wanted: cheap labour and freedom to plunder. It was therefore incumbent on the revolutionists to fight the autocracy, taking care not to sacrifice the distant goal to the nearer one. If the greater revolution could not yet be carried out, perhaps a less ambitious programme could be effected by conspirators striking a blow at the central Government. Terroristic acts were being committed in self-defence and in vengeance; could not terrorism be used as a weapon of offence, designed to wrest from the Czar liberal concessions? Would not heroic deeds shatter the apathy of the masses and destroy the prestige of the Government?

As the year 1878 opened this prestige was at a low ebb. The Russo-Turkish conflict had laid bare the incompetence and corruption of the bureaucracy, and the Treaty of Berlin, signed in July, was a humiliating conclusion to an inglorious and costly war. It seemed an easy matter to overthrow a régime so deficient in leadership. The first issue of *Land and Liberty*, dated October,

1878, had it that the revolution was a question of days, perhaps of hours. Even the patient liberals were stirring. Shortly after the assassination of Mezentzev the Emperor appealed to the population for assistance in combating the revolutionary movement. In response one *zemstvo* board hinted, in an address to the Czar, that the sovereign who had liberated the Bulgarians from the Turkish yoke and granted them a representative régime could do no less for the Russian people who had borne the burden of the war. There were liberals who went so far as to negotiate for a common front with the revolutionists. It is possible that the lull in terrorist acts during the winter of 1878–9 was the result of these discussions. A few arrests and deportations, and the flare-up of the constitutional movement was over, but it had encouraged the political orientation within Land and Liberty.

This orientation was strongest in the South. Radicals of Jewish birth, belonging as they did to a group that was denied elementary human rights, were apt to welcome a liberal régime more warmly than others. Aron Zundelevich, for one, said that he loved America. Civil liberties figure in the platform of the Northern Union of Russian Workers, printed early in 1879. In Plekhanov's words, it made the orthodox populists feel like a hen that had hatched a duckling. When in the pages of *Land and Liberty* the Union was gently but firmly upbraided for tainting Populism with political demands, it had the good sense to retort that there was nothing inconsistent about fighting for social revolution and fighting for 'political liberty', since the one would be served by the other.

The political trend found its most extreme expression in a splinter group, the Society of the People's Liberation, which originated late in 1877. It consisted of Tkachev and the handful of his fellow 'Jacobins' at home and abroad. *Nabat*, the little review which he ran, was its organ. According to its statutes, the organization aimed to overthrow the monarchy and, having seized power, decree an order based on political and economic equality. 'That the Society may flourish and achieve its great aims,' Section 12 runs, 'all means are considered good.' Land and Liberty professed the same belief, but adhered to the standards of ordinary morality, while the Society of the People's Liberation reverted to Nechayev's ways. Its allegedly all-powerful Central

Committee urged the members to spy on one another and to infiltrate other revolutionary organizations, so as to bore from within.

The few leaflets bearing the Society's imprint stress the conquest of political power and play down the social revolution. A pamphlet brought out soon after Vera Zasulich's shot is the earliest attempt to justify the tactics of systematic terror. It scorns 'anarchist chimeras and Utopias' as well as 'bourgeois theories of individual freedom', hails a return to the path followed by Karakozov and Nechayev, urges that type be melted down for bullets and shots be substituted for sermons.

It is uncertain if the Society of the People's Liberation attempted to put its theories into practice. Its following was very small, but not negligible, at a time when all the radical trends were represented by lilliputian groups. It claimed credit for the acts of terror which marked the year 1878. This the populists, including Vera Zasulich, Kravchinsky, and Stefanovich, flatly denied, declaring publicly that Russian social-revolutionaries could have nothing in common with the editors of *Nabat* or the theories they promote. It is not impossible that the group had a hand in some terrorist acts. The expropriation of the Kherson branch of the Imperial Treasury in the summer of 1879 was the work of a member of the Society. A million and a half roubles were taken, but the police recovered most of the money.

Late in 1878, at a conference of the editors of *Land and Liberty*, Morozov remarked that he intended to contribute an article to *Nabat*. A fellow editor recoiled in horror. 'There isn't a single revolutionary in Russia', he cried, 'who would approve the seizure of the government by a group of conspirators.' Morozov ventured to doubt this, and justly. 'If there are such,' was the response, 'they are our enemies!'

v

The question of the place of terrorism in the activities of Land and Liberty had become a storm centre. The advocates of the dagger and the pistol looked down upon the *derevenshchiks* ('villagists', i.e. partisans of work among the peasantry) as ne'er-do-wells, as peaceful triflers, while the latter regarded the terrorists as renegades. The unity of the organization was in jeopardy.

The lack of harmony was particularly glaring in the management of the review, *Land and Liberty*. The editorial board was a house divided against itself. It consisted of Kravchinsky, Klemenz, and Morozov. Kravchinsky, although he had himself carried out a spectacular political murder, held no brief for terror and was, indeed, like Klemenz, an orthodox *narodnik*. On the other hand, Morozov was an enthusiastic adherent of a terrorist conspiracy against the Government. A frail, gentle youth, he cast himself in the rôle of a Wilhelm Tell and walked around armed to the teeth.

When Kravchinsky escaped abroad, he was replaced by Plekhanov and Tikhomirov, a new member of the group. Tikhomirov kept to the middle of the road, but Plekhanov was an uncompromising enemy of the political orientation and of terror. As a result, Morozov found himself blocked. Yet the paper failed to maintain a consistent policy on the acute question of terrorism and presented a spectacle of ideological confusion. This by no means disconcerted those who, like Mikhailov, cared little for theory. What was important, he said, was not the contents of the journal, but the fact that it was printed and distributed in defiance of the law.

In March, 1879, the Society started another periodical, *Listok* (Bulletin), which came out at shorter intervals. Here Morozov had things rather his own way, except that he had to cope with the head printer, Maria Krylova, a fanatical 'villagist', who went into hysterics whenever she was handed copy with the tenor of which she disagreed. *Listok* was, in fact, the organ of the terrorist faction of the Society. Its second issue carried a paean to 'political assassination' as the most effective weapon in the revolutionary arsenal. The article brought home to all the conviction that the Society was headed for a split.

The terrorists were mostly active in the South. In a sense they were an organization—a very loose one—within an organization. Their link with the Petersburg Centre was weak. Never numbering more than fifteen, they styled themselves 'The Executive Committee of the Social-Revolutionary Party'. Its seal, showing an axe, a dagger, and a revolver crossed, was first used in a leaflet issued by the Committee on the occasion of the murder of a spy in Rostov on 1 February, 1878. Such leaflets, listing the charges against the victim, were usually issued after each terrorist act. The Committee also sent warnings and threats to officials.

Solovyov's attempted regicide caused a great stir in the Society. On arriving in the capital, he had applied to Land and Liberty for assistance in carrying out his plan. The meeting at which the matter was discussed witnessed a violent clash of the two factions. The orthodox populists argued that the people's veneration for the Czar should be respected, that an attack on him might result in a popular outburst against the propagandists settled in the villages and lead to reprisals threatening the existence of the Society. Some wanted the would-be regicide seized and tied up as a madman.

In the end it was decided that the Society could not offer the man any aid, but that neither could it forbid individual members to help him. He was refused the use of the racehorse that had whisked Kropotkin and Kravchinsky to liberty and that was kept in a livery stable for just such occasions. But several members enabled him to obtain the revolver he fired at the Czar and the dose of poison with which he unsuccessfully tried to kill himself.

As was anticipated, Solovyov's shot led to severe repressive measures, which hampered the Society's activities. Under these circumstances, was the attempt on the Czar's life to be repeated? And how was the factional struggle to be dealt with? Something had to be done. It was finally agreed to call a conference in Voronezh to decide the future policy of the organization. The city boasted a venerable shrine visited by throngs, and it was thought that the simultaneous arrival of a dozen or two men and women would not attract attention.

The partisans of political action overestimated the strength of their opponents. They believed that, being in the minority, they would simply be expelled from the Society. They resolved to organize beforehand, so as to be able to act as a group immediately upon expulsion. Accordingly, on 15 June, they gathered, secretly from the rest, at Lipetzk, not far from Voronezh. The meetings—they lasted three days—were held in a grove which was the town's picnicking grounds. In all a dozen persons participated in the deliberations. They included several activists who were not members of the Society, as well as Stepan Shiryayev, the moving spirit of a newly formed terrorist circle, which went by the name of 'Liberty or Death' and seems to have been loosely affiliated with Land and Liberty. The conferrers acted as though the schism had already taken place. On the other hand, they were willing to continue under the banner of the Society, provided they were free to carry on the fight in their own way. The gathering deviated sufficiently from populist orthodoxy to pronounce itself for a political revolution, with terror as part of its tactics. It also adopted the elaborate statutes of a conspiratorial society, centralized, hierarchical, close-knit. Mikhailov made a fiery speech, which was an indictment of the Czar and pointed to a continuation of the attempts at regicide.

From Lipetzk the conferrers made their way to Voronezh to take part in the conventicle there. Opening on 18 June, this went on for three or four days and was attended by a score of men and women. It happened that the 'politicals' were in the majority, so that their expulsion was out of the question. The spirit of compromise ruled the conference. Alone Plekhanov took an intransigeant stand, arguing that terror was incompatible with propaganda among the masses and indeed meant the death of revolutionary Populism. He stomped out of the conference in a huff and sent in his resignation, pointing out, among other things, that the 'disorganizing' activities were disorganizing not the Government but the Society.

The programme of Land and Liberty was left practically intact. Propaganda was placed on an equal footing with 'disorganizing' activities, which were to include a kind of agrarian terrorism, resembling Irish 'Ribbonism', and a majority voted for regicide. The Executive Committee, as the terrorist group continued to be known, was allotted one third of the funds and given full autonomy. Moreover, the 'politicals' managed to secure control of the Society's journal and to get two of their men, Mikhailov and Frolenko, on to a newly elected three-man Board.

After Solovyov's shot it became impossible to continue the propaganda among the Petersburg workmen, so Plekhanov, who had quit the Society, went to Kiev. Mikhailov, too, happened to be there. The former friends were now profoundly at variance. 'I loved the work among the people', Mikhailov told Plekhanov's wife, 'I was ready to carry it on at any cost, but . . . we are powerless to accomplish anything under the autocracy, all our people will perish without results. We have only one alternative: either to give up revolutionary activity or engage the government in single combat. We have enough strength, heroism, capacity for self-sacrifice to follow the latter course.'

For a while it looked as though Land and Liberty had weathered the storm. It was a storm in a tea-cup: at the time of the Voronezh conference the regular membership of the Society consisted of thirty-three men and women. But the peace that had been patched up was a bad peace. Friction between the two factions, far from ceasing, had increased. Reinforced by new arrivals from abroad, including Stefanovich and Vera Zasulich, who, curiously enough, abhorred the emphasis on terror and the trend toward political revolution, the 'villagists' started planning to resume work among the peasants, but no serious effort was possible: energy was used chiefly to remove misunderstandings and stop wrangles. Not a single issue of either *Land and Liberty* or *The Bulletin* appeared after the conference. There was no mending the breach. So distressing was the schism that it is said to have driven one youth to attempt suicide. The situation was all the graver as arrests had nearly wiped out the cells in the South and had weakened the Northern Centre.

There was no alternative but to sever the ties that connected the 'Executive Committee' with the Society. A commission was appointed to liquidate the organization and divide the assets between the two factions. On 15 August, 1879, Land and Liberty ceased to exist.

CHAPTER XII

THE PEOPLE'S WILL

A SEPARATE existence was now assumed by what had been the two factions of Land and Liberty. It had been agreed that neither should use that name. Accordingly, the group of orthodox populists called itself *Narodnaya Partiya* (Popular or People's Party), but was better known as *Chornyi Peredel* (Black Repartition), a phrase describing the periodic redistribution of land and taxes by the *mir*. It was also the title of the organization's journal which bore the motto, 'Land and Liberty!' on its masthead.

When it was formed, in the autumn of 1879, Black Repartition consisted of a score of men and women. Of organizing talent there was little, except for Pavel Axelrod, a former member of the Chaikovsky Circle, later a *buntar*, successful in propagandizing factory hands. Plekhanov, a born idéologue, was the brains of the group. It also included Yakov Stefanovich and Lev Deutsch, 'the Orestes and Pylades of the revolution'. The fact that Vera Zasulich, who had returned from abroad in 1879, was a member of the group did most to raise its prestige. In the division of the assets of Land and Liberty it had come off rather badly. The other faction got 'the Foreign Office' in the person of Zundelevich, as well as the Heavenly Chancery and the printing press. The loss of this last was particularly serious. After some weeks another press was obtained. The business of setting it up, preparing the text of the opening number of the new journal and collecting the funds necessary to cover the cost of the issue absorbed most of the group's energies during the first months of its existence.

The new year brought disaster. Plekhanov, as well as Stefanovich, Deutsch and Vera Zasulich fled to Switzerland, and this they did not merely to escape arrest. They withdrew from the battlefield in a mood of discouragement and apathy. *Chornyi Peredel* was left practically leaderless. And then, a typesetter on the secret press having turned informer, the police seized it, together with all the copies of the first issue of the journal, and arrested the four people who ran the press, including 'the Mother of God'. Other arrests followed, and it looked as if it was all up with the group.

It survived the crisis, chiefly owing to Axelrod's energy and devotion. He kept it alive by making a number of proselytes, mostly students and young naval officers. The first issue of *Chornyi Peredel*, with the original date, 15 January, 1880, but with some additions to the text, was reprinted in London and copies smuggled into Russia. The editors proclaimed their anarchist faith and in the next breath swore allegiance to 'the principles of scientific socialism'. The leading article, by Plekhanov, was a vigorous restatement of the populist thesis. A large proportion of the slim issue was given over to an account of the Chigirin affair, from the pen of Stefanovich himself. An editorial note stated that the publication of the piece implied no approval of exploiting 'the political idols' of the masses.

The second number of *Chornyi peredel* carried 'the Programme' of the group. It did not differ much from that of the defunct Land and Liberty. The organization set itself the long-term task of agitating for an agrarian revolution, which was to be the first step toward a complete reconstruction of society on socialist foundations. This, however, did not mean the teachings of Marx and Engels, but the platform of the Bakuninist wing of the International, which had not survived its founder and was then largely a memory. Political action was described as 'necessary', but given a subordinate place, as was propaganda among industrial workers. In commenting on the Programme, Plekhanov took exception to this last point. It was wisest, he wrote, to distribute available energies rather evenly between town and country, choosing the slogan: 'Worker, take the factory; peasant, take the land.' The centre of gravity in Russia was shifting toward industry, so that 'we cannot determine beforehand from what classes of the working population the main cadres of the social-revolutionary army will be recruited when the hour of the economic overturn strikes'.

Axelrod, who had gone to Geneva to submit the draft of the statutes to the expatriate members, failed to return. The arrest, in July, of Yelizaveta Durnovo was another serious blow to the group: she was its chief 'angel'. The daughter of a wealthy army officer and the niece of the Governor of Moscow, she is said to have turned over to the Society the sum of sixteen thousand roubles. Against odds, the work was carried on, largely by new converts, of whom there were about thirty. In addition to the main circle in Petersburg, there was a branch in Moscow, as well as handfuls of adherents in Kazan and in several southern centres. The distaste for subordination prevalent among the people who gravitated toward Black Repartition made the provincial cells virtually independent.

The situation was fraught with irony. The groups were supposed to centre their efforts on the peasantry, and the membership waxed eloquent on the need of getting closer to the rural masses. Yet they failed to secure a foothold in a single village. Propaganda outside intellectual circles was confined to city workers. Study groups were formed for factory hands, and aid was offered to strikers. The society helped, in the spring of 1880, to revive the Union of South-Russian Workers, which had been in suspended animation since 1875. Its new phase lasted no more than a year, but in that period it had a membership of some six hundred in Kiev alone. The Union adhered to orthodox Populism, but advocated terrorism, though only against economic exploiters, not against officials. To assist the propagandist, Black Repartition printed half a dozen issues of a review, *Zerno* (Seed), written down to the level of the simple workman and offering him popular essays in Marxist economics and stories with a message.

Three more numbers of *Chornyi peredel* came out, the last one dated December, 1881. The journal gave the organization whatever body and substance it possessed. A number of leaflets and a revised version of the Programme, dated 7 April, 1881, were also issued. Here nationalization of the land, the factories, and the other major means of production is substituted for 'redistribution of the land', the objective that had figured in the earlier text. Further, the document recognizes the existence of a proletariat with interests and ideals different from those of the peasantry. All these publications were run off on a clandestine press in Minsk under idyllic circumstances made possible by the laxity of the local police. An emissary from the capital discovered to his horror that on a vacant lot near the house where the press was located boys flew kites with discarded sheets of *Chornyi Peredel*.

II

The other faction, which espoused political revolution and the tactics of terror, took the name of the Party (or Society) of the People's Will (*Narodnaya Volya*). The term *volya* means 'freedom' as well as 'will'. It was used here in the latter sense. A member of the Party was a *narodovoletz*.

Structurally the new society was closely patterned on Land and Liberty. The People's Will was organized as an association consisting of a central nucleus exercising a measure of control over local chapters, which functioned in the provinces, and over special units which confined their activities to occupational groups, such as workmen, students, army officers. The hard core of the organization was known as 'the Executive Committee'. This was the direct descendant of the cell of that name which had existed within Land and Liberty and which had formally constituted itself at the Lipetzk Conference in June, 1879. The statutes adopted by the Conference became the statutes of the People's Will.

The Executive Committee was a misnomer: it was a self-appointed and self-perpetuating body. The Committee had a monopoly on the more ambitious terroristic enterprises, but by no means limited itself to them. It formulated the policies of the Party and sought to maintain its ideological unity. Every effort was made to build it into a myth, to create the impression that it was an august, inaccessible, all-powerful body carrying on its activities behind an impregnable wall of secrecy. The fewest persons came in direct contact with the members. In dealings with the outside world these were required to pass themselves off as its 'agents'. It also had real agents: activists connected with subsidiary groups who were called upon to assist the centre. A Managing Board, elected by the Committee, acted during the intervals between its sittings. Once admitted to the Committee, one could not resign. This rule, like others, seems to have remained on paper.

In the half dozen years of the Executive Committee's existence, fewer than fifty men and women served on it. Because of arrests, the number of members who were active at any one time was considerably smaller. The total membership was authoritatively estimated at five hundred. This figure apparently does not include fellow travellers. A list of persons associated, however tenuously, with the People's Will, compiled by a group of survivors of the movement, comprises over two thousand two hundred names. The register covers the entire period of the Party's life, including the 1886–96 decade when its existence was nominal.

The strength of the People's Will lay in the fact that the membership included a few dedicated spirits, men and women animated by the faith that makes heroes and martyrs. The biographies of those who made up the revolutionary *élite* were apt to have certain features in common. Such a man would early be responsive to radical ideas and hospitable toward populist sentiment; while at school or in the university, he would be active in a reading club or a propagandist group; his studies would be interrupted, because he would be deported for participation in academic disturbances, or else he would abandon the lecture hall to 'go to the people'. He would suffer exile or imprisonment, which would enhance his sense of martyrdom, and nourish dreams of violent upheavals; on being released, he would join Land and Liberty, unless preferring the part of a free-lance *buntar*; finally he would find himself in the ranks of the People's Will. Not that the social background of the activists, men and women, was the same. Frolenko was the son of a charwoman; Shiryayev was born into the family of a serf. Trigoni's father was a Major-General, and Sofya Perovskaya was the daughter of the Governor of Petersburg. But in the main, the People's Will, like the rival faction, was an organization of intellectuals or semi-intellectuals recruited from the middle-class, the clergy, the lower gentry. Even those who were of peasant or proletarian stock had had the benefit of an education. If culturally it was a rather homogeneous group, it reflected the ethnic variety of the vast country. In addition to Great Russians, the Executive Committee included a Ukrainian, three Jews, several persons of Germanic stock, the offspring of a Russian-Norwegian marriage, another of a Russian-Georgian union, a woman of Polish descent and the son of a Greek.

Alexander Mikhailov was perhaps the greatest asset the organization possessed. He was its watchdog. Day in, day out, he preached and practised discipline and caution, fighting tooth and nail for centralized control. He devoted himself to building up the apparatus of the People's Will, as he had previously built up that of Land and Liberty. No detail capable of menacing the safety of the Party escaped him. He knew how to order and use men, and he obeyed the rules he laid down. A stutterer, like many earnest people, he had no private ambitions, no personal ties. His room was enlivened solely by the motto: 'Do not forget your duty.' The cause was his religion. It was inseparable from his belief in God, that is, he said, in truth, justice, love. But there was something businesslike and matter-of-fact about the way he worshipped his deity. His last testament was a set of practical injunctions to his comrades. Although he was aware that as a revolutionary he was a doomed man, he considered himself particularly fortunate. 'From my earliest youth,' he wrote at the end of his career, 'a lucky star has shone over my head.' Annihilation held no terrors for him. 'Who does not fear death,' he liked to say, 'is almost omnipotent.'

Mikhailov exemplified the sober, puritanical, ascetic type of revolutionary. Among his fellows the antipodal type of the dare-devil, exuberant romantic, acting out of an impulse to live fully and strenuously, was also represented. Such was Alexander Barannikov, born, like Mikhailov, into a family of gentlefolk. Finding military school uncongenial, he escaped from it by making the authorities believe him drowned. He was then eighteen. Leaving the capital, he fell in with a group of agitators in the Don region and worked as a field hand, a fisherman, a stevedore. Then he joined a village settlement planted by Land and Liberty, but soon grew impatient with peaceful activities. When the Serbs rose against Turkey, he went to Montenegro to learn how partisans fight and saw some action. Returning to Russia, he took part in the assassination of Mezentzev, and he naturally found himself in the ranks of the People's Will. His character was in keeping with his appearance: jet-black hair—his mother was a Georgian—eyes so dark that they seemed without pupils, a tense, passionate air. Living in the moment, reaching out for experience, he yet gave the impression of a tightly wound spring. An avenging angel, as he was called, he was a figure out of a Byronic romance. His testament, penned in prison in the expectation of execution—he was actually given in 1882 a life term of hard labour, from which death delivered him a year later—ends with this rhetorical apostrophe to his comrades: 'Live and triumph; we triumph and die.'

Another striking figure was Mikhail Grachevsky, a former divinity student turned village teacher and, later, mechanic. With his nominal wife he occupied the flat in which one of the Party's printing presses was installed. He was a fanatic, a spiritual descendant of the schismatics who burned themselves to death rather than yield an iota of their faith. Sentenced to a life term of hard labour, he was kept in a Schlüsselburg prison. As a protest against the régime there, he ended his life, in 1887, by setting himself on fire after soaking his clothes with kerosene from his lamp.

The Executive Committee was a band of conspirators and political assassins. Andrey Zhelyabov reluctantly accepted this rôle, but it did not fit him. Powerfully built, full-blooded, magnetic, possessed of great drive and energy, somewhat histrionic yet capable of clear thinking, he had the makings of a tribune or a leader of men. 'There was about him,' wrote a comrade, 'a certain ruthlessness, of the kind that goes with strength moving forward irresistibly and pushing others before it.'

For an unusually long time he was content to remain an obscure soldier in the ranks. And then, overnight, he found himself among the top commanders of the small cohort of the revolution. Born a serf, he grew up in the Crimea, a frontier region where the peasantry was less cowed than in central Russia. His former owner saw him through secondary school, and a scholarship enabled him to study law at the University of Odessa. He had come under the sway of radical ideas while still at school, and as a student he held clandestine classes for seamstresses, reading to them Hood's 'Song of the Shirt'. His academic career came to an end in 1871, when he was twenty-one, because he had led a student protest against a tactless professor.

He eked out a meagre living in Odessa by teaching school and tutoring. His circumstances did not improve when he married the daughter of a well-to-do industrialist. Nor did marriage dampen his interest in the revolution. He leaned toward Lavrovism, but did not 'go to the people'. In the winter of 1874–75 he spent some months in prison. Released, he resumed his former mode of life, except that during the summer he would be farming in his native village. His wife worked with him in the fields, but sometimes she would lie down in a ditch and cry, remembering her piano. For a *narodnik*, he showed a curious interest in the political radicalism professed by the groups of Ukrainian nationalists that existed at this time, though he could not work up any enthusiasm for their programme of turning the Empire into a federation of states.

A defendant in the Great Trial of 1877–78, he was acquitted. He returned to farming, but soon reappeared in Odessa, where he assumed the status of an illegal. Though aware of the objections to it, he had come to the conclusion that the use of terror was unavoidable. 'History moves terribly slowly,' he told a friend, 'we must give it a push.' At the Lipetzk conference, where his appearance was something of a surprise, he leapt to the fore. Both at that gathering and at the Voronezh meetings he espoused a political orientation so warmly that he scandalized the orthodox populists. 'He is a constitutionalist!' they cried, appalled, after listening to one of his speeches. A novice among veterans, he was soon the moving spirit behind the activities of the People's Will.

Its feminine members rendered the organization indispensable services in various auxiliary capacities. The top leadership included at least three women. A conspirator by both temperament and conviction was Maria Oshanina (née Olovennikova), the eldest of three sisters, all of whom were in the revolutionary movement. Among her plain, blowsy female comrades she stood out because of her looks and her manners. She had character and courage and intelligence, but, sceptic that she was, lacked the moral integrity and austere devotion to the cause that distinguished Vera Figner and Sofya Perovskaya. The former had given up peaceful propaganda and was elected to the Executive Committee. A rather mediocre organizer, she was an effective agitator. In her bearing there was something that suggested the figure of Victory.

Perovskaya joined the People's Will after much hesitation, but once in its fighting ranks, she became irreplaceable. Like Mikhailov, she embodied duty and discipline. If she was severe with others, she was even more so toward herself. She not only planned and directed; she was the first to go under fire, and she chose the most responsible and dangerous post. The blonde, thin-lipped, big-browed, self-possessed slip of a girl, who in spite of her severe garb looked younger than her twenty-six years, concealed a heart of steel under her gentle exterior. A comrade must have had her in mind when he observed to a fellow revolutionary: 'Have you noticed that our women are more cruel than we men?'

During the Land and Liberty days she had, among other things, taken charge of correspondence with political prisoners. She would also visit them in an effort to keep up their morale. In this way she came to know Tikhomirov. The two fell in love and indeed, decided to get married. But nothing came of it. According to Tikhomirov, she could submit in love only to a man stronger than herself, which he was not. He added that when she met a strong man in the person of Zhelyabov, she became his slave. A comrade called Zhelyabov her first and only love. Presumably, it was not an unrequited passion. When Zhelyabov joined the terrorists he had abandoned his wife and infant son, while breaking the other ties that bound him to the old existence.

Although emotionally involved, Sofya Perovskaya shrank from accepting personal happiness as long as comrades were languishing behind bars or perishing on the scaffold, and while the people were suffering under the yoke of despotism. Some of her fellow activists held that love and marriage were incompatible with work for the revolution. Yet a professed Amazon, Olga Lubatovich, fell madly in love with Morozov. It was said that when they were together Fate itself could not touch them. He was arrested while she was in Geneva, where she had gone to be delivered of their child. Men and women, thrown together in this dangerous life, not unnaturally entered into intimate relations. Unions were formed, with or without benefit of clergy. Barannikov married Maria Oshanina. Children were born, sometimes in prison or in Siberian exile. A nominal marriage on occasion turned into a real one. It would seem that in personal relations the same intensity often obtained that marked the feeling for the cause.

III

The beginnings of the People's Will were not inauspicious. It started out with a nucleus that had been in existence for some years. There was money in the cashbox, and a sizable printing-

press was at its service. It lost no time in making itself heard.
Early in October, 1879, the first issue of its organ, also called
Narodnaya volya, was being eagerly if stealthily read. The opening
statement was a declaration of loyalty to the slogan of 'Land
and Liberty'. But the keynote was sounded in an article from the
pen of Tikhomirov, entitled '*Delenda est Carthago*'. The Czar's
autocratic régime was the Carthage that must be utterly destroyed.
The cry reverberates throughout the literature put forth by the
Society. It was repeated with what was practically its dying
breath in the editorial dated 1 October, 1885, which appeared
in the last issue of *Narodnaya volya*.

Here was a sharp departure from populist orthodoxy. Several
considerations were advanced to justify the political orientation.
The Russian State, it was argued, was the chief exploiter and
oppressor and the mother of all exploitation and oppression. As
long as it existed, the lot of the masses could not be bettered. In
Russia reform meant revolution. A representative government
was bound to benefit the people. Again, the despotic system
must be annihilated before a powerful middle-class was formed
under its aegis. In the West the monarchy had been overthrown
by the bourgeoisie. In Russia the historic task fell to the masses
and their vanguard, the Party. And let there be no fear that in
attacking the State the revolutionaries would be pulling chestnuts
from the fire for others: there was no organized force in the
country capable of snatching the fruits of victory from the people.
In fact, the Society's spokesmen asserted that in Russian circumstances a political revolution could not but be also a social
revolution. The theory did much to help a *narodnik* overcome
his taste for political action.

The People's Will did not share the anarchist animus against
all centralized political authority. On the other hand, the idea
of the Party seizing power and dictatorially effecting an economic
revolution was generally repudiated as 'a despotic Utopia'.
Narodnaya volya did not consider its break with the apolitical
stand as a betrayal of Populism. Its 'Programme', printed in the
third issue of its organ, dated 1 January, 1880, opened with the
statement: 'According to our fundamental convictions, we are
socialists and populists.' To the framers of this document
Populism was, above all, a democratic faith in the will of the
people as the only source and sanction of social institutions,

while Socialism was a vague ideal of justice and equality ensuring the material welfare of the community and the spiritual self-realization of the individual. Belief in the collectivist instincts of the Russian masses was unshaken. Socialism and Populism acting as guarantors of each other—such was, indeed, the philosophy of the People's Will. 'The people's welfare and the people's will are our two most sacred and inseparable principles.'

'It is important for the masses to achieve a better social order,' reads an article in the fourth issue of *Narodnaya volya*, 'but it is even more important for them to achieve it *by their own efforts*. . . .' A popular revolution replacing the monarchy with a régime permitting the masses to express their will through elected representatives was a consummation ardently desired. But the Programme, mentioned above, called upon the Party to take the initiative in effecting the overturn without waiting for a popular uprising and, indeed, without counting on it. The People's Will obligated itself, however, to see to it that the Provisional Government created by the triumphant revolution should promptly hand over its power to a Constituent Assembly. The Programme declared that the Party would submit to the people's will, as expressed through this democratically elected body, but would support a platform of its own in the electoral campaign and in the Assembly. A postscript to the document had it that in fighting the government, all means were permissible, that the forces of the opposition, whether affiliated with the Society or not, would be aided and abetted, and finally that 'individuals and groups standing outside our struggle with the government were considered neutral: their persons and property were inviolate.'

The aims, structure, and activities of the organization were also outlined in another official statement entitled 'The Preparatory Work of the Party'. Here the overthrow of the autocracy through a popular rising preceded by a series of terroristic acts was designated as the immediate task. 'The Party must have the strength to create for itself a moment favourable to action, to start the enterprise and bring it to a successful conclusion.' The ultimate goal was a political and social order under which the people's will is the sole source of law. It was, however, explicitly stated that the Party did not presume to be the bearer of that will.

It would be misleading to give the impression that there was anything monolithic about *Narodnaya volya*. Both ideologically and organizationally it was a loose body. As in the case of its rival, *Chornyi Peredel*, there were divergent trends in it. A prospective member of the Executive Committee was not asked about the exact tenor of his views, but whether he was ready to lay down his life for what was vaguely referred to as the cause of freedom. Some accepted the theory that the political and social revolution would occur simultaneously, others envisaged a long interval between the two. The most that Zhelyabov, for one, expected from the Party's efforts was a régime that would hamper its activities less severely. There were those who would wrest concessions from the government rather than overthrow it, and for whom the ultimate goal of Socialism was eclipsed by the nearer objective of political democracy. On the other hand, several people were receptive to the idea that the Party should seize power and decree Socialism into existence. In an article contributed to the Party organ Mikhailovsky observed that the vicissitudes of the coming struggle were unforeseeable, adding prophetically: 'The Russian popular uprising may produce an ambitious man of genius, a Caesar, a demigod, before whom our unhappy country will bow its head.'

Nor was there complete unanimity on tactics. Terror had its enthusiasts like Morozov, who attempted to erect it into a philosophy, if not into a mystique. He exalted systematic political assassination as the most equitable and suitable form of revolutionary struggle. For the most part, however, the membership regarded it, not without misgivings, as a matter of policy dictated by Russian conditions, as a measure which enabled strength to come forth out of weakness. At the news of President Garfield's death the Executive Committee prepared a statement protesting in the name of the Russian revolutionaries against political assassination in a country like the United States where 'the free popular will determines not only the law, but also the person of its administrators'.

IV

'The Preparatory Work of the Party' assigned great importance to city workers as a potential revolutionary force. The efforts to secure a foothold among them were not without success. Workers' circles sprang up in the two capitals and in several provincial cities. By the time the People's Will was constituted, the Northern Union of Russian Workers had been broken up, yet the seeds it had planted had not all been lost. The beginning of the 'eighties was marked by an industrial depression which resulted in lay-offs, and there was much unrest among factory hands. Several hundreds of them lent an ear to the propagandists. Along with lessons in the 'three R's', proselytes were offered indoctrination in economics according to Marx and Lassalle, as well as talks on such subjects as the struggles of the Irish peasantry, the French Revolution, the Paris Commune. The cells had statutes of their own, drafted in the autumn of 1880, but they did not differ much from the Party's Programme. At the end of the year the first issue of *Rabochaya gazeta* (The Workers' Gazette) made its appearance, thanks chiefly to Zhelyabov's initiative and energy. One of the policies of this publication during its brief existence— it lasted a little over a year—was opposition to the building of railways and factories, on the ground that they undermined peasant trucking and village crafts!

Theoretically, the rural masses bulked large in the plans of the organization. Only they could insure the victory of the revolution, it was argued, even if the initiative was to come from another quarter. The Party had no doubts that its programme would be welcomed by the villagers. It was conceded, however, that only outstanding individuals from among the peasantry could be won over in the immediate future. *Narodnaya volya* gave up all thought of 'going to the people' and no longer clung to the belief that Cossacks and sectarians were apt to be particularly hospitable to the message of revolution, though Alexander Mikhailov, for one, long cherished the plan of incorporating the clandestine organization of the schismatics into the Party.

The People's Will managed to devote some of its energies to proselytizing among the intelligentzia and the student youth. These exertions were not very fruitful. Not many individuals from among the educated public were induced to join the ranks of the activists, though a number contributed money and on occasion carried out minor assignments. The student body provided the Executive Committee with several agents. Zhelyabov was instrumental in forming a student group with cells in more than one school of higher learning in the capital. On 8 February, 1881, during the annual convocation at the University of Petersburg, the group got up a protest demonstration against the Minister of Education who had been appointed the previous spring. A leaflet was distributed among the audience, one student made an incendiary speech, and another walked up to the Minister and slapped his face. The unfortunate affair was condemned by the majority of the students. As a matter of fact, the policy followed by the new Minister, compared with that of his predecessor, was rather liberal.

Infiltrating the armed forces was held to be a vital and urgent task. Propaganda among common soldiers and sailors devolved upon the workers' circles, and apparently no headway at all was made in that direction. But a number of cells with a membership confined to commissioned officers were established in scattered army and navy units. In the autumn of 1880 Zhelyabov, with the aid of three Midshipmen, succeeded in welding these groups into an autonomous body, the Military-Revolutionary Organization of the People's Will, with a central board located in the capital and represented on the Executive Committee. Time was when army men had been urged to resign their commissions and 'go to the people'. They were now exhorted to stay in the service and seek to gain the confidence of the men under their command, without trying to win them over to the cause. The officers were to wait for the call from their Board, meanwhile carrying out certain orders issued by the Executive Committee. They obligated themselves to take up arms in support of a popular rising or of a military insurrection aiming to seize supreme power in order to set up a representative government. 'Popularization of socialist teaching' was included in the propaganda conducted by the Military-Revolutionary Organization.

The People's Will was not averse to a united front with the liberals. The statutes recommended seeking to persuade them that for the time being their interests were identical with those of the revolutionaries, both being forced 'to act together against the Government'. There was no actual attempt, however, to make common cause with the moderate opposition. As a matter of fact, it was held that the monarchy was in a moribund state and that its overthrow would prove an easy task.

In its proselytizing efforts the Party depended to a considerable extent on the printed word. As has been seen, shortly after it was constituted, it began issuing a journal. On 18 January, 1880, in the small hours, the secret press was raided. The half a dozen people who ran it offered armed resistance to arrest. One man shot himself dead to avoid being taken, and the rest were seized, together with the equipment and all but two hundred copies of the third issue of *Narodnaya volya*. While the police was being held off, most of the compromising papers were destroyed, so that the arrests did not spread, and by the time spring came, another press was functioning. It produced several issues of *Listok* (*The Bulletin*), and in the autumn the printing of *Narodnaya volya* was resumed, while toward the end of the year *Rabochaya gazeta* was launched. Extraordinary precautions were taken to safeguard the printing establishment from the gendarmes.

Like previous groups, the People's Will maintained several secret flats in the capital and elsewhere. Security demanded that such quarters should be used for one purpose only and by the fewest people, that as far as possible they should be isolated, so that the loss of one flat should not lead to the loss of others. Lack of funds often made this impossible. Meetings might take place in a *kvartira* where explosives and excavating tools were stored and where sheets of publications were stitched together and passports forged. One of the flats in the capital was reserved for the headquarters of the Executive Committee, but sometimes it was forced to meet under conditions that violated the safety rules worked out by Alexander Mikhailov.

He was the Party's bursar. The rental of the secret quarters, the printing, the maintenance of professional revolutionaries who lacked means of subsistence, travelling, and particularly terrorist activities demanded the outlay of rather substantial sums of money. Kravchinsky estimated that three of the attempts on the life of Alexander II involved the expenditure of thirty to forty thousand roubles. While information about the income of the organization is fragmentary, there can be no doubt that it was not seldom in financial straits. In June 1879, while the Executive Committee was still nominally part of Land and Liberty, its cashbox held two thousand five hundred roubles. Vera Figner recalled that the People's Will received a portion of Lizogub's fortune amounting to eight thousand roubles. An equal amount was contributed by the Subbotina sisters. The possessions of the members of the Executive Committee were at its disposal, but there were no moneyed people among them. In fact, many of them were apparently supported by the Party. The subsidiary groups were under obligation to turn over to the Committee a portion of what they took in, but this was a meagre and uncertain source of revenue. The sale of publications and photographs of revolutionary martyrs was a more reliable way of getting cash. Probably the largest source of income was the purses of sympathizers. A memoirist mentions a donation of ten thousand roubles from a *zemstvo* leader. The contributions from 'sympathizers with the struggle for the people's liberation'— they were listed thus in the Party's organs—included substantial sums. Between 1 March and 15 July, 1881, they amounted to over twenty-seven thousand roubles. Tikhomirov estimated the Party's annual budget at eighty thousand roubles.

Land and Liberty had rejected the method of obtaining funds by robbing—'expropriating' was the term used—State banks. The People's Will adopted this procedure, on the ground that since it was at war with the government, the latter's property was a belligerent's legitimate booty. In December, 1880, preparations were started to expropriate the Treasury in Kishinev, but the enterprise was abandoned. In 1882 an attempt at expropriation was made at Gori, Georgia, the birthplace of Joseph Stalin, but proved a fiasco. Hopes of securing some funds from abroad were entertained, but it is uncertain if these materialized.

v

There was little factional strife between the People's Will and Black Repartition. The members visited each other's secret quarters, borrowed money from one another, shared information, and helped each other in various ways. The assassination of an informer, carried out in February 1880, was decided upon jointly by both organizations. The hope persisted that the two groups would sooner or later compose their differences and reunite.

The schism was hardly six months old when an attempt was made to effect such a merger. Axelrod, who represented Black

Repartition in the negotiations, argued that fighting the government was not fighting for Socialism and that not to make this clear was to create confusion. Accordingly, he demanded that the organ of the People's Will should declare itself candidly to be a journal of political revolution. The Executive Committee offered instead to add Axelrod to the editorial staff of *Narodnaya Volya* and give him a free hand in preaching Socialism. Nor did Axelrod's other condition, namely, that the group for which he spoke should retain freedom of action after the merger, prove acceptable. The parley came to nothing, and the two organizations continued to carry on independently. From time to time orthodox populists joined the People's Will, but only as individual converts.

The members of the two factions were separated by differences of temperament, not unlike those that kept apart the *buntars* and the Lavrovists. The ideological causes of the rift have already been indicated, except the attitude toward the nationality problem. Like its parent body, Black Repartition advocated the political self-determination of the ethnic groups which the Empire had absorbed in the course of its expansion. In Russian radical circles the idea became current in the 'sixties and gained further authority in the next decade. A journal published in 1878 in Geneva by 'Populists-Bakuninists' pleaded for the break-up of the Empire, pointing out, among other separatist tendencies, that Eastern Siberia, because of its economic interests, might in time gravitate toward the United States rather than toward Petersburg or Odessa. The revised programme of Black Repartition included the demand for 'the independence of the nationalities mechanically bound together in the united all-Russian Empire'.

The orthodox populists accused their adversaries of standing for a centralized State dominated by the Great Russian nationality. The People's Will rejected the impeachment, insisting that it favoured the widest application of the principle of local autonomy and indeed did not deny the subject nationalities the right to secede from the Empire, but admitted that the disintegration of Russia was not its ideal. It preferred to keep out of its platform a demand that, on the one hand, had bitter enemies and, on the other, was, as the Executive Committee put it, 'an invention.' 'Where,' asked Zhelyabov, 'are our Fenians, our Parnell?'

Indeed, at this time the non-Russian population of the Empire evinced but little interest in local autonomy along ethnic lines, let alone secession. Poland alone harboured a powerful separatist movement. Yet the few socialist groups that existed in Warsaw in the late 'seventies were not interested in the restoration of Poland's independence. They held this to be a deviation from the class struggle, to which their efforts were confined. The so-called Ukrainian movement, which had lingered on among the intellectuals of Kiev, Kharkov, and Odessa since the 'forties, aimed only at cultural autonomy and held aloof from both Socialism and revolution. Men and women of Little Russian (Ukrainian) stock were prominent among the *narodniks*, but they were apt to think of themselves as Russians first and foremost. Hardly any propaganda literature in the Ukrainian vernacular was produced by the revolutionaries. The appearance of such literature would have been a double challenge to the authorities, for on 18 May, 1876, a *ukase* made the printing and importation of Little Russian publications a criminal offence.

Among the revolutionaries there was a scattering of men and women belonging to the other national minorities, but they were for the most part alienated from their own people. This was especially true of the Jews.

Very few Jews worked for the radical cause in the 'sixties. In the following decade the number increased. Among the politicals arrested between the middle of 1873 and 1 January, 1877, Jews constituted seven per cent of those placed under police surveillance, fifteen per cent of those deported and four and a half per cent of the serious offenders who were tried in court—sixty-six persons in all. Of the members of the People's Will who were given a court trial over fourteen per cent were Jews. They constituted fifteen per cent of all the politicals arrested in 1884–90 (579 out of 4,307 persons). Jews were outstanding among the radical leadership. Mark Natanson founded the Chaikovsky Circle and rallied the scattered forces of revolution under the banner of Land and Liberty; Lev Ginzberg headed the Lavrovist faction; Pavel Axelrod saved the frail barque of Black Repartition from foundering; Savely Zlatopolsky was prominent in the 'Executive Committee'; his brother Lev invented the code used by the People's Will.

Like their Gentile comrades, most of the Jewish radicals were of the intellectual type. They had received an education in the government schools thrown open to their people by Alexander II. The nihilist philosophy of the liberation of the individual from the bonds of authority and tradition held a strong appeal for youths eager to escape from the ghetto. Indeed, the trend represented by Pisarev had a repercussion in the neo-Hebrew literature of the period. Of the several hundred Jews who attended the Russian universities in the 'seventies, many embraced with a newcomer's zeal the world of advanced ideas into which Russian books carried them.

Only a few of the proselytes attempted to carry the socialist message to Jewish artisans and wage-earners in their own language. Aaron Liberman argued in the pages of *Vperiod!* (in 1875) that his people offered grateful soil for the socialist seed: 'Revolution is our tradition; the community is the basis of our legislation. Anarchy was our oldest social order. . . .'

In 1876 a group of 'Jewish socialist-revolutionaries' issued an appeal to Jewish intellectuals, in Russian and Hebrew, urging them to turn their attention to their own people. The call fell on deaf ears. By and large, the intellectuals subscribed to the then current notion that their own people were a parasitic body of shopkeepers and money-lenders who could not be expected to play any part in building the socialist future. They overlooked the fact that a considerable proportion of the group belonged to the working class. It was true, however, that the poverty-stricken Jewish masses, living their traditional life in ghetto seclusion, were even less accessible to ideas of political and social insurgency than were their Gentile neighbours, while the moneyed people—a small group of *nouveau-riche* merchants, bankers and railroad magnates—were completely loyal to the existing order.

Years were to pass before it was borne in on the Jewish radicals that there was work for them in their own vineyard. In the meantime they were eager to 'go to the people'—to the Russian people. Osip Aptekman, for one, was so determined to remove all barriers between himself and the Russian peasants that before he made his pilgrimage to the people he joined the Orthodox Church. 'And let me tell you,' he recalled, 'I felt as though I had been regenerated. "I am going to the people," I thought, "indeed not as a Jew but as a Christian; I am at one with the people." '

Others submitted to baptism in order to conclude a marriage, real or fictitious, with a person of Christian faith—mixed marriages occurring frequently in radical circles and the law forbidding marital union between Jew and Gentile. They severed the ties that bound them to their own people apparently without compunction. Jewishness was not a vexing problem to them, and if it did trouble them, they said to themselves that the social revolution would liquidate the Jewish question for good and all.

Baptism may have given an Aptekman spiritual satisfaction. It is doubtful if it added to his effectiveness as a propagandist. The barrier between the common people and the intellectual was, of course, even greater when the latter was of alien stock and tradition. Where Jews could be of most service was in the printing and distribution of literature and in organizational work. They found themselves in the faction that embraced the political orientation. A democratic régime assuring equality before the law to all citizens could not but attract members of a group deprived of elementary civil rights. Populism, with its Slavophil roots, its cult of the peasantry, its sense of indebtedness to the masses, could have only a superficial hold on the Jew.

The People's Will generally was not overmuch concerned with the country's ethnic heterogeneity. It held that the united efforts of all the sections of the population should be directed against the common enemy, the autocracy. The alleged nationalist aspirations of the minorities seemed a threat to the cause. It was only after the achievements of the revolution had been securely established by the Constituent Assembly that the component nationalities should be allowed freely to determine their status. Thus the People's Will differed from Black Repartition only in that it relegated the self-determination of national minorities to the post-revolutionary period. There were members of both factions, however, who held nationalism to be a divisive force, harmful to the cause of social emancipation. Fundamentally, Russian radicalism had no room in its scale of values for cultural pluralism. It was believed that the imminent social upheaval would wipe out all national differences, turning them, as Lavrov put it, into 'a pale tradition of history'.

CHAPTER XIII

MAN HUNT

FROM the first, the 'Executive Committee' was a fighting body designed to carry on a kind of guerrilla warfare by means of acts of terror. Foremost among these was the assassination of the Czar. In a society where all political authority ultimately derived from the monarch, the resentment of the the enemies of the existing order was bound to centre on him. Since the days of the Decembrists, and even earlier, the thought of regicide had haunted many heads like some archetypal urge.

The Ishutin group had produced Karakozov, and Nechayev, too, had played with the idea of killing the Emperor. In the summer of 1878 Solomon Wittenberg, a former engineering student who was the son of a poor Jewish artisan, procured a quantity of pyroxilin. With the aid of a comrade who was a sailor, he was planning to lay a mine in the Odessa harbour where the Czar was expected to land. Arrested, he was sentenced to death. He turned down a scheme for his escape from prison because it involved danger for one of the guards, and he refused to consider embracing Christianity as a means of having his sentence commuted, though his mother implored him to do so. In his last testament he wrote: 'Of course, I do not want to die, and to say that I die willingly would be a lie on my part, but this should not cast a shadow on my faith and the strength of my convictions. Consider that the highest example of loving kindness and self-sacrifice was undoubtedly the Saviour, and yet even He prayed: "Let this cup pass from me!" . . . Nevertheless, in the same spirit I say to myself: "If it cannot be otherwise, if, in order for Socialism to triumph, it is necessary that my blood be shed, if the transition from the present order to a better one is impossible without stepping over our corpses, then let our blood be shed, in redemption, for the good of humanity. And that our blood will serve as a fertilizer of the soil upon which the seed of Socialism will sprout, that Socialism will triumph, and soon—this is my faith!" ' And he concluded with a private word to a friend begging that all thought of vengeance be laid aside.

On 11 August, Wittenberg was hanged, together with his accomplice, at a public ceremony attended, under official orders, by the entire school population above the age of twelve.

Alexander Solovyov's attempt on the Czar's life has already been dealt with. The repressions unleashed by the Government after that event did anything but discourage the thought of regicide. Plans to kill the Governors-General were abandoned in favour of the more ambitious enterprise. The Executive Committee condemned the Emperor to death on 25 August, 1879, or on the following day, which happened to be the anniversary of his coronation.

The design was to dynamite the train carrying the Czar from his summer residence at Livadia (near Yalta) back to the northern capital. The idea of employing Alfred Nobel's invention seems to have originated among southern hotheads as far back as 1873 or 1874. In those days dynamite was something of a novelty in Russia. The use of it in the Russo-Turkish War made it popular. A sample of it was brought from Switzerland, but it was found impossible to import the stuff or purchase it at home, and the Party had to have it manufactured by its own technicians. This work had been started while Land and Liberty was still in existence. Soon after the formation of the People's Will, the Executive Committee had at its disposal about a hundred kilograms of dynamite. It was prepared chiefly by Nikolay Kibalch-ich, a former engineering student who was the son of a priest. He had served a three-year prison term for having subversive literature in his possession, and when in 1878 he regained his liberty, he decided that he could best serve terrorism by devoting his life to the study of explosives.

At first it was believed that the Czar would proceed from the Crimea to Odessa by sea, and the decision was to blow up his train as it left the seaport on its northward journey. Having secured the position of a trackman on the Odessa railway, Frolenko, aided by several men, including Vasily Merkulov, a carpenter, began excavating a tunnel under the track. Early in November it became known, however, that the Emperor had abandoned his sea trip to Odessa. The weather was foul, and he was a poor sailor. So the preparations were discontinued.

The Czar proceeded north by rail from Simferopol via Kursk and Moscow. Such an eventuality had been foreseen, and it was decided to blow up the imperial train near Alexandrovsk (now Zaporozhye). On 1 October Zhelyabov appeared in this small town and gave himself out to be a merchant who intended to set up a tannery there. He secured a plot of ground, bought a wagon and a team of horses, and moved into a modest flat with his 'wife' (Anna Yakimova, the daughter of a village priest, who looked like a sturdy young peasant woman). With them were two 'workmen' (Tikhonov, a weaver, and Okladsky, a carpenter). Zhelyabov played the part of a small tradesman admirably.

The plan was to mine the track at a point where the railroad ran on top of an embankment seventy-five feet high. Two metal cylinders containing dynamite and provided with electric detonators were to be placed under the sleepers some eighty yards apart. The cylinders and the explosive were brought from Kharkov, the detonators were filched from a powder plant by an employee. Kibalchich and another technician had a hand in these preparations, but the work proper was performed by Zhelyabov and his 'workmen'.

Running parallel to the railway track was a road separated from it by a ravine. To channel off the water that accumulated at the bottom there was a culvert under the embankment. Several times during the night guards with lanterns examined the culvert to make sure that it was not clogged up, and the track, too, was patrolled periodically. The conspirators had to work during the intervals between inspections. Zhelyabov was at this time suffering from night blindness and was helpless in the dark, so that he had to be led by the hand to and from work. Yet he insisted on taking part in the actual digging and in placing the mines himself. The autumn rains had come and the nights were chilly. He had to work sprawling in the mud, wet to the bone and shivering with cold. Sometimes the men lost their way and fell into pits filled with water.

When the second mine was being laid, the conspirators came near being discovered by a trackman. The nervous tension grew intolerable. The men were sure that they were being watched. And what if snow came, showing their footprints plainly? One night Zhelyabov leapt from bed in his sleep several times and crawled on the floor, shouting: 'Hide the wire! Hide the wire!'

The work was completed during the night of 17 November, since word had come the previous day that the imperial train was scheduled to pass Alexandrovsk on the 18th. That morning the three conspirators drove out to the spot on the road opposite the mines, taking with them an electric battery and an induction coil. The ends of the wires that led to the mines were connected with the apparatus, and then the men waited. When the train reached the spot over the mines Okladsky shouted: 'Go to it!' and Zhelyabov closed the circuit. There was no explosion as the cars thundered on.

Zhelyabov was sick with disappointment. The cause of the failure has remained a mystery. Immediately after the train had passed, the men examined the apparatus and the wiring and were unable to detect anything wrong. Okladsky eventually turned informer, entering the service of the police, and lived long enough to be tried by a Soviet court as a former secret service agent. The prosecutor suggested that the man had intentionally sabotaged the enterprise by cutting the wire, but no evidence has come forth to substantiate this theory.

It proved impossible to salvage the mines, and they were left undisturbed. Perhaps the Committee entertained the idea of using them a second time if the Czar passed that way the following year.

II

The conspirators did not rely on the Alexandrovsk mines alone. Farther along the Emperor's route another charge was to be fired under his train. Should the one fail, the other might succeed.

The locality was chosen by Alexander Mikhailov, who headed the enterprise. It was a Moscow suburb—a place of scattered cottages and wide, unpaved, grassy streets—of which the police took small notice. A two-storey house situated near the railway track some two miles south of the Moscow station was purchased in the name of one Sukhorukov, merchant. This was Lev Hartmann, the son of a German immigrant. Hartmann was an activist, of scanty schooling and mature years, who had recently been admitted to the Executive Committee. On 22 September the merchant and his 'wife', who was none other than Sofya Perovskaya, took possession. The two of them were to be assisted by half a dozen other comrades beside Mikhailov, all of them quartered in the city. The dynamite had been manufactured and brought to Moscow by Stepan Shiryayev, who was in charge of preparing, laying, and wiring the mine.

Explaining to the neighbours that they wanted to build an ice-cellar, the new owners had two hired labourers dig a deep pit in the kitchen. Then came the real work: the excavation of a tunnel to the railway embankment, a distance of some one hundred and fifty feet. It was decided to give it a triangular shape, shoring the sides with boards and leaving the floor bare. None of the conspirators had any experience in mining, and they had only the simplest tools: a large shovel, an 'English spade', a trowel. There was room in the tunnel for just one person at a time. He could move in it only by crawling and had to work in a crouching position. As the gallery lengthened, it became necessary to instal a primitive ventilator, but the cold, damp air was still so close that the men could stay at work for a short time only. At first, the earth was shovelled out, later it was hauled out with the aid of a windlass and scattered in the yard at night, in the hope that by morning it would either be partly washed away or snowed under.

A difficult problem was presented by the neighbours, who had the inquisitiveness of small-town folk. But the master of the house acted his part well, and the mistress was even cleverer in keeping suspicion at bay. The couple dressed, gestured, spoke in their assumed character of tradespeople, and the rooms were appropriately provided with icons and portraits of czars and metropolitans. The conspirators who were staying in the city would arrive early in the morning and leave late at night as inconspicuously as possible. A quantity of nitroglycerine sufficient to blow up the cottage was kept in two bottles under a bed. Perovskaya was to explode it with a shot at the appearance of police. The group had vowed not to be taken alive.

Progress was slow. There were unforeseen delays. Early in November came a heavy snowfall, followed by a thaw, and the pit in front of the gallery was turned into a puddle, while the gallery itself was flooded. Some of the water was baled out, and thereafter the men worked sitting in thin, icy mud. Then one morning the company made an appalling discovery. The tunnel crossed a rough dirt road that ran parallel to the railway track. Because of heavy autumn rains a washout had formed on the road, and through the hole the roof of the gallery was in plain sight. However, the water wagon that usually passed that way failed to appear, and the men were able to fill the hole without arousing any suspicion. Luck was with them again when a conflagration broke out in a neighbouring house: the fire was put out before it could endanger the Sukhorukov cottage.

Meanwhile it was getting more and more difficult to remove the earth, and the air in the shaft was so bad that sometimes the digger's lantern went out and he himself fainted as he crouched in the ooze. The situation became even more trying as the tunnel got closer to the railway embankment. Because of faulty construction, the mouth of the gallery was somewhat higher than its rear, and there the water tended to accumulate. To get rid of it, a low dam was made and the water baled over it. The dam turned the rear of the gallery into the semblance of a tomb. The worker was in constant danger of being buried alive, for the earth there was crumbly, and when a train passed overhead a cave-in was a definite possibility, all the more so since that part of the tunnel was not shored up. In fact, Hartmann is said to have carried poison with him to put an end to his sufferings in case of a catastrophe. But the physical wretchedness and the anxiety were matched by a rare exaltation. Mikhailov said that as he sat in the mud digging away, his back against the dam, for the first time in his life looking into the cold eyes of death, he remained calm. Indeed, he was rather thrilled by the weight and might of the train as it thundered overhead, shaking up everything like an earthquake. The company did not lose the ability to laugh and crack jokes at their mishaps. Jollity reigned at the dinner table around which all would gather at two o'clock.

They had hoped to reach the tunnel by the beginning of November, but when November came there was still much digging to be done. Time was getting short. It was decided to get a steel drill to reach the tracks. Probably in order to buy it, they mortgaged the house—a risky step, since it involved a preliminary inspection of the premises in the presence of a police officer. But the transaction was carried out without a hitch.

They worked feverishly now, fighting exhaustion and sickness. Sofya Perovskaya's endurance was amazing. All were buoyed up by a passion that defied physical obstacles. 'The conflict here was not between man and man,' Mikhailov testified, 'not between the weak and the strong, but between embodied idea and material force.'

Finally, with infinite pains, the brass cylinders containing some eighty pounds of dynamite were set in place and wired. The experts feared that the charge was not sufficiently powerful and that the mines had not been pushed far enough under the track, but that could not be helped.

Word came that the imperial train was due to reach Moscow at about ten p.m. on 19 November. The six regular members of the group and two visitors held a celebration on the eve of the fateful day. Their emaciated faces lit by the ghastly flame of burning alcohol, they drank to the success of the enterprise and sang revolutionary songs around a table in which eight daggers 'were stuck cross-wise' above eight revolvers. Thus runs an account of the evening that Hartmann wrote for the *New York Herald* some two years later. It may be presumed that some of these lurid details, meant to impress a gullible foreign public, were the product of his imagination.

In the morning all except Shiryayev and Perovskaya left the cottage. He was to close the circuit; she was to watch the track through a slit in the wall of a shed and give the signal at the approach of the Czar's train. She was proud and happy to be thus honoured.

Extraordinary precautions were taken to protect the Emperor while he was travelling. He was on board one train, while another carried his retinue, servants and baggage, and he would change trains secretly at stations. The story goes that the conspirators received a telegram in code to the effect that the Czar occupied the fourth car in the second train. A little after nine p.m. a train flashed by. Perovskaya decided that it was the imperial retinue train, which was usually sent ahead to test the safety of the way. At ten twenty-five the lights of another locomotive peered out of the darkness. Perovskaya gave the signal, and Shiryayev pressed the lever. There was a deafening report. The two locomotives and the first car broke away, a freight car loaded with Crimean fruit was overturned and smashed, many cars were derailed. No one on board the train was hurt. The Czar was not among the passengers. At the last moment the imperial train had been sent ahead of the one that carried the Czar's retinue.

Shortly after the explosion the police entered the Sukhorukov cottage. There was a fire in the stove, a candle was burning on the table, which was set for two, but there was no trace of the occupants.

A plan to mine one more spot on the road connecting the Crimea with the capital had been under consideration, but it had not been carried out.

On 22 November the People's Will issued a proclamation about the attempt on the Czar's life. It was the first such pronouncement of the Executive Committee which had become the nucleus of the newly formed secret society. Herein Alexander II is described as 'the embodiment of despotism, hypocritical, cowardly, bloodthirsty and all-corrupting . . . the main usurper of the people's sovereignty, the middle pillar of reaction, the chief perpetrator of judicial murders', with fourteen executions on his conscience. 'He deserves the death penalty for all the blood he has shed, for all the pain he has caused. . . . Only if he were to renounce his power and hand it over to a freely elected Constituent Assembly . . . would we leave him in peace and forgive his crimes. Until that time—war, implacable war, to the last drop of our blood!'

The article on the attempt in the issue of *Narodnaya volya* dated 1 January, 1880, had as its epigraph the words of Edouard Vaillant, member of the Paris Commune: 'Society has only one obligation toward monarchs: to put them to death.'

III

The attempts to wreck the Czar's train had failed. The conspirators could take heart from the fact that despite these efforts the Executive Committee was intact. The end must be reached by other means.

One of the two men who had headed the Northern Union of Russian Workers, mentioned earlier, was Stepan Khalturin, a cabinetmaker of peasant stock. In his teens he had belonged to a group of boys in his native Vyatka who were planning to emigrate to America. He reached Petersburg too late to embark from there with the others, fell in with the Chaikovsky Circle and became a propagandist among fellow workmen. When the Northern Union was smashed in 1879, he escaped the police net. By that time he had become a confirmed partisan of terrorism. The idea that the Czar should perish at the hand of a man of the people became an obsession with him. He decided to gain entrance to the Emperor's entourage in the capacity of a mechanic and kill him at the first opportunity. This plan he abandoned in favour of another, as daring as it was inept: blowing up the Winter Palace. He undertook to do this single-handed. All he asked of the Committee was a supply of dynamite.

He had at one time worked on the Czar's private yacht, and being a skilful craftsman—he could give a surface so high a polish that 'a flea could not take a jump on it', as the Russian saying goes—he found employment on the maintenance force of the Winter Palace. This was late in September, 1879. Together with three carpenters he lodged in the basement of the building. Directly overhead were the guards' quarters and above them the so-called Yellow Hall, where the Emperor usually dined *en famille*. The plan was to explode a charge of dynamite in the basement when the Czar was in the dining-room, in the hope of wrecking it and killing its occupants.

While the Emperor was in the Crimea, Khalturin's position was easy. Everyone liked the handsome, tall, thin youth—he was a consumptive—who acted the part of a yokel. There was little supervision of the staff. While the front entrances were strictly guarded, the back doors were open day and night to the servants and any stray companions they might choose to entertain in their quarters. Under these circumstances it was not difficult for Khalturin to smuggle in small quantities of the explosive in the guise of sugar.

The situation changed after the Czar's return from the south and particularly after the arrest, late in November, of Kvyatkovsky, the member of the Executive Committee who maintained contact with Khalturin. In addition to a quantity of dynamite and apparatus for the preparation of a mine, the police found among Kvyatkovsky's papers two plans of the Winter Palace with the dining-room marked by a red cross. The building was searched and, although nothing suspicious was found, extraordinary security measures were inaugurated. The entrances to the palace were closely guarded, the maintenance force was carefully screened, a gendarme moved into the carpenters' quarters which were subjected to sudden raids.

Khalturin continued to be held above suspicion. In fact, the aged gendarme took a special liking to him and even planned a match between the young man and his own marriageable daughter. Khalturin moved freely about the palace. On one occasion he found himself alone with the Czar in his study, where some repair work had to be done. He had a hammer in his hand and could easily have killed the monarch from behind. He could not bring himself to do it. On another occasion this man who plotted the Czar's death and firmly believed him to be the people's worst enemy, took a trifling object from his desk and treasured it as a souvenir.

In spite of the increased risk, Khalturin went on adding to his stock of dynamite. At first he had placed it under his pillow, although this gave him severe headaches. Later he transferred it to a chest where he kept his linen and clothes. Excavating, and laying a mine in the basement, or in any way directing the force of the explosion, was out of the question. The chest placed in a corner was to act as a mine. The chances of success were so slight that the enterprise verged on the fantastic. The Executive Committee may have realized this, but snatched at desperate measures.

By the beginning of February Khalturin had stored in his chest about a hundred pounds of explosive. He kept asking for more. Zhelyabov, who had replaced Kvyatkovsky after the latter's arrest, admired the man's pluck, but quoted the experts' opinion that the amount was sufficient to demolish the Czar's dining-room. He was thinking of the risk of detection that further delay would involve, and perhaps also of the innocent people who were bound to be injured by a bigger explosion. Finally the rumour spread that the carpenters were to be moved out of the palace, and it was decided to act.

Khalturin was to take advantage of the earliest moment that the carpenters would be out of the basement and the Czar in the Yellow Hall, Such an opportunity presented itself on 5 February, 1880. He knew that the imperial family dined about six-thirty. Finding himself alone in his quarters that evening, he fired a fuse connected with a detonator of fulminate of mercury placed in the chest and left the building.

At six-twenty he met Zhelyabov a short distance from the palace, and just as he greeted him there was an explosion. It shook the immense edifice, smashing over a thousand window panes and putting out all the lights. The guardroom above the basement was demolished, but the dining hall directly overhead was only slightly damaged: the floor sagged and one wall sprang a crack. The total number of casualties was eleven killed and fifty-six wounded, many of them soldiers on guard duty. The injured men refused to leave their posts until properly relieved. The Czar was not among the victims. At the moment of the explosion he was on his way to the Lesser Hall of Marshals to meet the Grand Duke of Hesse and the latter's son Alexander, Prince of Bulgaria, who had come to dine with the imperial family. Even had the Czar been in the dining-room, he would not have been harmed.

Khalturin managed to make his way quietly out of the capital. He was profoundly disheartened, and many months passed before he resumed an active rôle in the People's Will.

In its proclamation issued hot upon the event, the Executive Committee, trying to save its face, stated that the dynamite charge had been calculated correctly, but that the Czar was half an hour late for dinner and thus escaped alive, 'to the misfortune of our country'. It expressed deep regret over the death of the soldiers of the guard and concluded by declaring that the fight would go on until Alexander II abdicated in favour of the people and placed social reconstruction in the hands of a freely elected Constituent Assembly.

The explosion at the palace greatly added to the prestige of the Executive Committee. The public could not help being awed by this mysterious, redoubtable body that had dared to pit itself against all the resources of a mighty Empire.

IV

The acts of terror were beginning to give the Government a case of nerves. On 26 May, 1879, Count Valuyev, one of the most influential and less benighted members of the ruling hierarchy, made this entry in his private diary: 'It seems to me that everything is crumbling and collapsing piecemeal—and that I am powerless to arrest this process.' And a few days later: 'I feel that the ground is shaking, the house threatens to crash down, but the tenants don't seem to notice it.' A year passed, and he was writing: 'Alone a supernatural power can stop the land-slide. The Government is besieged, but imagines itself the besieger.'

On the day after the train had been blown up near Moscow the Czar received representatives of the various estates in the Kremlin. He promised the nobles to take energetic measures against subversion and wordless, with tears in his eyes, he passed through the halls where the members of the other estates were gathered. The organ of the People's Will noted the absence of patriotic demonstrations in the city. In the evening Alexander attended a rout given by the Governor-General. He looked old, his eyes were lustreless, his breathing laboured. 'In the hands of this flabby, cowardly, pleasure-loving, dissolute old man is the fate of a nation of a hundred million,' ran an account by an eye-witness printed in *Narodnaya volya*. The next day he took part in the traditional procession from the Uspensky Cathedral to the Chudov Monastery in the Kremlin. The two buildings are separated by a few dozen yards. In former years the Czar had walked this distance in plain view of the populace. This time he proceeded in a carriage surrounded by an armed escort. It was whispered in the crowd of onlookers that he had been led out of the cathedral under guard, like a prisoner.

The Winter Palace explosion threw the capital into a turmoil. People began to leave the city in panic. It was expected that grave disturbances would occur on 19 February, the twenty-fifth anniversary of Alexander's reign. The London *Times* reported the rumour that on that day the three principal avenues would be blown up. Nothing untoward happened, and the city soon quieted down. To mark the anniversary a reception was held at the palace. The Czar looked like 'a ghost', Viscount Vogüé thought. 'Never,' wrote the French diplomat in his diary, 'have I seen him so pitiful, aged, played out, choked by a fit of asthmatic coughing at every word. . . . Behind him another ruin, the old Chancellor [Gorchakov], who has been trotted out for this supreme occasion, like a mummy taken out for an airing. He leans against one of the columns of the Hall of Peter the Great so as not to fall, like the Empire that he directs;

he understands nothing, recognizes no one, and keeps repeating: "I'm done for. I'm done for." It looks as if he would have to be carried out by the spoonful. We are disturbed by the spectacle of these human ruins . . . in this palace that trembles.' In the evening there was a gala performance of Glinka's *A Life for the Czar*, and the diarist noted the empty boxes, from which 'no doubt fear had chased the tenants.'

A few days after the explosion the Emperor appointed a Supreme Commission for the Maintenance of State Order and Public Peace. At the head of this body, which was vested with practically unlimited authority, he placed Count Mikhail Loris-Melikov, a hero of the Turkish war and a brilliant administrator who, in spite of his lowly origin—he was the son of an Armenian merchant—was rapidly making his way to the top of the bureaucratic ladder.

Almost at once the Government had an opportunity to demonstrate its decision to deal ruthlessly with terrorists. Loris-Melikov had been in office hardly more than a week when there was an attempt on his life, which, however, left him without a scratch. His assailant was a former Yeshiva student by the name of Mlodecki who had embraced Christianity to make it easier for him to carry the message of revolution to the peasantry. In firing at the Count he had acted without the help and indeed the knowledge of the Executive Committee. The young man was seized *in flagrante delicto*, court-martialled and hanged two days later (22 February, 1880). Years afterwards Loris-Melikov asserted that the execution had been carried out against his will, at the Czar's instance. In March, two men were sent to the gallows in Kiev for distributing underground leaflets. Their execution figures in the uncensored text of Tolstoy's novel, *Resurrection*, as the shattering experience transforming an unpolitical, scholarly youth into a revolutionary.

Loris-Melikov's programme of combating sedition was not, however, confined to punitive measures and to increasing the efficiency of the police. He decided that to cut the ground from under the revolutionaries' feet it was necessary for the monarch to complete the reforms that had marked the beginning of his reign. The younger generation, he argued, should be treated with leniency, in the hope that it would make its peace with the State and with society. Above all, the population should be given a chance to participate, through representatives, in legislative work having to do with local matters. The bureaucracy was becoming aware of the danger of functioning in complete isolation from the people.

One of the first acts of the head of the Supreme Commission was to issue an appeal to the public, stating that he relied chiefly on its support in restoring law and order. Two years earlier, after the assassination of Mezentzev, a similar appeal had been made, but while that had remained an empty gesture, Loris-Melikov struck the keynote of a brief era of official liberalism which at the time was dubbed 'the dictatorship of the heart'. Certain security measures that inconvenienced the population without hampering the revolutionaries were repealed; some political deportees were set free; the censor's hand was stayed; Count Tolstoy, the reactionary Minister of Education, whom the General held chiefly responsible for the spread of radicalism, was dismissed

At this time the Executive Committee hatched two more plots against the Czar's life, of which later. They miscarried, and the police remained unaware of them. The policy of toughness with revolutionaries and concessions to loyal subjects seemed to work: acts of terrorism appeared to have ceased. By the end of the summer the authorities were sufficiently reassured to do away with the Supreme Commission. In reporting this measure, the correspondent of the London *Times* wrote that Loris-Melikov 'had broken the spirit, if not the backbone, of the revolutionary monster'.

The Count remained at the helm as Minister of the Interior. Without delay he obtained the abolition of the dreaded Third Division which, as he said in a private communication, 'for over half a century had stood outside and above the law'. This amounted to little more than a change of name, however, for the political police was not abolished. Its functions were merely turned over to a department of the Ministry of the Interior. This pattern was to be followed in a later generation, when the *Cheka*, a descendant of the Third Division, would be abolished, only to reappear under a succession of names.

The new Minister was largely responsible for another measure: teams of senators were dispatched to certain provinces to gather information about the needs of the population. The data were to be used in formulating reforms. He then suggested a further step, which he believed to be the most effective way to fight sedition. He proposed that a General Commission should participate in the legislative work entailed by the prospective reforms. In addition to civil servants and specially appointed experts, the Commission was to include—and this was a great innovation—delegates elected by the *zemstvo* boards and municipal councils of the larger cities. It was to function in a strictly consultative capacity. Nothing was further from the Minister's mind than the intention to set up an agency that would encroach on the monarch's absolute authority. Nevertheless, the plan was held to be a timid step toward a parliamentary régime. Alexander himself is variously reported to have likened the Commission to the *Etats Généraux* or the *Assemblée des Notables* convoked by Louis XVI, and to have added: 'We must not forget what followed.'

In previous years similar and even bolder proposals had been made by several statesmen, including the Czar's brother, Constantine, but they were all stillborn. The 'Loris-Melikov constitution', as the project of the Commission came to be called, was favourably reported on by a special committee of high dignitaries including the Heir Apparent and, on 17 February, 1881, it received the seal of approval from the Emperor.

V

Aside from the cessation of acts of violence, the authorities had yet another reason to feel reassured: by the spring of 1880 the cloak of mystery had fallen from the terrorist group.

On 14 November, 1879, a young man was arrested at the Yelizavetgrad (now Kirovo) railway station, and his suitcase proved to contain a quantity of dynamite. This was Grigory Goldenberg, known to his comrades as 'Beaconsfield', apparently in allusion to his Jewish origin, the only trait he shared with Dizzy. His experiences resembled those of most of the men who joined the small band of terrorists that was to be the core of the People's Will. In his early twenties, already an illegal with prison and exile in his past, he read in an underground pamphlet entitled *Buried Alive* about the treatment of politicals in the Kharkov prisons, and he decided to kill Prince Kropotkin,

Governor-General of Kharkov. When, after shadowing his man for days, he fired the fatal shots (on 9 March, 1879), he was in a state of intolerable tension. In fact, he had made up his mind to take his own life if there were further delay. He had intended to give himself up on the spot, so as to enhance the effect of the prince's death with that of his own. But the Executive Committee succeeded in making him abandon his idea, and he managed to evade arrest. Shortly thereafter he volunteered to assassinate the Czar, but his offer was rejected, and the attempt was carried out by Solovyov. He had knowledge of the Alexandrovsk enterprise and he participated in the mining of the track near Moscow. To that end he undertook to bring some dynamite from Odessa. It was this trip that landed him in jail.

Goldenberg was not unintelligent, but he was inordinately gullible and given to day-dreaming, in which self-exaltation played a large part. Furthermore, he alternated between spurts of rapturous elation and periods of abysmal depression. Just before he died he recognized that he had been 'mentally ill', a fact apparently not realized by the rest of the inner circle of conspirators.

At first, in spite of threats, the prisoner refused to make a deposition. He did, however, talk—and at great length—to a fellow political with whom he shared a cell. He did not suspect that his comrade was an informer planted by the police. In this way the authorities learned that the man they were holding was Prince Kropotkin's assassin. He admitted nothing. It was only in February (1880) that he prepared a statement, in which he confessed his crime. His main purpose in committing it, he wrote, was to lay bare in court Kropotkin's brutality. He did not regret his act: 'Let my blood, too, be the seed of Socialism, just as the blood of the early martyrs was the seed of the Christian Church'. He blamed the Government's white terror for the red terror. And he ended with an impassioned appeal to the Czar to stop 'the fratricidal war', warning him that blood would continue to be shed until the country had a régime guaranteeing the people freedom under law.

Yet when he was making this deposition, he was no longer sure that he and his comrades were on the right road. Now kept in solitary confinement, he had ample opportunity to subject his beliefs to a thorough scrutiny. Presently his uncertainty crystallized into the conviction that political terror was a tragic failure. It interfered with the work of enlightenment and organization, and if it demanded heroism, it also sowed the seeds of treason. Besides, the revolutionaries did not have the shadow of a chance to come out on top in the unequal struggle against the Government. They must lay down their arms, and before long the Czar would be sure to grant the country a democratic régime, and under the sun of freedom the way would be speedily prepared for the advent of Socialism.

Goldenberg did not reach this delightful conclusion unaided. The prompting of his questioners helped him to it. The secret service men were beginning to use rather sophisticated methods of handling prisoners. They played on the young man's credulity, flightiness, and self-regard. They succeeded in convincing him that they, too, had the interests of the people at heart. A reconciliation between the two warring camps was possible, they suggested, and he, Goldenberg, might personally bring it about. One officer hinted that a constitution was to be promulgated that very year. What gave a semblance of reality to the hint was that rumours of the great reforms associated with Loris-Melikov's name penetrated even the prison walls. The Count himself twice visited the prisoner in his cell and made a favourable impression. The repentant terrorist decided that Loris-Melikov was to be the saviour of Russia.

He was now possessed by one idea: it was his duty to stop the futile murders and the hangings that followed them. But how? Finally, he hit upon what seemed to him a stroke of genius— again not without the prompting of his astute examiners. He would tell the authorities all about his own revolutionary activities and all he knew about the activities of his fellow conspirators. This would disarm the Government, it would have no excuse for going on with the policy of repression, the hopeless fight would cease, and many precious young lives would be saved. True, his revelations would lead to a number of arrests, but at worst they would result in sentences of hard labour. Then a year or two later there would be a general amnesty, and the prisons would disgorge their inmates; before long, Russia would have a constitutional régime and a glorious era of freedom would commence. And he, Goldenberg, would have played no small part in bringing all this about.

In March he signed a formal confession. He spared neither himself nor his comrades. He gave names, real and assumed, addresses, identifying marks; he outlined the history of the People's Will as well as its organization and methods of propaganda; he told all he knew of the various attempts on the Czar's life. In April he was transferred from the Odessa prison to the Fortress of Peter and Paul. While he travelled north, he was put in irons. When he reached his destination, they were removed, much to his regret. 'In irons,' he wrote to his sister, 'it is somehow pleasanter, better, morally more satisfying.' Alone the fear of being declared insane prevented him from asking to keep his fetters. In his new prison he continued his revelations.

When he first resolved to turn informer, he had been ecstatically happy. He had given ample proof that he was ready to lay down his life for the cause. Now he was going to stake his honour, risk the reputation of a Judas. But events would vindicate him, and in good time it would be recognized that he had been prompted by the highest motives. He told his mother on one of her visits to him that she would have reason to be proud of her son. When in May two death sentences meted out to political offenders were commuted to hard labour, he attributed this to his disclosures. So firm was his conviction of having done the right thing that he believed that he might win over some of his comrades. He was permitted to talk without witnesses to Zundelevich, who was now a fellow prisoner. But far from being converted, Zundelevich apparently succeeded in raising terrible doubts in Goldenberg's mind.

The time of his trial drew near. He wrote to Loris-Melikov requesting that he be shown no clemency. The thought of being rewarded for his services to the authorities was intolerable to him. He also penned a lengthy confession addressed to 'Friends, comrades, honest people of the whole world, known and unknown to me', a confused and anguished apologia. Then, too, he wrote frantic little notes assuring his comrades that he had sought their happiness, not their ruin, and that he continued to be faithful to the cause.

He was already half aware that he had been tricked by the cunning of his examiners and his own *naïveté* and folly into becoming an ordinary informer. Perhaps a conversation he was permitted to have with Zundelevich on 10 July finally opened his eyes to the dreadful reality. On one occasion he had hinted to his questioners that if he ever came to repent his frankness even for a moment, he would commit suicide. On 15 July he managed to strangle himself with a towel attached to the faucet of his washstand.

Kletochnikov, the Party's counter-spy, was able to keep the Executive Committee informed about Goldenberg's disclosures and thus somewhat neutralize them. Nevertheless they had a disastrous effect on the fortunes of the People's Will.

CHAPTER XIV

SIC SEMPER TYRANNIS

As has been stated, during the first months of Loris-Melikov's ascendancy there were two additional and equally abortive attempts on the life of Alexander II. One occurred in Odessa. Rumour had it that he would pass through the city in the spring on his way to Livadia. Accordingly a couple, consisting of Sofya Perovskaya and a nominal husband of hers, opened a grocery on the street along which the Czar was bound to be driven on his way from the railway station to the harbour. The plan was to dig a tunnel from the store and lay a mine under the roadway. The work was actually begun, with the help of half a dozen men and women, including Vera Figner. In the latter part of May, however, it became known that the Emperor was not likely to go south just then, since the Empress lay on her deathbed (she died on 22 May). As a result, the operations were discontinued.

The conspirators then proposed that the work be completed to the end of doing away with Todleben, Governor General of the Odessa region. He had earned the hatred of the revolutionaries by his ruthlessness, and in any case there was a plan afoot to force the authorities to abolish the office of Governor General by systematically obliterating its incumbents. The Executive Committee decided, however, that the mine, as a method of assassination, should be reserved for the Czar. And so, traces of excavation having been removed, the grocery was abandoned. According to Vera Figner, Todleben escaped alive because he soon left the city for a post in Vilna.

The other attempt on the Czar's life was made that summer in the capital. It involved blowing up the Kamenny Bridge, as he crossed it on his way from the Tsarskoe Selo railway station to the Winter Palace. A team of activists, headed by Zhelyabov, managed to place in the water under the bridge four rubber sacks containing some two hundred and fifty pounds of dynamite and provided with detonators and wires. They fastened the loose ends of these to a float anchored nearby, on which women did their laundry. Acting on the intelligence that the Czar was expected to arrive in the capital from Tsarskoe Selo on 17 August, Zhelyabov arranged to meet Vasily Teterka, a labourer he had won over to the cause, at the bridge on that day. The latter was to bring with him a basket of potatoes, and Zhelyabov an electric battery. The two were to row out to the float, where Teterka was to go through the motions of washing the potatoes while Zhelyabov connected the wires with the battery. When the Czar's carriage was on the bridge, Zhelyabov was to detonate the charges.

It is not clear why the scheme fell through. One explanation is that Teterka, having no watch, was late for the appointment. The same day the Emperor left for the Crimea. He was accompanied by Princess Yuryevskaya, who, having been his mistress for fifteen years and having borne him three children, became his morganatic wife six weeks after the Empress's death—to the scandal of the court circles.

There was something half-hearted about this last effort, and it was followed by a lull in terrorist activities. But this was not because Goldenberg's comrades shared his faith in 'the dictatorship of the heart'. In *Narodnaya volya* Loris-Melikov was described as a cross between a wolf and a fox. Nevertheless, it is possible that the People's Will deliberately refrained from action, waiting to see if the Government would at last take the road of democratic reforms.

The unacknowledged truce was short-lived. As winter approached, it was increasingly evident that nothing was to be expected from Loris-Melikov's 'bobtailed constitution' as, in a quatrain that was on everybody's lips, a humorist dubbed the plan for a General Commission. Long terms of hard labour were meted out to political offenders, and the treatment of the convicts was such that one of them committed suicide. In all, 127 politicals were tried in 1880, and at the end of the year 1,770 persons were under police surveillance. In October sixteen terrorists who had been arrested at various times during the preceding twelve months faced a Petersburg military court. Many of the charges against them were based on Goldenberg's disclosures. Two of the defendants were hanged on 4 November. As long as there had been some hope that the sentence would be commuted, the hands of the Executive Committed were tied. Now it was free to act again. Zhelyabov testified that the hangings 'were hailed with joy, in spite of the fact that the death of the two men tore out the very nerves, as it were, of the Party, while the commutation of Adrian Mikhailov's death sentence was met with undisguised chagrin.'[1]

The proclamation issued by the People's Will on the occasion of the double execution urged its members to store up their strength, for 'the hour of judgment is not far'. The phrase had a clear meaning: the assassination of the Czar. All other tasks were pushed into the background. The enterprise had now become an obsession with most of the members of the Committee. They were no longer able to reason about it. Zhelyabov, for one, behaved like a man in a trance, as though under the urgency of an outside force. Yet they were by no means free from a gnawing sense of the futility of their undertaking.

In the early winter it was resolved to make one more attempt, the seventh since the Odessa project the previous year, to explode a mine in the Czar's path. A team of observers, reporting to Sofya Perovskaya, ascertained that on Sundays he usually attended the trooping of the colours in the Mikhailovsky Manège, a score of blocks from the palace, and that he was driven there up the Nevsky and along Malaya Sadovaya. Work was started on a plan to mine this side street.

In the midst of these preparations the organization suffered a crushing blow: at the end of November the invaluable Alexander Mikhailov was arrested. He had ordered a number of photographs of the two men who were hanged from a commercial studio, the owner of which was a secret service agent, and was seized when he called for the pictures. Although he had sensed that there was something suspicious about the place, he failed to live up to his own precept of unremitting caution and walked into a police trap like the merest tyro.

Shortly before he faced the court, with nineteen other defendants, over a year later, he admonished his comrades in letters not to be tempted by thoughts of vengeance or by beautiful theories. 'In Russia,' he wrote, 'there is only one theory: to win liberty in

---

[1] Adrian Mikhailov, who had driven the carriage in which Kravchinsky escaped after killing Mezentzev, was condemned to hang, but the sentence was changed to a term of hard labour because he had turned informer, a fact that was not known to his comrades at the time.

order to get land.' The only way to do it, he asserted, was 'to strike at the centre,' i.e. at the occupant of the throne. He and nine of his comrades were condemned to die. He had long been used to the thought of death, and during the fifteen months of solitary confinement he had succeeded in overcoming the last vestiges of aversion to it. The trial itself was a happy experience, for it gave him a chance to profess his deepest convictions freely. On the eve of the day when he expected to be executed he tasted intense exaltation. He pictured himself on the scaffold among comrades all calmly facing the end, and saw his own state in 'a most iridescent light'. It seemed to him that if he had been a composer, he would have produced immortal music that night. 'Involuntarily,' he wrote to his sister, 'you come to believe in the presence within man of that heavenly fire which, at such cost to himself, Prometheus ravished and gave to humanity.' Then euphoria yielded to serenity. An hour after midnight he went peacefully to sleep.

He woke up in the morning in the same placid mood. The news that in his case the Emperor had substituted a life term of penal servitude for the death penalty left him indifferent. But as the days went by and he remained in the dark as to the fate of his comrades, he was seized with anguish. He could not bear the thought that he alone had been spared. As a matter of fact, all the death sentences, except one, had been commuted. Instead of being shipped to Siberia, Mikhailov was incarcerated in the Alexis Ravelin of the Fortress of Peter and Paul. Less than two years later he sickened and died there.

II

On 2 December, a three-room front basement on Malaya Sadovaya Street was rented by Yevdokim Kobozev, tradesman, in reality Yury Bogdanovich, member of the Executive Committee. A dynamite charge under the roadway was again to be tried, but it was to be combined with a new form of attack: several bombs were to be tossed at the Czar's carriage, should he survive the explosion. Kibalchich and Isayev, another Party technician, had succeeded in producing such a missile. Finally, if both methods failed, Zhelyabov was to assail Alexander with dagger and pistol. The combination of mine, bomb, pistol, and dagger gave the conspirators the feeling that this time Alexander could not escape alive.

On New Year's Eve some of the activists who were in the capital got together to celebrate. Gleb Uspensky, the writer, was the host. The gathering was meagrely but genuinely gay. The life of the party was Zhelyabov. Sablin, who had acted the part of a grocer in Odessa, told anecdotes from the life of the clergy. Gesya Helfman made music on a comb. She was a homely girl with a high-pitched voice and a constant smile, who had run away from an Orthodox Jewish home at sixteen to avoid marriage to a groom chosen by her parents. There was singing and dancing: quadrilles, lancers, and the native *trepak*, a gallopade with plenty of stamping. Isayev made so much noise that the neighbours protested. He took off his shoes and kept it up. One guest did not join in the fun: she had witnessed the execution of Lizogub, and her imagination was fitting the shroud now to one, now to another dancer. A similar gathering had greeted the coming of the previous year. On that occasion the ghost of Nicholas I had informed the company through the instrumentality of an improvised ouijah board that his son would die by poison.

On 8 January, 1881, Bogdanovich and his 'wife', the Anna Yakimova who had played the part of Zhelyabov's spouse at Alexandrovsk, moved into the basement on Malaya Sadovaya. The couple opened a cheese store in one room and used another as living quarters. It was from there that the digging was started. Ten men, including Zhelyabov, lent a hand at various times. Operations went on smoothly until a wooden sewer was cut into, and the tunnel was filled with an overpowering stench. Nevertheless the work went on and late in February a passage of some fifteen feet extending to the middle of the street was completed.

While preparations for the dynamiting were in progress, experimentation with a hand bomb was also going forward. It was conducted by Kiblachich and Isayev, the Party's best technical brains. Who was to throw the missiles? Four men were selected: Ignaty Grinevitzky (Party name: 'Pussy'), twenty-six years old, a former engineering student, stocky, good-natured, taciturn; Timofey Mikhailov, a boiler maker, twenty-one years old; Ivan Yemelyanov, a boy of twenty, who after graduating from a trade school, had studied abroad on a grant from Baron Ginzburg, and was now a cabinetmaker; Nikolay Rysakov, a nineteen-year-old student. All were members of a 'fighting squad' formed as an adjunct to a workers' group primarily to carry on 'economic terror': to use strong-arm methods on informers and unpopular foremen. Zhelyabov was to testify in court that the Executive Committee had called for volunteers from the several 'squads' in existence and that forty-seven men had signified their 'willingness to sacrifice themselves'. He was generally candid in his testimony, but in this case he must have deviated from the truth. If he had all those volunteers to choose from, it seems odd that he should have selected Rysakov, a mere boy who had recently fallen under his influence. The People's Will was to pay dearly for having entrusted so dangerous a task to this raw youth.

One evening in mid-February the four bomb-throwers gathered in a newly rented *kvartira* on Telezhnaya Street, tenanted by Sablin and Gesya Helfman. Zhelyabov outlined the plan of attack, and Kibalchich lectured on the bomb—there was something professorial about this quiet man, with his lean, bloodless, sharp-nosed face and his habit of screwing up his eyes, which often had a faraway look. He demonstrated parts of the mechanism for the class, drew diagrams, described how the bomb worked and how it should be handled. The missile was a cylindrical affair weighing five to six pounds, the outer shell fashioned out of an empty kerosene can, and the explosive a combination of nitroglycerin and pyroxilin. Shortly after the meeting the bombs were tested in a suburban park. Two missiles were pitched, and one of them exploded.

Meanwhile, the affairs of the Party were going from bad to worse. It was using up its principal, as Zhelyabov put it. In addition to intelligence obtained from Goldenberg the previous year, the police now had the services of another informer: the young carpenter, Okladsky, who had taken part in the attempt at Alexandrovsk. Arrest followed upon arrest. Early in February Kletochnikov was trapped by gendarmes. The conspirators felt surrounded. Nerves were on edge. Then came the heaviest blow of all: in the evening of 27 February Zhelyabov was arrested in the lodging of an incautious comrade.

The shattering news reached Vera Figner the next morning. With Isayev as her 'husband' she was occupying a flat, which was the headquarters of the conspiracy. Later in the day word came that the cheese store had been visited by the police. It was a house search in the guise of a sanitary inspection. For some time the establishment had been under suspicion. The owners looked the part of petty tradespeople, he with his massive beard and his face the colour of a brass samovar, she with the manner and speech of a country wife, but they acted queerly, and there were too many young men coming to the basement at night. As it happened, luck was with the plotters: the examination of the premises was so perfunctory that the excavation was not discovered. This in spite of the fact that a barrel and a tub in the store were filled with earth from the tunnel; that in the store-room, too, there were sacks and boxes packed with earth, as well as heaps of it barely covered with straw or coke and mats; and that there was earth under the sofa in the living-room. For the moment the situation was saved, but it was obvious that the police had an eye on the place.

That afternoon all the members of the Executive Committee who could be reached met at headquarters. The situation that confronted them was a dismal one. Kletochnikov, the Party's shield, was gone. Zhelyabov, the heart of the conspiracy, was behind bars. The police were clearly closing in on them. True, the Malaya Sadovaya excavation was completed, but the explosive had not yet been placed in it. And not a single bomb was ready. Kibalchich, phlegmatic and absent-minded as usual, had been dilatory, perhaps not quite trusting the child of his brain. The culmination of the long effort, on which so many hopes were centred, hung by the thinnest of threads. A slight mishap might mean the final collapse of the enterprise for which so much had been risked and for which men had gone to the gallows.

In these desperate circumstances the Committee decided to act. Isayev was instructed to lay and wire the mine on Malaya Sadovaya. The meeting adjourned at three p.m. and two hours later in the same quarters work began on the bombs. The task was entrusted to Kibalchich, who had just returned with the prospective bomb-throwers from testing a half-loaded missile in an unfrequented spot beyond the Neva. Vera Figner and Sofya

Perovskaya also made themselves useful. The four bombers were told to report the following morning, 1 March, at the Telezhnaya Street flat. It was expected that on that day, as on two previous Sundays, the Emperor would be driven to the Manège to witness the trooping of the colours.

That night Grinevitzky set down what was in effect a letter to posterity. Only a fragment of it has been preserved. 'Alexander II must die,' he wrote. ' . . . He will die, and with him, we, his enemies, his executioners, shall die too. . . . How many more sacrifices will our unhappy country ask of its sons before it is liberated? . . . It is my lot to die young, I shall not see our victory, I shall not live one day, one hour in the bright season of our triumph, but I believe that with my death I shall do all that it is my duty to do, and no one in the world can demand more of me. . . .'

Next day, by eight a.m., after fifteen hours of feverish, un-interrupted work, four bombs were ready. There was no ex-plosive for any more, nor would there have been time to manufacture them. The men would have one apiece. Perovskaya took two missiles to the Telezhnaya Street quarters, and later Kibalchich carried the other two there. Grinevitzky, Mikhailov, Yemelyanov, Rysakov were there, waiting. They were dismayed to hear that Zhelyabov had been arrested. Perovskaya was now in command. She outlined the plan of action and drew on an envelope a rough chart of the streets adjacent to the Manège, marking with circles the spots where the bomb-throwers were to be stationed. It was believed that the Emperor would be driven up the Nevsky and along the mined block, which opened onto a small square in front of the Manège. Two men were to loiter at the corner of the Nevsky and Malaya Sadovaya Street, and two were to stand at the other end of the block, near the square. At the sound of the explosion all of them were to close in on the Czar's carriage from opposite directions and use their bombs if he was still alive.

Of course, he could take a different route, turning into Bolshaya Italyanskaya (now Rakov Street) which runs parallel to the Nevsky, thus avoiding the mined block. In that case no attack was to be made in the Manège Square, since it would be full of people. Instead, Perovskaya would walk past the men and by taking out a handkerchief and blowing her nose signal to them that they should abandon their posts and proceed to the Yekaterininsky (now Griboyedov) Canal, in the hope of attacking the Czar on his way back.

About an hour before noon all the conspirators filed out of the flat, each of the chosen four carrying a bomb wrapped in a handkerchief or a newspaper. There was little time to lose. The Emperor usually left the Palace in the early afternoon.

Since the previous night the mine on Malaya Sadovaya had been in place. On completing the work, Isayev had withdrawn. Sunday morning Bogdanovich too left the store, Yakimova alone remaining behind. Later in the morning she was joined by Frolenko. The imperturbable Ukrainian had been selected to turn on the current that would detonate the mine. The hope was that, being a stranger to the place, he might be able to get away in the confusion following the explosion. Yakimova, for her part, was to warn him of the approach of the imperial party and then leave without waiting for the mine to go off.

III

On Sunday morning, 1 March, the Emperor was in excellent spirits. Count Valuyev, who had an audience with him in the forenoon, noted in his diary that he hadn't seen the sovereign looking so well in a long time. The previous day, after the imperial family had attended Lenten service and taken communion, word had come that the redoubtable Zhelyabov had been arrested. This was glorious news. The cloud of fear under which the Czar and his wife had been living was at last lifting. Soon the rest of the terrorists would be rounded up. He felt a sense of well-being so keen that it frightened him. Nevertheless, Loris-Melikov, arriving about noon, pleaded with him not to leave the palace that day. The Minister spoke of rumours of another attack. After some hesitation, the Czar decided to attend the parade at the Manège. Their leader gone, he argued, the terrorists must have abandoned their plans. As a matter of fact, this view was shared by the security forces. That very morning the chief of police told his men that all was going well and that it was only necessary to seize two or three more conspirators to put an end to sedition for good and all. Thus Zhelyabov's arrest indirectly contributed to the success of the enterprise he had captained.

The Czar left the Palace in his two-seater drawn by a pair of horses a few minutes before one o'clock. It was a raw day; snow lay on the ground and was heaped up along the sidewalks; low clouds blanketed the sky. He had promised his wife that he would avoid Nevsky Prospect and the Malaya Sadovaya block with that peculiar cheese store. It filled her with apprehension, in spite of the fact that, as Loris-Melikov had assured her, the police found nothing suspicious there. Accordingly, the Emperor ordered his coachman to drive along Yekaterininsky Canal and up Bolshaya Italyanskaya. He was in the habit of naming the route at the last moment, so that no one knew it beforehand. Perovskaya was hanging about the Manège Square and two men with bombs were stationed nearby They made no move to attack the Czar: there was still the possibility that on his way back he might drive past the cheese store.

At the Manège, Alexander watched the manœuvres of two Guard battalions with obvious pleasure. He had a smile and a gracious word for his brother, Constantine, and the other dignitaries in his entourage. The brilliant ceremony lasted no more than thirty or forty minutes.

What route would he take on his way back? The terrorists waited feverishly for the answer. His carriage rolled down Bolshaya Italyanskaya, rendering the mine useless. This was Perovskaya's clue to give the signal that was to send the men with the bombs to the Yekaterininsky Canal. As she passed Grinevitzky, he gave her a barely perceptible wink.

Had the Czar driven home directly, he would have passed the quay before the bombers had time to reach it on foot. But he didn't. He paid a brief visit to his cousin, the Grand Duchess Catherine, and this enabled the men with the bombs to take up their new positions. Only three of them did so: Timofey Mikhailov lost his nerve, took his missile back to headquarters and went home. Astonishingly enough, none of the plotters, each carrying a queer parcel, attracted the attention of the police stationed along the Sovereign's route.

Emerging from the gates of the Duchess's palace, the Emperor's carriage proceeded at a clip down Inzhenernaya Street. On the box next to the coachman sat an orderly, and the vehicle was guarded by six mounted Cossacks. The rear was brought up by three sleighs, carrying Colonel Dvorzhitzky, district chief of police, and two officers of the Gendarmerie, charged with the security of the Emperor.

At the end of the block the two-seater turned right, on to the quay. It had gone little more than a hundred and fifty yards when it encountered a thick-set youth in a fur cap. This was Rysakov. He moved closer to the roadway and threw his bomb —it looked like a large snowball—between the horse's legs. It was then two-fifteen p.m.

There was a loud explosion, a spray of snow, earth and splinters fanned out from a spot on the pavement, and the scene was filled with bluish smoke. One of the Cossack escorts lay motionless on the ground, and nearby a butcher's boy, who had been on his way to deliver an order, was writhing and groaning. Both of them had been severely wounded and soon died. When the bomb went off, Colonel Dvorzhitzky's team reared and came to a sudden stop. He jumped out and hurried over to the Czar's carriage which had halted not many yards away. He was in time to help his Sovereign step out. The Colonel took in the situation at a glance: the floor and back of the carriage were shattered, the window panes broken, the orderly wounded, the Emperor himself, somewhat dazed, had suffered a slight cut on one of his hands, but was otherwise unharmed. He crossed himself and inquired if the criminal had been seized. The Colonel satisfied him on that score. Glancing back, he had noticed that several policemen and soldiers were holding a man pinned against the iron railing along the edge of the quay. This was indeed Rysakov. An eye-witness reported that on leaving his carriage, the Czar bent over one of the wounded. The coachman begged his master to get back into the carriage, but as it did not look safe, Dvorzhitzky took the liberty of offering to drive the Czar to the Palace in his sleigh. The Emperor consented, but said he wished first to have a look at his assailant.

By now not only policemen, but soldiers, sailors, cadets, and civilians were milling around on the quay. The Czar, flanked by Dvorzhitzky and the Cossack guards leading their horses, walked up to Rysakov. According to Dvorzhitzky, Alexander merely inquired about the youth's identity and turned away without a word. Another eye-witness thought he saw the Sovereign wag a threatening finger at his assailant.

The Colonel again urged the Czar to get into his sleigh and drive on to the palace. Alexander reflected a moment and said he wanted to have a look at the spot where the explosion had occurred. He walked over to the funnel-shaped pit formed by the bomb. The Cossack and the boy were still lying where they had fallen. He expressed solicitude for them.

His curiosity satisfied, he was ready to drive away. The delay amounted to five or six minutes. He had taken only a few steps when he came within two or three paces of a man leaning against the railing with a parcel in his hands. The man turned to face the Emperor and made a sudden movement. There was a second deafening explosion.

When the smoke cleared, on the dirty, blood-stained snow, pocked with splinters and littered with shreds of clothing, shoe leather, and other debris, lay nearly a score of wounded, moaning, crawling, trying to rise. Because people had crowded close to the Czar, the second bomb claimed many more victims than the first. On the shattered flagstones of the sidewalk near the railing the Czar crouched in a pool of blood. He was bare-headed, his fur-trimmed cloak and the uniform of the sappers of the Guard that he was wearing were in rags. His legs were splintered below the knee and blood was gushing from the wounds. Beside him lay his attacker, Grinevitzky, also gravely wounded and unconscious. Dvorzhitzky was in the same state but soon recovering consciousness, heard the Czar call weakly for help. The Colonel managed to lift him and with assistance place him in his own sleigh, but no one had sufficient presence of mind to see that he got first aid.

Alexander continued to bleed so profusely that the sleigh left a bloody trail as it made its way toward the Palace. When he was finally placed on a couch in his study and a physician summoned, his condition was hopeless because of loss of blood. He seemed to rally and received Holy Communion. At three-forty p.m. the flag flying over the Winter Palace was lowered to half mast.

At nine o'clock Grinevitzky, who had been carried to the infirmary attached to the Palace, regained consciousness. Determined to give no information to the police, he refused to disclose his name. An hour and a half later he was dead. His identity was established only posthumously. Of the innocent bystanders injured by the second bomb only one was wounded fatally. The affair of 1 March cost fewer lives than the Winter Palace explosion.

When Rysakov saw that the Czar was hurt, he expressed satisfaction, which earned him a punch in the head from one of the soldiers holding him. But he was turned over to the authorities unharmed.

The moment the second bomb went off, Yemelyanov, who was stationed some twenty paces down the quay, rushed to the scene of the explosion to see if Grinevitzky was alive and could be spirited away in the confusion. He realized at once that nothing could be done. Then, on impulse, he approached the Czar—he claimed to have been the first at his side—and helped prop him up in the sleigh. He did this with the bomb wrapped up in a newspaper under his arm. Then he made his way un-molested to the flat on Telezhnaya Street and turned in the missile.

IV

When Kibalchich and Isayev, who had been loitering near the Manège, found that the Emperor had not driven past the cheese store, they decided that the affair was a fiasco. Aloof and ab-stracted as ever, Kibalchich went to his furnished room and it was only in the evening that he learned of the event he had done so much to bring about. Isayev made his way to headquarters and reported failure. Vera Figner then went out to pay a visit, and while at her friend's learned of the Czar's death. She hurried back to the flat, where several comrades were gathered. Tears were in the eyes of all those present. Of that incredible moment she wrote later: 'The nightmare that had weighed down on Young Russia for ten years had vanished. . . . The Czar's blood shed by us had redeemed all the horrors of prison and exile, all the brutality and cruelty inflicted on hundreds and thousands of our comrades, all the blood of our martyrs, every-thing.'

Sofya Perovskaya was not at headquarters. Aside from the members of the bombing squad, she was the only conspirator to witness the attack. Standing on the other shore of the narrow canal, she had seen all that had happened on the quay. Straight from that scene she went to keep an appointment with two students. As she quietly entered the café where they were waiting, her bloodless face betrayed no emotion, and there was the usual concentrated look in her eyes. As yet she was unaware of the fatal outcome of the bombing. When she learned of Alexander's death, her exultation was crossed by deep anguish: Zhelyabov was in the hands of the enemy. The immense pressure under which she lived in the hours immediately following his arrest had riveted her mind to the tasks at hand. But now her thoughts turned to him. She was not unaware that the police dossier contained much against him, but it was possible that the authorities had no evidence of his connexion with the assassination. And, of course, he hadn't actually taken part in it.

Then came the news that he had confessed to having been responsible for the act. She read about it in an extra she bought as she walked along the Nevsky with a comrade. Clearly the fate of her beloved was sealed. Even at that terrible moment she did not lose hold of herself. She only lowered her head and slowed her pace, mechanically clutching the narrow sheet. 'Why did he do it?' asked her companion. 'I suppose it was necessary,' she replied.

Was it necessary? Interrogated immediately after his arrest, Zhelyabov answered the question about his occupation by declaring: 'I am employed in liberating my country.' He admitted membership in the People's Will—in subsequent statements he described himself as an agent of the Executive Committee—and he confessed to having organized the attempt at Alexandrovsk. He must have believed that Goldenberg had disclosed the fact to the police.

On Sunday afternoon, on his obligatory walk in the prison yard, he listened for the sound of an explosion. He did not hear it, and went to bed unaware of what had happened. At two a.m. he was aroused from sleep and brought face to face with Rysakov. They made no attempt to conceal that they knew each other. Zhelyabov was then told of the assassination and presumably of Rysakov's part in it. So this lad, a raw recruit whom he had only recently brought into the ranks, was the only one of those directly implicated in the affair to have been seized. Could he possibly let him take his punishment alone? Rysakov may have already worn the crestfallen look that presaged his breakdown.

Zhelyabov did not try to hide his joy at the momentous news from his captors. A giant step, he said, had been taken toward the liberation of the people. If he had not actually been involved in the attack, he declared, it was only because he was behind bars, but morally his participation was beyond question. And he added a threat: 'If, with the ascension of Alexander III to the throne, the Party's expectations are not fulfilled and if it meets with the same treatment as before, it will not hesitate to attempt his life, too.' The gist of these remarks he incorporated in a formal deposition. In another statement, dated 2 March, he explained that he had sponsored Rysakov as a regicide because he believed the youth to have 'the makings of a calm, manly terrorist and to be a person of rare moral strength.'

On the same day he addressed this communication to the public prosecutor:

'If the new sovereign, having received the sceptre from the hands of the revolution, means to follow the old system of treating regicides, if the intention is to execute Rysakov, it would be a crying injustice to spare my life, since I have made repeated attempts on Alexander II and since I did not actually take part in assassinating him merely because of a stupid accident. I demand to be included among those indicted in connexion with the affair of 1 March, and, if necessary, I will make such disclosures as shall convict me. I request that this statement be given appropriate consideration.' He added the following postscript: 'I am troubled by the fear that the Government, putting legality above justice, will adorn the new monarch's crown solely with the corpse of the young hero for lack of formal evidence against me, a veteran of the revolution. I protest against such an eventuality with all the strength of my soul and demand justice for myself. Alone, the cowardice of the Government will account for *one gallows, not two.*'

That very day Rysakov began to inform against his erstwhile comrades. What he said enabled the police to raid the Telezhnaya quarters the next night. Gesya Helfman alone was arrested, as Sablin killed himself after firing several shots at the gendarmes. The following morning Timofey Mikhailov was seized after he had wounded three police officers. Rysakov identified both prisoners.

In the weeks that followed, the frightened, bewildered boy continued to tell everything he could recall about his comrades. His experiences on the quay had had a shattering effect on him. He had envisaged the assassination of the Czar as a radiant event certain to work a magic transformation of life. Instead, he saw blood flow and heard the death rattle of innocent victims. He also discovered that his political convictions were rather shaky. And his questioner, the same astute detective who had handled Goldenberg, persuaded him that complete frankness would save him from the noose. He did try to justify his behaviour. He hinted that while he was still at liberty he had lost faith in terror. He argued lamely that he had joined the group in the hope of putting an end to terror, both red and white, and of preventing the horrors of a popular rising. And he blamed Zhelyabov for having misled him. Alleging sincere repentance, he said that he had turned against his former comrades in order to atone for his crime.

The Executive Committee had intended to maintain the cheese store with a view to using the mine eventually against the new Czar. The idea was given up after the Telezhnaya quarters had been discovered. On 3 March the couple who ran the establishment abandoned it, and the next morning the police searched the premises. On the counter they found one rouble left to pay the butcher for meat that had been bought for the cat. They also discovered the mine. This heightened the tension in the city. There were wild rumours of new plots. Cossack troops patrolled the streets. Railway stations and trains were watched, and so were roads. Wholesale house searches were conducted and arrests made under the slightest pretext.

Meanwhile a change had come over Sofya Perovskaya. Her composure and self-control were gone. She alternated between hope and despair, between apathy and furious activity. She was no longer the professional revolutionary for whom the cause was the be-all and end-all. She was possessed by the idea of arranging for Zhelyabov's escape. She made plan after plan, one more reckless and fantastic than the last. She had lost her head. She would not hear of leaving town, as her friends urged her to do. She grew neglectful of the most elementary rules of precaution. It was as though she craved to share the fate of her beloved.

Before long her unconscious wish was granted. On 10 March she was seized as she was being driven along the Nevsky. She had been spotted by the proprietress of a dairy who had known her as a customer. Rysakov established her identity and described the rôle she had played. She made no attempt to contradict him and readily signed a full confession. Rysakov also identified Kibalchich, who was arrested a week later. Speaking with perfect detachment, the latter calmly admitted his guilt. As a matter of fact, his mind was not on the subject. He was at this time deeply absorbed in designing a flying machine. As soon as he was installed in jail, he went on with his diagrams and calculations, using the walls of his cell until paper was brought to him. In the wake of his arrest came the capture of Frolenko.

V

At first the authorities had intended to try Rysakov alone. But as they gained a fuller insight into the plot that had resulted in the Emperor's death, it was decided to have a group trial. Four men: Zhelyabov, Rysakov, Timofey Mikhailov, Kibalchich, and two women: Sofya Perovskaya and Gesya Helfman, were to be arraigned before a tribunal made up of senators and representatives of the estates of the Empire. The case was to be heard in public.

In a communication addressed to the presiding Senator, Zhelyabov denied the competence of the court on the ground that it was an interested party. He demanded a trial by jury. The jurors, he concluded, were certain not only to acquit him and his comrades, but to offer them the gratitude of the fatherland. After due consideration, the court overruled this objection, and Zhelyabov accepted the ruling.

On 26 March the defendants faced their judges. The trial was conducted in strict accordance with legal procedure. The accused were provided with counsel, except for Zhelyabov, who chose to conduct his own defence. When the defendants were asked about their occupation, Perovskaya and Helfman replied: 'Revolutionary affairs,' while Zhelyabov said: 'I served the cause of the people's liberation. For many years this was my sole occupation, to which I am devoted with my whole being.'

Concerning his religion he stated that he adhered to the essence of Christ's teaching, and believed that it was the duty of every true Christian to fight for justice, for the rights of the oppressed and the weak, and, if necessary, to suffer for it.

After the bill of indictment was read, the prisoners were given a chance to explain their motives and state their views, as well as to confirm or modify their pre-trial testimony. All admitted membership in 'The Russian Social-Revolutionary Party' and, except for Mikhailov and Helfman, pleaded guilty of participating in the assassination of the Emperor. They made no effort to withhold damaging evidence. It is certain that these confessions were not extorted by means that in our day have been brought to such perfection by totalitarian régimes. They were made freely in proud defiance of the enemy. Foreign observers of the trial were amazed at the readiness with which the accused acknowledged their guilt and detailed their clandestine activities. An editorial writer of the *New York Herald*, in commenting on 10 April, 1881, on this disposition of 'the nihilist' to gratify 'the excusable curiosity of justice in regard to all he has done,' concluded that there existed 'some profound and radical difference between Russian nature and human nature generally as known in our part of the world'.

Although the accused made it easy for the prosecutor to ascertain the facts of the case, the State produced over sixty witnesses. The prosecutor's oration, which lasted for hours, rose to its rhetorical peak when he voiced his horror at the crime of 1 March. In dealing with the case of Gesya Helfman he made no attempt to turn anti-Jewish prejudice to account. He found all the defendants guilty as charged and deserving the supreme punishment. Then the lawyers for the defence spoke. Mikhailov's counsel offered the curious argument that since his client did not seem to prize his life, he should not be deprived of it. Zhelyabov, speaking as his own counsel, was at pains to lay bare the conditions that turned peaceful propagandists into terrorists. Necessity alone, he repeated, had forced him to use violence.

The prisoners were entitled to a last word before judgment was pronounced. Rysakov was incoherent. All through the trial he looked like an ill-prepared schoolboy at an examination. Kibalchich, composed as ever, took advantage of the opportunity to mention his flying ship.

The trial reached its expected denouement at three a.m., 29 March, when all the defendants were found guilty, and at six-thirty a.m. they were sentenced to be hanged.

They did not exercise their right of appeal. Kibalchich was refused permission to consult a member of the committee that was studying his paper on a flying machine. He had handed it to the authorities and was told that it had been turned over to experts for examination. As a matter of fact, it was sealed up in an envelope, which lay in the police archives unopened for thirty-six years. Published in 1918, it proved to contain a suggestion for the application of the rocket principle to aviation—hardly a contribution to aeronautics, since it did not even attempt to solve the engineering problems connected with the construction of a rocket plane.

As the trial was drawing to an end, Vladimir Solovyov, a young instructor at the University of Petersburg who was to become Russia's greatest systematic philosopher, suggested in a public lecture that the Czar, as a Christian and ruler of a Christian nation, ought to forgive his father's assassins. He was wildly cheered by some of his hearers, An appeal to the same effect was made by Tolstoy. He anticipated the outcome of the trial with dread. One afternoon he dozed off and dreamed that he was at once executioner and executed. Waking from his nightmare, he wrote to Alexander III, urging him to summon the regicides, give them money and send them away somewhere, say to America. Whether or not the letter reached the addressee, he was not likely to have heeded it. In reply to Pobedonestzev, Procurator of the Holy Synod, who had warned him not to yield to counsels of Christian extremism, Alexander III wrote: 'I give you my word that all six will hang.'

One of the six did not hang. The day after the end of the trial Gesya Helfman informed the authorities that she was with child. The court postponed her execution until forty days after her delivery, and in July the Emperor, chiefly to placate foreign public opinion, commuted her sentence to hard labour for life. She gave birth to a girl in a prison hospital, and it is alleged that the baby was provided with a luxurious layette by an anonymous American donor. Gesya died a few months later, under circumstances suggesting malpractice by the Court accoucheur who had delivered her, and the infant did not long survive her. It was never seen by the father, a member of the Executive Committee, who was also to die in prison.

The execution of the other five was set for 3 April. The previous day Rysakov offered his services to the police in a last desperate effort to save his neck. His plea was ignored. Kibalchich composed a long communication to the Czar in an effort to suggest 'a peaceful way out of the present impossible situation'. Sofya Perovskaya's last extant letter is addressed to her mother. 'Believe me, dearest Mummy,' she wrote, 'my lot is not at all such a dark one. I have lived as my convictions have prompted me; I could not do otherwise; therefore I await what is in store for me with a clear conscience.'

In the evening the Church offered its ministrations. Both Zhelyabov and Perovskaya refused to see a priest. Kibalchich engaged the Father in a dispute and would not be shriven. Mikhailov made his confession. Rysakov confessed and received the Eucharist.

The next morning the hangman and his assistant placed the condemned in two tumbrils and strapped them to their seats with their backs to the horses. On the chest of each hung a placard with the single word: 'Regicide'. By eight o'clock the carts were jolting over the cobblestones, on their way to Semenovsky Square, where the execution was to take place. Rysakov's head was bent, the others appeared self-possessed. A disdainful smile contorted Perovskaya's pinched, slightly flushed face. Mikhailov, his massive form bulking large, kept bowing to the people, as was customary for those on their way to the scaffold. He shouted to them, but his words were drowned out by the drummers who formed part of the military convoy. To at least one sympathetic eye-witness the condemned looked like victors riding in triumph. Carriages occupied by five priests brought up the rear of the procession. The mood of the crowd that lined the route of the cortège was far from friendly. Indeed, two young women who waved handkerchiefs at the condemned would have been torn to pieces by the mob, if not for the intervention of the police.

At eight-fifty the tumbrils reached the square, a vast unpaved plaza, and a muffled murmur rose from the crowd, estimated at a hundred thousand by the correspondent of the London *Times*. Lumbering down an aisle flanked by Cossacks, the carts drew up in front of a scaffold surmounted by gallows, which loomed black against a clear, pale sky. The wooden structure was surrounded by troops. The hangman, with four helpers, unstrapped the prisoners and led them to the pillories in the rear of the scaffold. Zhelyabov kept turning his head to Perovskaya, who stood next to him. The air of detachment and imperturbable calm did not abandon Kibalchich. Rysakov was deathly pale. Big Mikhailov wore a petrified look.

An official read the verdict from a low platform nearby, the paper shaking in his hand. The priests mounted the scaffold. All the condemned kissed the crucifix, and the priests, having signed them with the cross, withdrew. Then they kissed each other good-bye, but Perovskaya turned away from Rysakov. The hangman and his helpers slipped over each of the condemned a loose garment which covered the head and face. Rysakov's knees gave way. All the while the drums kept up a steady rumble. The hangman took off his blue peasant coat, revealing his red shirt. He was ready for business.

The first to be hanged was Kibalchich. Mikhailov was second. Twice the rope broke under the weight of his big body and he crashed to the floor of the scaffold with a thud. In the half century and more that had elapsed since the execution of the Decembrists the efficiency of the executioners had not noticeably increased. The crowd that had been so hostile to the regicides a few minutes earlier was now buzzing with indignation and saying that it was a sign from heaven that the man should be pardoned. As the rope was about to break the third time, the executioner hastily reinforced it with another noose. It worked. The hanging of the remaining three prisoners went off without a hitch. Rysakov had to witness the execution of all his companions before being dispatched to his own death.

At nine-fifty the bodies were cut down from the gallows and placed in the black wooden coffins that had been waiting for them. They were buried in a nameless common grave.

CHAPTER XV

A PYRRHIC VICTORY

THE more sanguine among the terrorists had hoped that the execution of the Czar would touch off a mass uprising. The soberer souls had expected that the authorities would be frightened into liberal reforms, which would facilitate the work of the Party. On the other hand, conservatives had predicted that should the plot against the Emperor succeed, the enraged populace would exterminate the revolutionaries and indeed make short shrift of the educated class from which they stemmed. The course of events belied all expectations.

Immediately after the explosions there was great excitement in the streets of the capital, but it was brief, and before midnight Nevsky Prospekt had assumed its usual look. At first the officers in charge of the troops garrisoned in the city were vaguely apprehensive of trouble in the ranks. Nothing untoward happened. The soldiers cursed the assassins, and by ten o'clock all were snoring. On 2 March Count Valuyev wrote in his diary: 'Our army is still healthy. . . .'

In the days that followed, a few students were manhandled by ruffians, perhaps not without police connivance. Two men who bought a portrait of the deceased monarch and tore it up in the street were beaten within an inch of their lives by passers-by. A group of shopkeepers, in a letter published in the newspapers, dared the terrorists to come out into the open and promised to lynch them. For a while students avoided wearing their uniforms in the street, while young women let their hair grow and put on kerchiefs. Wild reports about plots and reprisals were in circulation. But both rumours and acts of violence soon ceased. Moscow and the provincial cities remained quiet. Of course, there was a plethora of protestations of loyalty to the throne on the part of public bodies.

In the countryside on the whole the news was met with puzzlement or composure verging on indifference. A widespread notion was that the Czar had been murdered by the gentry because he had been on the side of the people. For a while a district in the province of Tver was an unhealthy place for a traveller who looked like a *barin* (master). The villagers were apt to stop his carriage, smash the bell on his shaftbow, and beat him up. According to a correspondence printed in *Chornyi peredel*, it was rumoured that the new Czar had turned all the mileposts between Petersburg and Moscow into gallows for the murderers of his father, that he had confiscated their lands and would distribute them among the peasants on the day of his coronation.

If the response of the masses was disappointing to the People's Will, that of the intelligentzia was no more encouraging. True, at the University of Moscow the attempt of some students to collect money for a wreath to be placed on the Czar's coffin resulted in disturbances which led to the expulsion of over three hundred youths, and in Kazan, while the citizenry was taking the oath of allegiance to Alexander III, hundreds of students attended a meeting on the campus, at which the late Czar was excoriated and monarchic government condemned. Several *zemstvo* and municipal boards and even one or two assemblies of nobles respectfully urged the Emperor not to deviate from the path of reform followed by his august father. Two or three newspapers made bold to express themselves in a similar vein. On the other hand, it soon became apparent that the event of 1 March had frightened and alienated many of the liberal fellow travellers. In sum, nothing approaching a revolutionary situation developed as a result of the assassination.

Naturally, the few groups of intellectuals and workmen who moved within the orbit of the People's Will and Black Repartition were deeply stirred. They wanted to know what was coming next; they offered their services. Eager for action, some of the factory hands that had been proselytized by Zhelyabov turned to Sofya Perovskaya for guidance. Before she could respond, she was behind bars. The Executive Committee, which was rapidly depleted by arrests, had scanty funds, no arms, no plan and could furnish no leaders to the rank and file. All it did was to print several leaflets, one of them urging all and sundry 'to send petitions from towns and villages'. The Party had scored a brilliant victory, but it was a Pyrrhic victory.

Nikolay Sukhanov, a rather flighty naval officer who had been co-opted by the Committee from the military branch of the organization, proposed an immediate attack on the life of Alexander III. The proposal could not be seriously entertained. Instead, Tikhomirov, who had had no hand in the assassination, suggested an appeal to the new ruler. The Committee consented, though without enthusiasm.

'The Letter from the Executive Committee to Alexander III', dated 10 March, is couched in respectful, if forthright, language. It indicates that there are two ways out of the existing situation: revolution or 'the voluntary turning of the sovereign to the people'. It is curious how tenaciously the Russian radical mind clung to the idea that the autocrat was capable of becoming the people's Czar, 'a crowned revolutionary', as Herzen had put it a generation earlier. To avoid the fearful waste and suffering entailed by revolution, the Committee urges the Emperor to choose the second alternative. 'As soon as the Government ceases to be arbitrary and resolves to carry out the demands of the people's conscience and consciousness, you can get rid of the spies, send your bodyguard back to the barracks, and burn the gallows that deprave the people. The Executive Committee will disband of its own free will. . . . Peaceful efforts will replace violence, which is more repugnant to us than to your ministers, and which we practise from sad necessity.'

Speaking to the Emperor as to 'a citizen and a man of honour,' the Committee sets forth the measures that would make it abdicate as a revolutionary body. They are two: political amnesty and the calling of a Constituent Assembly charged with the task of 'reviewing the existing forms of political and social life and altering them in accordance with the people's wishes'. Also, to insure freedom of elections, civil liberties must be granted, but only as 'a temporary measure'. Apparently it was held that the Constituent Assembly might regard civil liberties as too much of a luxury. This peculiarly moderate programme is followed by a solemn declaration that 'our Party' will unconditionally submit to the decisions of the Assembly. 'And so, your Majesty, decide,' the letter concludes. 'There are two ways before you. The choice is yours. We, on our part, can only beg of Fate that your mind and conscience prompt you to make a decision consistent with the good of Russia, your own dignity and your duty to our country.'

Thirteen thousand copies of this communication were run off, and a few copies, intended for the Emperor and the highest official, were printed on special paper.

The hangings on Semenovsky Square were a reply to the Committee's letter. Another, and equally unequivocal answer came at the end of April.

It will be recalled that less than a fortnight before his death Alexander II had endorsed Loris-Melikov's plan for a General Commission. Half an hour before he started on his fatal trip to the Manège, he approved the text of a manifesto announcing the establishment of the Commission. The approval was tentative, for he ordered the document read, possibly for reconsideration, at a session of the Council of Ministers to be held 4 March. He seems to have had misgivings about his action. After the Minister left, he turned to his sons and said: 'I have consented to this measure, although I do not conceal from myself the fact that this is the first step toward a constitution.'

He had no sooner breathed his last, than those at the top of the bureaucratic hierarchy were ranged in two opposed camps. One was headed by Loris-Melikov; the other, by Pobedonostzev, recently appointed Procurator of the Most Holy Synod. He had been a tutor to the Heir Apparent and had maintained a hold on his former pupil. On the evening of 1 March, the thirty-six-year-old Alexander III sobbed on the Procurator's shoulder 'like a big baby.' Pobedonostzev spared no effort in trying to win over the Emperor to a programme of intransigeant absolutism. Not concessions to public opinion, he argued, but a policy of 'blood and iron' would destroy the evil seed of sedition. Loris-Melikov must be dismissed, he insisted, and indeed, the whole administration purged from top to bottom, for treason lurked everywhere. A prime necessity, he repeated, was immediate and firm action, putting an end to the prattle about liberty and representative government.

At first the Emperor did not show his cards. He gave Loris-Melikov no reason to doubt the security of his position, although the Minister realized that the event of 1 March was a grave blow to his prestige. Nor was he apprehensive about the fate of the General Commission, for the Czar as heir had been a member of the committee that favoured the creation of that body. Both at home and abroad it was generally expected that the new reign would witness the beginning of representative government in the Empire. In fact, the aged Emperor Wilhelm wrote to Alexander III describing 'the underwater reefs one must steer clear of in granting a constitution'.

The General Commission came up for consideration on 8 March at a meeting of Ministers presided over by the Czar, and was quickly shelved by him, after Pobedonostzev had violently attacked the measure. In the ensuing weeks there was some uncertainty as to the course the Government would follow. And then, on 28 April, the Council of Ministers was confronted with the printed text of an Imperial manifesto, composed by the Procurator, which was promulgated the next day. The Emperor had approved it without consulting his Ministers, in flagrant violation of a decision adopted a few days previously. It proclaimed the Czar's determination to govern 'with faith in the might and justice of Autocratic Rule, which for the good of the people we are called to strengthen and defend from any encroachment'.

Loris-Melikov's first reaction on reading the manifesto was that it had been faked by the revolutionaries in order to arouse widespread indignation. He resigned, and several other administrators followed suit. They were replaced by advocates of reaction and repression. Pobedonostzev's triumph was complete. Commenting on the manifesto, the London *Times* wrote that it 'rudely shattered the hopes aroused by the new reign'. A statute issued in August was, as one historian put it, 'the *Magna Carta Libertatum* granted to the police against the citizenry'. The course that was to be followed for a generation was set. The People's Will had offered the Czar two alternatives. He made his choice.

II

The blast on Yekaterininsky Canal was heard round the world. The press lamented the loss of 'a far-seeing and beneficent prince,' as the *New York Herald* had it, and Government bodies, including the Senate of the United States, extended official condolences to Alexander III. A small segment of the public, however, felt differently. Marx and Engels hailed the assassination as an event that 'must inevitably lead, even though after prolonged and cruel struggle, to the creation of the Russian Commune'. In

London, Copenhagen, Vienna, Chicago, public meetings were held to celebrate the triumph of the Russian terrorists. On 15 March (New Style) four hundred persons gathered in New York at the Steuben House on the Bowery, listened to speeches in English, German, Polish, and Russian, and 'in the name of humanity' adopted a resolution congratulating the world on 'the overthrow of the absolutism of feudal autocracy in Russia' and the people of Europe on 'the removal of the greatest obstacle to the establishment of the Western Republic or the United States of Europe'.

The press accounts of the trial of the regicides made the names of Zhelyabov and Sofya Perovskaya known far and wide. While to many they meant the horrors of 'nihilism,' a few pronounced them with reverence. A California newspaper carried a ballad by Joaquin Miller, entitled 'Sophie Perowskaja,'[1] the concluding stanza of which read as follows:

> The Czar is dead; the woman dead,
>   About her neck a cord.
> In God's house rests his royal head—
>   Hers in a place abhorred.
> Yet I'd rather have her bed
>   Than thine, most royal lord!
> Yea, rather be that woman dead,
>   Than this new living Czar,
> To hide in dread, with both hands red,
>   Behind great bolt and bar—
> While, like the dead, still endless tread
>   Sad exiles tow'rd their star.

One of the first steps taken by the Executive Committee after 1 March was to issue a statement to the Western public, which described the execution of the Czar as an episode in the struggle against a despotism that injured not only the Russian people but all mankind. The Committee's letter to Alexander III made a favourable impression abroad. Marx and Engels found it proved that there were 'people with a statesmanlike bent of mind' in the ranks of the Russian revolutionaries. Yet the Party failed to take

---

[1] From *The Californian* the poem was reprinted in the *New York Herald*, 31 July, 1881, and it figures, minus two initial stanzas, in *The Poetical Works* of Joaquin Miller under the title, 'The Dead Czar'.

advantage of this fund of sympathy on the part of the liberal and radical circles in the West. It received no help from abroad. And that in spite of the fact that several émigrés publicly championed the terrorists and that it had its own emissary in foreign parts.

One of the aims of the People's Will was to dispose Western public opinion in its favour. Several men identified with the revolutionary struggle in Russia and articulate enough to reach a foreign audience lived abroad, but they all objected strongly to one or another feature of the Party's programme or tactics. As a result the organization turned, in May, 1880, to an expatriate settled in Geneva, who was a relative stranger to the movement. This Mikhail Dragomanov, a former professor at the University of Kiev, whom Zhelyabov had known in his Odessa days, was a Ukrainian nationalist of democratic sympathies. As he found the People's Will too centralist to suit him and as he abhorred terror, he refused to plead the Party's cause before the European public. The Executive Committee then decided to make one of its members ambassador to the West. Leo Hartmann, who had taken part in the Moscow attempt on the life of Alexander II, was selected for the purpose. The choice was anything but a happy one.

The credentials issued to him under date of 25 October, 1880, charged him with the task of informing and winning over public opinion abroad by means of meetings, lectures, and articles in the press, and empowered him to collect funds for the revolution, including contributions from workers for Russian strikers. He crossed the border safely and went to Paris. He seems to have done nothing in France to carry out the tasks entrusted to him. On 3 February, 1881, he was arrested at the request of the Russian authorities. Because of public agitation, however—in which Victor Hugo participated—he was not extradited, but merely expelled from the country. Thereupon he crossed over to London, where he frequented the households of Marx and Engels. He made vast plans for raising funds and for publishing an English daily entitled *Nihilist*, which was to come out '*at the same hour*' in London, Paris, and Geneva, and become the main source of information about Russia for the West. None of his schemes materialized.

On 6 June, 1881, Marx was writing to his eldest daughter: 'Hartmann left for New York on Friday, and I am glad he is now out of danger [he had apparently been threatened with extradition]. Several days before his departure he asked Engels for the hand of Pumps [a niece of Engel's wife; a brainless, pleasure-loving young thing whom the couple were bringing up], declaring that he was sure of Pumps's consent. She did indeed flirt violently with him, but that was merely to arouse Kautsky. And Tussy [Marx's youngest daughter] has just told me that the same Hartmann had proposed to her before he left for Jersey. But the worst thing is that the famous Perovskaya, who died for the Russian revolution, had lived with Hartmann in a free union. . . . From Perovskaya to Pumps—that's too much, and Mama is now disgusted with him and the entire male sex.'

It will be recalled that Hartmann and Perovskaya were the 'married' couple that had occupied the house in the Moscow suburb from which mining operations were conducted. Either Marx misunderstood the situation or was misled by Hartmann.

He landed in New York early in July and made no secret of the nature of his mission. The papers carried long interviews with him, articles over his own signature in the form of letters to the editor, as well as the text of the appeal of the Executive Committee to the American people, which he had brought with him. 'The abolitionists,' it ran, 'were your dearest and best sons. . . . We are the Russian abolitionists. . . . Your sympathy, like that of other nations, is dear to us.' To secure it, the document went on, Leo Hartmann had been dispatched to the hospitable land of America so that its people might get acquainted with 'the condition of affairs in Russia'.

The emissary of the People's Will told the readers of the *New York Herald* (29 July) through his interviewer that the success of the 'nihilist' movement was assured, since it had the support of all classes of the population. 'Has not one of your noblest and best citizens,' he exclaimed, 'has not Wendell Phillips publicly expressed his respect and sympathy for the nihilists? Has he not spoken the noble words: "If liberty cannot be gained by any other means but the dagger, then welcome the dagger!"?' The following day in the columns of the same paper Hartmann offered a highly coloured account of his career and a defence of terrorism. A fortnight later he again wrote at great length to the editor of the *Herald*. Among other things, he asserted that the late Czar had twice tried to expatriate himself, but was prevented from doing so by the Executive Committee, which was in fact the real government of Russia.

At the time when this letter was printed, its author was in Canada. When he had first arrived in the United States he had been assured by a lawyer that his extradition to Russia was out of the question. He had disregarded the demands voiced in certain Republican newspapers for his surrender to Russia, but became alarmed when Assistant Secretary of State Hitt was quoted in the press to the effect that the extradition of a would-be regicide was not ruled out. Secretary of State Blaine disavowed his subordinate's opinion, but was rather evasive about the matter. Thereupon Hartmann became something of a storm centre. The newspapers collected opinions of jurists on his extradition. A large meeting of protest against it was held in Brooklyn. Wendell Phillips accused the Secretary of State of being ready to act as 'sheriff to the Czar'. The *World* contended that 'in the sight of George III George Washington was as atrocious a criminal as Hartmann'. On the other hand, the *Tribune* wrote of him (on 10 August): 'He deserves no more pity or protection than the snake whose head it is the right and duty of humanity to crush.'

Hartmann did not long remain under the protection of the British flag. The issue of the *Herald* of 17 August carried a letter from him to the effect that he had returned to New York ready to contest his extradition. A week later he was writing to Engels that Russia had demanded his surrender, but that he was hopeful, since he had the support of Wendell Phillips, John Swinton (an editor of the *Sun*, described by Engels as 'an American Communist') and other 'big people'. As a matter of fact the Russian authorities did not apply for his extradition. Instead, they spread a report that the person who claimed to be Hartmann was an impostor and that the real Hartmann was in Russia and had offered his services to the police as an informer.

When Hartmann had first been interviewed he told the *Herald* reporter that he would soon return home 'to continue to the end the struggle against despotism'. He mentioned this on several other occasions. Yet on 19 August, to everyone's amazement, he declared his intention of becoming a United States citizen. Nothing is known about his further efforts, if any, to carry out his mission. The following year he showed up in London, but he returned to the States and spent the rest of his days there. It is said that he worked in a machine shop and then went into business for himself as a manufacturer of electric appliances, inventing a tie pin with a tiny bulb that could be turned on. He died in New York or Florida at a ripe age.

III

In the weeks that followed the event of 1 March the situation of the People's Will deteriorated rapidly. The rounding up of activists proceeded apace. The police made good use of the information supplied by Goldenberg and Rysakov. In March alone nearly fifty men and women were put behind bars. In ferreting out and identifying revolutionists, the secret service was assisted not only by Okladsky, the carpenter who had participated in the Alexsandrovsk attempt and who, as has been said, had turned informer on being arrested, but also by another one of the workmen whom Zhelyabov had proselytized. Accompanied by a detective, this Merkulov walked the streets of the capital and pointed out men and women to be seized. One of his first victims was Yemelyanov, the only member of the bombing squad to have survived. On 1 April, Isayev, the Party's sole remaining technician, was arrested. Before the end of the month Lieutenant Sukhanov and Anna Yakimova—the latter had run the cheese store on Malaya Sadovaya—were caught in the dragnet. In May the secret press was discovered.

Meanwhile the Emperor had retired for safety to the town of Gatchina, where he kept himself practically incommunicado in the gloomy palace erected by his great-grandfather Paul. It was not until April that he felt sufficiently secure to make his first public appearance by reviewing a military parade.

The membership of the Executive Committee had by now dwindled to five men and three women, of whom one, Maria Oshanina, was seriously ill. The auxiliary forces at the disposal of this handful of not particularly effective people had also shrunk. The situation had been anticipated by Zhelyabov. At one of the meetings of the Committee shortly before his arrest he had observed that whether or not the attempt on the Czar's life succeeded, after it was over most of the participants in the attack would be casualties. The gathering was attended by two organizers who had come from Moscow, where they had succeeded in forming a fairly strong group with cells in factories and schools. Zhelyabov had shown great interest in their report. He wanted to have all the details. What was the quality of the human material in Moscow? Would it be able to carry on, once the Petersburg centre was smashed? 'Remember,' he had told the pair, 'if your Moscow doesn't come to our rescue, it will go badly with us.'

Moscow did attempt to come to the rescue, but failed. In the summer the headquarters of the People's Will were transferred to that city. The removal was an admission of defeat. Vera Figner called it 'exile'. Opposition to the existing order centred in the northern capital, which, besides being the seat of the Government, was the brain of the country. No other city possessed its material and spiritual resources. None other had a revolutionary tradition going back to the Decembrists. But the police in Moscow were less vigilant than in Petersburg, and for some months the tiny contingent of revolutionaries carried on in relative safety. Their financial situation improved, and a new secret press was set up, so that the printing of leaflets and of the Party organ was resumed. The gaps in the membership of the Executive Committee, however, remained unfilled. The immediate result of the shift of headquarters to Moscow was the weakening of the local organization, some of whose active members were dispatched to other centres.

The few groups that marched, or rather marked time, under the populist banner of Black Repartition, were also hit by arrests. The organization had hailed the assassination of the Czar jubilantly. Paradoxically enough, the leaflets it issued on the occasion were less moderate in tone than the proclamations of the Executive Committee. The burden of their message to the people was: 'If you want land and liberty, take them by force.' The Union of Southern Workers, which gravitated toward Black Repartition, announced in a proclamation dated 14 March that it had sent to the Emperor a demand for the enactment of a number of reforms, including an eight-hour workday. 'We shall wait a month for an answer,' the leaflet concluded. 'Should we convince ourselves that we can get no help from the new Czar either, then we will act on our own, and let the blood shed by us be upon the heads of those who could have brought about reconciliation, but did not.' The Union was boasting when it spoke of shedding blood. It was moribund and soon vanished from the scene.

Not many months had elapsed after the assassination of the Czar when the thin ranks of Black Repartition were ready to pursue political objectives, though assigning them a secondary rôle. The issue of *Chornyi Peredel*, dated September, 1881, while making it clear that political democracy was not the aim of the People's Party, conceded that such a régime had its points. The time seemed ripe for the two factions to reunite, on a platform combining political and economic demands. But the merger did not take place, perhaps because Black Repartition was in an advanced stage of disintegration. In fact, it did not survive the year. The issue of *Chornyi Peredel*, dated December, 1881, was the last. Thereafter only a few scattered groups, clinging to the tenets of orthodox Populism, carried on socialist propaganda in the provinces.

Axelrod, like Plekhanov, and other leaders of Black Repartition, had remained abroad. Vera Zasulich had been with them since the previous year. Yakov Stefanovich, who had long felt that they should all return to Russia and compose their differences with the People's Will, was the exception. By September he was in Moscow and a member of the Executive Committee. A few other adherents of the populist faction joined the People's Will, without, however, strengthening that organization to any marked degree.

Vera Figner, arriving in Moscow from the South in the late autumn, found a distressing state of affairs. The Executive Committee was no longer a fighting body. It could only carry on propaganda and organizational work. Morale was so low that precaution was thrown to the winds—with disastrous results. Alone, Tikhomirov ostentatiously wore mourning for Alexander II and further to avert suspicion went on a pilgrimage to a venerated shrine. 'Both brain and brawn were lacking,' wrote Vera Figner retrospectively, 'there were neither leaders capable of initiative nor skilful executants.'

IV

As yet the authorities were unaware of the extent to which their adversary had been weakened. They did not question the ability of the Executive Committee to carry out the threat of renewed terrorism implied in its public pronouncement. This may be inferred from the fact that the Government aided and abetted, if it did not actually initiate, a quasi-secret society of militant monarchists. This so-called Holy League (*Svyashchenaya Druzhina*) was a voluntary association of men banded together to furnish a bodyguard for the Emperor, as well as to spy on the terrorists, infiltrate their ranks, sow discord among them, demoralize them, assassinate their leaders—in a word, to combat the underground with its own weapons.

It came into being shortly after 1 March in an atmosphere of general distrust of the ability of the police to safeguard the Czar and cope with the menace of revolution. A minor railway official who years later as Count Witte, Prime Minister, negotiated the Russo-Japanese peace treaty, laid claim to having originated the idea of the League. Its statutes, dated 1 June, 1881, provided for a centralized hierarchical organization of bewildering complexity, headed by a five-man Council of First Elders. The Czar's brother, Vladimir, may have been a First Elder.

The League affected the secrecy of a conspiratorial society and the ritualism of a Masonic lodge. Each member ('brother') went through a ceremony of initiation, in the course of which he took an oath in the name of the Father, the Son, and the Holy Ghost to dedicate himself wholly to 'the protection of the Sovereign and the eradication of sedition, which disgraces the Russian name'. The brethren were recruited from among the higher officialdom, the aristocracy, the world of finance. The exclusive Yacht Club in the capital served as headquarters, and there were branches in Moscow and in several provincial centres. In October, 1881, the League broadened its base by forming the Voluntary Guard (*Dobrovolnaya Okhrana*), a semi-autonomous auxiliary society. If the League was an *élite* body, the Guard approximated a mass organization. Acting openly, though unofficially, the latter looked out for the safety of the Emperor and his family at home and on their travels. Such protection was also provided by the League. For this purpose both societies hired strong-arm men and detectives. Late in 1881 the League counted 729 brethren and the Guard no less than 14,672 members.

Large funds were at the disposal of the League. It had no other assets. Miserable bunglers were at the helm, and the ranks were infested with patrioteers, promotion seekers, and shady characters interested in easy pickings. In co-operation or competition with the regular secret service, the organization carried on extensive espionage at home, and since it believed, quite mistakenly, that the terrorist activities were directed from abroad, it maintained a network of sleuths in Paris and Geneva. Huge sums of money were spent, reams of paper covered with reports, every trick of the trade was used, even to the employment of a Mata Hari— all to no purpose. Arrangements for the assassination of Hartmann and Kropotkin also came to nothing. There was something of *opéra bouffe* about the League's enterprises. Needless to say, its existence was an open secret, although no mention of it was permitted in the press. In commenting on its activities *Narodnaya volya* observed: 'The Government is openly taking the form of a secret conspiracy against the people's freedom.'

The League was also out to combat the revolutionary movement 'ideologically'. To this end it maintained three periodicals. Two of them were printed in Geneva. *Volnoe Slovo* (*Free Word*), which began to appear in August, 1881, was intended to wage war on the People's Will from the point of view of moderate political radicalism. By disguising their identity, its backers were able to engage as editor Dragomanov, to whom Zhelyabov had appealed for help. Under the guidance of this sincere democrat it advocated a parliamentary and federalist régime for Russia. A year later another journal was launched, under a title which the Bolsheviks were to make notorious: *Pravda* (*Truth*). It was a publication 'of the most fiery kind', in the words of its editor, a former rural police officer first employed by the League as a detective. The wretched sheet passed itself off as the mouthpiece of a newly formed secret society with a programme which called for an orgy of destruction in the manner of Bakunin at his most ferocious. *Pravda*'s favourite occupation was baiting the League's other organ, in an effort to win the confidence of the extremist elements. The issues were filled with bloodthirsty abuse and invective directed against the secret police, the administration, and particularly the Czar and all his kin. The editor went out of his mind, he wrote to his superiors, as he reread what was printed in his journal about 'those dearer to him than life itself', but was consoled with the reflection that this was done 'for a holy purpose and out of loyalty to the Sovereign'.

Furthermore, the League, acting through a dummy, resuscitated a progressive Moscow daily that the authorities had driven out of existence. In its columns liberalism was to be expounded, and then a blow was to be delivered to it by disclosing the identity of the paper's backers. This measure was not carried out, and the liberal cause suffered no damage. It was also planned to issue openly a journal of monarchist opinion, but this, strangely enough, never materialized.

By means of these publications the League hoped to discredit the doctrine of revolutionary Populism and demoralize the membership of the Party. There was also the hope of infiltrating the Executive Committee and the ranks of the liberals, who were suspected of having an organized core affiliated with the underground. None of these assorted objectives was achieved. The editor of *Pravda* had a vision not only of gaining entrée to the inner sanctum of the People's Will, but indeed of heading the Party, with a view to delivering it into the hands of his employers. As a matter of fact, he didn't come near a single activist. In a joint statement the more prominent political émigrés publicly repudiated both the programme and the tactics of *Pravda*. All that the League's inept Machiavellianism succeeded in doing was to poison with mutual suspicion the atmosphere breathed by the handful of Geneva expatriates.

The constituted authorities supported the League, but at the same time held it in suspicion, in spite of its credo. For was it not, after all, a manifestation of public initiative? A close watch was kept on its activities. The regular secret service eyed the organization's members and agents with mingled hostility and contempt as competitors and meddlesome amateurs who helped rather than hindered sedition. Its venture into underground journalism was a farce. Most of the copies of the Geneva publications that were smuggled into Russia were destroyed by its own agents in obedience to an unfathomable logic. Some of the literature did get through to the public, not without unlooked-for effects.

As the months went by, the enemies of the League grew in number. Apparently the suspicion arose that some of its leaders intended not to destroy the revolutionary movement, but to use it, together with the League's machinery, in order to advance their political ambitions, that they had, indeed, entered into a secret alliance with the revolutionaries. The possibility is not excluded that some highly-stationed 'brethren' were not averse to seeing their monarch's authority limited by an aristocratic constitution. Others may have gone even further. Prince Meshchersky, who dabbled in literature, published a satirical tale, the hero of which, a transparent caricature of one of the pillars of the League, dreams of becoming Prime Minister, perhaps president of the Russian Republic. The book is said to have been called to the Czar's attention by Pobedonostzev. Allegedly one of the most exalted leaders of the organization, the Procurator of the Holy Synod now sharply turned against it.

On 23 November, 1882, he addressed a forceful message to the Emperor, warning him that the League in its arrogance was about to make the position of the legitimate Government impossible. 'As I look around me,' he concluded, 'the conviction grows upon me that great as is the danger to you from the conspirators, the danger from the Holy League is even more serious.'

Yielding to pressure from this and other foes of the League, the Czar acted without delay, and by the end of the year the organization was liquidated. A little later its organs folded up. The Voluntary Guard lasted until the coronation, which took place on 15 May, 1883. Thus ended the grand effort of the Russian aristocracy to defend the principle of monarchy.

V [1]

Before proceeding with the account of the waning fortunes of the People's Will, something should be said about an episode that chroniclers of the Russian revolutionary movement have tended to slur over.

In the spring of 1881 a wave of anti-Jewish riots swept over Southern Russia. Before the end of the summer pogroms had

[1] This section, with some changes, was printed in *The Chicago Jewish Forum*.

occurred in over a hundred localities. Later there were more disorders, and only in 1884 did mob violence cease. The pogroms were not spontaneous outbreaks. That they should have followed closely upon the death of Alexander II was no accident. The smoke had scarcely lifted over the scene of the assassination when a certain portion of the press began to point an accusing finger at the Jews. There is reason to believe that a campaign of incitement and provocation was conducted by forces intent on diverting the attention of the masses from the real causes of their misery, though exactly who the instigators were is not known. It may have been the work of the Holy League. Certainly the guardians of law and order were guilty of inaction and, in some cases, of connivance with the rioters.

At the outset, officialdom promoted the idea that the pogroms had been fomented by the revolutionaries to give the masses an object lesson in rebellion, or as a convenient way of starting a general upheaval. The view had a brief but considerable vogue. It figured in a report from the United States Minister in Petersburg to the Secretary of State. Writing on the subject of the anti-Jewish riots on 24 May, 1881, John W. Foster observed: 'It is asserted that the nihilist societies have profited by the situation to incite and encourage the peasants and lower classes of the towns and cities in order to increase the embarrassment of the Government. . . .' He went on to say, however, that the charge was 'not based on very tangible facts'. Count Kutaisov, the official investigator of the riots, denied that the social-revolutionary party had instigated the anti-Jewish movement. Another theory then won approval in high places: the Jews themselves were to blame; they had brought down on their heads the wrath of the masses whom they had been plundering.

A former student who was under police surveillance reportedly attempted single-handed to launch a pogrom in Yekaterinoslav in order 'to arouse the masses to protest against exploitation'. Such incidents must have been exceedingly rare. Unquestionably neither Black Repartition nor the People's Will had a hand in starting the riots. It is equally certain that not a few radically-minded individuals condemned the pogroms on both humanitarian and political grounds. Yet it is a fact that at least initially the prevalent attitude in revolutionary circles was one of sympathy with the perpetrators, not with the victims of the

Alexander II (1818–1881)

The Regicides on the scaffold.

Left to right:
Rysakov, Zhelyabov, Sofya Perovskaya, Kibalchich, Timofey Mikhailov

looting and the butchery, and indignation was likely to be directed chiefly at the police for manhandling and arresting the rioters. The wish being father to the thought, the pogroms appeared to be a prelude to a broader movement, indeed a harbinger of the revolution. For here was an authentic mass protest, violent, unbridled, sweeping aside the barriers of law. The Jews were attacked not so much on racial or religious as on economic grounds, people argued, for were not these money-lenders and venders of vodka a set of exploiters battening on the body of the people? It was held that the movement was bound to grow in scope and reveal its revolutionary nature. 'The Party,' wrote a commentator on the subject in *Narodnaya volya*, 'cannot take an indifferent, let alone negative, attitude towards a genuinely popular movement. The French Revolution,' he added, 'had its excesses, but its leaders did not therefore repudiate it.'

A leaflet issued by the South Russian Workers' Union mildly upbraided the rioters for attacking the Jews 'indiscriminately', pointing out that not all of them were exploiters. *Zerno,* the journal sponsored by the Black Repartition, sounded a similar note and reminded its readers that the workers, irrespective of nationality and religion, must unite against their common enemy. In the same breath, however, it described the outbreaks as just retribution and made the point that only the rich with their minions had interceded for the Jews. 'The anti-Jewish movement,' runs a passage in the *Bulletin* (*Listok*) of the People's Will, 'which was not originated or shaped by us, is, nevertheless, an echo of our activity.' The tenor of the discussion indicates that this statement is a claim to credit. Its anti-Jewish animus finds further expression in the charge that to win over the wealthy and the powerful, the Jews were deliberately spreading the idea that the mobs were bound to turn against the Gentile propertied classes. Leo Hartmann, soon after his arrival in New York, contributed to the local German Socialist paper an article in which he wrote: 'It is a fact that in South-Western Russia the Jew is not only the pothouse-keeper and money-lender, but also for the most part a secret service agent.'

Clearly, the attitude toward the pogroms reflected a readiness to welcome the revolution, no matter what ugly guise it took. But the anti-Jewish prejudice also counted for a great deal.

During the second half of the nineteenth century, in Russia as elsewhere, extreme Radicalism was sometimes tinged with anti-Semitism. Bakunin, for one, was not free from it. In 1876 a *narodnik* of Jewish birth complained of its presence among his comrades. 'They make no distinction between Jews and gentry,' he wrote, 'preaching the extermination of both.'

There was but a step from the hopeful view of the riots to an attempt to exploit them for the benefit of the cause. This step the revolutionaries did actually take. While the reactionaries would use Jewish blood to put out the fire of rebellion, an interested contemporary observed, their adversaries were not averse to using it to feed the flames. A proclamation of the Executive Committee, dated 30 August, 1881, told the Ukrainian masses in their own vernacular that the Jew was their worst enemy. They were everywhere, 'the vile Judases' that had grabbed everything both in town and country; they had bought the officials; the Czar was the landowners' Czar, but also the Jews' Czar. When the people attacked their exploiters, he brought in soldiers, and Christian blood flowed. 'You have already begun to rise against the Jews,' the leaflet concluded. 'That is fine. For soon a revolt will start all over Russia against the Czar, the landowners and the Jews.'

The leaflet was the work of a member of the Executive Committee who eventually deserted the revolutionary camp for that of black reaction. It is reported that the Committee's imprimatur for this proclamation was obtained by 'trickery' and that its circulation was soon stopped. Yet *Narodnaya volya*, No. 6, dated October, 1881, carried a discussion of the anti-Jewish movement by the same writer and of the same tenor. What is more, the Ukrainian leaflet was reprinted the following year by a local group of the People's Will. Though never formally repudiated, it was implicitly disavowed in the leading article of *Narodnaya volya*, No. 8/9, dated February, 1882. Nevertheless another leaflet in the vernacular, bearing the imprint of the People's Party and dated 18 March, 1883, urged the people to recall their glorious ancestors who had driven the Jews and the gentry out of the Ukraine with fire and sword.

In the summer the Executive Committee issued a proclamation which was so distasteful to the couple who operated the press—the wife was a Jewish woman who had embraced Christianity in order to contract a fictitious marriage—that they ran it off under protest and without the Party imprint. The sheet blamed the Jews for the pogroms and condemned the authorities for putting them down by force. In discussing the disorders in another Party publication, a contributor noted indignantly that in one town the troops had fired on the rioters, and expressed the hope that the news would reach other towns and start riots there, too. 'We do not think that the disorders will achieve their end,' he admitted, 'but we rejoice in the educational effects of such occurrences.' Disregarding the experience of the preceding three years, he persisted in conjuring up a vision of the mobs turning on their other enemies, once the Jews had been disposed of. 'Let us remind our readers', he wound up, 'that the French Revolution, too, began with massacres of Jews (Taine). It is a sad fate, which is apparently unavoidable.' On an earlier occasion a similar reflection had been offered the pogrom victims as solace in the organ of Black Repartition.

The following year the People's Will once more reversed itself, branding the anti-Jewish outbreaks as 'an erroneous formula', that could not benefit the people and admitting that in this matter the judgment of the revolutionaries had been hopelessly clouded. They had at last freed themselves from the aberration which had led them to condone what August Bebel called 'the socialism of fools'.

The émigrés showed themselves to be less opportunist and politically immature regarding the Jewish question. Alone, Trachev's *Nabat* perceived in the pogroms all the symptoms of an approaching social revolution. The 1881 leaflet caused dismay and indignation among them. Under the fresh impact of the pogroms, Plekhanov had started an essay on Socialism and Anti-Semitism, but gave it up, becoming 'unbearably ashamed', as he put it later, 'of demonstrating elementary truths'. Axelrod proposed that the Executive Committee publish a pamphlet addressed to the Jews to reassure them morally and to show them that not everyone was against them. As such a publication did not materialize, he began an article on the Jewish question in which he advocated, among other measures, a systematic campaign against anti-Semitism by the revolutionary factions. His comrades objected. Lavrov wrote to him guardedly that it was difficult for Russian socialists to take a stand in the matter because they had to have the masses on their side. Lev Deutsch, in a postscript to Lavrov's letter, dotted the 'i'. The revolutionaries, he conceded, must fight for racial equality, but to take such an idea to the masses would be impolitic: the peasants would say that the socialists had not only killed the Czar, but also sided with the Jews. He admitted that the situation chagrined him, but he personally felt no obligation toward his fellow Jews: he was above all a member of the Russian revolutionary party, and its interests were paramount.

His position was by no means typical. True, the revolutionaries of Jewish extraction at first apparently shared the attitude toward the outbreaks which prevailed in radical circles. But the fact that the riots had failed to assume a revolutionary character and that in the West, too, anti-Semitism was on the increase gave them pause. In some cases the result was a change of heart and mind. They discovered a new solidarity with their own people. 'Deep down in the soul of each one of us, revolutionaries of Jewish birth,' Plekhanov's wife was to recall, 'there was a sense of hurt pride and infinite pity for our own, and many of us were strongly tempted to devote ourselves to serving our injured, humiliated and persecuted people.' Jewish university students, long alienated from the ghetto, took a leading part in organizing self-defence units in Odessa, and demonstratively appeared in the synagogues on the fast-day proclaimed by the Rabbinate in protest against the pogroms. The assimilationist trend suffered a serious setback, and there were those who lost their enthusiasm for the revolution together with their belief in Socialism as a solution of the Jewish question.

CHAPTER XVI

THE AGONY OF
THE PEOPLE'S WILL

LATE in 1881 a conference of activists was held in Moscow. The results of its deliberations were meagre. Undismayed by the failure of previous efforts in that direction, the Party resolved to set up a special organization, the Christian Brotherhood, to be made up of Old Believers and sectarians converted to the cause of revolution. In the name of this non-existent body, an encyclical was issued, in which the Czar's laws and regulations were declared 'contrary to God's commandments and the spirit of Christian teaching'. This was the last attempt dictated by the old notion that religious dissenters were particularly susceptible to revolutionary propaganda. Nothing further was heard of the Brotherhood.

The conference also decided to assassinate General Strelnikov, the exceptionally brutal prosecuting officer in the military courts of the South. All the preliminary preparations were made by Vera Figner, who had in fact proposed the measure, and on 18 March, 1882, in Odessa, an agent of the Executive Committee, fatally wounded the General. Khalturin, who two years previously had blown up the Winter Palace, was waiting in a carriage nearby to drive the assassin to safety. Both men were seized on the spot and hanged four days later under assumed names—they had refused to disclose their identities.

Few other acts of violence were carried out or attempted during the lifetime of the People's Will. The work of the Party was practically confined to socialist propaganda among factory hands, conducted by a few local groups independently and without central direction.

When the Party's fortunes were at this low ebb there occurred a significant and rather paradoxical shift in its ideology. The issue of its organ dated 5 February, 1882, contained a striking statement. If the masses spontaneously effect a social revolution, at the time when the conspirators seize political power, the leading article read, then the task of the Provisional Government

311

will be merely 'to sanction the economic equality wrested by the people from their age-old oppressors and exploiters'. But the people may fail to act. In that case the Provisional Government will not only establish a free political order but will make an economic revolution by abolishing the right of private property in land and other means of production. Only then will the Constituent Assembly be made up of 'true representatives of the people'.

The same stand was taken, and more boldly, in a letter that the Executive Committee addressed about the same time to 'emigré comrades', urging them to return home and join the People's Will. 'We ascribe enormous importance to political power', the communication read. 'The revolution will occur only when this power is in good hands, and that is why we strive to seize it. . . . Should we obtain it as a result of an overturn, we would not let go of it until we had assured the people a firm footing.' The Committee hastened to add that it did not intend to perpetuate this 'tutelage of the people', but it was vague about the conditions under which the Party would be ready to turn the reins over to the Constituent Assembly. The long missive ended on a Machiavellian note: for fear of repelling the moderates the addressees were requested not to expatiate in public on the seizure of power, 'at least not in our name'. [1]

Two years later in an article entitled 'What Are We to Expect from the Revolution?' Tikhomirov stated that while the Party wished to secure political power, it had no intention to use it in order to *force* the benefits of Socialism or Communism on the people. This denial notwithstanding, it would appear that in its decline the People's Will was headed by persons no longer committed, as most of them had been in the past, to the plan of either compelling the Czar to liberalize his régime or replacing it with a Provisional Government which would forthwith hand over its power to a democratically elected Constituent Assembly. Instead, the leadership had developed a leaning toward the 'Jacobin' programme first broached in the *Young Russia* manifesto back in 1862 and later advocated by the Tkachev faction: that of seizing power by conspiracy and bringing Socialism into existence by decree—a programme which adumbrated the

[1] In her reminiscences, published in 1926, Anna Pribyleva, a then surviving member of the Executive Committee, argued that the letter was spurious.

Bolshevik revolution. Maria Oshanina asserted that the members of the Executive Committee toward the end of its existence 'had all become Jacobins, more or less.'

The letter to 'the émigré comrades' was addressed chiefly to the handful of former leaders of Black Repartition who stayed abroad. As a matter of fact, the Tkachevist trend in the Executive Committee was no news to them. The previous autumn a communication from Stefanovich, who had returned to Russia, had apprized them of it.

The expatriates did not relish the message. They were moving toward a position resembling that of Western social democracy, which assumed a long interval between the political and the social revolution. Kravchinsky took a particularly dark view of the 'Jacobin' tendency. Its advocates, he said, were 'already getting drunk on the ambrosia of power. . . . They want power not for the cause, but for power's sake.' He was also extremely critical of the Committee's inclination to claim 'papal infallibility'. That disposition, he wrote to Axelrod, could do the Party the greatest harm, for its future largely depended on 'the right to free thought and free criticism. This right,' he observed with truly prophetic insight, 'is the only bulwark against that terrible development of centralism which, given Russian extremism, could assume monstrous proportions and kill everything that is alive.'

Nevertheless, the émigrés' reply, though somewhat evasive, was that they would go home and lend a hand. But because of the wave of arrests that swept both capitals in the spring, they were advised to wait. A little later, the arrival in Geneva of a loquacious member of the Executive Committee opened their eyes to the lamentable state of the Party of which they had been unaware, and they chose to stay on abroad. They contented themselves with printing pamphlets for home consumption and collecting money for the Red Cross of the People's Will, a new organization dedicated to alleviating the lot of political prisoners. Vera Zasulich returned to Russia in 1905, dying fourteen years later, a bitter enemy of the Soviet régime. Plekhanov did not repatriate himself until the revolution of 1917, after an absence of thirty-seven years.

The talk about 'seizing power' verged on the ludicrous in view of the condition of the Party. The arrests just mentioned brought the activities of the Executive Committee to a virtual standstill. The printing-press had been given up. The police raided the flat where passports were forged and seized the forgers and their equipment. Maria Oshanina crossed the border, joining the ranks of the émigrés, and so did Tikhomirov and his wife, in spite of Vera Figner's protests.

In the northern capital work continued a little longer. The leading figure in Petersburg was Mikhail Grachevsky, who had come to the fore after the event of 1 March. Owing to his efforts, the manufacture of dynamite was resumed in May. The following month, however, he and most of his comrades were in prison. Aside from those who had expatriated themselves, the sole member of the Executive Committee now left at liberty was Vera Figner.

The arrests were due to the efficient detective work of Major Sudeikin, head of the secret service in the capital, of whom more will be heard later. With the death of Strelnikov, the revolutionaries saw in him the arch-enemy, as subtle as he was ruthless. They particularly resented his persistency in corrupting his captives. He would introduce himself to them as an old-time *narodnik* and a student of Marx, critical of the tactics of the People's Will but not of its aims. He made it a rule to urge every political he encountered to join the secret service, and he was not unsuccessful, especially with young people.

Vera Figner fully realized the seriousness of the situation. But she would not give up. After all, some local cells were still active. She took into her confidence a leading member of the Kiev group and another activist, a retired army captain, who had been a trusted agent of the Executive Committee. With the aid of these two men she set about restoring the core of the People's Will. A slight break in the clouds occurred when one of the Subbotina sisters, then an exile in Siberia, turned over to the Party the remnant of the family fortune, eleven thousand roubles, according to one statement. It was now possible to resume printing. In November a press was set up in Odessa.

In casting about for people capable of replacing the arrested members of the Executive Committee the trio turned their minds to the Party's military branch. In April, 1881, it had lost two of its most active members—one of them, Lieutenant Sukhanov, was subsequently executed by a firing squad. Nevertheless it continued to hold its own and indeed to grow. The fact that its numerical strength was not impressive did not daunt the leadership. This was given to formulating fantastic plans in the belief that a handful of resolute men in a commanding position could work miracles. For example, there was talk of seizing Kronstadt and the naval vessels stationed there and bombarding the capital.

The military organization had been set up to give support to a spontaneous popular uprising or, if that failed to materialize, to head an insurrection engineered by the Party. Since both eventualities had now moved off into the dim future, its existence seemed no longer justified. Vera Figner was not ready to suggest that it disband, but she felt no compunction about attempting to divert the best men in the military branch to more important tasks. Accordingly, half a dozen of them were requested to retire from the service, sever their connexion with the military organization, and join the Executive Committee. Only two men fell in with this plan. The situation at the centre did not improve. Behind a serene façade Vera Figner was in a panic.

The authorities were still unaware of the helplessness to which their adversary had been reduced. The Executive Committee continued to loom as the general staff of a formidable force that was lurking in the shadows of the underground. Its very quiescence was ominous. Fearing that some act of violence might be perpetrated at the coronation, they conceived the notion of making terms with the revolutionaries for the cessation of terrorism at least until the ceremony was over. To that end the police approached more than one political prisoner, urging them to state the conditions of an armistice. These efforts came to naught. Yakov Stefanovich, who was arrested in February, 1882, would not speak for the People's Will. Another prisoner responded by writing a long memorandum in which he tried to convert Alexander III to Socialism, arguing that an autocracy could be a workers' as well as a feudal or bourgeois State.

Later in the year the negotiations were taken over by the Holy League. Two separate attempts to arrange a truce seem to have been made. An emissary of the organization actually came to terms with Lavrov, who was still regarded by the uninitiated as the head of the revolutionary movement. An elaborate agreement was drafted in Paris, as well as the text of a proclamation to be issued by the Executive Committee. There was an element of pure comedy in the proceedings: while Lavrov acted for a practically non-existent Party with which he was not affiliated, the man he dealt with, concealing the identity of his backers, spoke in the name of a wholly mythical *Zemstvo* Association. The *pourparlers* were suddenly broken off on the ground that the Association had lost its influence in high places.

While negotiating with Lavrov, the League was duplicating its efforts with the aid of an outsider, a journalist by the name of Nikolay Nikoladze. He was told by Count Vorontzov-Dashkov, Minister of the Court and one of the pillars of the League, that it might be able to persuade the Government to make certain liberal concessions in return for a temporary cessation of terror. Nikoladze then gained the ear of several left-wing authors, including Mikhailovsky. The latter travelled a thousand miles to Kharkov to lay the matter before Vera Figner. She was rather sceptical, suspecting a police trap. In any event, she could make no decision without the consent of the members of the Committee who were abroad. Accordingly, she sent a trusted agent to Geneva to consult Tikhomirov and the others.

The emissary arrived there about the same time as Nikoladze. The latter made contact with Tikhomirov and laid his cards on the table. Saying that he spoke for a group of politically influential personages, he asked on what terms the terrorists would agree to a truce. Tikhomirov was elated. An armistice would supply the Executive Committee with a plausible excuse for the inaction which impotence had forced upon it. In exchange for fictitious self-restraint, the Party would receive real concessions. This was a godsend.

As the price of the armistice Tikhomirov demanded that the coronation manifesto should include the following provisions: amnesty for political prisoners; civil liberties, specifically freedom of socialist propaganda; a larger measure of *zemstvo* and municipal self-government. Furthermore, he requested that Nikoladze's backers, by way of an earnest of their intentions, deposit the sum of one million roubles with some individual enjoying the confidence of the Party, this money to be forfeited if they failed to keep their side of the bargain. Also an important political prisoner was to be freed before the coronation.

The negotiations were proceeding smoothly when, in the

last days of 1882, Nikoladze abruptly broke them off and returned
to Russia at the request of the League. This is Tikhomirov's story.
Nikoladze has it that an agreement had actually been concluded,
but that on returning to Petersburg he was told by Vorontzov-
Dashkov to drop the whole matter.

In undertaking his mission Nikoladze, who was a man of
liberal views, had stipulated as his sole reward, irrespective of
the outcome of his efforts, that Chernyshevsky should be included in the amnesty that was expected at the coronation. The
amnesty granted in connexion with that event, which went off
without a hitch on 15 May, 1883, failed to cover Chernyshevsky's
case, but some months later the exile was allowed to return to
European Russia after his sons had addressed a petition to the
Czar.

II

The Holy League had broken off negotiations with Lavrov
and Tikhomirov because by the end of 1882 the authorities had
lost interest in treating with the People's Will. The regular police
had succeeded unaided not only in learning what the true state
of the Party was, but also in taking over the little that remained
of it. This is how it happened.

As has been noted, when Vera Figner found herself the sole
active member of the Executive Committee she turned for help
to two men. One of them was Sergey Degayev. Coming of a
cultivated middle-class family, he, like his younger brother,
Vladimir, fell under the influence of radical ideas, eventually
joining the People's Will. Vladimir was in his teens when, early
in 1881, he was arrested. He was questioned by Sudeikin himself
and invited to enter the secret service. This he did, intending to
step into the boots of Kletochnikov, who had just been seized.
Of course, the shrewd detective saw through the would-be
counter-spy. Far from being of help to the Party, the rather dull-
witted boy may have been instrumental in causing the many
arrests that occurred in February, 1882. In the spring Sudeikin
dispensed with his services, and the following year Vladimir
expatriated himself, eventually settling in the United States and
repudiating the radicalism of his youth.

Sergey, born in 1854, graduated from a military college, but retired from the army at an early age and attended an engineering school when, at the end of the 'seventies, he first became involved with revolutionaries. He conducted propaganda among his fellow students and as a leader of the military organization of the People's Will stood close to the Executive Committee. He was implicated in the event of 1 March, having had a hand in the mining operations conducted from the cheese store. After the assassination of the Czar he remained active. When in the spring of 1882, it was decided to kill Sudeikin, he took part in shadowing the detective with whom he had become acquainted through his brother.

It must have given him great satisfaction to be chosen by Vera Figner as her associate. To be a member of the Executive Committee had long been his ambition. He believed himself destined to do great things. In his new rôle he took charge of a secret press in Odessa. Within a few weeks, on 18 December, he was in prison. He was seriously compromised and threatened with a term of hard labour. Sudeikin questioned him without witnesses and was gratified with the results.

A statement printed later in *Narodnaya volya* offered this explanation of Degayev's conduct: 'He took it into his head to buy the Government's gratitude at the price of betraying his former friends and its bitterest enemies, and then, having secured the complete confidence of the autocracy, to deal it a decisive blow when the occasion presented itself.' In his memoirs Tikhomirov presented Degayev's motive in a somewhat different light. According to him, Degayev fell in with Sudeikin's curious idea that an alliance between the secret service and the People's Will would accomplish what the Party had failed to bring about: a liberal régime. Degayev's sister, who was in his confidence, substantially corroborated this version. 'Sudeikin told the prisoner,' she wrote, 'that only with his [Sudeikin's] help could the People's Will seize power. He spoke less like a police officer than like a fellow populist, admitting that the existing order was in need of a thorough overhauling, but arguing that the Party's tactics were wrong and hence it was getting nowhere.' Degayev realized that his pact with Sudeikin involved the loss of certain comrades, but he told himself that no revolutionary enterprise had ever succeeded without sacrifices.

To achieve their end, Sudeikin and his prisoner agreed that

the latter must rejoin his comrades. Accordingly a fake escape was conveniently arranged for him while he was being transferred from one prison to another. This occurred on 14 January, 1883, and a week or two later he turned up in the capital as a representative of the Executive Committee. He was not the first activist to turn State's evidence. Treason dogged the People's Will, as it had its predecessors. But for the first time the police had an informant who belonged to the inner core of the Party.

Sudeikin had apparently assured Degayev that his primary interest was not in making arrests, but in directing the activities of the People's Will in accordance with the plans the two had laid. But before long he changed his tune. Arguing that it was necessary, first of all, to protect the Government from the terrorists, he seized Vera Figner and her associates.[1] He then attacked the Party's military organization. So numerous were the arrests among its leading members that it was utterly crushed.

Except for some groups on its loose periphery, the People's Will was now completely at the mercy of the police. Indeed, it functioned under the ægis, as it were, of the head of the secret service in the capital, Lieutenant-Colonel Sudeikin. The forged passports used by 'illegals' were supplied by his office. It has even been said that he had edited the two issues of the Party's *Bulletin* printed in 1883.

The relations between him and his 'ally' were unusual, to say the least. Though he had every reason to be suspicious, he trusted Degayev fully and confided to him his secret ambitions. He belonged to the race of men with a giant appetite for power and no scruples about getting it. He dreamed of making himself indispensable to the Czar and the highest dignitaries of the realm by convincing them that he alone stood between them and death at the hands of the revolutionaries. To that end he planned to organize, with Degayev's help, a terrorist group, and then under some pretext, such as disability caused by a fake attack on his life, resign from the service. Then one or two key notables, such as the Minister of the Interior, would be assassinated. Panic-stricken, the Emperor would recall him, and under the circumstances it would be easy for him to get the Minister's post. He

[1] Vera Figner was condemned to death, but her sentence was commuted to a life term of hard labour. Actually she spent twenty years in prison and died in 1942 at the age of ninety.

would become the most powerful man in the land, the all-Russian dictator, before whom even the Czar would quake. Through Degayev he would also rule the underground. The two of them would constitute the real Government of the Empire.

At first Degayev may have been impressed with this grandiose scheme, in which a place was duly reserved for him. But as the weeks slipped by and the arrests caused by his disclosures multiplied, while Sudeikin did nothing to keep his side of the pact, the future duumvir perceived that his own rôle remained that of a mere informer. Moreover, his position was becoming more difficult. To shield him, the police spread the rumour that a young woman who had been arrested with him and subsequently set free was turning State's evidence. Nevertheless he was not altogether above suspicion. A Colonel of the gendarmerie gave away the secret of Degayev's escape to an army man, who, while in his cups, repeated what he had been told within the hearing of someone who passed the word on to the local group of the People's Will. There were those who dismissed the story, but others were ready to believe it.

Degayev was beginning to labour under a severe mental strain. Perhaps to get respite from contacts with his comrades, perhaps to find out how he stood with the leadership, he persuaded Sudeikin to send him abroad. His trip appears to have taken place in May. He went to Geneva with the object of luring Tikhomirov from there to Germany, where the expatriate was to be kidnapped and taken to Russia. The two men had several unhappy talks. On one occasion Tikhomirov observed that the condition of the Party was hopeless and that some sort of compromise with the Government was perhaps the best way out. Degayev, deciding that he was talking to a man who might be won over to his side, spoke freely and before he knew it, he found himself revealing his compact with Sudeikin. Tikhomirov listened impassively. Degayev talked on, looking for some sign of indignation at his treachery, some token of admiration for his noble intentions. But the host in no way betrayed his emotions. Finally Degayev exclaimed that his fate was in Tikhomirov's hands. It was for the Executive Committee—he was still in awe of that body, which was now little more than a name—'either to mete out to him the punishment he deserves,' as the above-mentioned statement in *Narodnaya Volya* has it, 'or to allow him to make amends for his crime, at least to some extent, by doing the Party a signal service.'

Tikhomirov was in a quandary. His visitor had said that he had given Sudeikin information about certain individuals, which had not as yet been acted upon. To denounce the informer and have him assassinated would mean to expose these people to arrest. He agreed not to disclose Degayev's secret if the latter would save those who had not been seized by arranging for their escape abroad. Furthermore, Degayev was to execute Sudeikin with his own hands.

The only person Tikhomirov took into his confidence was Maria Oshanina, the sole other member of the Executive Committee. Perhaps he was not sure that there would be approval of the conditions he had imposed on Degayev, dictated as they were by expediency rather than by moral scrupulousness.

He made no attempt to warn the remnant of the membership: he kept his side of the bargain. Degayev, on the other hand, was slow in keeping his. Accordingly, in August he was summoned abroad, presumably to be reminded of his promise. Nothing more fully attests the confidence which Sudeikin had in him than the fact that he was allowed to leave the country for the second time.

On his return to Russia he continued to play his double rôle undisturbed. He dominated the conference of activists which took place in October and he was elected to a directorate that included three more members, all, of course, known to Sudeikin and completely at his mercy (one of them eventually also turned informer). Unaware of the obligation Degayev had taken upon himself, the conference decreed Sudeikin's liquidation.

About this time one more person learned Degayev's secret. This was Hermann Lopatin, a free-lance revolutionary of whom more will be heard presently. Questioned about the details of his escape from his guards, as the two sat over glasses of tea in Palkin's Restaurant, Degayev became confused and blurted out the truth, including the fact that he had obligated himself to kill Sudeikin. Thereafter Lopatin kept close watch over the informer.

Sudeikin had toyed with the idea of having a fake attempt made on his life. At first Degayev had planned to take advantage of this and turn the feigned attack into a genuine one, but had given up the scheme as too chancy. Finally, on 16 December, 1883, he received Sudeikin in his flat on a suitable pretext and there with the aid of two accomplices (one of them eventually became a police agent) who knew nothing of their comrade's real rôle, killed him and severely wounded the henchman who accompanied him. Degayev was the first to fire, and the other two finished the job with sawed-off crowbars. One of the men had been groomed by Sudeikin, in furtherance of his ambitious plan, for the rôle of assassin of the Minister of the Interior.

It had been expected that, in destroying Sudeikin, Degayev would meet his own end. But luck was with him. He succeeded in escaping abroad. In Paris his case was examined by a tribunal consisting of Tikhomirov and two other comrades. He was forbidden on pain of death ever to rejoin the ranks of Russian revolutionaries or to return to Russia. As the Government was offering a large reward for his capture, there was no great inducement for him to go back.

Without delay he and his wife embarked for America, landing in Canada and later making their way to the United States. For a while they stayed in St. Louis, where he resumed his studies, and in 1897 received his Ph.D. from Johns Hopkins. For ten years he taught at the University of South Dakota. Professor Alexander Pell, as he now called himself, Dean of the College of Engineering, was a popular man on the campus, not only because of his interest in college athletics. 'He was one of the most humane men I have ever known,' one of his students said of him. The issue of the college magazine for 25 March, 1901, contained this notice: 'Dr. and Mrs. Pell entertained the class of which he is class father. From the head of the table beamed the jolly countenance of Jolly Little Pell [he was rather short] cracking jokes faster than the freshmen could crack nuts.' A childless couple, the Pells surrounded themselves with young people whom they housed and helped through college. From South Dakota the professor was called to the Armour Institute of Technology.

On the death of his wife, he married one of his students, an American girl, and when his failing health obliged him to retire from the Armour Institute he went to live first at South Hadley and later at Bryn Mawr, where his wife was teaching. He is said to have hailed Russia's defeat by Japan and to have viewed

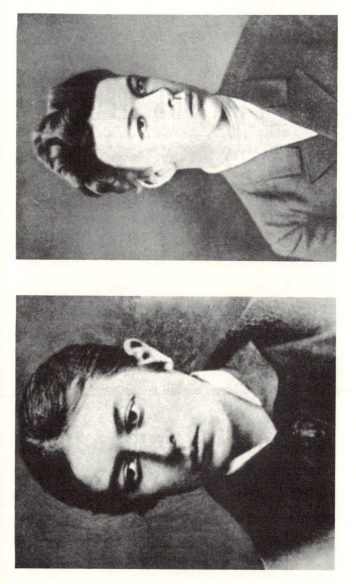

Vera Figner

Alexander Ulyanov, Lenin's elder brother, who was hanged in 1887 for an unsuccessful attempt on the life of Alexander III

A poster offering rewards of 5,000 and 10,000 roubles for information
leading to the apprehension of Sergey Degayev

the Bolshevik Revolution with aversion. His Russian past was apparently a sealed book to his American associates. To protect himself against embarrassing disclosures, he had his brother Vladimir send a dispatch to a Russian newspaper in 1909 or 1910, to the effect that Sergey Degayev died in New Zealand. His actual death occurred in 1921. An obituary of him by a former colleague concluded thus: 'His generosity and loyalty will live long in the hearts of those who were privileged to know him.'

III

A statement by the Executive Committee denouncing Degayev was drafted shortly after Sudeikin's assassination, but was not published till nearly a year after. Almost immediately, however, the news of Degayev's treachery leaked out. A storm of indignation swept the thin ranks of the People's Will. Why, they asked, had he not been brought to book after his confession? Why had they not been warned? In the absence of an authoritative account of the affair, there were those who concluded that Degayev had done his infamous work with the approval of the Executive Committee.

For some time dissatisfaction with the organization and programme of the Party had been on the increase, particularly among the younger proselytes. The Degayev incident, in damaging the prestige of the Executive Committee, strengthened the opposition. Early in 1884 the revisionist ferment resulted in the formation of a dissident faction, which adopted the name of the Younger People's Will. It looked upon itself not as a junior adjunct to the Party, but as its heir and successor.

The Young focused their attention on the urban proletariat. They favoured terrorism, but they wanted it directed against economic exploiters near at hand, rather than against political oppressors far away. Their immediate objective was to force the Czar to convoke a Constituent Assembly and they were opposed to the idea of dictatorship by the Party. Above all, they advocated rebuilding the People's Will along more democratic lines. They argued that the Executive Committee, self-perpetuating, authoritarian, was a brake on the growth of the movement and should be replaced by a directorate, representative of and responsible to the membership. While the Old Guard stood for a strong central authority, an organization directed from above, the Young clamoured for local autonomy, an organization growing from below. This was the very rock on which, in a later generation, the Russian Social-Democratic Labour Party was to split into the Bolshevik and Menshevik factions.

The Old Guard was not ready to give up the fort without a struggle. Tikhomirov made a half-hearted attempt to reassert the authority of the shadowy Executive Committee. Before he had expatriated himself, he had intended to bid farewell to revolution. Degayev's confession had made him change his mind. Since the Party at home was completely under the thumb of the police, he had decided that it was incumbent on him to try and create abroad a nucleus of the tried and true, around which a resurrected *Narodnaya Volya* might eventually grow. Accordingly, he joined Lavrov in Paris, and together they launched a new journal. At first it was planned as a forum for the various shades of revolutionary thought. But when the new review made its bow, in September, 1883, it bore the title, *Vestnik Narodnoi Voli* (Messenger of the People's Will), and the sub-title: *Organ abroad of Russian Socialism as it expresses itself in the People's Will*. Of the two editors, Lavrov was not a member, but, as it were, an ally of the Party, while Tikhomirov was already in the grip of that crisis which eventually led to his withdrawal from the revolutionary camp. The *Vestnik* was a heavy-handed, academic affair, and its bulky issues, appearing at long intervals, made little impression on the public to which it addressed itself.

In February, 1884, delegates of the several groups that were still active met in Paris. The opposition was not represented and the authority of Tikhomirov and Maria Oshanina was not challenged. They appointed a three-man Commission, which was instructed to proceed to Russia and try to revive the Party without changing a jot or tittle in its programme or organization.

The trio included Hermann Lopatin, who has already been mentioned. A man of about forty, he had been on the fringe of the movement since his student days, but, unable to submit to party discipline, he avoided formal affiliation with any group. During his stay in London he became friendly with Marx and Engels. A knight errant of the revolution, he had been repeatedly arrested, and on several occasions managed to break jail. He had helped Lavrov escape abroad and had unsuccessfully attempted to free Chernyshevsky from his Siberian bondage. The People's Will acquired in him an adherent of unusual resourcefulness and irrepressible spirit, with a dash of amateurishness and frivolity in his make-up.

He reached Petersburg in March and was soon joined by his two associates. They found the opposition in a truculent mood and firmly entrenched both in the capital and in the provinces. The Young People's Will denied the authority of the expatriates and treated their emissaries as impostors. Lopatin took a conciliatory attitude toward the dissidents. He humoured them, he argued with them, he tried to show them that a breach was both harmful and unnecessary. The *pourparlers* were conducted in an atmosphere of mutual irritation and downright hostility. Things were at such a pass that the arrest of a member of one faction was met by the other with a sigh of relief.

Nevertheless, by June an uneasy peace had been patched up. The schismatics gave up the idea of bringing out a journal of their own, destroyed most of the copies of their programme that had been run off on their own press, and returned to the fold, not without some mental reservations. The Petersburg Workers' Group, a mainstay of the opposition, chose to remain outside the Party. What seems to have put an end to the conflict was a succession of arrests. They were particularly numerous among the Young: the two agents planted by the police in that group earned their keep.

The feud over, the activists were now able to concentrate on rehabilitating the Party. The task was difficult. It was necessary to get rid of informers, to ascertain who had been betrayed to the police by Degayev, to deal with the deviations that had arisen during the absence of central control, to raise funds. In order to replenish the cashbox, attempts were made to rob the mails, and during one of them a postman was killed. These exploits were not approved by the Commission of Three. Lopatin argued that the post was a public institution, the neutrality of which the Party should scrupulously respect.

He lacked neither energy nor initiative. He spent the summer touring provincial centres in an effort to renew contact with the old groups and establish new ones. His labours were not very fruitful. There was no want of proselytes, but much energy was wasted in petty quarrels. Nevertheless two printing presses were set up, and copy was assembled for an issue of *Narodnaya volya*, which had been in a state of suspended animation since February, 1882. The long-awaited number of the journal, dated September, 1884, appeared in the autumn. It contained the belated and rather lame statement on Degayev, which has already been mentioned—in fact, two somewhat contradictory statements. It also presented a declaration by the Young People's Will, describing its position and explaining that it had merged with the Party because the two factions were separated by a divergence of theoretical views, which 'for the time being' was not likely to lead to such a disagreement on practical matters as would result in a split. In an effort to placate the Young and reaffirm his populist faith, Lopatin wrote that whether the masses were summoned to have their say 'from the height of the throne shaken by the blows of revolutionaries', or by the Party, after it had seized political power 'for a moment', the ultimate result would be the same: 'We firmly believe that on our soil the coming transformation cannot degenerate into a purely political constitution, but will surely bring with it all the agrarian and other economic and social reforms which are compatible with the present intellectual development of mankind.' He was thus restating the thesis Tikhomirov had advanced in the article mentioned earlier in the chapter, namely, that in Russia the overthrow of the monarchy was bound to usher in the socialist organization of the country's economy.

The feeling was that the Party should give more telling evidence of its existence than an issue of its journal and the execution of a spy, which occurred early in 1884. Lopatin was a believer in terrorism. What wouldn't he give, he said, for a couple of 'butchers' like the pair that had helped Degayev dispatch Sudeikin. He would have liked to direct a blow at the occupant of the throne, but compromised on a lesser target: Count Dmitry Tolstoy, the arch-reactionary Minister of the Interior.[1] Chance had saved the man from the poisoned dagger of one member of the Young People's Will and from the pistol

[1] The previous year the Count had told Prince Bernhard von Bülow that should the autocracy, which admittedly had its shortcomings, be overthrown, the result was sure to be not a parliamentary régime but 'naked Communism' the doctrine that Karl Marx had preached.

of another. Now it was decided to use bombs on him. Several missiles, of a rather faulty construction, made at Lugansk,[1] in the South, with dynamite stolen from a Government plant, were brought to the capital by Lopatin himself. In the midst of these preparations, on 6 October, he was arrested.

Lopatin had many qualities useful to a conspirator. Elementary caution was not one of them. When he was seized, he was carrying two bombs. Besides, he had in his pockets a dozen scraps of paper scribbled with passwords and keys to the codes used by the organization, as well as with names and addresses forming a miniature Who's Who of the movement. He had been certain that in an emergency he would manage to swallow these papers, but he was prevented from doing so by the detectives who apprehended him. As a result, there were arrests in thirty-two cities. They were all the more numerous since, as usual, more than one prisoner lost heart and turned informer. Not only activists, but also fellow travellers were hit. The fruits of the organizational work of the previous months were destroyed. Aside from a group of expatriates, all that remained of the People's Will was a handful of individual adherents here and there and, in the larger centres, some scattered cells isolated from each other.

IV

And still the ghost of the People's Will refused to be laid. One more attempt was made to resuscitate the Party. The moving spirit behind this effort was a youth with a fiery temperament who was a born organiser. In 1882, at the age of eighteen, Boris Orzhikh entered the university in his native Odessa and immediately plunged into extra-curricular activities. They assumed such a character that in the summer of 1884 he became an 'illegal'. Then came Lopatin's arrest and débâcle.

As Orzhikh watched the collapse of the Party, he had moments of despair, but he did not succumb to it. The destruction was not as complete as had appeared at first. In the southern provinces the secret service was incredibly amateurish, and in such centres as Kiev, Kharkov, Odessa, entire cells remained intact. Here and there a bundle of underground literature had been saved, or the

[1] Now Voroshilovgrad.

implements for forging passports. Moreover, among the ruins new life was stirring: there were converts, awkward, inexperienced, yet full of ardour for the cause. With the help of a few fellow students and factory hands, he set to work.

His immediate aim was to revive the local groups in the South. He visited several cities and was somewhat encouraged by what he found. His ambitions soared when he discovered a dozen bombs available for use. They had been made with dynamite stolen from the same plant that had supplied the explosive for the missiles found on Lopatin. Having learned that Count Tolstoy, Minister of the Interior, was going to the Crimea for a rest, Orzhikh decided to attack him at a southern railway station. This was in the spring of 1885. With several bombs in his luggage he went to Kharkov, more than once during his trip barely escaping catastrophe. But when he reached Kharkov he heard that the Count was being taken South in a state of acute mental derangement. Orzhikh decided to let well alone.

Frustrated but undismayed, he busied himself with other matters, such as the resumption of secret printing. A small press was set up in Kharkov, but the police, tipped off by an informer, promptly seized it. The printer resisted arrest, killing an officer, and was hanged. Two other presses were set up in out-of-the-way towns and Orzhikh began to get together copy for a new issue of the organ of the non-existent Party. He had the help of two young students, Lev Sternberg and Natan Bogoraz. Both, eventually exiled to farthest Siberia, were to become noted ethnographers. Like the Young People's Will before them, Orzhikh and his comrades did not feel that they were accountable to the expatriates and did not apprize Tikhomirov of the plan. The text of the projected number of *Narodnaya volya* was approved at a meeting of half a dozen representatives of the more active cells. The 'conference', as the gathering was grandiloquently styled, elected a committee which was to co-ordinate the activities of local groups throughout the South. A definite step was thus taken toward restoring the Party.

The printing of the issue was not completed until December. The leading article repeated the old slogan: *delenda est Carthago*: the autocracy must be crushed and replaced by a democratic régime. The prevalent black reaction was dismissed as the last desperate effort of a doomed despotism. True, the downfall of the monarchy would not mean a political and social revolution in one—'life had smashed that hope'. But neither would it be a mere scene-shifting, the dawn of a bourgeois era, a new way of exploiting the people 'under cover of an illusory freedom'. Great changes would follow, above all the long-awaited re-distribution of land. And let 'our Olympians dwelling in the beautiful faraway'—a thrust at expatriates who had embraced Marxism—be reassured: the fears of these doctrinaires that the agrarian reform would delay the advent of Socialism were without foundation. In the West every summons to social revolution had fallen on deaf ears, because the farmers there had been bred to the belief in private property. Not so in Russia, where the peasants 'to a man' held that the land belongs to him who works it.

The issue of the journal—it was to be the last—made a great stir. It was incontrovertible proof that the Party had not been wiped out. The group was now able to enlarge the scope of its activities. His luggage weighed down with copies of *Narodnaya volya*, Orzhikh visited the central and northern provinces, travelling as far as Dorpat (now Tartu). His ambition was to revive the local circles there and set up regional boards, like the one that existed in the South. To a limited extent he was success-ful. He was instrumental in establishing the nucleus of an organiza-tion in Moscow, though not in Petersburg, where only one group, a workmen's circle, was functioning.

The year 1886 opened calamitously. A Southern activist, arrested, turned State's evidence. One of the secret presses was discovered, and the other had to be abandoned. Arrests multiplied. In February Orzhikh himself was seized. Another informer turned up in Moscow, with disastrous results for the group there. Shortly before his arrest, which occurred in December, Bogoraz succeeded in printing the last issue of the Party *Bulletin*.

Late that year the Geneva organ of the People's Will also folded up. Tikhomirov, its co-editor, had long since lost his faith in revolution, but continued to advocate it by inertia, as it were, and without betraying his change of heart. Consequently, when two years later he publicly performed a complete volte-face by writing a pamphlet, *Why I Have Ceased to Be a Revolutionary*, his defection came like a bolt from the blue. In September, 1888, he addressed an abject petition to the Emperor, protesting his sincere repentance and begging permission to repatriate himself, so that he could atone for his past by conduct befitting a faithful communicant and loyal subject. His wish granted, he returned to Russia. Eventually the pillar of the legendary Executive Committee, the spokesman of the band of terrorists who had assassinated Alexander II, became an influential reactionary journalist. The last Czar presented him with a golden inkpot in recognition of his service to the Throne.

v

While the police were mopping up the last vestiges of the organization set up by Orzhikh and his comrades, a new group of militants was forming in the northern capital. They called themselves the Terrorist Section of the People's Will, though they were fully aware that the Party was no more. Nor did they seek to establish contact with any of the remnants of the society to which they nominally belonged, such as the local workmen's circle that had once been part of the Young People's Will. They proposed to act entirely on their own.

At the University of Petersburg there was a secret committee of representatives of a dozen fraternities (*zemlyachestva*), each made up of men hailing from the same province. In defiance of a police order this committee held a demonstration on the occasion of the twenty-fifth anniversary of the emancipation of the serfs. Late in the year an attempt was made to mark similarly another anniversary: that of Dobrolubov's death. But when the marchers, wishing to lay a wreath on the grave, reached the cemetery, they found that the police had locked the gate. The procession was surrounded by Cossacks and the names of some of the students were taken down. Feeling ran high on the campus. A leaflet was brought out, which ended by declaring that 'we' would oppose force rooted in spiritual solidarity to brute force used by the Government.

Pyotr Shevyryov, who was chiefly responsible for the leaflet, seems to have initiated the Terrorist Section. The core of it was a handful of students, mere tyros, ignorant of conspiratorial methods, unused to the atmosphere of the underground.

Shevyryov himself was a consumptive youth, fanatical and rather unscrupulous, who was not above mystifying and deceiving his comrades in a manner reminiscent of Nechayev. He entertained an ambitious plan to set up a vast revolutionary organization embracing both intellectuals and manual workers.

A leading part was played by Alexander Ulyanov, a reserved, serious young man who majored in zoology. Like several of his comrades, he was a dedicated soul who calmly accepted the prospect of self-immolation in the service of the cause. The most articulate member of the group, it was he who drew up its credo. This deviates from *narodnik* orthodoxy in holding the working class to be the mainstay of the Party and the chief object of its activities, yet affirms the populist dogma that Russia may achieve Socialism without going through the capitalist phase. Fighting for free institutions, hand in hand with the liberals, is proclaimed the immediate task of the Party, and as long as it lacks mass support, political assassination is declared virtually the sole weapon in its arsenal.

Of course, terror meant regicide. This was an obsession with Shevyryov. Another member transferred from the University of Kazan to that of Petersburg for the express purpose of killing the Emperor. All agreed that the deed had the strongest moral justification. By January, 1887, a plot against the life of Alexander III was well under way. He was to be attacked by bombs, as his father had been. To render them lethal, hollowed-out leaden pellets filled with strychnine were crammed into the space between the inner metal container holding dynamite and the outer cardboard case. Expenses were defrayed with money from the pockets of the conspirators. Ulyanov, who had a hand in the manufacturing of the dynamite, pawned the gold medal he had been awarded by the university for a paper on the organs of fresh-water Annelida. Late in February three missiles were ready.

The plan was to toss a bomb under the Emperor's carriage while he was being driven along Nevsky Prospect. As rumour had it that he was about to depart from the capital, haste was essential. Ulyanov learned by heart a proclamation announcing the monarch's assassination by the (non-existent) Party and made arrangements to have it run off on the group's small press, if the attempt succeeded. Three men, who for days had been studying the Czar's movements, were to give the signal for the attack. Three others made up the bombing squad. They paced the avenue with the bombs held in readiness on 26 February, but the Czar did not emerge from the palace that day. Nor were the plotters luckier on 28 February. When on the afternoon of 1 March—a memorable date—bombers and signallers appeared on the avenue for the third time, all of them were arrested. It happened that the previous month a member of the bombing squad had broadly hinted at the impending attack in a letter to a friend. The police had intercepted the missive and identified the author. As a result, detectives grew suspicious when, on 28 February, they noticed that he loitered on the avenue all afternoon, apparently carrying a heavy object under his overcoat and keeping in touch with several other young men. When the same strollers had reappeared the following day, the plain-clothes men seized all of them. 'The second March the first', as the affair is sometimes designated, had come to nothing.

The prisoners at once pleaded guilty of attempted regicide, and two of them became very communicative, so that other arrests followed. Before they occurred it had been hoped that a second terrorist band, headed by a workman, would repeat the attempt. A small quantity of dynamite was available for the purpose. But as arrests multiplied, all such plans were abandoned. By the end of the month the Terrorist Section had ceased to exist.

Behind closed doors twelve men and three women faced a tribunal consisting of a special panel of senators. Most of the defendants concealed nothing from their judges. Shevyryov was one of the few who tried to minimize their guilt. Ulyanov took upon himself the blame for organizing the group. In his final statement he defended terror as the only weapon at the disposal of a small minority which, in defying a powerful police state, had nothing to lean upon but spiritual strength and the consciousness that it was fighting for justice. 'Among the Russian people,' he concluded, echoing Karakozov's words, 'there will always be found a dozen men and women who are so devoted to their ideas and feel so keenly their country's plight that they will not consider it a sacrifice to lay down their lives for the cause.'

The accused were condemned to death, but capital punishment was commuted to penal servitude or imprisonment for all except five men. The death sentence would probably have been commuted for these too, had they agreed to petition the Emperor for mercy. In refusing his mother's entreaty that he do so, Ulyanov told her that a duelist, having fired his shot, could not very well beg his adversary not to use his weapon.

Three defendants were given only ten years of hard labour in Siberia in consideration of the fact that they were minors, that they sincerely repented their misdeeds and that 'from the first they had helped the authorities to uncover the crime,' as the final verdict put it. (One of the men eventually committed suicide out of remorse, it is said, for having betrayed his comrades.) For the same reasons Bronislaw Pilsudski, who had supplied the poison for the bombs, received a fifteen-year term of hard labour, while his brother, Josef, who was only slightly involved in the affair, was exiled to Siberia for five years by administrative order. He lived to be the head of resurrected Poland and, as commander-in-chief of the Polish troops, he saved his country from Soviet conquest in 1920.

On 8 May the five who had been condemned to death were hanged. One of them managed to shout from the scaffold, 'Long live the People's Will!' Among the executed was Alexander Ulyanov. His family lived in Simbirsk (now Ulyanovsk), where his father, until his death the previous year, had held the post of superintendent of elementary schools in the province. Alexander's younger brother, Vladimir, learned the news of the execution from a newspaper. It is reported that the seventeen-year-old boy whom the world was eventually to know under the assumed name of Lenin, flung the sheet aside and exclaimed: 'I swear I will revenge myself on them!'

EPILOGUE

Official reaction and public lethargy ruled the 'eighties. The drab decade contented itself, on the one hand, with what a contemporary satirist called 'pigsty ideals' and, on the other, with the brighten-the-corner-where-you-are philosophy. Nevertheless, the fires of rebellion continued to smoulder, if precariously. Here and there small, ephemeral revolutionary circles managed to carry on. Recruited for the most part from the student youth as well as from among army and navy officers and cadets, they were isolated from each other and in a state of flux.

Following in the footsteps of the Terrorist Section of the People's Will, certain groups advocated the tactics of political assassination, now a policy of despair, and did not limit themselves to talk about it. In 1888 at Zürich several émigrés were conducting experiments with the preparation of bombs. These were to be smuggled into Russia and used by a nucleus of a projected nation-wide revolutionary organization. It owed its existence chiefly to the initiative and energy of a young woman by the name of Sophia Ginzburg. One February day in 1889, while staying in the capital, she happened to leave her purse in a store. The shopkeeper found in it the draft of a proclamation announcing the execution of the Czar, which he handed over to the police. Before long she was arrested together with several comrades, and since one of them turned informer, the entire group was wiped out, Sophia Ginzburg committing suicide in prison.

The making of bombs in Zürich ended disastrously, an explosion killing one man and wounding another. Thereupon the terrorists transferred their activities to Paris and established contact with another circle of conspirators at home. As one of the expatriate plotters was a secret service agent, arrests, in 1890, put an end to the activities of both groups.

In the ideological confusion that prevailed in those years two main trends were discernible. One was continuous with militant Populism as represented chiefly by the People's Will. Without accepting its entire platform, not a few activists and would-be

334

activists chose the label *narodovoltzy*, adherents of *Narodnaya Volya*. The Party was now no more than 'the shadow of a great name'. Yet for at least a decade after it had ceased to exist it continued to be a feeble rallying cry in an age of dispersion and discouragement. The other trend meant a break with tradition, espousal of a doctrine rather new to the intelligentzia: Marxism.

The writings of Marx and Engels and the social-democratic movement dominated by their ideas had not been unknown in Russia. Marx's *Critique of Political Economy* had a larger sale there than anywhere else. As has been said, in 1869 a translation of *The Communist Manifesto*, made, oddly enough, by its authors' arch-enemy, Bakunin, came from a Geneva press. Three years later a rendering of *Das Kapital* was openly published in Petersburg, the censor feeling that few would read the tome and fewer would understand it. The book did find a considerable public— nine hundred copies were sold during the first fifty days—but failed to impress itself on radical thinking. Marx was chiefly prized as a detractor of capitalism. His emphasis on the economic factor appealed to those whose orientation was apolitical. For the rest his doctrine was held inapplicable to Russia. With the collapse of the People's Will this attitude underwent a change.

In the autumn of 1883 a few expatriates living in Switzerland formed an Association which called itself Liberation of Labour. Its objectives were to spread 'scientific Socialism' among the intelligentzia and to create the nucleus of a Russian labour party modelled on that of Germany. Ironically enough, these converts to Marxism were the former leaders of Black Repartition, that champion of populist orthodoxy. In the words of one of them, Black Repartition died in childbirth, having brought forth Russian social-democracy.

The members of the group could be counted on the fingers of one hand. But it included a man, already mentioned in these pages, who combined a subtle and richly equipped intellect with a literary gift and who, moreover, was possessed of the temperament of a revolutionary and the zeal of a missionary: Georgy Plekhanov. In two pamphlets, which came out in Geneva in 1883 and 1884 respectively, he subjected the populist ideology, the programme of the People's Will and the 'Jacobin' trend within it, to a withering critique. The industrial proletariat, not the peasantry, was the hope of Socialism in Russia, as elsewhere, he argued; the immediate future in Russia belonged to capitalism, a progressive and 'historically inevitable' phase; the coming upheaval was bound to be a purely political change-over—to act on the assumption that the end of the monarchy would coincide with the socialist revolution was 'to retard the achievement of both goals'; the *obshchina* was moribund and, in any case, it could not set the country on the way to Communism.[1]

The propositions elaborated in Plekhanov's spirited essays, which offered the earliest formulation of Russian Marxism, were presented succinctly in the group's platform. This was printed in 1884, a revision of it appearing in 1888. The earlier text calls for a democratic constitutional régime as the first objective of the labour party. The possibility of a spontaneous revolutionary movement among the peasants is not excluded, and it is stated that the association by no means ignores their interests. On the contrary, the second version of the platform declares that the *muzhik* neither understands nor sympathizes with the revolutionaries and is indeed the chief support of the monarchy. By way of a sop to populist sentiment, however, the hope is held out that the overthrow of the old régime would arrest the dissolution of the peasant commune.

A few copies of these publications, as well as some social-democratic literature in the original German, found their way into Russia. There was then but little good soil for the seed. The industrial depression that started in 1881 had arrested the growth of the infant labour movement, and the prevalent apathy was not favourable to the spread of the new gospel. Among radicals, both at home and abroad, the term 'social-democrat' was in bad odour. Furthermore, though Populism as a political movement had been reduced to impotence, some of its tenets continued vigorously to be championed. In articles and books that had wide circulation a number of publicists and economists defended with new conviction the old thesis that in a backward country, like Russia, capitalism was a predatory, wholly destructive force, but no more a threat than a promise, since it could not possibly grow and was in fact stillborn. In the teeth of increasing evidence to

[1] On this point there was disagreement within the group. Vera Zasulich, for one, held that capitalism would be wiped off the face of the earth before the disintegration of the *obshchina*, and that the latter would then be of inestimable value to Russia.

the contrary, these theorists affirmed their belief that the collectivist and equalitarian tradition of the Russian folk had sufficient vitality to defy and eventually to defeat 'the rule of capital'. The country's future, they maintained, lay with a socialist economy, developing out of the native *obshchina* and *artel*.

At this time the populist ideology received encouragement from a most unlikely quarter. The year 1886 saw the posthumous publication of a letter written by Karl Marx nearly a decade earlier as a rejoinder to an article in a Petersburg magazine. Therein he admitted to sharing Chernyshevsky's view that by preserving the *obshchina* Russia might enjoy the fruits of capitalism without suffering its torments. And he took occasion to protest against interpreting his sketch of the origin of capitalism in Western Europe as a pattern which all nations must inevitably follow in the course of their history. He had expressed himself similarly in a communication to Vera Zasulich, dated 8 March, 1881, but the letter had remained unknown outside the circle of her intimates. The *obshchina*, he had written, was the mainstay of Russia's 'social renascence', but to function as such it must be guaranteed 'conditions of free development'. He was more explicit in his and Engels' foreword to the second Russian translation of the *Communist Manifesto*, printed at Geneva in 1882.[1] 'Should the Russian revolution be the signal for the workers' revolution in the West,' they wrote, 'so that the two complement each other,' then the *obshchina* might prove 'the starting point of communist development'.

It should be noted that at the time Marx held the days of Western capitalism to be numbered. He, as well as Engels, also greatly overestimated the chances of revolution in Russia. In handing down his sanguine opinion on the rôle of the rural commune, he may have been guided by the desire not to injure the morale of the Russian activists, who, he knew, had pinned their faith to the *muzhik's* collectivist habits. Be that as it may, Marx appeared to lend his great authority to the basic proposition of populism, namely, that Russia might bypass capitalism on its way to the socialist order. It was Marx against the Russian Marxists.

In one respect did the theorists mentioned above deviate from

[1] That year there appeared two more Russian editions of the *Manifesto*, one hectographed secretly in Petersburg, the other lithographed in Moscow.

militant populism: they implied that its objectives could be achieved within the framework of the existing order. The sole requirement was for the Government to stop fostering large-scale industries and to protect the interests of peasants and artisans. Also it was necessary to raise the cultural level of the masses. The cry: '*delenda est Carthago*' was muted, and that not only because the writings of these authors had to stand the censor's scrutiny. Temporarily, populism assumed the character of a moderate, reformist doctrine. In every way it was opposed to the principles of the Liberation of Labour group.

The circles that adhered to its tenets in the 'eighties were small, few, and short-lived. Their membership, like that of the other groups, came for the most part from the student body. They were chiefly busy indoctrinating the few factory hands they could reach, with a view to preparing leaders of the future labour movement. Some of those who called themselves social-democrats were content to leave the fight against the monarchy to the bourgeoisie, holding that their own task was to make the proletariat ready to use the freedom won by their class adversary. Between the Marxist and non-Marxist coteries relations were still rather amicable. In fact, a merger of the two was held possible. There were circles with programmes that were an amalgam of Populism and Marxism. Not a few heads held a jumble of ideas derived from the *Communist Manifesto*, on the one hand, and from the writings of Herzen and Lavrov, on the other.

The Liberation of Labour group itself failed to grow in size. By the end of the decade it still counted fewer than a dozen members. Boating on the Lake of Geneva with several comrades, Plekhanov would joke: 'Be careful, if we drown, Russian Socialism will perish.'

II

In the winter of 1891–92 famine gripped the eastern and south-eastern provinces, an area of half a million square miles with a population of thirty million. A severe epidemic of cholera followed. The measures taken by the authorities and private organizations were pitifully inadequate. Here and there young men and women abandoned their studies and made their way to the villages to help the starving and the sick. It was another 'going to the people', though on a small scale. At least some of these volunteer relief workers vaguely contemplated the possibility that the stricken peasantry would revolt, and they hoped to have a hand in the risings. They were disappointed. Violence did flare up, but it took the form of 'cholera riots', crowds smashing hospitals and dispensaries set up to combat the epidemic, and attacking doctors as poisoners. A group of *Narodovoltzy* printed *A Letter to the Starving Peasants*, but it is doubtful if the message reached any of the addressees, and in any case, all it urged them to do was to get in touch with their well-wishers in the cities.

If the disaster failed to arouse the masses to active protest, it had wide and deep repercussions nevertheless and in fact came close to being an historic turning-point. It helped to exorcise the spirit of apathy and political indifferentism that had possessed the previous decade. It focused the public mind on broad national problems, the condition and prospects of the peasantry, above all. In revealing the precarious state of agriculture the famine greatly weakened the belief, which had penetrated liberal and certain populist circles during the preceding years, in the possibility of progress under the existing régime. Nicholas II dealt another blow to that belief when, in a speech made in January, 1895, shortly after his ascension to the throne, he dismissed all hopes for a constitution as 'senseless dreams'. The need for the forcible replacement of the autocracy by a democratic order took on new urgency. A major item in the legacy that the People's Will left to both populists and Marxists was the conviction that the monarchy must be destroyed.

How was this vital task to be accomplished? A united front of all the elements of the opposition, including the liberals, was one answer. Such a policy, involving as a tactical manoeuver abandonment of the socialist objective, was advocated by a number of former populists both at home and abroad. Mark Natanson, who had returned from Siberian exile, attempted, with another one-time member of Land and Liberty, to set up a 'revolutionary' party on this basis. In April, 1894, he was arrested, before it had done little more than bring out a manifesto, and therewith *Narodnoe Pravo* (The People's Right), as the incipient organization called itself, was liquidated.

A programme of political democracy pure and simple could

muster but scant support. The radicals who gravitated toward Populism envisaged the overthrow of the monarchy as the outcome of a popular revolution spearheaded by a terrorist conspiracy and resulting in the triumph of a socialist order not evolving from an imported industrialism but springing from indigenous roots. The Marxists had a different answer to the question of the country's political emancipation. The intelligentzia, they argued, were powerless; the behaviour of the peasants during the famine had demonstrated once more that the revolution could not count on them; salvation was bound to come from the growing industrial proletariat: in fighting for its class interests it would crush the autocracy.

In the last years of the century a new vibrancy could be sensed in the political air. Plainly the country had emerged from the doldrums. Discontent with conditions was beginning to lose its passive character. The students demonstrated in the streets, demanding a liberal academic régime; a wave of great strikes swept the more industrialized western and central provinces; in the countryside there were outbreaks of violence against landlords and local authorities. By the middle of the 'nineties a score of populist groups were in existence. Scattered all over the country, including Siberia, they were strongest in the southern centres. The revolutionary cadres were swelled by the reappearance of some of the politicals, like Catherine Breshkovsky, who had served their terms in prison or exile. The volume of underground literature was on the increase. Much of it was supplied by the Free Russian Press, organized in London in 1892, and by the Group of Old *Narodovoltzy* which functioned in Paris.

By this time the *narodniks* had managed to set their intellectual house in order. To begin with, they had high regard for the revolutionary past and in fact believed themselves to be the heirs of the People's Will, in duty bound to carry on its work. Like the social-democrats, they held 'the working-class' to be the sole force capable of destroying the existing order, but in 'the working class' they included the peasantry. While paying lip service to 'scientific Socialism', they were wary of such Marxist dogmas as economic determinism and the capitalist filiation of Socialism. In the drama of history they assigned a leading part to intellectually superior individuals, and they continued to adhere to tactics requiring personal heroism and total dedication: terror.

The latter was largely a mere desideratum. Two provincial governors were unsuccessfully assaulted, and in 1895 a circle started preparations for an attempt on the life of Nicholas II, but the enterprise was nipped in the bud. A major terrorist act was not carried out until 1903, when the Minister of Education was assassinated.

To the label, *narodovoltzy* or *narodniki*, some of the populist groups preferred that of 'Socialists-revolutionaries'. The term had been used occasionally since the days of Lavrov's *Forward!* It was now intended to underline the militant character of resurgent Populism, in contradistinction to social-democracy. Writing in 1896, 'An Old *Narodovoletz*' scorned the latter as a philosophy for 'tired revolutionaries', a quietist doctrine leaning on automatic historical forces instead of man's moral duty to fight for justice. In the heat of polemics the Marxists were accused of wishing to promote the growth of capitalism and the proletarization of the peasantry, indeed of urging the intelligentzia to serve the interests of the propertied classes. There were also, however, attempts to fraternize with the social-democrats. As late as 1900 a pamphlet issued by a group of Socialists-revolutionaries argued that their own party, in aiming at immediate political action, was a party of the present, while the social-democrats, in stressing economic demands and in organizing the masses for a struggle with capitalism, formed the party of the future. But if the ways of the two parties differed, their goal was the same. 'We shall help them with our left hand,' the pamphlet ran, 'since our right hand is occupied by the sword.'

Meanwhile Marxism was gaining ground. Secret social-democratic groups were proliferating in the larger urban centres, but they were unconnected and their bond with the labour movement was tenuous. Some of them were at first committed to the populist creed. Such was the case of a circle of *narodovoltzy*, which for several years was active in both capitals. From its clandestine press came, among other items, a reprint of the programme of the late Party, but minus the second term in the opening formula: 'According to our basic convictions, we are socialists and *narodniks*.' Nevertheless, the populist outlook dominated the first two issues of the *Bulletin of the People's Will* that the group put out in 1892 and 1893 respectively. A Marxist note was sounded in the third issue, printed in 1895, but it also contained a pæan to terror in line with the practice of *Narodnaya Volya*. (At the time the members had under consideration a plan of exterminating the Czar and his kin by poisoning the water supply of the Winter Palace.) The fourth and last issue, run off at the end of the year, was consistently Marxist.

The effort to bring the Marxist groups together into one organization resulted in the founding of the Russian Social-Democratic Labour Party. The event took place in 1898. The previous year a conference of delegates from half a dozen groups formed the Party of Socialists-Revolutionaries. Arrests played havoc with some of its constituent elements, but could not halt the integration of the populist circles, a process initiated at the grass roots level. In the first years of the century the organization, like its social-democratic counterpart, was a going concern. The revolutionary movement was no longer a matter of a few small groups of intellectuals and semi-intellectuals plotting underground. It was acquiring a mass base. Yet, far from marching shoulder to shoulder, for the next score of years the Party of Socialists-Revolutionaries and the Social-Democratic Party lived in the atmosphere of a bitter feud, the latter organization soon splitting into two irreconcilable factions, the Menshevik and the Bolshevik. In the end the upheaval for which both parties had worked toppled the monarchy, and before long brought about the proscription alike of the Socialists-Revolutionaries and the Mensheviks by the régime that the Bolsheviks had set up. The final stretch of the road to the revolution that has proved one of the most fateful events in history is beyond the scope of the present book.

SELECT BIBLIOGRAPHY

ABBREVIATIONS

A   *American Slavic and East European Review.*
B   *Byloe.*
BA *Bazilevsky* (pseud.), ed. *Gosudarstvennye prestupleniya v Rossii v 19 veke.*
     Stuttgart-Paris, 1903–5, 3v.
C   *Chernyshevsky, Polnoe sobranie sochineniy,* 1906, 10v.
CS *Chernyshevsky, Polnoe sobranie sochineniy,* 1939–53, 16 v.
F   *Vera Figner, Polnoe sobranie sochineniy,* 1928–9, 6 v.
GM *Golos minuvshevo.*
GR *Gruppa Osvobozhdenie Truda.*
H   *Herzen, Polnoe sobranie sochineniy i pisem,* 1919–25, 22 v.
HS *Herzen, sobranie sochineniy v 30 t.,* 1954–7, v. 1–12.
K   *Katorga i ssylka.*
KA *Krasnyi arkhiv.*
L   *Literatura Partii Narodnaya Volya,* Paris, 1905, sup. to *Bazilevsky,* ed.
     Gosudarstvennye prestupleniya v Rossii.
LN *Literaturnoe nasledstvo.*
T   *Nevsky,* ed. *Ot Zemli i Voli k Gruppe Osvobozhdeniya Truda,* 1930.
N   *Tkachev, Izbrannye sochineniya,* 1932–7, 6 v.

Note:—When Moscow or Leningrad (St. Petersburg, Petersburg, Petrograd) is the place of publication, the word is omitted from the imprint.

CHAPTER I

Polnoe sobranie sochineniy (Radishchev), 1938–52, 3 v.
Radishchev (Blagoy), 1948.
Mémoires (Ségur), Paris, v. 2, p. 170.
Russkaya starina, 1900, 9, p. 544.
Rossiya i Frantziya v 1789–92 gg., in *LN* 33/34.
Arkhiv Vorontzova, v. 18, p. 44; v. 9, pp. 267–8, 273.
Istorichesky vestnik, 1903, v. 92, p. 907.
Ocherki i rechi (Kluchevsky), 1913, p. 304.
Radikalnye i politicheskie protzessy kontza 18 veka (Svetlov), in *Iz istorii russkoy filosofii 18–19 vekov,* 1952.
Obshchestvennoe dvizhenie v Moskve vo vtoroy polovine 18 veka (Alefirenko), in *Izvestiya Akademii Nauk, Seriya istorii i filosofii,* v. 4, no. 6, 1947.

CHAPTERS II–III

Vosstanie dekabristov (Chentzov), *bibliografiya,* 1929.
Vosstanie dekabristov, 1925–54, v. 1–6, 8–11.

Vosstanie dekabristov (Nechkina), 1955, 2 v.
The First Russian Revolution, 1825. (Mazour), Berkeley, California, 1937.
Izbrannye sotzialno-politicheskie i filosofskie proizvedeniya dekabristov (Shchipanov, ed.), 1951, 3 v.
Arkhiv Vorontzova, v. 8, p. 297.
Correspondance (Napoléon I), Paris, v. 24, pp. 399, 469.
Molodaya gvardiya, 1938, 2, p. 51.
The Russian Military Colonies (Pipes), in the *Journal of Modern History*, 1950, 9.
Voennye poseleniia v Rossii (Levintov), in *Istorichesky zhurnal*, 1940, 6.
Russky arkhiv, 1912, 7, p. 364.
Griboedov i dekabristy (Nechkina), 1947, p. 381.
Politicheskie i obshchestvennye idei dekabristov (Semevsky), 1909.
Russkaya pravda (Pestel), 1906.
Politicheskaya doktrina nakaza Pestelya (Syromyatnikov), in *Sbornik statei posvyashchennykh Kluchevskomu*, 1909.
The Character of Pestel's Thought (Adams), in *A*, 1953, 4.
Obshchestvennye dvizheniia v Rossii v pervoi polovine 19 veka, 1905, v. I, pp. 412, 305.
Iz pisem i pokazaniy dekabristov (Borozdin), 1906, p. 23.
Vosstanie dekabristov, v. 3, p. 278; v. 9, p. 47; v. 4, p. 124.
Dekabristy (Shchegolev), 1926, p. 241.
Zapiski (Gorbachevsky), 1916, pp. 34, 431.
Report of the Commission of Inquiry, 1826, p. 103.
Severnoe obshchestvo dekabristov (Aksenov), 1951, pp. 222, 243, 318.
Imperator Alexander I (Schilder), 1905, v. 4, p. 420.
14-oe Dekabrya, 1825 g. (Presnyakov), 1926, p. 121.
Dekabristy na Ukrayini, Kiev, 1926–30, 2. v.
Zapiski (Zavalishin), 1906, v. I, p. 255, *n.*
Vospominaniya Bestuzhevykh, 1931, p. 83.
The Decembrist Conspiracy through British Eyes (Lang), in *A*, 1949, 12.
Jefferson and the Russian Decembrists (Dvoichenko-Markov), in *A*, October 1950.

CHAPTER IV

Obzor russkoy istorii (Pushkarev), New York, 1953, p. 389.
Krestyanskie dvizheniya (Morokhovetz), 1827–69, 1931, v. I, p. 9.
Stikhotvoreniya i poemy (Ogarev), 1938, v. 2, p. 274.
Sobranie sochineniy i pisem (Bakunin), 1934–5, v. 2, p. 177; v. 3, p. 296.
Istoriya russkoy obshchestvennoy mysli (Ivanov-Razumnik), 1907, v. I, p. 315.
Pisma (Belinsky), 1914, v. 2, pp. 218, 262.

Russkie nochi (V. F. Odoevsky), 1913.
Literaturnye vospominaniya (Annenkov), 1928, p. 231.
Obshchestvo propagandy v 1849 g., Leipzig, 1875, p. 80.
Kirillo-Mefodievskoe obshchestvo (Bortnikov), in *Trudy istoricheskovo fakulteta Kiev. univ.*, 1940, v. 1.
Delo petrashevtzev, 1937–51, 3 v., v. 2, pp. 428, 438, 233; v. 1, pp. 525, 280, 91, 33, 421.
Petrashevtzy (Semevsky), in *GM*, 1916, *Vestnik Yevropy*, 1916.
Russkie zapiski, 1916, 10, p. 32.
Revolutzionnaya praktika petrashevtzev (Leikina-Svirskaya), in *Istoricheskie zapiski*, 47, 1945.
Russky fourierizm 40-kh gg. (Blyumin), in *Izv. Akad. nauk. Otd. obshchestvennykh nauk*, 1938, 1–2.
Russkaya starina, 1900, No. 5, p. 279; No. 3, pp. 561, 568.
Golosa iz Rossii, London, 1858, 1, p. 13.
H, v. 5, p. 243–4; v. 7, p. 252.
HS, v. 6, p. 58; v. 5, p. 199.
Herzen and the Peasant Commune (Malia), in *Continuity and Change in Russian and Soviet Thought* (E. J. Simmons, ed.), Cambridge, Mass., 1955.
Revue des Deux Mondes, 1880, v. 37, p. 771.
La Russie et la Révolution (Tyutchev, F.), in his *Polnoe sobranie sochineniy*, 1913.

CHAPTER V

GM, 1916, 5/6, p. 353.
Sotzialistichesky vestnik, New York, 1954, 2, p. 81.
Pismo k izdatelyu, in *Golosa iz Rossii*, London, 1858, v. 1.
K, 14, p. 109.
CS, v. 14, p. 456.
Arkhiv Marksa i Engelsa, v. 4, p. 388.
Das Kapital (Karl Marx), 2nd ed., v. 1, P.S.
C, v. 4, p. 329; v. 5, p. 305.
Ocherki osvoboditelnovo dvizheniya (Lemke), 1908, p. 420.
Prolog (Chernyshevsky), 1936, p. 327.
Otmena krepostnovo sostoyaniya v Rossii (Zaionchkovsky), 1954.
Krepostnoe naselenie v Rossii (Troinitzky), 1861, p. 26.
Obshchestvennoe dvizhenie pri Alexandre II (Kornilov), 1905, pp. 109, 92.
K, 33, p. 46.
Iz vospominaniy proshlovo (Panteleyev), 1924, p. 708.
Chernyshevsky v gody revolutzionnoy situatzii (Nechkina), in *Istorichesky zhurnal*, 10.

Ogarev v gody revolutzionnoy situatzii, in *Izvestiya Akademiya Nauk, Seriya istorii*, 1947, 2.
Novye materialy o revolutzionnoy situatzii, in *LN*, 61.

CHAPTER VI

GM, 1915, 4, p. 198.
Kruzhok Zaichnevskovo i Argiropulo (Kozmin), in *K*, 1930, 7–9.
Molodaya gvardiya, 1924, 2/3, p. 244.
Vstrechi s Leninym (Valentinov), New York, 1953, pp. 117, 103, 106.
Chernyshevsky i Lenin (Valentinov), in *Novyi zhurnal*, New York, v. 26–7.
Peterburgskie pozhary (Reiser), in *K*, 1932, 10.
Rol Chernyshevskovo v sozdanii 'Revolutzionnoy Partii' (Taubin), in *Istoricheskie zapiski*, 39.
Elitism in Chernyshevsky (Bowman), in *A*, 1954, 4.
Protzess Chernyshevskovo (Alekseyev), Saratov, 1939.
Chernyshevsky (Steklov), 1928, 2 v.
C, v. 4, p. 156.
CS, v. 4, p. 328.
Mirovozzrenie Chernyshevskovo (Baskakov), 1956.
Pisarev et l'Idéologie du Nihilisme Russe (Coquart), Paris, 1946.
Nihilisme—Mot et idée (Hepner), in *Synthèses*, Bruxelles, January, 1949.
Pisarev i literaturno-obshchestvennie dvizhenie 60-kh gg. (Plotkin), 1945.
Politicheskie protzessy (Lemke), 1923.
Iz otcheta 3-vo otdeleniya, in *K*, 1924, 10.
LN, 61, p. 515.
Kolokol, London, 1 July, 1861.
H, v. 15, p. 404, 375.
A Russian Anarchist Visits Boston (Handlin), in *New England Quarterly*, 1942, 3.
Bakunin (Steklov), 1926–7, 4 v.
Michael Bakunin (E. H. Carr), London, 1937.
Kazansky zagovor (Kozmin), 1929.
The Memoirs of Herzen, London, 1926, v. 5, pp. 154, 157.

CHAPTER VII

H, v. 21, p. 187; v. 17, p. 37; v. 18, pp. 136, 107, 7.
Herzen, Ogarev i revolutzionnaya emigratziya, in *LN* 41/42.
Nashi dom. dela (Alex. Serno-Solovyovich), Vevey, 1867.
Pokushenie Karakozova, 1928–30, 2 v.
The Congressional Globe, Washington, 1866, p. 2384.

KA, 33, p. 213.
Tkachev i revolutzionnoe dvizhenie 60-kh gg. (Kozmin), 1922.
Iz proshlykh let (Annenskaya), in *Russkoe bogatstvo*, 1913, 1, p. 62.
T, v. 1, pp. 445, 429.
Istoriko-revolutzionnaya khrestomatiya, 1923, v. 1, p. 81.
Materialy dlya istorii revolutzionnovo dvizheniya v Rossii v 60-kh gg.,
    Paris, 1905, sup. to *BA*.

CHAPTER VIII

KA, 1, pp. 153, 148.
Egalité, 17 April, 1869.
Revolutzionnye proklamatzii zhenevskikh tipografiy, in *LN* 41/42.
H, v. 18, p. 277; v. 20, p. 132; v. 10, p. 117; v. 3, p. 395.
HS, v. 6, p. 125.
Herzen and the Grand Inquisitors (Berlin), in *Encounter*, 32.
Katekhizis revolutzionera, in *Borba klassov*, 1924, 1/2, p. 268.
BA, v. 1, p. 298.
B, 1922, 18, p. 42.
Avtobiografii revolutzionnykh deyateley, in *Entziklopedichesky slovar
    Granat*, v. 40, s.v. *Kuznetzov*.
Ispoved (Pryzhov), in *Minuvshie gody*, 1908, 2.
Nechayev i nechayevtzy (Kozmin), 1931.
LN 41/42, p. 65.
Alexeyevsky Ravelin (Shchegolev), 1929.
V sporakh o Nechayeve (Gambarov), 1926.
Russkaya revolutziia v sudebnykh protzessakh (Kovalensky), 1923, p. 11.
Istoriya ili fantastika (Kozmin), in *Pechat i revolutziya*, 1926, 6.

CHAPTER IX

Bakunin (Steklov), v. 2, p. 119.
Istoriya russkoy intelligentzii (Ovsyanikov-Kulikovsky), 1909, v. 2,
    p. 95.
Opravdanie narodnichestva (Vishnyak), in *Novyi zhurnal*, New York,
    30.
Intelligentziya i sotzializm (Tugan-Baronovsky), in *Intelligentziya v
    Rossii*, 1910.
Lavrov i Mikhailovsky (Vityazev), 1917.
Sochineniya (Mark i Engels), v. 24, p. 295.
LN, 1, p. 154.
Ot buntarstva k terrorizmu (Debagori-Mokrievich), 1930, v. 1, ch. 3.
Zapiski chaikovtza (Sinegub), 1929.

Kruzhok chaikovtzev (Levin), in *K*, 1929, 12.
Literaturnye vospominaniya (Skabichevsky), 1928, p. 337.
Kolokol, London, 1 November, 1861.
Russkie v Zurich'e (Sazhin), *in K*, 1932, 10.
Bakunin and Russian Jacobins (Varlamov), New York, 1955.
Istoricheskoe razvitie Internatzionala (Bakunin), 1873, p. 355.
Politicheskoe pismo sotzialista [Grognard (Mikhailovsky)], in *L*, p. 170.

CHAPTER X

Khozhdenie v narod (Ivanchin-Pisarev), 1929.
V narod! (Lukashevich), in *B*, 1907.
Hidden Springs of the Russian Revolution (Catherine Breshkovsky), London, 1931.
Dolgushintzy (Kunkl), 1931.
Narodniki, 1873–8 (Lavrov), Geneva, 1895–6.
Vperiod!, London, 1875, p. 462.
Istoriya revolutzionnovo dvizheniya v Rossii (Balabanov), 1925, p. 184.
Memoirs of a Revolutionist (Kropotkin), Boston, 1899, p. 358.
Povesti moyei zhizni (Morozov), v. 2, p. 118.
B, 1907, 10, p. 173.
Obshchina, Geneva, 1878, 5, 8/9.
B, 1912, 14, p. 50.
Chigirinskoe delo, in *Chornyi peredel*, 1880, 1–2.
B, 1906, 12, p. 257; 10, p. 198.
Vperiod!, 1875, 1 July, 1 March.
T, v. 3, pp. 91, 224.
A Forerunner of Lenin (Karpovich), in *Review of Politics*, Notre Dame, Ind., 1944, 6.
Na chuzhoy storone, Prague, 10, p. 201.
Uspekhi revolutzionnoy propagandy v Rossii (Palen), in *B*, 1906, 9.
Statisticheskie svedeniya o propagande 70-kh gg. (Sidorov), in *K*, 1928, 1.
Protzess 50-i (Dzhabadari), in *B*, 1907, 8–10.
BA, v. 3.

CHAPTER XI

KA, 19, p. 196.
Obshchestvo Zemlya i Volya (Serebryakov), Geneva, 1894.
Obshchestvo Zemlya i Volya (Aptekman), 1924.
Revolutzionnaya zhurnalistika 70-kh gg. (Bazilevsky ed.), Paris, 1905, sup. to *BA*.
Arkhiv Zemli i Voli i Narodnoy Voli (Valk ed.), 1932.
Perekhodnyi moment (Axelrod), in *Obshchina*, Geneva, 1878, 8/9.
Sviatoy revolyutzii (Kravchinsky), 1917.

Pervaya rabochaya demonstratziya v Rossii (Korolchuk), 1927.
Briv (Liberman), New York, 1951, p. 114.
B, 1907, 8, p. 277.
Povesti moyey zhizni (Morozov), v. 2, p. 64.
Vospominaniya (Zasulich), 1931.
Vospominaniya o dele V. Zasulich. (Koni), 1933.
Le Procès de Véra Zassoulitch, in *Revue des Deux Mondes*, 1878, 5.
KA, 19, p. 200.
Iz istorii Obshchestva narodnoe osvobozhdenie (Kusheva), in *K*, 1931, 4.
Neobkhodimoe razyasnenie, in *Obshchina*, Geneva, 1878, 8/9.
Lipetzky i voronezhsky syezdy (Frolenko), in his *Sobranie sochineniy*, 1931, v. 2.
Gruppa Svoboda ili smert (Yakimova), in *K*, 1926, 3.
Pered burey (Chernov), New York, 1953.

CHAPTER XII

Chornyi peredel, 1880–1, 1923.
Chornyi peredel (Deutsch), in *Istoriko-revolutzionniy sbornik*, 1924, v. 2.
Yuzhnorussky rabochy soyuz (Kovalskaya), 1920.
Revised programme of Chornyi Peredel, in *Istoriko-revolutzionniy sbornik*, v. 3.
Opyt ukazatelya literatury po istorii partii Narodnaya Volya (Drey), 1929.
Ustav ispolnitelnovo komiteta Narodnoy Voli (Nikolaevsky), in *Na chuzoi storone*, 1924, 7.
Vospominaniya (Tikhomirov), 1927, p. 95.
Uchastniki narodovolcheskovo dvizheniya, in *Narodovoltzy* (Yakimova-Dikovskaya ed.), 1934.
Narodovolcheskaya zhurnalistika (Kuzmin), 1930.
Mikhailov (Pribyleva-Korba and Figner), 1925.
Barannikov (Figner), 1935.
Zhelyabov (Voronsky), 1934.
B, 1906, 5, p. 159; 4, p. 219.
Perovskaya (Asheshov), 1921.
Vospominaniya (Tikhomirov), p. 98.
Terroristicheskaya borba (Morozov), London, 1880.
L, p. 401.
Sobranie sochineniy (Figner), 1928, v. 1, p. 165.
Pervye dni narodnoy voli (Jochelson), 1922, p. 57.
Iz istorii politicheskoy borby v 70-kh i 80-kh gg. 19 Veka. Partiya Narodnoy Voli [Bogucharsky (pseudonym)], 1912.
Na rodine (Rusanov), 1931, p. 193.

Iz vospominaniy starovo narodnovoltza (Jochelson), p. 27. (MS. in the New York Public Library).
Pismo Zhelyabova k Dragomanovu, in *Zvenya*, 1935, v. 5.
Ocherk deyatelnosti Min. Yustitzii (Slukhotzky), in *Istoriko-revolutzionnyi sbornik*, 3.
Staticheskie svedeniya o propagande (Sidorov), in *K*, 1928, 1.
Narodovolcheskie protzessy (Nikitina), in *Narodnaya Volya v dokumentakh i vospominaniyakh* (Yakimova-Dikovskaya and others, eds.), 1931, v. 2.
Yidn-revolutzionern in Russland (Cherikover), *Historishe shriftn* (Yivo), Wilno, 1939, v. 3.
Obshchestvo Zemlya i Volya (Aptekman), p. 168.

CHAPTER XIII

Wittenberg (Semionov), in *B*, 1925, 6.
Kibalchich, s.l. (1903).
Hartmann, Letter to the Editor of the *New York Herald*, 30 July, 1881.
Mikhailov (Pribyleva-Korba and Figner), pp. 140, 136.
Russky arkhiv, 1894, 3, p. 270.
B, 1906, 12, p. 32.
Khalturin i Alexeyev (Mishev), 1928.
Journal (Vogüé), *1877–83*, Paris, 1932.
Ispoved (Loris-Melikov), in *K*, 1925, 2.
Konstitutziya Loris-Melikova, London, 1893.
Iz istorii 'Konstitutzionnykh' veyanii (Shchegolev), in *B*, 1906, 12.
L'Empire des Tzars (Leroy-Beaulieu), v. 2, p. 509.
K, 1924, 13, p. 145.
Ispoved Goldenberga (Kantor, ed.), in *KA*, 1928, 5.

CHAPTER XIV

Khronika sotzialisticheskovo dvizheniya v Rossii, *1878–87* (Shebeko), 1906, p. 136. (A translation of a confidential publication, in French, printed under official auspices in St. Petersburg, 1890.)
Alexander Mikhailov v dni ozhidaniya kazni, in *B*, 1918, 4/5. (A special number devoted to the event of 1 March, 1881.)
Zhelyabov, London, 1882, p. 37.
L, p. 971.
Rysakov (Asheshov), 1920.
Dnevnik sobytii s 1 Marta po i Sentyabrya 1881 g., 1882.
1 Marta 1881 g. (Dvorzhitzky), in *Istorichesky vestnik*, 1913, 2.
F, v. 1, p. 248.

K Sobytiyu 1 Marta 1881 g. (Tyrkov), in *B,* 1906, 5.
Pokazaniya pervomartovtzev, in *B,* 1918, 4/5.
Proyekt vozdukhoplavatelnovo apparata (Kibalchich), *ibid.*
Delo 1-vo Marta 1881 g. (*Lev. Deutsch*, ed.).
Protzess Zhelyabova, Perovskoi i dr., 1906.
Moi vospominaniya (Ilya Tolstoy), Berlin, 191?, p. 140.
Pobedonostzev i yevo korrespondenty, 1923, v. 1, part 1, p. 47.
K sudbe Gesi Helfman (N. Tyutchev), in his *Statyi i vospominaniya,*
    1925, v. 1.
Kazn tzareubitz (Planson), in *Istorichesky vestnik*, 1913, 2.

CHAPTER XV

1 Marta 1881 g. (Yakimova-Dikovskaya and others, eds.), 1933.
Narodnaya Volya v dokumentakh i vospominanyakh (id.), 1930–31, 2 v.
L, p. 903.
1 Marta 1881 g.; proklamatzii i vozzvaniya (Tyutchev, ed.), 1920.
Dnevnik (Milutin), 1950, v. 4, p. 61.
Pisma Pobedonostzeva k Alexandru III, 1923, v. 2.
Konstitutziya Loris-Melikova, London, 1893, p. 31.
Borba dvukh gruppirovok (Gautier), in *Istoricheskie zapiski,* 1938, 2.
Polnoe sobranie zakonov, sobr., 3, v. 1.
The Times, London, 16 May, 1881.
Yevrei v Rossii i zapadnoy Yevrope (Dubnov), 1923, p. 11.
Letopisi Marksizma, 7/8, p. 56.
Actes et Paroles (Victor Hugo), Paris, v. 3, p. 385.
Chaikovsky (Titov ed.), Paris, 1929, v. 1.
B, 1917, 7, p. 51; 1907, 6, p. 6.
F, v. 1, pp. 282, 287.
The Memoirs of Count Witte, Garden City, New York, p. 22.
Vzvolnovannye lobotryasy (Zaslavsky), 1931.
Obshchestvo svyaschennoy druzhiny (Sadikov), in *KA,* 1927, 2.
Svyashchennaya druzhina, in *Minuvshie gody,* 1916, 1.
Mosk. otdelenie Svyaschennoy druzhiny (Fedorov), in *GM,* 1918, 1/3.
Knyaz Nony (Meshchersky), 1882.
House of Representatives, 51st Congress, First Session, *Executive
    Document No. 470,* Washington D.C., p. 53.
Zapiski narodnovoltza (Bach), 1929, p. 84.
L, p. 438.
Materialy dlya istorii anti-yevreiskikh pogromov, v. 2, p. 225.
N, p. 413.
L, p. 386.
New Yorker Volkszeitung, 3 July, 1881.

Lieberman et le Socialisme Russe (Sapir), in *International Review for Social History*, Leiden, 1938, v. 3.
Unzer Zeit, Warsaw, 1929, No. 1/2, p. 3.
K, 1928, 48, p. 50.
Narodnaya Volya (Pribyleva-Korba), 1926, p. 197.
Za sto lit, Kiev, 1928, v. 3, p. 124.
Letuchaya tipografiya Narodnoy Voli v 1883 g. (Shebalin), 1926, p. 17.
L, p. 622.
Geshikhte fun der yidisher arbeter bavegung (Cherikover), New York, 1945, v. 2, p. 177.
Sovremennyi mir, 1912, 5, p. 173.
Iz arkhiva Akselroda, Berlin, 1924, p. 29.

CHAPTER XVI

Narodovoltzy 80-kh i 90-kh gg. (Yakimova-Dikovskaya and others, eds.), 1929.
Narodovoltzy posle 1 Marta 1881 g. (id.), 1928.
Narodovoltzy (id.), 1934.
GR, sb, 3, p. 143.
Pokazaniya; k istorii Partii Narodnaya Volya (Polonskaya), in *B*, 1907, 6.
O sblizhenii i razryve s narodovoltzami (Deutsch), in *Proletarskaya revolutziya*, 1923, 8.
Zapiski narodovoltza (Bach), 1931, p. 31.
Voyennaya organizatziya Narodnoy Voli (Ashenbrenner), 1924.
Peregovory Svyaschennoy druzhiny s partiey Narodnoy Voli v 1882 g. (Nikoladze), 1917.
L, p. 656.
Sudeikin i Degayev (Makletzova), in *B*, 1906, 8.
Protzess 21-vo, Geneva, 1888, p. 36.
Neizdannye zapiski (Tikhomirov), in *KA*, 29.
Vestnik Narodnoy Voli, Geneva, 2, p. 91. (Second pagination.)
Provokatory i terroristy (Lev Deutsch), Tula, 1923.
Vstrecha s Degayevym (Serebryakova), in *B*, 1924, 25.
Predatel Degayev v Amerike (Genkin), in *K*, 1939, 9.
Dr. Alexander Bell (Akeley), in the *Alumni Quart. of the University of South Dakota*, April 1924.
Molodaya partiya Narodnoy Voli (Valk), in *Problemy Marksizma*, 1930, 1.
Rasporyaditelnaya komissiya i molodaya partiya Narodnoy Voli (id.), in *K*, 1932, 2.
Lopatin (Shilov), 1922.
Protzess, 21-vo, Geneva, 1888, p. 22.
K istorii protzessa 21-vo (Valk), in *KA*, 36.

V ryadakh Narodnoy Voli (Orzhikh), in *Narodnovoltzy* (Yakimova-Dikovskaya ed.), 1934.
Denkwürdigkeiten (Bernhard von Bülow), Berlin, 1930-1, v. 4, p. 537.
1 Marta 1887 g. (Shilov, ed.), 1927.
Vospominaniya o dele 1 Marta 1887 g. (Lukashevich), in *B*, 1917, 1-2.
Pokushenie na Alexandra III (*Govorukhin*), in *GM na chuzhoy storone*, 1926, 3.
Ulyanov i delo 1 Marta 1887 g. (Ulyanova-Yelizarova), 1927.
Rannie gody Lenina [*Brat Lenina—A. Ulyanov*] (Valentinov), in *Novyi zhurnal*, New York, v. 40.
K godovshchine smerti Lenina, 1925, p. 83.

EPILOGUE

Proniknovenie idey marksizma v Rossii do 1882 g. (Gagarin), in *Iz istorii russkoy filosofii 18–19 Vekov*, 1952.
Russkaya ekonomicheskaya mysl 60-kh i 70-kh gg. i Marksizm (Reuel), 1956.
Pisma Marx'a k Kugelmanu, 1928, p. 53.
KA, 1933, 1, p. 6.
Plekhanov on Russian Capitalism and the Peasant Commune, 1883–85 (Baron), in *A*, Dec. 1953.
Populism and Early Russian Marxism on Ways of Economic Development of Russia (Schwarz), in *Continuity and Change in Russian and Soviet Thought* (Simmons, ed.), Cambridge, Mass., 1955.
Sovremennyi mir, 1912, 5, p. 168.
Perepiska Marx'a i Engels'a s russkimi politicheskimi deyatelyami, 1947, p. 178.
Arkhiv Marx'a i Engels'a, 1924, v. 1, p. 286.
Fate of Capitalism in Russia: Narodnik Version (Laue), in *A*, February 1954.
Gruppa osvobozhdenie truda i marksistskie kruzhki (Sergievsky), in *Istoriko-revolutzionnyi sbornik*, v. 2.
Narodovoltzy na pereputyi (Kudelli), 1925.
S rodiny i na rodinu, No. 6/7, Geneva, 1896, p. 475.
K istorii vozniknoveniya partii sotzialistov-revolutzionerov (Sletov), 1917.
Partiya sotzialistov-revolutzionerov i yeyo predshestvenniki (Spiridovich), 1920.

GENERAL WORKS

Avtobiografi revolutzionnykh deyateley russkovo sotzialisticheskovo dvizheniia 70-kh–80-kh gg., in *Entziklopedichesky Slovar Inst. Granat*, 7th ed. v. 40.

Burtzev, *Za sto let*, London, 1897, 2 v. Selected passages from the literature of Russian Radicalism, 1825–96, and a chronology of the 'Political and Social Movements in Russia, 1801–96'.

Kennan, George, *Siberia and the Exile System*, New York, 1891, 2 v.

Klevensky and others, comp., *Russkaya podpolnaya i zarubezhnaya pechat*, 1935, v. 1, fasc. 1. A catalogue of books, pamphlets, and leaflets, 1831–79.

Kulczycki, *Geschichte der Russischen Revolution. Ubers. aus dem Polnischen*, Gotha, 1910–14, 3 v. Period covered, 1825–1900.

Livshitz, *Podpolnye tipografii 60-kh–80-kh gg.*, in *K*, 41 and ff.

Obzor sotzialno-revolutzionnovo dvizheniya v Rossii, 1880. Published by the Third Division; the earliest survey of the Russian revolutionary movement (from the 1840's until 1879).

Pazhitnov, *Razvitie sotzialisticheskikh idey v Rossii ot Pestelya do Gruppy osvobozhdenie truda*, 1924.

Pokrovsky, *Ocherki po istorii revolutzionnovo dvizheniya v Rossii 19 i 20 vekov*, 1924.

Rozhanov, *Zapiski po istorii revolutzionnovo dvizheniya v Rossii*, 1913. Published by the Russian Police Department.

Scheibert, Peter, *Von Bakunin zu Lenin; Geschichte der Russischen Revolutionären Ideologien, 1840–95*, Leiden, 1956, v. 1 (of three projected).

Shilov, *Chto chitat po istorii russkovo revolutzionnovo dvizheniya?* 1922.

Shilov and others, comp., *Deyateli revolutzionnovo dvizheniya v Rossii*, 1927–33. Only v. 1–2 of this bio-bibliographic dictionary, covering the period from the end of the eighteenth century to 1879, a part of v. 3, covering the 1880's, and of v. 5, listing the social-democrats, have been published; an indispensable reference work.

Stein, V. M., *Ocherki razvitiya russkoy obshchestvenno-ekonomicheskoy mysli 19–20 vekov*, 1948.

Stepniak (pseudonym of Kravchinsky), *Underground Russia*, New York, 1883.

Thun, *Geschichte der Revolutionären Bewegungen in Russland*, Leipzig, 1883. There are several editions—the latest dated 1923—of Russian translations of this pioneer study.

Franco Venturi, *Storia del Populismo Russo*, Torino, 1952, 2 v. Deals with the period from the 1840's to 1881 in great detail; ample bibliographical footnotes.

INDEX

ABC of the Social Sciences, The (Bervi), 177

Argiropulo, Pericles, 112-13

Aksakov, Ivan, 107

Aksakov, Konstantin, 66

Alexander, I, Emperor of Russia, initial liberalism of, 15–17, 24; repressive régime of, 17–18, 21; military settlements of, 18–19; liberator abroad but despot at home, 20; plots to assassinate, 23, 26, 29, 32, 34–5, 44; and Semyonovsky affair, 25; death of, 36, 44

Alexander II, Emperor of Russia, accession of, 86, 125; early concessions of, 86; Herzen's open letter to, 87; and emancipation of serfs, 88–9; reforms of, 131, 142, 248; attempts on life of, 138–41, 142, 222, 251–6; plans to assassinate, 161, 168, 250, 263, 269, 272–7; death of, 168–9, 279–80; appeals for help against revolutionary movement, 224, 263; cost of attempts on life of, 244; effect on, of attempts on life, 261–2, 277; on 'Loris-Melikov constitution', 264, 293; morganatic wife of, 270; goes to parade at Manège, 276–8; reactions to assassination of, 290–1, 294–5

Alexander III, Emperor, and 'Loris-Melikov constitution', 264, 293–4; appeals to, for clemency to regicides, 287; and Pobedonestzev, 287, 291–2; urged to follow path of reform, 291–3, 300; determines on autocratic rule, 294; first public appearance of, 299; voluntary associations to protect, 302–5; liquidates Holy League, 305; coronation manifesto of, 316–17; Sudeikin's plans regarding, 319–20; plot against life of, 331–2

Alexandrov, V., 180

Alexandrovsk, attempt to blow up train at, 252–3, 265, 282

Alexeyev, Pyotr, 206–7

All-Russian Social-Revolutionary Organization, 196–7, 207

'Analysis of the New Serfdom, An' (Ogarev), 105

Anarchism, motto of international, 62–3; Bakunin's, 134, 144, 151, 184

Anna, Empress of Russia, 8

Aptekman, Osip, 248–9

Arakcheyev, Count, 18–19

Army, dissaffection in, 20–1, 25, 34; revolutionaries seek to sway ranks of, 29, 37, 45; part of, in Decembrist rising, 41–3; punishment of rebels in, 49; spirit of opposition dead in, 59; reforms in, 142; and People's Will, 243

Artel, theorizing on, 64, 84, 171; reality of, 172, 193

Astrakhan, 217

Axelrod, Pavel, 230–1; discusses merger with People's Will, 245–6; Jewish nationality of, 247; remains abroad, 301; and anti-Semitism, 309; mentioned, 313

Bakhmetev fund, 133, 153, 162, 165

Bakunin, Michael, 127; Hegel's influence on, 62; arrested, 80; supports Land and Liberty, 127, 129; believes in imminent revolution, 127; and Polish revolt, 129, 131; on young emigrés, 133; anarchism of, 134, 144, 151, 184; journal of, 144; and Nechayev, 150–2, 156, 161–2, 164–5; Herzen's open letters to, 154–6; translates *Communist Manifesto*, 163, 335; influence of, on Populism, 172; Marx's feud with, 175; advocates proselytizing masses, 182; in Zurich, 183; *Statehood and Anarchy* of, 184–5; last years and death of, 185; Soviet opinion of, 185; anti-Jewish feeling of, 308; mentioned, 60, 212

Bakuninists, *versus* Lavrovists, 184–7, 202; 'go to the people', 187–8, 191–3, 198–201; journal of, 201–2; oppose Blanquists, 203; disillusionment among, 210; in Land and Liberty, 213

Balts, preferential treatment of, 20, 24

Baptized Property (Herzen), 84

Barannikov, Alexander, 235–6, 238

Bardina, Sofya, 195, 206–7

Beideman, Mikhail, 167 *n*

357

Sovremennik—contd.
emancipation of serfs, 108; suspension of, 114–15; *What's to Be Done?*
appears in, 115; in 'sixties, 131; suppression of, 143
Speransky, Count, 15, 52
Speshnev, Nikolay, 73–4, 77–8
Staël, Madame de, 20
Statehood and Anarchy (Bakunin), 184–5
Steinheil, Baron, 28
Stefanovich, Yakov, 194; and Chigirin affair, 200–1, 231; arrest of, 201, 315; escape of, 219; opposes terrorism, 229; member of Black Repartition, 230; flees to Switzerland, 230; returns to Russia, 301; mentioned, 225
Sternberg, Lev, 328
Strelnikov, General, 311
Strogonov, Count Paul, 7–8
Subbotina, Madame, 195
Subbotina sisters, 195, 207; fortune of, 245, 314
Sudeikin, Lieutenant-Colonel, methods of, with political prisoners, 314, 317; uses Degayev, 318–20; runs People's Will, 319, 321; plans for self-aggrandisement, 319–20; murder of, 321–2, 326
Sukhanov, Nikolay, 291, 299, 314
'Sunday schools', 112, 114
Supreme Commission for the Maintenance of State Order and Public Peace, 262–4
Susanin, Ivan, 140
Svyashchenaya Druzhina. See Holy League
Swinton, John, 298
Switzerland, Herzen naturalized citizen of, 83; Russian émigrés in, 132–3, 144, 165, 183, 313, 316; Nechayev in, 150–2, 161–2, 164–5; Russian students in, 183, 195; leaders of Black Repartition in, 230–1

Taganrog, 36, 44
Tambov province, 102
Terrorist Section of People's Will, 330–2
Teterka, Vasily, 270
Théorie de l'Unité Universelle (Fourier), 76
Third Division of His Majesty's Chancery, 57–8; report of head of (1869), 123, 125, 145; Land and Liberty's agent in, 215; abolition of, 263

Tikhomirov, Lev, 180, 226; Sofya Perovskaya and, 238; suggests appeal to Czar, 292; wears mourning for Czar, 301; on revolution and the People's Will, 312, 326; joins émigrés, 314; negotiates for armistice, 316–17; on Degayev's motives, 318; Degayev and, 320–2; tries to revive People's Will, 324; becomes a renegade, 329–30
Tikhonov, 252
Times, The, reports rumors of grave disturbance, 26; on Loris-Melikov's measures, 263; on Imperial manifesto, 1881, 294
Timkovsky, Konstantin, 72
Tkachev, Pyotr, 146–8; wife of, 148; trial of, 178; opposed to Lavrov, 203–4; his conception of revolution, 204–5; Lenin on, 205; and Society of People's Liberation, 224; 'Jacobin' programme of, 312–13
To the Younger Generation, 109–10
Tocsin (Nabat), 204–5, 224, 309
Todleben, Governor General of Odessa, 269
'Toilers' theory', 96
Tolstov, student, 74, 77
Tolstoy, Count Leo, populist motif in works of, 171; *Human and Divine* of, 215 n; *Resurrection* of, 262; appeals for clemency to regicides, 287
Tolstoy, Count Dmitry, 263, 326–8
Tovarishchestva, 96
Trepov, General, attempted assassination of, 219–20
Trilesy, 45
Trubetzkoy, Prince Sergey, 26, 33; plans insurrection, 35; 'Dictator', 38; fails conspirators, 40, 42; arrest of, 49; pleads for life, 51; mentioned, 53
True and Faithful Sons of the Fatherland, Society of, 22
Truth (Pravda), 303–4
Tsarkoe Selo, 23, 41
Tulchin, 24
Turgenev, Ivan, social protest in works of, 68; imprisonment of, 79; and Ogarev's appeal to Czar, 108; *Fathers and Children* of, 117, 122; on *artèl,* 172
Turgenev, Nikolay, on Decembrists, 55
Turkey, closes straits, 20; and Crimean War, 84
Tver province, petition of nobles of, 107, 176; attempt to proselytize